Federal Lobbying

Federal Lobbying

Jerald A. Jacobs, Editor

Leland J. Badger
Benjamin Beiler
William B. Bonvillian
John H. Broadley
Anthony C. Epstein
Paula C. Goedert
Mary Jane Graham
D. A. Handzo
Carl S. Nadler
Toni Prestigiacomo
Christopher Vaden
David E. Zerhusen

Jenner & Block
Washington, D.C.

The Bureau of National Affairs, Inc. • Washington, D.C.

Library of Congress Cataloging-in-Publication Data

Federal lobbying/Jerald A. Jacobs, editor; Leland J. Badger . . . [et al.].
   p. cm.
   Includes index.
   ISBN 0-87179-623-6
   1. Lobbying—Law and legislation—United States. I. Jacobs, Jerald A.
II. Badger, Leland J. III. Bureau of National Affairs (Washington, D.C.)
KF4948.F43   1989
342.73′05—dc20
[347.3025]   89-17347
                                                                          CIP

Published by BNA Books
1231 25th Street, N.W., Washington, D.C. 20037

International Standard Book Number: 0-87179-623-6
Printed in the United States of America

Foreword

Federal Lobbying analyzes the areas of law and policy that affect lobbying at the federal government level. It is intended to be used by professionals in business corporations, nonprofit organizations, and law firms to assist in evaluating and resolving issues that arise in connection with federal lobbying. It is a guide through the thicket of complex, vague, overlapping, and inconsistent requirements that have been imposed over the years by each of the three branches of the federal government—legislative, executive, and judicial.

Issues of lobbying law and policy are often raised, by government officials, by the media, and by citizens, whenever an accusation of lobbying misconduct is made, a proposal for lobbying reform is introduced, or a particularly stunning lobbying victory or defeat occurs. Popular misconceptions are common, particularly the misconception that there are no rules to govern lobbying.

Until now there has appeared no comprehensive review of what precisely the federal government provides in its law and policy with respect to lobbying. This book is intended to shed light on the subject. It attempts to identify clearly what is black and what is white in this area, and it attempts to narrow as much as possible that which must remain grey.

The book covers lobbying registration, the best known of the federal requirements that apply to federal lobbying. The present system of disclosure has existed since 1946, but its details continue to confound both novices and experts in the lobbying field.

The book addresses lobbying for foreign interests, an area in which a broad scheme of prohibitions and disclosures exists and is enforced.

There is a chapter on lobbying and ethics of federal officials, a subject that must be understood not only by those in government who are the subjects of lobbying but also by those who engage in lobbying the government officials.

One chapter treats corporate lobbying communications, since both business and nonprofit corporations issue pronouncements in many forms about their government affairs policies and positions.

The book explains the relationship between lobbying and antitrust. While lobbying ususally enjoys an exemption from the anti-

v

trust laws, the exemption is not without limits. There is tension between the constitutional right to redress grievances through approaches to government and the statutory prohibition against restraint of trade among competitors.

There is a chapter on lobbying and defamation. Once again a privilege against illegality exists for lobbying, but the privilege is not unqualified.

The subject of lobbying by government contractors is covered. Here there is a matrix of prescriptions and proscriptions applicable not only to those that contract with the federal government but also to those that receive grants and awards.

Finally, there are two chapters on federal income tax ramifications of lobbying endeavors. One of these deals with tax deductibility of lobbying expenses. The other covers lobbying by charitable organizations.

Federal Lobbying is authored by 13 attorneys of the law firm of Jenner & Block. One of the authors, Bill Bonvillian, is formerly with the firm. He has recently joined the community of those who are lobbied, as Legislative Director and Chief Counsel for a U.S. Senator. The authors brought special expertise and experience to their assignments; equally important, they brought enthusiasm and dedication. The Editor most appreciates the enormous contributions made by all of the co-authors of *Federal Lobbying* and trusts that readers will agree that they have advanced considerably the opportunity for understanding federal law and policy on lobbying.

JERALD A. JACOBS
EDITOR

Washington, D.C.
July 1989

About the Authors

Leland J. Badger, the author of Chapter 7, is a partner in the Washington office of Jenner & Block. His degrees are from Harvard Law School (J.D., 1973) and Dartmouth College (A.B., *summa cum laude,* 1970). He served as a member of the *Harvard Journal on Legislation.* He is admitted to practice in Illinois, the District of Columbia, and several U.S. district courts and U.S. courts of appeals. He is a former Attorney-Advisor to the Assistant General Counsel to the Secretary of the Air Force and was in the Honors Program of the Office of Air Force General Counsel. He has authored numerous legal articles. His practice areas include associations, health care, government procurement contracts, and legislative, civil, and antitrust litigation.

A co-author of Chapter 8, *Benjamin Beiler* is a partner in the Chicago office of Jenner & Block, where he specializes in federal income taxation, acquisitions, joint ventures, debt financing, venture capital financing, and other business transactions. He has written for various tax and legal publications and has spoken at various seminars on these subjects. He received his J.D. degree from Columbia University, his LL.M. in Taxation degree from New York University, and his B.A. degree from the University of Wisconsin.

William B. Bonvillian, co-author of Chapter 3, is a former partner in the Washington office of Jenner & Block. He is Legislative Director and Chief Counsel to U.S. Senator Joseph Lieberman of Connecticut. He is admitted to the bar in Connecticut and the District of Columbia. His degrees are from Columbia University (A.B., *cum laude,* 1969), Yale University (M.A.R., 1972), and Columbia University (J.D., 1974). He served as a member of the Board of Editors of the *Columbia Law Review* and has authored law journal articles on securities and environmental law issues. He served as Law Clerk to Chief Judge Jack B. Weinstein, U.S. District Court, Eastern District of New York, and as Director, Congressional Affairs and Liaison Officer (1977–1979) and Deputy Assistant Secretary (1980–1981), U.S. Department of Transportation.

The author of Chapter 2, *John H. Broadley,* is a partner in the Washington office of Jenner & Block. He is a member of the bars of California and the District of Columbia. He received his undergraduate education at the Massachusetts Institute of Technology and legal education at the University of California at Berkeley. He served as Special Counsel for Rail Litigation, U.S. Department of Justice (1976–1981), Chief Counsel, Federal Railroad Administration (1981–1982), and General Counsel, Interstate Commerce Commission (1982–1984). He concentrates his practice in transportation, transportation bankruptcy, and litigation.

A co-author of Chapter 5 and author of Chapter 6, *Anthony C. Epstein* is a partner in the Washington office of Jenner & Block. He is admitted to practice in the District of Columbia and Maryland, in several U.S. district courts and U.S. courts of appeals, and in the U.S. Supreme Court. His education was at Yale College (B.A., *summa cum laude,* 1974) and Yale Law School (J.D., 1977). He served as law clerk to Hon. Charles B. Renfrew, U.S. District Court for the Northern District of California (1977–1978); attorney, Antitrust Division, U.S. Department of Justice (1978–1979); Special Assistant to the Deputy Attorney General, U.S. Department of Justice (1980–1981); and Special Assistant U.S. Attorney, Eastern District of Virginia (1981).

Paula Cozzi Goedert, a partner in the Chicago office of Jenner & Block, is the author of Chapter 9. She graduated from Mundelein College, *summa cum laude,* in 1973, and from Northwestern University School of Law, *magna cum laude,* 1976. She concentrates her practice in the tax aspects of nonprofit organizations. She is a frequent lecturer on topics raised by nonprofit organizations and the author of numerous articles and seminar outlines.

Mary Jane Graham is an associate attorney in the Washington office of Jenner & Block and co-author of Chapter 3. She graduated *magna cum laude* from the Georgetown University Law Center, holds a Bachelor of Science from Cornell University in Engineering and Applied Physics, and received a Master of Engineering from the University of Virginia in Nuclear Engineering. She is a former reactor inspector with the Nuclear Regulatory Commission, and a former nuclear licensing engineer employed by a public utility to maintain relations with state and federal government agencies. She is admitted to the bar in the District of Columbia.

David Handzo, co-author of Chapter 1, is an associate attorney in the Washington office of Jenner & Block. He received his undergraduate degree from Princeton University in 1976 and his law degree, *magna cum laude,* from the University of Michigan in 1980. He has served in the trial division of the District of Columbia Public Defender Service.

Jerald A. Jacobs is a partner in the Washington office of Jenner & Block. He is the Editor of this book as well as co-author of Chapter 1. His education was at Georgetown University (A.B., *cum laude,* 1967; J.D., 1970) and at the University of Fribourg, Switzerland. He is admitted to practice in the District of Columbia and Illinois, in several U.S. district courts and U.S. courts of appeals, and in the U.S. Supreme Court. He concentrates his practice in association, antitrust, health care, legislative, and administrative law. He is the author of *Association Law Handbook* published by The Bureau of National Affairs, Inc. He has authored several other books as well as law journal and other articles on legal and government affairs topics.

Carl S. Nadler is an associate attorney in the Washington office of Jenner & Block and co-author of Chapter 5. He concentrates his practice in litigation, antitrust, and telecommunications law. He is a member of the bars of Illinois and the District of Columbia. He graduated from Washington University School of Law in 1982 and served as Law Clerk for Judge Alvin B. Rubin of the U.S. Court of Appeals for the Fifth Circuit.

The co-author of Chapter 8, *Toni Prestigiacomo,* is an associate attorney in the Chicago office of Jenner & Block. Her degrees are a B.S. from Northwestern University, a J.D. from Chicago Kent College of Law, and an LL.M. in Taxation from New York University. She concentrates her practice in tax law.

Christopher S. Vaden, who authored Chapter 4, is an associate attorney in the Washington office of Jenner & Block. He is a graduate of the University of Virginia School of Law (J.D., 1982) and of Amherst College (B.A., 1978). He is a member of the bars of the District of Columbia and several U.S. district courts and U.S. courts of appeals. He is active in many areas of civil and administrative litigation, particularly in the areas of antitrust, railroad regulation, and insurance.

A co-author of Chapter 5, *David E. Zerhusen* is a partner in the Washington office of Jenner & Block. He graduated from the University of Chicago Law School in 1980. He is admitted to practice in Maryland, the District of Columbia, and Pennsylvania, as well as in several U.S. district courts, U.S. courts of appeals, and the U.S. Supreme Court. He served as Law Clerk for federal judge Joseph Young (Maryland) and served as Maryland Assistant Attorney General, Civil Litigation Division. He is an experienced commercial litigator with extensive recent concentration in special governmental investigations.

     *   *   *   *   *

The authors acknowledge with appreciation the assistance of Mark D. Schneider and Theresa A. Chmara in the preparation of Chapter 3, John S. Di Bene for his assistance in the preparation of Chapter 5, and James A. Wilson, a student at the University of North Carolina Law School, in the preparation of Chapter 7.

Summary Contents

Detailed Contents

1

Lobbying Registration

Jerald A. Jacobs, David A. Handzo

Since 1946, the Federal Regulation of Lobbying Act has governed lobbying of the United States Congress.[1] At heart, the Act is designed to let Congress and the public know who is lobbying, how much they are spending, and where the money is coming from. Consequently, the Act requires that certain people and entities register as lobbyists and disclose basic financial information about their lobbying activities. Nothing in the Act prohibits or limits lobbying, nor does the Act affect the substance of lobbying efforts. Indeed, because lobbying is a form of speech directly protected by the First Amendment to the Constitution, any statute placing substantive limits on the right to lobby Congress would face a formidable constitutional challenge.[2]

To date, the Act remains the only legislation broadly regulating the lobbying of Congress. Other lobbying statutes, narrower in scope and coverage, regulate special situations such as lobbying by the agents of foreign governments.[3] The focus of this chapter, however, is limited to the Act and its interpretation. In particular, this chapter outlines the requirements of the Act, identifies the persons and activities that fall within the scope of the Act, and provides assistance in submitting the forms required by the Act. The chapter concludes with a discussion of legislative proposals to broaden and toughen the regulation of lobbying at the federal level.

Registration and Reporting Requirements

In general, some of those individuals or organizations to which the Federal Regulation of Lobbying Act applies must register with Congress as lobbyists. But all individuals and organizations to which the law applies must periodically disclose certain financial information and must retain for two years the records documenting that information.

First, there is the registration obligation. Registration is required of an individual or an organization that engages for pay in efforts to influence the passage or defeat of legislation in Congress.[4] Any individual or organization that fits this description—discussed in detail later in this chapter—must register with the Secretary of the Senate and with the Clerk of the House of Representatives.

Registration is accomplished by submitting, in writing, information describing the registrant's employer or client, disclosing the amounts paid for expenses and received as salary or fees, and identifying the sources of the funds from which compensation is paid. If an individual or organization lobbies on behalf of more than one client or employer, separate registration forms must be filed for each client or employer.

Next, there is the reporting obligation. An individual or organization that lobbies must file quarterly reports itemizing financial receipts and disbursements made in furtherance of lobbying activities, naming those to whom disbursements were made, and describing the legislation supported or opposed by the reporting lobbyist or lobbying organization.[5] This information is compiled and published periodically in *The Congressional Record*. Here again, a lobbyist or lobbying organization must file a separate quarterly report for each of its clients or employers. More broadly, quarterly reports must also be filed by any individual or organization that solicits, collects, or receives money for lobbying purposes, so long as lobbying is the principal function of the individual or organization, or the principal purpose for which the money is used. In other words, only those who lobby Congress "for pay" are required to register, but even those who do not lobby "for pay" must nevertheless file quarterly reports if they fit the specified criteria; i.e., they solicit, collect, or receive money for lobbying purposes and their principal purpose, or that of the money, is lobbying. Quarterly reports are filed with the Clerk of the House of Representatives and with the Secretary of the Senate, and must inform those offices of each contribution exceeding $500 received by the filer during that quarter, the names and addresses of those who made the contributions, the total amount of lesser contributions received during the quarter, and an accounting of expenditures made.[6]

Lastly, those who have a duty to file quarterly reports must retain for two years all records and accounts regarding the financial items appearing in those reports.[7]

Overall, the Act is relatively straightforward in terms of what information those covered by the Act must report, when they must report it, and to whom. On these questions, one need only read the text of the Act in order to obtain answers. The threshold question as to what persons or organizations are covered by the Act is far more difficult to answer.

Persons and Activities Covered by the Act

In general, the Act applies to any "person" who "solicits, collects, or receives money or any other thing of value," where the "principal purpose" of the person *or of the contribution* is to "influence * * * the passage or defeat of any legislation by the Congress." Thus, Section 307 of the Act, which contains this language, defines the universe of persons to whom all other sections of the Act apply.[8] Any individual or organization that does not fit the criteria of Section 307 has no obligations under the Act.[9]

The coverage of the Act as it was originally drafted was broader than the language of Section 307. However, in 1954 the U.S. Supreme Court was called upon to consider the constitutionality of the Act, and responded in the *Harriss* case by limiting its reach to those "persons" described by Section 307.[10] Every subsequent interpretation of the Act has taken the *Harriss* decision as its point of departure.

In light of *Harriss,* Section 307 is generally understood to establish a three-part test for coverage by the Act:

(1) the individual or organization must have solicited, collected, or received contributions;
(2) the principal purpose of the individual or organization, or the principal purpose the contribution, must have been to influence the passage or defeat of legislation by Congress; and
(3) this lobbying effort must have been accomplished by means of direct communication with Congress.

Because the language of Section 307 from which this test derives is not free from ambiguity, each of the operative phrases in that section must be examined closely.

"Any Person"

The word "person," as used in Section 307, is broadly defined to include individuals, corporations, partnerships, associations, and other organizations or groups. The only people or entities that Section 307 categorically excludes from coverage are public officials and newspapers.

With respect to public officials, so long as they act in their official capacity they may have any manner of contact with members of Congress without registering or reporting. The "public official" exemption includes state and municipal officials. Indeed, one court decision extended the exemption to include incorporated associations of cities, counties, and mayors that lobby Congress on behalf of their members. Because these organizations were funded solely by public money and exclusively represented entities which were themselves entitled to the public official exemption, a federal district judge found that the associations were likewise exempt.[11] It is safe to assume, therefore, that agents of public officials are ordinarily exempt to the same extent as their principals.

Newspapers or similar periodicals which publish, in the ordinary course of their business, articles and advertisements taking a position on pending legislation are not considered lobbyists under the Act. This is true even with respect to editorials and advertisements which urge the passage or defeat of pending legislation.

"Who * * * Solicits, Collects, or Receives Money"

The full text of Section 307 makes clear that any type of contribution or compensation is covered, including in addition to money "any thing of value." One who is a lobbyist "for pay" and therefore subject to the registration requirements of the Act necessarily falls within the scope of this language, although the converse is not necessarily true. For example, someone who works on a voluntary basis soliciting money for lobbying purposes may be subject to the reporting and record-keeping requirements, even though not a lobbyist "for pay."[12]

The expenditure of money for lobbying purposes does not, by itself, trigger coverage by the Act. Although the government once claimed that spending as well as receiving money mandated compliance with the Act, the Supreme Court rejected this argument in *Harriss*.[13] Thus, lobbyists who do not solicit, collect, or receive money are not obligated under the Act. Obviously, however, few can spend who do not also solicit, collect, or receive; therefore, the real limitation on the coverage of the Act stems from the requirement, discussed below, that the funds be solicited, collected, or received for the "principal purpose" of influencing legislation or by an individual or organization that has the "principal purpose" to influence legislation.

"To Be Used Principally to Aid"

In order for the Act to apply, the individual or organization that solicits, collects, or receives money must either obtain the money "principally to aid" lobbying activities, or else lobbying must be the "principal purpose" of the individual or organization. This so-called principal purpose test is nebulous at best. The Supreme Court's effort to elucidate added only the explanation that an individual has the "principal purpose" of lobbying if the individual's activities are "in substantial part" directed to influencing legislation.[14] Likewise, a contribution which is expended in substantial part on lobbying activities meets the principal purpose test.

Under this test, a business corporation normally need not register or report pursuant to the Act. Lobbying is not normally a substantial part of the corporation's business; the money expended on lobbying typically comes from general revenues not originally solicited, collected, or received for the purpose of lobbying. Therefore, because the expenditure of money for lobbying purposes is not alone sufficient to trigger coverage by the Act, the corporation need not register or report so long as the funds spent on lobbying efforts were not originally obtained by the corporation for that purpose.

On the other hand, nonprofit organizations such as affinity groups, labor unions, trade associations, and professional societies are more likely than most business corporations to have a principal purpose of lobbying for their members or for their cause. Likewise, such a nonprofit organization may be more likely than other entities to have solicited, collected, or received money in order to use that money entirely or in substantial part for lobbying purposes. An organization involved in lobbying, therefore, must realistically evaluate the principal purpose of the organization and its income to determine whether the organization is subject to the requirements of the Act.

Finally, a coalition of business corporations, nonprofit organizations, or other entities formed for lobbying purposes may well be subject as an entity to the Act if the coalition solicits, collects, or receives money for its lobbying or if the coalition's principal purpose is lobbying.

This evaluation may be easier to perform where individuals, rather than organizations, are concerned. An individual who has received any payment specifically as compensation for performing lobbying services has obviously "solicited, collected, or received" money for the principal purpose of lobbying, no matter how small the payment or limited the lobbying effort, and is therefore subject to the Act's registration and reporting requirements. This includes attorneys or other consultants engaged or retained to provide lobbying services.

If the individual receives a salary for a job that includes lobbying as only one of its duties, the question of coverage turns on whether lobbying is a substantial enough part of the job that the individual "would be relieved of his position if he failed to carry on his work in connection with legislative interests."[15] For example, a corporate officer whose primary function within the corporate structure involves something other than lobbying need not register, even though an ancillary part of his or her job involves lobbying activities. On the other hand, a corporate officer who has substantial responsibility for government relations, including lobbying, would likely have to register despite the presence of incidental nonlobbying duties.

When one or more individuals in an organization are covered by the Act, and they are compensated by an organization that itself is also covered by the Act, generally it has been found acceptable for the organization to register and report, naming the individuals as lobbyists.

Given that reporting under the Act occurs on a quarterly basis, common sense suggests that an individual's or an organization's "principal purpose" should be evaluated on a quarterly basis as well. That is, any individual or organization that engages in substantial lobbying activity during a calendar quarter should register and report, even if lobbying activity for the balance of the year is *de minimus*.

"The Passage or Defeat of Any Legislation by the Congress"

Assuming that an individual or organization has "solicited, collected, or received" money for the "principal purpose" of lobbying, coverage by the Act turns finally on the question of whether the lobbying activities are those contemplated by the Act. In general, the Act covers only the lobbying of the U.S. Congress. Lobbying the executive branch of the federal government, therefore, is not within the ambit of the Act. This is true even if the subject of the communication between the lobbyist and the executive branch official is pending legislation in Congress.

The Act sweepingly defines the term "legislation" to include virtually any matter "which may be the subject of action by either House."[16] Lobbying for or against the Senate's confirmation of a nominee to the U.S. Supreme Court or its ratification of a treaty, for example, is covered by the Act.

In the *Harriss* decision, the Supreme Court repeatedly noted that the Act applies only to "direct communication with members of Congress."[17] With that single phrase, the Supreme Court seemingly excluded from the Act *indirect* communications, such as contact with the staff of the legislators, grassroots lobbying, and general communications and publicity.

With respect to grass-roots lobbying, the general opinion appears to be that such activity is indeed excluded from the Act,[18] even though a close reading of *Harriss* leaves the reader less than certain of that conclusion. The Court suggested in its *Harriss* opinion that Congress intended the Act to extend to communications with Congress "through an artificially stimulated letter campaign."[19] The Court, after noting this intention, did not clearly indicate whether its construction of the statute would give effect to the intent of Congress. The result of this ambiguity has been that grass roots lobbying is not considered by commentators to fall within the purview of the Act.

On the other hand, while the language of *Harriss* suggests that contact with the staff of legislators is not "direct lobbying," members of Congress tend to a contrary view, and consider contact with staff equivalent to direct communication with the legislator. While this view is at odds with the language of *Harriss*, which speaks in terms of communications with "members" of Congress, it does recognize the reality that staff members play a key role in the functioning of today's Congress. Consequently, the better practice may be to comply with the requirements of the Act even where contact with staff constitutes the sole lobbying activity. Failure to do so, however, is likely defensible under the language of the *Harriss* decision.

Certain other types of ostensible lobbying are excluded by the express terms of the Act. Witnesses appearing before Congress and its committees to give testimony or to present written statements are exempted from the Act. Those who help prepare the witness to testify or assist in formulating the witness's written statement are included within this exemption. Any ambiguity regarding this latter point was resolved by a federal district court case.[20] In *United States v. Slaughter,* the trial court acquitted a defendant charged with violating the Act after the evidence established that the defendant's activities "consisted largely of preparing statements for witnesses to be given by the witnesses before congressional committees."[21] The court concluded that the exemption for witnesses includes those who assist the witnesses.

Procedures for Reporting and Registering

The procedures for registering and reporting are straightforward. The offices of the Clerk of the House and Secretary of the Senate use a single form for both registration and reporting.[22] Registration is accomplished by filling out the front of the form and submitting it; quarterly reports are accomplished by filling out both sides of the form and submitting it.

The quarterly reports are due by April 10 (for January, February, and March), July 10 (for April, May, and June), October 10 (for July, August, and September), and January 10 (for October, November, and December). Quarterly reports need not be filled out for any calendar quarter in which no reportable activity has occurred. The lobbyist may simply omit filing in that quarter, and will begin filing again at the end of the next quarter in which lobbying activity occurs.

Information from a previous filing should not be incorporated by reference in a current filing; for each separate filing the form must be filled out completely. Completed forms must be filed with *both* the Clerk of the House and the Secretary of the Senate, and both copies must bear an *original* signature.

Most items on the form are self-explanatory. The following items can cause confusion:

1. Preliminary filing. When filling out the front of the form in order to register, check the box marked "P" at the top right of the form, which indicates that it is a "preliminary" filing.

2. <u>Identification number.</u> For a lobbyist that has several clients, a different "identification number" is assigned for each client that the lobbyist represents. Therefore, when filing the initial registration, the lobbyist obviously will not yet know the identification number and should leave this blank. After receiving the registration, the congressional office will send out a postcard with the identification number on it. This should be used by that lobbyist on all subsequent filings for that particular client.

3. <u>Employer.</u> For a lobbyist representing a client, the name of the client will be entered here, along with the other information requested. If an organization is lobbying on behalf of itself, and if the report is filled by that organization, this space will be left blank. If the report is filed by an individual employed by that organization, the organization's name is inserted here. If an individual is employed by an organization which is itself engaged by a client to perform lobbying services (e.g., a lawyer employed by a law firm that is engaged to provide lobbying services), the names of both the direct employer and the client should be inserted in this space.[23]

4. <u>Legislative interests.</u> This should be filled in as specifically as possible, including the titles and numbers of bills that the lobbyist will support or oppose. However, it is not uncommon for this information to be unavailable when filing the initial registration; in that case, the registration can be amended later.

5. <u>Line D(5).</u> If the lobbyist receives a salary for performing duties which include, but are not limited to, lobbying, then the amount inserted in this section should be that amount of the lobbyist's remuneration attributable to lobbying. For example, if the lobbyist spends 60 percent of his or her time lobbying, then the amount entered on line D(5) would be 60 percent of the lobbyist's quarterly remuneration.

6. <u>Line D(12).</u> Any expenses reflected in Section E for which the lobbyist later receives reimbursement should be entered on this line.

7. <u>Line E(2).</u> Some lobbyists make the mistake of entering their own remuneration on this line. It is intended, instead, to reflect remuneration paid by the lobbyist to others in connection with lobbying activities.

8. <u>Line E(15).</u> The Act requires that all expenditures of $10 or more be itemized. Ten dollars does not, however, buy as much as it did in 1946 when the Act was passed. In view of this fact, the congressional offices will permit certain minor expenses to be aggregated. For example, one could report an aggregate expense of $70 for transportation to and from airports without concern that the congressional offices would object.

Any questions not addressed above can be easily answered by telephoning the offices of the Clerk of the House (202–225-1300) and Secretary of the Senate (202–224-0322). The staff of those offices are available to answer questions and are extremely helpful.

Enforcement

The Act is a criminal statute, and the willful violation of its requirements is a misdemeanor punishable by up to one year in jail and a fine of up to $5,000. In addition, a criminal conviction under the Act automatically bars the convicted lobbyist from any further congressional lobbying for three years after the conviction.[24]

In some sense, judicial interpretation of the Act has been shaped by the fact that the Act carries potential criminal penalties. Because constitutional due process principles require that a criminal statute "give a person of ordinary intelligence fair notice that his contemplated conduct is forbidden," courts have struggled to place a clear and definite limit on the potentially broad reach of the Act's hopelessly ambiguous language.[25] Perhaps it is a measure of the courts' lack of success in this endeavor that only six prosecutions under the Act have been reported, and only one of those was successful. No reported criminal prosecution has been initiated since the decade of the 1950s, possibly in recognition of the fact that the Act's coverage remains so vague that fairness dictates remedying violations informally without prosecution.

Obviously, however, criminal sanctions remain a possibility; compliance with the Act is not a matter to be taken lightly.

The Future of Lobbying Regulation

The Act is often criticized as vague and inadequate.[26] As a result, periodic efforts have been made to enact more stringent lobbying disclosure legislation. In general, these efforts have focused on: (1) expanding the people and activities covered by the statute to include lobbying of congressional staff, lobbying of certain members of the executive branch, and grass-roots lobbying activities; (2) substituting specific registration and reporting thresholds, based on either lobbying expenditures or on time spent on lobbying activities, or both, in place of the principal purpose requirement; (3) requiring organizations meeting the registration and reporting thresholds to disclose information about lobbying activities in greater detail than is now required; (4) transferring administrative authority for registration and reporting to the General Accounting Office and the Comptroller General; and (5) providing for detailed enforcement provisions, with both civil and criminal penalties, and vesting in the Department of Justice and the Attorney General investigatory authority for alleged violations.

Interest in enacting comprehensive lobbying disclosure legislation appears to have waned in recent years. Two bills were introduced in the 99th Congress, referred to committee, and never enacted. One bill, H.R. 3150, expanded substantially on the provisions of the current statute. The second, H.R. 3151 and S. 1564, took an entirely different approach and provided for voluntary registration and reporting of lobbying activities. Both bills expanded coverage to include grass-roots lobbying, as well as communications with legislative staff members and certain executive branch officials.

Presumably, any amendment to the current Act and any new legislation will contain features similar to those of the recently proposed statutes. However, no new legislation has been introduced since the 99th Congress. The 1946 Act, despite its flaws, thus continues to govern the lobbying of Congress.

Notes

1. The Act is codified at 2 U.S.C. §§261-70. The text of the Act is included in Appendix A.
2. For example, an attempt by the Massachusetts legislature to prohibit corporations from spending money to influence the outcome of voter referendums was struck down by the U.S. Supreme Court on First Amendment grounds. Finding that the First Amendment protects both a corporation's right to make its views known and the public's right to hear those views, the Court threw out the Massachusetts statute because it abridged the right to free speech in a manner not justified by any compelling state interest. *First Nat'l Bank of Boston v. Bellotti,* 435 U.S. 765 (1978).
3. For example, see Sec. 12(i) of the Public Utility Holding Company Act of 1935, 15 U.S.C. §79(l)(i), Sec. 807 of the Merchant Marine Act of 1936, 46 U.S.C. §1225, and the Foreign Agents Registration Act of 1938, 22 U.S.C. §§611 *et seq.,* the latter of which is covered in Chapter 2.
4. 2 U.S.C. §267(a).
5. The complete list of information required for registration and quarterly filings appears at 2 U.S.C. §267(a).
6. The list of information to be included in these filings appears at 2 U.S.C. §264.
7. 2 U.S.C. §262.
8. Sec. 307 of the Act is codified at 2 U.S.C. §266.
9. While the registration, reporting, and record-keeping requirements of the Act must be observed only by those who meet the test of Sec. 307, the registration requirements are further limited by Sec. 308 of the Act to those who are "engage[d] * * * for pay" in lobbying.
10. See *United States v. Harriss,* 347 U.S. 612, 619 (1954).
11. *Bradley v. Saxbe,* 388 F. Supp. 53 (D.D.C. 1974).
12. As a practical matter, the offices of the Clerk of the House and Secretary of the Senate make no distinction between those who must report and those who must register. Their view is inconsistent with the Supreme Court's treatment of this issue in *Harriss,* 347 U.S. at 623. However, because registration is easily accomplished, the better practice is to file a registration statement in all instances where reporting is required.
13. 347 U.S. at 619-20.
14. *Harris, supra,* 347 U.S. at 622.
15. HOUSE SELECT COMM. ON LOBBYING ACTIVITIES, REPORT AND RECOMMENDATIONS ON THE LOBBYING ACT, H.R. REP. 3239, 81st Cong., 2d Sess. 27 (1951).
16. 2 U.S.C. §261(e).
17. *Harriss, supra,* 347 U.S. at 620, 623 (emphasis added).
18. See, e.g., Boggs & Boyce, *Federal Regulation of Lobbying,* ASSOCIATION ISSUES 85, 87 (1983); CONGRESSIONAL QUARTERLY, THE WASHINGTON LOBBY 23 (4th ed. 1982); Land, *Federal Lobbying Disclosure Reform Legislation,* 17 HARV. J. ON LEGIS. 295, 300 & n.22 (1980); COMMON CAUSE, THE POWER PERSUADERS iv-v (1978); *Lobby Reform Act of 1977: Hearings Before the Senate Committee on Governmental Affairs,* 95th Cong., 2d Sess., 251, 260-61 (statements of Andrew A. Feinstein and David E. Landau) (1978).

19. 347 U.S. at 620.

20. *United States v. Slaughter,* 89 F. Supp. 876 (D.D.C. 1950).

21. 89 F. Supp. at 877. Many of the facts of the *Slaughter* case are recounted in an earlier opinion from the same case. *United States v. Slaughter,* 89 F. Supp. 205 (D.D.C. 1950).

22. Forms can be obtained from the Clerk of the House of Representatives, Office of Records and Registration, 1036 Longworth House Office Building, Washington, D.C. 20515. The forms are reproduced in Appendix B.

23. Alternatively, because the employer must also register in these circumstances, it is considered acceptable for the employee not to register so long as the employer registers and names the employee as its lobbyist.

24. In turn, a violation of the three-year suspension provisions of the Act carries a criminal penalty of up to five years in prison and a fine of up to $10,000.

25. *Harriss, supra,* 347 U.S. at 617.

26. See, e.g., Land, *Federal Lobbying Disclosure Reform Legislation,* 17 HARV. J. ON LEGIS. 295, 300–04 (1980); AMERICAN ENTERPRISE INSTITUTE, PROPOSALS TO REVIEW THE LOBBYING LAW (1980); COMMON CAUSE, THE POWER PERSUADERS (1978); Comptroller General of the United States, The Federal Regulation of Lobbying Act—Difficulties in Enforcement and Administration (1975), *in Public Disclosure of Lobbying Act: Hearings Before House Subcomm. on Administrative Law and Governmental Relations,* 94th Cong., 1st Sess. 870 (1975).

2

Lobbying for Foreign Interests

John H. Broadley

The many changes in the domestic and in foreign economies over the past 30 years have resulted in a substantial increase in the interest and knowledge of foreign states and corporations in the U.S. political process. Foreign entities understand that decision making in the American system is decentralized and competitive and that diplomatic contacts with the Department of State no longer suffice as the sole means of influencing the U.S. decision makers.

Recognition of the complexity of the American political process has led foreign states and commercial enterprises to turn to specialists to ensure that they have an effective input in decisions affecting their interests. However, as with many domestic organizations, few foreign states and companies have the volume of business with the American political process to warrant "in-house" staff for all their needs. Foreign interests increasingly rely on third parties for assistance.

Thus, the American lobbyist often may represent either a foreign state or a foreign business. Representation of such foreign interests presents unique regulatory and legal problems. In particular, the lobbyist must deal with the Foreign Agent Registration Act ("FARA" or the "Act").[1]

Background

FARA was originally enacted in an entirely different era to deal with activities far different from those undertaken by the lobbyist today. Unfortunately, FARA's markings and language reflect its origin. FARA was first enacted in 1938[2] to deal with what Congress perceived to be the problem of German and Soviet propaganda in the United States. In the language of the House Report on the bill, it was

12

designed to turn the "spotlight of pitiless publicity" on to the activities of foreign propagandists in order to "serve as a deterrent to the spread of pernicious propaganda" and to allow the people "to know the sources of such efforts, and the person or persons carrying on such work in the United States."[3]

The statutory language fully reflects the framers' essentially pejorative view of the activities against which FARA is directed. Individuals subject to the Act's requirements are referred to as "agents of a foreign principal," and much of their work is referred to as "political propaganda."

The approach of the Act similarly reflects the time during which it was written. FARA does not *prohibit* activities; instead it requires *public disclosure* of the identity of agents of foreign principals and the foreign principals as well. It similarly requires disclosure in an agent's work that it was undertaken or produced on behalf of a foreign principal.

Because of both the pejorative tone of the Act, and the burdensome nature of the disclosure requirements, a lobbyist should seek, if possible, to ensure that he or his activities on behalf of his client either are not subject to FARA or fall within one of the statutory exemptions. Once the lobbyist believes he may be subject to the Act, he should obtain professional advice, unless he is familiar with FARA's registering, record-keeping, labeling, and other disclosure requirements.[4]

Foreign Principal

FARA does not come into play unless the lobbyist has a "foreign principal," as defined in Section 1(b) of the Act.[5] A useful way to approach the issue is to analyze first whether the lobbyist has a direct foreign principal, and second whether he has an indirect foreign principal. Neither the Act nor the regulations[6] promulgated by the Attorney General (the "Attorney General's regulations") now use the terms direct foreign principal or indirect foreign principal. However, use of the concepts simplifies the analysis of the issue of whether the lobbyist has a foreign principal.

Direct Foreign Principal

Section 1(b) of FARA identifies three sets of foreign principals. The first set, according to Section 1(b)(1), consists of foreign governments and foreign political parties.[7] Although a lobbyist usually has little difficulty in determining whether his client is a foreign government or a foreign political party, the Act's definitions of these terms give them a broader scope than the lobbyist first might recognize.

The term "foreign government" is defined in Section 1(e) of the

Act.[8] That section defines the term to include any person or group of persons exercising sovereign *de jure* or *de facto* political jurisdiction over any country other than the United States. The definition also includes a group exercising sovereign *de jure* or *de facto* political jurisdiction over any part of a country, as well as any subdivision of any such group, and any group or agency to which sovereign *de facto* or *de jure* authority or functions are delegated. The definition specifically states that "[s]uch term shall include any faction or body of insurgents within a country assuming to exercise governmental authority whether such faction or body of insurgents has or has not been recognized by the United States."

The term "foreign political party," defined in Section 1(f) of the Act,[9] includes any organization or other combination of individuals in a country other than the United States, or any unit or branch of such organization, which has the aim or purpose, or which is engaged "in any activity devoted in whole or in part to, the establishment, administration, control, or acquisition of administration or control of a government of a foreign country or a political subdivision thereof, or the furtherance or influencing of the political or public interests, policies, or relations of a government of a foreign country or a subdivision thereof."

Section 1(b)(2) defines a second set of foreign principals to include "a person outside the United States."[10] Because Section 1(a) defines "persons" to include individuals, partnerships, associations, corporations, organizations, "or any other combination of individuals," the Section 1(b)(2) definition of foreign principal is quite broad. It encompasses U.S. citizens domiciled abroad, as well as U.S. corporations that have their principal place of business abroad. It also includes subsidiaries of American corporations that are organized under foreign laws, even though they may be wholly owned by a U.S. corporation.

The sweep of Section 1(b)(2) is narrowed by two exceptions. The first exception applies if a person can establish that he is (1) an individual, (2) a U.S. citizen, and (3) domiciled in the United States. The second exception to the Section 1(b)(2) definition applies if a person can establish that it (1) is not an individual, (2) is organized or created under the laws of the United States, any state, or other place subject to the jurisdiction of the United States, and (3) has its principal place of business within the United States.[11]

The third set of foreign principals, specified by Section 1(b)(3) of the Act,[12] includes partnerships, associations, corporations, organizations, or other combinations of persons that are either (1) organized under the laws of a foreign country or (2) have their principal place of business in a foreign country. This set of foreign principals overlaps to some degree with Section 1(b)(2), and resolves any doubt that foreign corporations doing business in the United States and American corporations that have their principal place of business abroad are foreign principals within the Act.

The Act's definition of foreign principal does not include individual citizens of foreign countries who are in the United States. Thus, an alien who is permanently resident in the United States is not considered to be a foreign principal under the Act, solely because he is an alien.

Indirect Foreign Principal

The concept of the indirect foreign principal stems from the language of Section 1(c) of the Act.[13] That section brings within the scope of the Act (as a potential "agent of a foreign principal") not only every person who acts as an agent of a foreign principal, but also every person who acts as the agent of another person "any of whose activities are directly or indirectly supervised, directed, controlled, financed, or subsidized in whole or in major part by a foreign principal * * * ."[14] This person shall be called the "intermediary."

Thus, whether a lobbyist is an "agent of a foreign principal," as that term is used in the Act, depends on not only whether the lobbyist's direct principal is a statutory foreign principal, but also whether the lobbyist's principal is an intermediary. If the lobbyist's principal is an intermediary as set forth in Section 1(c) of the Act, the intermediary's foreign principal becomes the lobbyist's indirect foreign principal.

In *Attorney General of the United States v. The Irish People*[15] the court of appeals pointed out that different tests determine whether an entity is an intermediary and whether an entity is an agent of a foreign principal). In that case, the Irish Northern Aid Committee (INAC) had been enjoined to register as a foreign agent of the Irish Republican Army (IRA) on the grounds that it acted as a representative for or at the request of the IRA.[16] The court of appeals found that this relationship did not necessarily qualify INAC as an intermediary of the IRA because that relationship was dependent upon showing that INAC's activities are "directly or indirectly supervised, directed, controlled, financed, or subsidized in whole or in major part by a foreign principal."[17]

The court was also careful to state that Congress did not intend registration to stifle internal debate on political issues by citizens sympathetic to the view of foreigners. The court also pointed to the legislative history of the 1966 amendments to FARA, particularly the House Report which stated that "mere receipt of a bona fide subsidy not subjecting the recipient to the direction or control of the donor does not require the recipient of the subsidy to register as a foreign agent."[18]

Thus, from the lobbyist's perspective, it is not sufficient simply to determine whether his principal falls within one of the Section 1(b) categories. He must further determine whether his principal is an intermediary for a foreign principal, in which case the lobbyist may be required to register as an foreign agent. While on its face this might appear to be an onerous burden, in fact the difficulty of identifying an indirect foreign principal is alleviated by the fact that the lobbyist does not come within the reach of the Act unless his activities are conducted "for or in the interests of" the underlying foreign principal.[19] Particularly where the lobbyist is retained by a person, such as a law firm or an association, which is clearly not the real party in interest, further investigation regarding the nature of the real party or parties in interest would be prudent, especially where the subject matter of the representation suggests the presence of a foreign interest.

An Agent of a Foreign Principal

Once it becomes clear that the lobbyist has entered into a relationship, directly or indirectly, with a foreign principal, he must determine whether he is an "agent of a foreign principal" within the meaning of Section 1(c) of the Act.[20] The statutory test to determine whether the lobbyist is an agent of a foreign principal has two parts. The first part focuses on whether there is a particular type of relationship between the lobbyist and the foreign principal (the "relationship test"), and the second part focuses on the activities to be undertaken on behalf of the foreign principal (the "activities test").

The Relationship Test

To be considered an agent of a foreign principal under the Act, a lobbyist must act either as an agent, representative, employee, or servant of a foreign principal, or at the order, request, or under the direction or control of a foreign principal. Whether one is an agent, representative, employee, or servant of a foreign principal is unlikely to present significant difficulties. Where there is a formal contractual arrangement providing for the lobbyist to further the interests of the foreign principal or of the foreign principal's intermediary, there is unlikely to be any doubt that the necessary relationship exists.

More difficult issues arise when existence of the necessary relationship depends on the lobbyist's acting at the "order, request, or under the direction or control" of a foreign principal. It is well established that the relationship need not be one of formal agency.[21] While the exact limits of the necessary relationship have not been spelled out, one court has described them as follows:

> "While we acknowledge that the Act requires registration by a person who acts, in specified ways, at a foreign principal's 'request,' we caution that this word is not to be understood in its most precatory sense. Such an interpretation would sweep within the statute's scope many forms of conduct that Congress did not intend to regulate. The exact perimeters

of a 'request' under the Act are difficult to locate, falling somewhere between a command and a plea."[22]

The same court provided some guidance to determining whether a "request" falls within the meaning of the Act. One factor considered by the court was whether those requested to act were identified with specificity by the foreign principal. The court noted that when members of large ethnic, racial, or religious groups respond to pleas for contributions or general political assistance, they do not become "agents" within the meaning of the Act. In contrast, when a particular individual or a sufficiently limited group of identifiable individuals is asked to act, the court concluded, the surrounding circumstances may show that those "requested" are in some way authorized to act for, or to represent, the foreign principal. However, the court made clear that even where a specific individual has been made the target of a request by a foreign principal, if the individual is acting independently, he does not become an agent under the Act, even if the foreign principal is indirectly benefited.[23]

In another case, a district court held that a U.S. partnership was not subject to the control of a foreign principal.[24] The foreign principal had only a 25 percent interest in the partnership formed under New York law, while a New York corporation that was unconnected with the foreign principal had a 75 percent interest and was designated as managing partner. The court focused solely on the control issue and did not decide whether the partnership was acting at the request of the foreign principal, although it was clearly furthering the interests of the foreign principal by attempting to secure legislation favorable to both the foreign principal and the partnership.[25]

In the absence of a formal agency or representation agreement, the existence of the necessary relationship with the foreign principal will depend on the facts. A relationship in which the lobbyist is acting independently of a foreign principal, even while serving the foreign principal's interests, will not meet the requirement.[26]

The Activities Test

Once the necessary relationship has been found, the activities test must be met. Only certain activities undertaken by the agent on behalf of his foreign principal qualify the agent as the "agent of a foreign principal" within the meaning of the Act. Activities satisfying the test fall into four groups.

Political Activities

The first type of activities that meets the activities test is "engag[ing] within the United States in political activities for or in the interests of the foreign principal."[27] The Act defines political activities as any activity which the person undertaking it "believes will, or which he intends to, prevail upon, indoctrinate, convert, induce, persuade, or in any other way influence" an agency or official of the U.S. government, "or any section of the public within the United States with reference to formulating, adopting, or changing, the domestic or foreign policies of the United States or with reference to the political or public interests, policies, or relations of a government of a foreign country or a foreign political party."[28]

The intent of the Act with respect to political activities is spelled out succinctly in the House Report on the 1966 amendments, which added the definition of political activities now found in Section 1(o).

> "The basic point of reference in determining whether an agent's efforts for his principal fall within the intent and meaning of the definition [of political activities] is the end objective of his activities. If the agent disseminates political propaganda or engages in any activity with the objective of influencing a Government agency or official, or any portion of the public with reference to—
> "(1) formulating, adopting, or changing the foreign or domestic policies of our Government, or
> "(2) the political or public interests, policies or relations of a foreign government or a foreign political party, the agent is engaged in political activities and must register* * *."[29]

The House Report makes clear that political activities do not include the routine administration and application of existing policies, but only matters relating to changing or preserving policies. It points out that matters within the purview of the judiciary cannot be the subject of political activities on the grounds that the courts do not make "policy" as that term is used in FARA. As examples of policy matters within the meaning of political activities, the House Report refers to existing or proposed legislation, treaties, executive agreements, proclamations and orders, and decisions relating to or affecting departmental policy.[30] The Attorney General's regulations have incorporated this distinction.[31] The Attorney General's regulations also state that the routine implementation of existing policies, as in a request for administrative action where the policy itself is not in question, is not "formulating, adopting or changing" policy.[32]

The House Report on the 1966 amendments draws a similar distinction between policy making and implementation in explaining the phrase "political or public interests, policies or relations of the government of a foreign country or a foreign political party." Policy matters fall within the meaning of the terms, while "questions calling for decision at the level of government or of a political organization charged with the administration of existing laws, regulations or other policies"[33] are not encompassed. Thus, activities intending to influence the U.S. public with reference to the routine administration of existing laws or policies of a foreign government would not fall within the definition of political activities, so long as those activities did not also attempt to influence the public in formulating, adopting or changing the domestic or foreign policies of the United States.

While the Act refers only to "formulating, adopting, or changing" policies, both the House Report[34] and the regulations of the Attorney General make clear that the preservation of existing policy is encompassed within those terms.[35] Similarly, activities intended to influence government officials directly can fall within the definition of political activities, as can activities directed to the general public or to a segment of the general public (activities that might be characterized as grass-roots lobbying). Thus, a direct approach to an official to influence policies and an indirect approach to the general public, or a segment of the public, constitute political activity within the meaning of the Act.

The Act also classifies as political activity the dissemination of "political propaganda."[36] As defined by the Act, political propaganda consists of any communication or expression which is reasonably adapted to, or which the person disseminating it believes will, or which he intends to, influence either the recipient or any section of the public within the United States with respect to (1) the political or public interests, policies, or relations of the government of a foreign country or a foreign political party, (2) the foreign policies of the United States, or (3) the promotion of racial, religious, or social dissensions in the United States.

The statutory definition includes two components—one objective and one subjective. First, the material is political propaganda if it is reasonably adapted to influence either the recipient or the general public with respect to one of the specified subject matters. Second, the material is political propaganda if the disseminator believes it will influence the recipient or the general public with respect to one of the specified subject matters, or the disseminator intends that it influence the recipient or the general public with respect to one of the specified subject matters.

The Act also classifies as political propaganda communications which advocate, advise, instigate, or promote "any racial, social, political, or religious disorder, civil riot, or other conflict involving the use of force or violence in any other American republic or the overthrow of any government or political subdivision of any other American republic by any means involving the use of force or violence."[37]

Dissemination of political propaganda within the meaning of the Act includes transmitting it or causing it to be transmitted in the U.S. mails or by any means or instrumentality of interstate or foreign commerce or offering or causing it to be offered in the U.S. mails.[38]

Public Relations Counsel, Publicity Agents, Information-Service Employees, and Political Consultants

The second type of activities that meets the activities test consists of acting as a public relations counsel, publicity agent, information-service employee, or political consultant within the United States on behalf of a foreign principal.[39] All four activities are further defined in the Act.

The term "public relations counsel" is defined to mean persons who are engaged, either directly or indirectly, in informing, advising, or representing a principal in any public relations matter that pertains to political or public interests, policies, or relations of the principal.[40] Simply advising a foreign principal regarding public relations matters does not bring an activity within the statute. The advice must pertain to political or public interests, policies, or relations of the principal. The expression "political or public interests, policies or relations," used elsewhere in the Act,[41] appears to be limited to matters of policy, and not to the routine implementation of existing law of a foreign country.[42]

The term "information-service employee" is defined to mean persons "engaged in furnishing, disseminating, or publishing information with respect to the political, industrial, employment, economic, social, cultural, or other benefits, advantages, facts, or conditions" of any country other than the United States, any foreign government or political party, or any partnership, association, corporation, organization, or "other combination of individuals organized under the laws of, or having its principal place of business in, a foreign country."[43] While the definition of "public relations counsel" limits covered subject matters to the "political or public interests, policies, or relations of the principal," the definition of "information-service employee" contains much broader subject-matter limitations.

As defined in the Act, a "publicity agent" is

"any person who engages directly or indirectly in the publication or dissemination of oral, visual, graphic, written, or pictorial information or matter of any kind, including publication by means of advertising, books, periodicals, newspapers, lectures, broadcasts, motion pictures, or otherwise."[44]

This activity appears to have no subject-matter limits; indeed, it appears to include anything not covered in the definition of "information-service employee."

The fourth activity in this group is that of the "political consultant." The Act states:

"The term 'political consultant' means any person who engages in informing or advising any other person with reference to the domestic or foreign policies of the United States or the political or public interest, policies, or relations of a foreign country or of a foreign political party."[45]

On its face this provision is both sweeping and unambiguous. However, the legislative history of the 1966 amendments to the Act suggests that Congress may have had in mind a considerably narrower definition than is suggested by the actual language of the definition. The House Report on the 1966 amendments says:

"The definition of the term 'political consultant' would apply to persons engaged in advising their foreign principals with respect to political matters. However, a 'political consultant' would not be required to register as an agent unless he engaged in political activities, as defined, for his foreign principal. A lawyer who advised his foreign client concerning the construction or application of an existing statute or regulation would be a 'political consultant' under the definition, but unless the purpose of the advice was to effect a change in U.S. policy he would not be engaged in political activities and would be exempt from registering with the Department of Justice."[46]

The Attorney General's regulations provide that the term "domestic or foreign policies of the United States" as used in the definitions of "political activities" and "political consultant" in Section 1 of the Act

"shall be deemed to relate to existing and proposed legislation, or legislative action generally; treaties; executive agreements, proclamations, and orders; decisions relating to or affecting departmental or agency policy, and the like."[47]

This provides little assistance in resolving the dilemma. However, the Registration Unit in the Department of Justice advises that registration is not required unless the purpose of the advice is to effect a change in U.S. policy, as stated in the House Report.

As a practical matter, many of the activities that would fall within the statutory definition of acting as a political consultant would be exempt from registration.[48] Availability of an exemption, however, does not entirely resolve the matter. Even with respect to exempt activities, there may be some disclosure requirements.

Collecting and Dispensing Money and Other Things of Value

The third type of activities that meets the "activities test" to establish that a person is an agent of a foreign principal within the meaning of the Act is the solicitation, collection, disbursement, or dispensing of contributions, loans, money, or other things of value in the United States for or in the interest of the foreign principal.[49] This type of activity is reasonably straightforward and does not appear to be subject to any subject-matter limitations.

Representing a Foreign Principal Before an Agency or Official of the United States

The fourth category of activities that satisfies the "activities test" is the representation of a foreign principal, in the United States, before any agency or official of the U.S. government.[50] The Attorney General's regulations make clear that the term "agency" includes every unit in the legislative and executive branches of the government, including the committees of Congress. Similarly, "official" is defined by the regulations to include members and officers of both Houses of Congress as well as officials of the executive branch. The regulations do not indicate whether legislative staff is encompassed within the meaning of the term "official."[51]

In addition to the person who has both the prescribed relationship with a foreign principal and performs one or more of the specified activities for that foreign principal, the Act also designates as an agent of a foreign principal anyone who agrees to act as or holds himself out to be an agent of a foreign principal.[52] This section brings within the statute persons who either have the necessary relationship with the foreign principal and agree to perform any of the acts previously discussed and set forth in Section 1(c)(1)(i)-(iv) of the Act, and persons who hold themselves out to be agents of the foreign principal, regardless of the existence of a formal contractual relationship.

Section 1(d) of the Act limits the definition of "agent of a foreign principal" by specifically excluding therefrom certain news or press services or associations organized under the laws of the United States, and certain newspapers, magazines, periodicals, or other publications, provided that specified requirements are met.[53] This exclusion is of interest only to the limited number of specialized entities to which it applies.

Exemption From Registration

Because FARA's coverage is so broad, in the absence of exemptions, almost ever person involved in representing an entity with foreign connections would be considered an agent under the Act and required to register. Fortunately, a number of exemptions are available which substantially reduce the probability that the lobbyist will have to register. The most important exemption is set forth in Section 3(d) of the Act.[54]

Section 3(d) exempts from registration an agent of a foreign principal whose activities fall into either of two groups: (1) private, nonpolitical activities in furtherance of the bona fide trade or commerce of the foreign principal; and (2) other activities not serving predominantly a foreign interest.

Commercial Exemption

An agent of a foreign principal is exempt if he engages in or agrees to engage in only private and nonpolitical activities in furtherance of the bona fide trade or commerce of the foreign principal. Two of the key terms of this exemption—"private" and "bona fide trade or commerce"—are amplified in the Attorney General's regulations.

The Attorney General's regulations make clear that the term "trade or commerce" includes the exchange, transfer, purchase, or sale of commodities, services, or property of any kind. They also make clear that "private" activities means, at a minimum, that the activities do not directly promote the political or foreign policy interests of a foreign government. The regulation further states that private activities promoting bona fide trade or commerce do not lose that status simply because the foreign principal is owned or controlled by a foreign government, if the activities do not directly promote the foreign government's political or foreign policy interests.[55]

The term "nonpolitical" is not defined in either the Act or the regulations. However, the logical deduction that "nonpolitical" covers those activities that are not "political activities" as defined in Section 1(o) of the Act gains some limited support from language in the House Report on the 1966 amendments which could be read as implying that the two terms are exclusive.

> "Section 3 would amend Section 3(d) of the Act to exempt from registration foreign agents engaging in private and nonpolitical activities with a bona fide commercial purpose, or in political activities when the activities do not serve predominantly a foreign interest."[56]

Other Activities Not Serving Predominantly a Foreign Interest

The second exemption found in Section 3(d) of the Act provides that an agent need not register when engaged in "other activities not serving predominantly a foreign interest."[57] Arguably, this is the most important exemption for the professional lobbyist because it relates to circumstances likely to arise in the case of a domestic client that has either a foreign subsidiary or foreign parent.

On its face this exemption seems to be the height of ambiguity. Section 1(q) of the Act, however, gives some concrete guidance; in many respects, it can be viewed as providing a "safe harbor." Section 1(q) ensures that most lobbying activities undertaken on behalf of a U.S. subsidiary of a foreign corporation or on behalf of a U.S. corporation that has a foreign subsidiary will not require registration of the lobbyist as a foreign agent.[58]

Section 1(q) provides that activities will not be considered to serve predominantly a foreign interest within the meaning of Section 3(d) if those activities further the bona fide commercial, industrial, or financial interests of a domestic person that is engaged in substantial commercial, industrial, or financial operations in the United States. The section specifically provides that is the case even if the activities also benefit the interests of a foreign person engaged in bona fide trade or commerce and the foreign person is either owned or controlled by the domestic person, or owns or controls the domestic person.

There are, however, limits to the safe harbor. The domestic person must be engaged in substantial commercial, industrial, or financial activities in the United States. It cannot be an empty shell used as a lobbying vehicle. Moreover, the activities undertaken by the agent must be in furtherance of the commercial, industrial, or financial interests of the domestic person. Finally, the foreign person must be engaged in bona fide trade or commerce and must either own or control the domestic person, or be owned or controlled by the domestic person.

Three further restrictions apply. First, a foreign person that owns or controls the domestic person cannot be a foreign government or a foreign political party. Second, the activities undertaken by the domestic person cannot be directly or indirectly supervised, directed, controlled, financed, or subsidized in whole or in substantial part by a foreign government or a foreign political party. Third, if the foreign person owns or controls the domestic person, the activities undertaken by the agent must be substantially in furtherance of the commercial, industrial, or financial interests of the domestic person.

Section 1(q) raises an issue discussed briefly earlier in this chapter. Once a person meets the definition of an "agent of a foreign principal," there are consequences, even if exemptions *from registration* are available. Section 1(q) requires that the identity of the foreign person benefited by the activities undertaken by the agent be disclosed to the agency or official (as those terms are defined in the Attorney General's regulations) before the activities take place. The burden is on the agent to establish that the disclosure was in fact made.

The statutory provisions do not resolve all the issues in this complex area. For example, can relationships other than that of one entity either owning or controlling the other be brought within the safe harbor? What level of domestic activity is required to meet the "substantial commercial, industrial, or financial operations in the United States" part of the safe harbor definition? And what constitutes "activities substantially in furtherance of the bona fide commercial, industrial, or financial interests of [the] domestic person"? Notwithstanding Congress's apparent intent to provide a safe harbor for the agent of the multinational entity, there appear to be no clear answers to these questions.

Practice of Law

The second most significant exemption under the Act for the lobbyist is probably that contained in Section 3(g), which exempts from registration any agent who is qualified to practice law, but only insofar as he engages or agrees to represent a disclosed foreign principal before any court or any agency of the U.S. government. Attempts by the agent to influence or persuade agency personnel other than in the course of established formal or informal agency proceedings are not covered by the exemption.[60]

The Attorney General's regulations provide that only attempts to influence agency personnel with respect to (1) the domestic or foreign policies of the United States or (2) the political or public interests, policies, or relations of a government of a foreign country or of a foreign political party outside the course of established proceedings will be excluded from this exemption.[61] The Attorney General's regulations reemphasize the statutory requirement that in order to come within this exemption, the agent must disclose the identity of the foreign principal, even if it would not otherwise be required in the proceeding. The attorney agent must make the disclosure to each of the agency's personnel or officials before whom, and at the time when, his legal representation is undertaken. The burden of establishing that the disclosure took place is on the agent.[62]

Diplomatic Exemptions

The Act contains three exemptions which apply to the diplomatic representation of foreign governments in the United States. Section 3(a) exempts duly accredited diplomatic or consular officers of a foreign government recognized by the State Department as such, but only while the officer is performing within the scope of the officer's functions that the State Department recognizes.[63] The Attorney General's regulations state that the exemption of the consular officer commences only when the officer has received formal approval, either provisionally or permanently, from the State Department. The exemption is a personal one, and does not apply to any office, bureau, or other entity.[64]

Closely related to the diplomatic and consular exemption is an exemption in Section 3(b) of the Act for officials of a foreign government, if that government is recognized by the United States.[65] This exemption is more limited than that afforded to diplomatic and consular officials. As with the diplomatic and consular exemption, the exemption for officials of a foreign government only applies after the name, status, and character of the duties of the official are filed with the State Department. The official must be engaged in activities which the State Department recognizes as within his duties. In addition, this exemption does not apply to any person who is acting as a public relations counsel, a publicity agent, or an information-service employee as those terms are defined in the Act.[66] Finally, the exemption does not apply to any person who is a citizen of the United States. The Attorney General's regulations require that a formal Notification of Status with a Foreign Government be filed with the State Department on form D.S. 394 before this exemption becomes effective.[67]

Section 3(c) of the Act exempts staff members and persons employed by a duly accredited diplomatic or consular officer of a foreign government.[68] The limitations on this exemption are similar to those applicable to foreign government officials. The foreign government must be recognized by the United States; the employee must have notified the State Department of his status on form D.S. 394; the employee must not be a public relations counsel, publicity agent, or information-service employee; and the exemption extends only to those activities which the State Department recognizes as being within the scope of the employee's functions. By its terms, this exemption does not exclude U.S. citizens.

Other Exemptions

Section 3(d) of the Act exempts from registration any person engaging in the solicitation or collection of funds or contributions in the United States "for medical aid and assistance, or for food and clothing to relieve human suffering, if the solicitation or collection of funds and contributions is made in accordance with subchapter II of chapter 9" of Title 22.[69] As with other exemptions, the burden of establishing entitlement to the "relief agency" exemption is on the agent.[70]

Section 3(e) of the Act also exempts from registration any person engaging in "activities in furtherance of bona fide religious, scholastic, academic, or scientific pursuits or of the fine arts."[71] The Attorney General's regulations deny this exemption to any person who engages in political activities as defined in Section 1(o) of the Act on behalf of his foreign principal.[72]

Requirements Under FARA

Registration

Section 2 of the Act provides that before acting as the agent of a foreign principal, the agent must register with the Attorney General.[73] A registration statement must be filed with the Attorney General within 10 days of becoming an agent. The obligation to register continues beyond the tenth day, and indeed survives the termination of an agent's status as such. Thus, where an agent fails to file a registration statement when required, terminating the agent's status does not eliminate the obligation to file a statement for the period during which he was an agent.

The Attorney General's regulations require that the agent file an initial registration statement (Form OBD-63) with the Registration Unit of the Internal Security Section of the Criminal Division of the Department of Justice in Washington, D.C.[74] It is beyond the scope of this chapter to detail the mechanics of registration. A brief overview of the process is presented.

Form OBD-63 seeks detailed information concerning the registrant. It asks for (1) identification of the registrant's foreign principal, (2) a description of activities the registrant is undertaking to benefit his foreign principal, (3) financial information relating to the registrant's relationship with his foreign principal, and (4) information regarding the nature of any political propaganda intended to be disseminated on behalf of his foreign principal.

The Attorney General's regulations also require that certain exhibits be filed with the initial registration statement.[75] Exhibit A, which must be filed on Form OBD-67, requests information regarding the foreign principal. Exhibit B, which must be filed on Form OBD-65, requests information relating to the agreement between the foreign principal and the registrant, the nature and method of performing the agreement, and the existing or proposed activities to be undertaken by the registrant, including political activities. Any changes in the information furnished on Exhibits A or B must be reported to the Registration Unit within 10 days of the change, and the Assistant Attorney General may require the filing of new exhibits.

Exhibit C, which does not have a standard form, consists of documents relating to the corporate existence of the registrant. Thus, the regulations call for the filing of the registrant's charter, articles of association or incorporation, or constitution, as well as its bylaws.[76] Exhibit C also must contain a copy of every other instrument or document, and a statement about every oral agreement, relating to the organization, powers, and purposes of the registrant. Where the registrant is a law firm, Exhibit C must contain a copy of its partnership agreement. The Assistant Attorney General may waive, wholly or partially, the filing of Exhibit C.

Exhibit D, required by the regulations, is a statement that must be filed when the registrant receives or collects contributions, loans, money, or other things of value as part of a fund-raising campaign in the United States.[77] The agent must set forth the names and addresses of the persons who contributed the money or things of value, the amount of money or things of value collected, the amount of money or things of value transmitted by the registrant to the foreign principal, and the manner and time of such transmittal. The regulations specify no form for Exhibit D.

The Attorney General's regulations require the registrant to file supplemental statements every six months during the course of the representation. Supplemental statements are required even though no activities may have taken place during the six-month period. Supplemental statements are filed on Form OBD-64.[78]

Every partner, officer, director, associate, employee, and agent of the registrant is also required to file a registration statement.[79] However, unless the Assistant Attorney General directs otherwise, this requirement can be satisfied by filing a "short form" registration statement on Form OBD-66.[80] The short form registration procedure requires that the registrant report any change in the services to be performed or the compensation to be received for those services by filing a new short form within 10 days of the change. There is no requirement to file exhibits with a short form registration statement, nor is there a requirement for filing supplemental statements.[81]

The Attorney General's regulations exempt from the requirement of filing a short form registration statement any partners, officers, directors, associates, employees, or agents of a registrant who do not engage directly in activity in furtherance of the interests of the foreign principal. The regulations also exempt from the requirement to file a short form registration statement employees whose services in furtherance of the interests of a foreign principal are of a clerical, secretarial, or similar nature.[82]

Amendments due to deficiencies in an initial, supplemental, or final statement are to be filed on Form OBD-68. Certain changes in information must be reported to the Assistant Attorney General as amendments.[83]

The registrant must also file a final statement on Form OBD-64 (the same form used for supplemental statements) within 30 days of the termination of his obligation to register under the Act. The final statement must cover the period not covered by any previous registration statement.[84] The regulations explicitly provide that the registrant may file a termination statement notwithstanding the continuation of his agency relationship if that relationship becomes limited to activities which are exempt from registration under Section 3 of the Act.[85]

Political Propaganda

An agent required to register must also comply with certain requirements relating to political propaganda, as defined by the Act.[86] The agent must meet a filing requirement, a labeling requirement, as well as certain other requirements.

The Filing Requirement

According to Section 4(a) of the Act, the agent must file two copies of each item of political propaganda with the Attorney General, accompanied by a statement describing the places, times, and extent of transmittal of the political propaganda. This requirement is applicable when:

(1) the political propaganda is transmitted in the United States by an agent required to register, or at his direction;

(2) the political propaganda is transmitted in the mails or by any means or any instrumentality of interstate or foreign commerce;

(3) the political propaganda is transmitted for or in the interests of the foreign principal; and

(4) the political propaganda is either (a) in the form of "prints" or (b) in any other form reasonably adapted to being, or which the agent believes will be, or which the agent intends to be, disseminated or circulated among two or more persons.[87]

Section 1(n) of the Act defines the word "prints" to mean

"newspapers and periodicals, books, pamphlets, sheet music, visiting cards, address cards, printing proofs, engravings, photographs, pictures, drawings, plans, maps, patterns to be cut out, catalogs, prospectuses, advertisements, and printed, engraved, lithographed, or autographed notices of various kinds, and, in general, all impressions or reproductions obtained on paper or other material assimilable to paper, on parchment or on cardboard, by means of printing, engraving, lithography, autography, or any other easily recognizable mechanical process, with the exception of the copying press, stamps with movable or immovable type, and the typewriter."[88]

Whether more recent technological developments such as electronic mail would fit within the definition of "prints" is an intriguing question. However, Section 4(a)(ii) renders most such questions moot. The language "any other form which is reasonably adapted to being, or which he [the agent] believes will be, or which he intends to be, disseminated or circulated among two or more persons" would encompass almost any transmittal of political propaganda.

The two copies of each item of political propaganda must be filed with the Registration Unit.[89] Once the two copies of an item have been filed, additional copies need not be filed when further dissemination takes place.[90] The regulations do not require that copies of motion pictures be filed, provided, however, that either a filmstrip showing the required labeling, or an affidavit that such label is affixed, is filed, and so long as monthly reports on its dissemination are filed.

A dissemination report must be filed for each item of political propaganda that is transmitted. The dissemination report must be filed on Form OBD-69 within 48 hours of transmittal of the political propaganda. However, if periodic transmittals of the same material are made, the regulations permit a monthly dissemination report to be filed.[91]

The Labeling Requirement

Section 4 of the Act also requires that political propaganda be labeled.[92] Before transmitting political propaganda, the agent must conspicuously mark, preface, or accompany the material with a

"true and accurate statement, in the language or languages used in such political propaganda, setting forth the relationship or connection between the person transmitting the political propaganda or causing it to be transmitted and such propaganda; that the person transmitting such political propaganda or causing it to be transmitted is registered under this subchapter with the Department of Justice, Washington, District of Columbia, as an agent of a foreign principal, together with the name and principal; that as required by this subchapter, his registration statement is available for inspection at and copies of such political propaganda are being filed with the Department of Justice; and that registration of agents of foreign principals required by the subchapter does not indicate approval by the United States Government of the contents of their political propaganda.[93]

The Attorney General's regulations deal primarily with the mechanical aspects of the labeling required by the Act. Prints are to be marked or stamped at the beginning with a statement containing the information required by the Act. Other political propaganda not in the form of prints must be accompanied by a statement setting forth the information required by the Act. Televised or broadcast materials must be introduced by a statement which is reasonably adapted to convey to the viewers or listeners the information required by the

Act. Still or motion picture film must contain at the beginning a statement reasonably adapted to convey to the viewers the information required by the Act.[94]

A constitutional challenge to the labeling requirement of the Act was rejected by the Supreme Court in *Meese v. Keene*.[95] The plaintiff, who was not an agent, argued that characterization of a film the plaintiff wanted to exhibit as "political propaganda" was pejorative and an unnecessary and therefore invalid abridgment of free speech. The Court rejected the argument.

There are two other requirements relating to political propaganda. Section 4(e) of the Act makes it unlawful for any person required to register under the Act to transmit, convey, or furnish to any U.S. agency or official (including a member or committee of Congress) any political propaganda for or in the interests of the foreign principal[96] or *to request* from an agency or official, for or in the interests of his foreign principal,

> "any information or advice with respect to any matter pertaining to the political or public interests, policies or relations of a foreign country or of a political party or pertaining to the foreign *or domestic* policies of the United States unless the propaganda or request is prefaced or accompanied by a true and accurate statement to the effect that such person is registered as an agent [of the foreign principal under the Act]."[97] (Emphasis added.)

The statement that must accompany the political propaganda or request made to the agency or official must be in writing.[98] It is not clear how telephonic requests for information should be handled.

Finally, Section 4(f) of the Act contains a requirement that whenever an agent of a foreign principal required to register under the Act testifies for or in the interests of his foreign principal before any congressional committee, he must supply the committee with, for inclusion in the record as part of his testimony, a copy of his most recent registration statement filed with the Department of Justice.[99]

Maintenance of Books and Records

Section 5 of the Act and the Attorney General's regulations prescribe the records that a registered agent of a foreign principal is required to keep.[100] The record-keeping requirements are quite detailed, going beyond ordinary financial and tax record-keeping requirements. This chapter covers a few requirements from the Attorney General's regulations to illustrate their broad scope.

The registered agent must keep all correspondence, memoranda, cables, telegrams, teletype messages, and other written communications to and from all foreign principals and *all other persons,* relating to the agent's activities on behalf of or in the interest of any of his foreign principals.[101] In addition, he must keep all written communications to and from all persons (other than foreign principals) "relating to the registrant's political activity, or relating to political activity on behalf of any of the registrant's foreign principals."[102] Thus, the record-keeping requirement extends to other political activities of the agent, including those on his own behalf, in addition to those performed on behalf of his foreign principal.[103]

Other provisions require keeping records of the names and addresses of persons to whom political propaganda has been transmitted,[104] financial records of the agent's activities for or on behalf of his foreign principals,[105] minute books,[106] and records of the names and addresses of all employees and agents, including former employees and agents of the registered agent.[107]

Records are to be kept in such a manner as to render them accessible for inspection as permitted under Section 5 of the Act.[108] They must be kept for three years following the termination of the agent's registration,[109] though an agent may seek the Assistant Attorney General's permission to destroy records supporting registration statements filed more than five years prior to the date on which he seeks permission.[110]

Officials of the Criminal Division of the Department of Justice and the Federal Bureau of Investigation are authorized by Section 5 of the Act to inspect the records.[111] In addition, materials filed with the Department of Justice are available for public inspection pursuant to Section 6 of the Act and the Attorney General's regulations, and copies of such materials can be obtained from the Department of Justice upon payment of a nominal fee.[112]

Enforcement

Section 8(a) of the Act provides that any person who

"(1) willfully violates any provision of this subchapter or any regulation thereunder, or
"(2) in any registration statement or supplement thereto or in any statement under section 614(a) of this title concerning the distribution of political propaganda or in any other document filed with or furnished to the Attorney General under the provisions of this subchapter willfully makes a false statement of a material fact or willfully omits any material fact required to be stated therein or willfully omits a material fact or a copy of a material document necessary to make the statements therein and the copies of documents furnished therewith not misleading, shall, upon conviction thereof be punished by a fine of not more than $10,000 or by imprisonment for not more than five years, or both, except that in the case of a violation of subsection (b), (e), or (f) of section 614 of this title or of subsection (g) or (h) of this section the punishment shall be a fine of not more than $5000 or imprisonment for not more than six months, or both."[113]

Section 8 of the Act contains other elements of both an enforcement and substantive nature. Section 8(c) makes an alien convicted of violation of the Act subject to deportation;[114] Section 8(e) makes the failure to file any registration statement or supplement required by Section 2(a) of the Act a continuing offense, notwithstanding any statute of limitations.[115]

Section 8(f) gives the Attorney General the right to seek an injunction against continued violation of the Act, to require compliance with the Act, and to enjoin a person from continuing to act as the agent of a foreign principal. Most of the recent litigation under the Act has arisen as a result of injunction actions brought by the Attorney General.[116]

Section 8(g) of the Act permits the Attorney General to notify a person that a registration statement does not comply with the requirements of the Act or the regulations.[117] Thereafter it is unlawful for that person to continue to act as an agent at "any time ten days or more after receipt of such notification" unless the person has filed an amended registration statement in full compliance with the requirements of the Act and regulations. The Attorney General's regulations provide that depositing an amended registration statement in the mail no later than the tenth day after receipt of the notice satisfies the requirement, and that the agent can continue to act beyond the 10-day period unless he receives a Notice of Noncompliance from the Registration Unit.[118]

The final provision of the Act, Section 8(h), makes it unlawful for an agent of a foreign principal to enter into any arrangement with his foreign principal, expressed or implied, under which the agent's compensation is contingent in whole or in part upon the success of any political activity carried on by the agent.

Other Considerations

While the lobbyist who has a foreign client will be concerned primarily with compliance with FARA, there are other statutes applicable to foreign interests and their representation.

The lobbyist should be particularly aware of the provisions of 2 U.S.C. §441(e) which prohibits contributions by foreign nationals, directly or indirectly, to an election campaign. The term foreign national is defined to include a "foreign principal" as defined in Section 1(b) of FARA, except that it does not include any individual who is a citizen of the United States. The definition of a foreign national also includes any individual who is not a citizen of the United States and is not admitted to permanent residence in the United States.

Another statute of which the lobbyist should be particularly aware is 18 U.S.C. §951, which makes it an offense for any person other than a diplomatic, consular officer, or attache to act in the United States as an agent of a foreign government without first notifying the Secretary of State. This notification requirement is in addition to the registration requirements of FARA.

Notes

1. The Foreign Agent Registration Act was at one time referred to as the "McCormack Act." The reference is rarely, if ever, used now. It is found at 22 U.S.C. §§611-618 and reprinted in Appendix C.

2. 52 Stat. 631, ch. 327 (1938).

3. H.R. Rep. No. 1381, 75th Cong., 1st Sess. 1-2 (1937).

4. Because of the complexity of FARA, this chapter can provide only an overview sufficient to identify the principal issues. The practitioner whose client encounters a problem in this field will find great assistance in *The Registration of Foreign Agents in the United States: A Practical and Legal Guide,* edited by Joseph E. Pattison and John L. Taylor and published by the District of Columbia Bar in 1981. As well as containing a detailed discussion of FARA, the publication contains invaluable advice regarding registration and recordkeeping.

5. 22 U.S.C. §611(b).

6. The regulations implementing FARA are found at 28 C.F.R. Part 5, Administration and Enforcement of the Foreign Agents Registration Act of 1938, as amended. See Appendix D.

7. 22 U.S.C. §611(b)(1).

8. 22 U.S.C. §611(e).

9. 22 U.S.C. §611(f).

10. 22 U.S.C. §611(b)(2).

11. *Id.*

12. 22 U.S.C. §611(b)(3).

13. 22 U.S.C. §611(b)(3).

14. The House Report on the 1966 amendments to FARA makes it clear that "the mere receipt of a bona fide subsidy not subjecting the recipient to the direction or control of the donor does not require the recipient of the subsidy to register as an agent of the donor. However, the amendment would insure, in order to curtail the use of subsidies as a means of avoiding the act's requirements, that where the foreign principal subsidizes a domestic person to the extent that the subsidy involves, as outlined above, direction and control of the activities subsidized, then the domestic person or group as well as any agents employed to carry out the functions subsidized will be treated as acting for the foreign principal." H.R. Rep. No. 1470, 89th Cong., 2d Sess. 5-6 (1966), *reprinted in* 1966 U.S. Code Cong. & Admin. News 2397, 2402-03.

15. *Attorney General of the U.S. v. The Irish People,* 796 F.2d 520 (D.C. Cir. 1986).

16. *Attorney General of the U.S. v. Irish Northern Aid Comm.,* 530 F. Supp. 241, 256-60 (S.D.N.Y. 1981), *aff'd,* 668 F.2d 159, 161 (2d Cir. 1982).

17. 796 F.2d at 525.

18. *Attorney General of the U.S. v. Irish Northern Aid Comm.,* 796 F.2d 520, 524 (D.C. Cir. 1986), *citing* H.R. Rep. No. 1470, 89th Cong., 2d Sess. 5-6 (1966), *reprinted in* 1966 U.S. Code Cong. & Admin. News. 2397, 2401. See also *Figli v. Fisheries Dev. Corp.,* 499 F. Supp. 1074, 1081-82 (S.D.N.Y. 1980) (corporation that receives financial support from foreign principal without being subject to its control and whose lobbying efforts benefit a foreign government but are not subject to the foreign government's control is not an agent under FARA).

19. 22 U.S.C. §611(c).

20. 22 U.S.C. §611(c).

21. See *Attorney General of the U.S. v. Irish Northern Aid Comm.,* 530 F. Supp. 241 (S.D.N.Y. 1981), *aff'd,* 668 F.2d 159 (2d Cir. 1982). In this case, the district court rejected the defendant's argument that the Act required an agency relationship conforming to the *Restatement (Second) of Agency* §1. It looked instead to the defendant's relationship with the foreign principal and concluded that the defendant in fact acted as a representative of or at the request of its foreign principal, the Irish Republican Army.

    On appeal, the court concurred with the lower court that control of the agent by the foreign principal within the meaning of the law of agency is not the appropriate standard, but "whether the relationship warrants registration by the agent to carry out the purposes of the Act." 668 F.2d at 161.

22. 688 F.2d at 161.

23. *Id.* at 161-62.

24. *Figli v. Fisheries Dev. Corp.,* 499 F. Supp. 1074 (S.D.N.Y. 1980).

25. *Id.* at 1081-82.

26. This issue is one that may arise in the context of trade associations with foreign members. Where the foreign members control the association, the relationship test between the association and the foreign members, or groups of foreign members appears to be satisfied. It is not clear whether actions taken by the association at the request of its foreign members (where they do not have the necessary control to compel the action) satisfies the relationship test, although applying the principles outlined in *Attorney General v. Irish Northern Aid Comm.*, 668 F.2d 159 (2d Cir. 1982), would suggest it does, at least where the action to be taken is solely for the benefit of the foreign members.

27. 22 U.S.C. §611(c)(1)(i).

28. 22 U.S.C. §611(o).

29. H.R. REP. No. 1470, 89th Cong., 2d Sess. (1966), *reprinted in* 1966 U.S. CODE CONG. & ADMIN. NEWS 2397, 2402.

30. *Id.*

31. 28 C.F.R. §5.100(f).

32. 28 C.F.R. §5.100(e).

33. H.R. REP. No. 1470, 89th Cong., 2d Sess. (1966), *reprinted in* 1966 U.S. CODE CONG. & ADMIN. NEWS, 2397, 2403.

34. H.R. REP. No. 1470, 89th Cong., 2d Sess. (1966), *reprinted in* 1966 U.S. CODE CONG. & ADMIN. NEWS 2397, 2402.

35. See 28 C.F.R. §5.100(e).

36. 22 U.S.C. §611(j).

37. 22 U.S.C. §611(l). The Act defines "American republic" to include any of the states which were signatories to the Final Act of the Second Meeting of the Ministers of Foreign Affairs of the American Republics at Habana, Cuba, June 30, 1940.

38. 22 U.S.C. §611(j).

39. 22 U.S.C. §611(c)(1)(ii).

40. 22 U.S.C. §611(g).

41. See 22 U.S.C. §611(j) and (o).

42. In the definitions of "political activities," "political propaganda," "political consultant," and "foreign political party," the expression is applied to "a foreign government" or a "foreign political party." It is not clear whether use of the term in connection with the work "principal" causes it to have a different meaning in the definition of "public relations counsel." See H.R. REP. No. 1470, 89th Cong., 2d Sess. (1966), *reprinted in* 1966 U.S. CODE CONG. & ADMIN. NEWS 2397, 2403, where the Committee states:

    "The phrase 'political or public interests, policies, or relations,' relating to activities on behalf of a foreign government or foreign political party, has been carried over from existing law. It is the committee's understanding that the phrase refers to matters which on the domestic governmental level would be called a policy matter, in the international context may be called questions concerning a country's foreign relations, and in the context of party politics may be termed matters involving the national interest. All of these facets of national policy, whether called policy matters, foreign relations, or matters of national interest, are to be distinguished from questions calling for decision at the level of government or of a political organization charged with the administration of existing laws, regulations or other policies."

43. 22 U.S.C. §611(i).

44. 22 U.S.C. §611(h).

45. 22 U.S.C. §611(p).

46. H.R. REP. No. 1470, 89th Cong., 2d Sess. (1966), *reprinted in* 1966 U.S. CODE CONG. & ADMIN. NEWS 2397, 2403.

47. 28 C.F.R. §5.100(f).

48. 22 U.S.C. §613.

49. 22 U.S.C. §611(c)(1)(iii).

50. 22 U.S.C. §611(c)(iv).

51. 28 C.F.R. §5.100(c) and (d).

52. 22 U.S.C. §611(c)(2).

53. 22 U.S.C. §611(d).

54. 22 U.S.C. §613(d).

55. 28 C.F.R. §5.304(a) and (b).

56. See H.R. REP. No. 1470, 89th Cong., 2d Sess. (1966), *reprinted in* 1966 U.S. CODE CONG. & ADMIN. NEWS at 2397.

57. 22 U.S.C. §613(d).

58. 22 U.S.C. §611(q).

59. See 28 C.F.R. §5.304(c).

60. 22 U.S.C. §613(g).
61. 28 C.F.R. §5.306(a).
62. 28 C.F.R. §5.306(b).
63. 22 U.S.C. §613(c).
64. 28 C.F.R. §5.301.
65. 22 U.S.C. §613(b).
66. 22 U.S.C. §611(g), (h), and (i).
67. 28 C.F.R. §5.303.
68. 22 U.S.C. §613(c).
69. 22 U.S.C. §613(d). Sec. 448(a) of Title 22 prohibits the solicitation of funds for or on behalf of a belligerent government designated by the President pursuant to 22 U.S.C. §441, or on behalf of their agents or instrumentalities. Sec. §448(b) of Title 22 grants an exception to that prohibition, provided that the funds are to be used exclusively for medical aid or assistance or for food and clothing to relieve human suffering, and further provided that the solicitation or collection is made for or on behalf of a person or organization that is not acting on behalf of a belligerent government.
70. See *Attorney General v. Irish Northern Aid Comm.*, 530 F. Supp. 241, 254-55 (S.D.N.Y. 1981), *aff'd,* 668 F.2d 159 (2d Cir. 1982).
71. 22 U.S.C. §613(e).
72. 28 C.F.R. §5.304(d). Another exemption contained in 22 U.S.C. §613(f) exempts persons whose foreign principals are governments of a foreign country whose defense the President deems vital to the defense of the United States. At this time no countries are so designated.
73. 22 U.S.C. §612(a).
74. 28 C.F.R. §5.200.
75. 28 C.F.R. §5.201.
76. 28 C.F.R. §5.201(c).
77. 28 C.F.R. §5.201(e).
78. 28 C.F.R. §5.203.
79. 28 C.F.R. §5.202.
80. 28 C.F.R. §5.202(e).
81. *Id.*
82. 28 C.F.R. §5.202(b) and (c).
83. 28 C.F.R. §5.204.
84. 28 C.F.R. §5.205.
85. 28 C.F.R. §5.205(c).
86. 22 U.S.C. §611(j).
87. 22 U.S.C. §614(a).
88. 22 U.S.C. §611(n).
89. 28 C.F.R. §5.400(a).
90. 28 C.F.R. §5.400(b).
91. 28 C.F.R. §5.401.
92. 22 U.S.C. §614(b).
93. *Id.*
94. 28 C.F.R. §5.402(a)-(e).
95. *Meese v. Keene,* 481 U.S. 465 (1987).
96. 22 U.S.C. §614(e).
97. 22 U.S.C. §611(e).
98. 28 C.F.R. §5.402(f).
99. 22 U.S.C. §614(f).
100. 22 U.S.C. §615; 28 C.F.R. §5.500.
101. 28 C.F.R. §5.500(a)(1).
102. 28 C.F.R. §5.500(a)(2).
103. This requirement may present constitutional problems, but has not been challenged. It is also not clear that this regulation is permitted by the Act.
104. 28 C.F.R. §5.500(a)(4).
105. 28 C.F.R. §5.500(a)(5).
106. 28 C.F.R. §5.500(a)(6).
107. 28 C.F.R. §5.500(a)(7).

108. 28 C.F.R. §5.500(b).
109. 28 C.F.R. §5.500(c).
110. 28 C.F.R. §5.500(d).
111. 22 U.S.C. §615.
112. 22 U.S.C. §616; 28 C.F.R. §§5.600-01.
113. 22 U.S.C. §618(a).
114. 22 U.S.C. §618(c).
115. 22 U.S.C. §618(e).
116. 22 U.S.C. §618(f).
117. 22 U.S.C. §618(g).
118. 28 C.F.R. §§5.800-01.

3

Lobbying and Ethics of Federal Officials

William B. Bonvillian, Mary Jane Graham

The laws, regulations, and official pronouncements on the ethics of government officials affect lobbying at the federal level in many ways. They provide direction to officials in the areas of honoraria, conflicts of interest, future employment,[1] and financial disclosure. All of these areas can be important to those who seek to influence the decisions of federal officials. This chapter explores separately the ethics requirements for congressional officials and administrative officials.

Congressional Officials

An understanding of the ethical constraints placed on the legislative branch of the federal government is important to anyone who deals with the Senate and House of Representatives. Most of the statutes and rules of legislative ethics regulate the conduct of members, officers, and employees of the House and Senate. A few, such as the federal bribery statute, also restrict the activities of outsiders who are involved in unethical conduct. Even if a rule directly addresses only persons within the legislative branch, in the closely monitored Capitol Hill environment, considerable adverse press coverage can follow unethical legislative behavior, indirectly penalizing outsiders who are involved. Unwitting violations of the legislative ethics requirements are easy to commit. The rules do not simply reflect conventional morality. They are not intuitive, nor are they consistent throughout the legislative branch. The House and Senate have different codes of conduct, and members, officers, and employees are treated differently within those codes. The rules must simply be studied and applied. To assist in understanding the network of statutes and rules of ethics, the ethics committees of both the Senate and House have collected rules, statutes, and their formal interpretations in publicly available publications.[2]

In addition, both committees urge members, officers, and employees to seek clarification of the rules whenever necessary by posing written or telephone questions to the committee staffs.[3]

Background

Congress has exempted itself from many of the federal conflict of interest statutes that govern the behavior of employees and officers of the executive branch.[4] Only the prohibitions against outside compensation for the performance of official duties,[5] legal representation by members of Congress before the Court of Claims or Federal Circuit,[6] and representational activities by officers and employees of Congress (as opposed to Senators and Representatives)[7] are applied to Congress, its officers, or employees. The financial disclosure requirements of the 1978 Ethics in Government Act also apply to high-level staff and members of the legislative branch.[8]

In addition to these conflict of interest statutes, members of Congress and their staff are subject to other federal statutes that define ethical conduct. The most notable for purposes of this chapter are the federal bribery statute, 18 U.S.C. §201, and the statutory limit on the receipt of honoraria, 2 U.S.C. §31-1. The Federal Election Campaign Act, 2 U.S.C. §§431-441, also governs the behavior of members of Congress and their staff by defining acceptable means of receiving funds.[9]

The statutory framework defining ethical behavior in the legislative branch is limited. These statutes are supplemented by official codes of conduct promulgated separately by the Senate and the House of Representatives. These codes are the product of standing committees of both houses of Congress, and typically govern those areas of behavior which are beyond the scope of the federal statutes. In addition, they contain statements reaffirming statutory requirements as rules of the House or Senate.

Rules XXXIV through XLII of the Standing Rules of the Senate comprise the Senate Code of Official Conduct. These rules, and the committee decisions which interpret them, are published in the *Interpretive Rulings of the Select Committee on Ethics ("Senate Interpretive Rulings")* of the U.S. Senate. The Select Committee on Ethics has made over 400 rulings on specific questions raised by members of the Senate regarding interpretation of the rules. These advisory opinions may be relied upon by individuals in similar situations.[10] Most[11] are published chronologically in that volume with cross-references to the related rule or statute.[12]

Various House rules, statutes, and regulations governing the conduct of members, officers, and employees of the House of Representatives have been collected and interpreted by the House Committee on Standards of Official Conduct in the *Ethics Manual for Members, Officers, and Employees of the U.S. House of Representatives ("House Ethics Manual").* The *House Ethics Manual* outlines standards of conduct topic by topic, rather than rule by rule. Each discussion is based on applicable rules, statutes, regulations, and interpretive rulings of the Committee. Because the interpretive material is extensive, and the Committee's preferred form of counseling is responding to telephone inquiries, the House Committee has issued far fewer advisory opinions than its Senate counterpart. Key advisory opinions are cited in the *Manual* and published in its appendices. The *Manual* also summarizes recommendations of the Committee and rulings of the full House on ethical charges brought against Representatives and their staffs.

In addition to the statutes and codes of conduct which govern behavior by virtue of position in the legislative branch, members, officers, and employees are still bound by any professional standards of conduct relevant to their training and occupation. Standards such as the rules of professional conduct for lawyers promulgated by the American and other Bar Associations may impose different or additional obligations on some individuals.

The enforcement of ethical standards for the legislative branch is accomplished in a variety of ways. Counseling of members and staff by the ethics committees of both houses is a prophylactic enforcement mechanism. If violations do occur, both houses have internal penalties which may be imposed. The type of penalty depends on the position of the violator within the legislative branch and the severity of the violation.

The House Committee on Standards of Official Conduct and Senate Select Committee on Ethics investigate alleged violations of any law, rule, or regulation by members, officers, and employees of their respective houses of Congress, and recommend action to the full house.[13] Each house is authorized by the U.S. Constitution to punish its members for disorderly conduct and, by two-thirds vote, to expel a member.[14] In addition, the House of Representatives procedures provide for punishment of a member by censure, reprimand, fine, condemnation, suspension, demand of an apology for misconduct, or other action as appropriate, and permit administrative action to be taken to penalize House officers and employees.[15] Similarly, at the recommendation of the Senate ethics committee, the full Senate may punish a Senator by censure or expulsion, by recommending to the Senator's party loss of seniority or responsibilities, or by other action as appropriate. The Senate may punish its employees by suspension or dismissal.[16] Employees may also be reprimanded or removed from their positions at the discretion of the employing member, committee, or a supervising officer.[17]

With the approval of the House or Senate, the ethics committees may report substantial evidence of violations of statutory ethical requirements to the appropriate criminal law enforcement authorities.[18] Only these authorities can prosecute persons involved in the wrongdoing who are not members, officers, or employees of Congress. Violations of criminal statutes, such as the federal bribery laws, may result in fines or imprisonment.

A final, unofficial form of enforcement is recognition of the role of the press in matters of congressional ethics. Significant adverse consequences are possible as a result of an appearance of conflict of interest, both to members of Congress or legislative employees and to other parties involved.

Applicability

In general, the legislative ethics statutes and rules apply to members, officers, and employees of the House and Senate.[19] Where appropriate to the subject of the rule, applicability is extended to candidates and prospective appointees for these positions, or to past officeholders and employees. In most cases, it is easy to determine whether an individual is bound by the rules. The identities of members and officers of the House and Senate are known. Salaried staff of members and of committees in permanent positions are obviously "employees" subject to all ethics rules.

In some cases, however, it is not clear whether a person should be considered a congressional employee. Some individuals volunteer their services as unpaid staff. Others may be contractors, short-term employees, or employees of other branches of the government on special assignment to provide services to a House or Senate committee.

To remove potential ambiguity, Senate Standing Rule XLI requires that any individual performing full-time services for senatorial offices or committees for more than 90 days in a calendar year must be Senate or government officers or employees, or must agree in writing to be bound by the Code. Full-time service includes service as an employee or a contractor. Government officers or employees assigned to provide services to the Senate must also agree in writing to be bound by the Code. If applicability of a rule depends on the salary of the individual, the salary paid for the services rendered is used to determine whether the rule applies, irrespective of the source of the salary.

Accepting Things of Value

Bribes, Gratuities, and Compensation for the Use of Influence

The federal bribery statutes make it illegal to give or receive a thing of value given with the intent to influence an official act, or for or because of an official act.[20] The "public official" who is prohibited from being bribed is broadly interpreted,[21] and includes members, candidates, officers, potential appointees, employees, and persons who do not fit the definition of employee but are acting "for or on behalf of" the United States or a department, agency, or branch of the federal government.[22] In addition to the statute, Senate Standing Rule XXXVII and House Rule XLIII, clause 3, prohibit any member, officer, or employee of the Senate or House from receiving compensation for the use of influence. The House prohibits accepting benefits which even give the appearance of compensation for the use of influence.[23]

Outside Income

There are several ethical concerns which arise whenever a member, officer, or employee receives income other than salary from the legislative branch. The first question is whether the individual is really being compensated for the use of influence. If so, the income is inappropriate as described above. The second question is whether persons in the legislative branch may ever receive compensation for performance of their governmental duties. Finally, if the outside income is in return for other types of services, the question arises whether outside employment is appropriate.

Compensation for Legislative Duties. There is no statutory requirement that the full compensation paid to members, officers, or employees of the Congress come from appropriated funds.[24] Prohibitions against receiving compensation for the use of influence, and against maintaining unofficial office accounts, discussed elsewhere in this chapter, effectively prohibit most forms of outside compensation for official duties.

Senate Standing Rule XLI clearly contemplates permitting outside compensation for official tasks in that it requires persons who receive compensation from other sources to comply with the Code of Official Conduct. In addition, both ethics committees have determined that payment of all or part of an intern's salary by a sponsoring organization does not violate the restrictions of either house, provided that (1) the purpose of the internship is primarily to educationally benefit the intern and (2) the sponsoring organization is not given an undue advantage.[25]

Compensation for Other Services. Outside employment is permitted by both the House and Senate, though many limitations apply. Outside services raise questions of conflict of loyalties in providing adequate services in both positions. There may also be a conflict of interest if the second employer or the individual (by virtue of the second position) has a financial interest in undertaking legislative duties. The rules of the House and Senate regarding outside employment address these concerns.

Senate Standing Rule XXXVII prohibits members, officers, and employees of the Senate from engaging in any outside employment "inconsistent or in conflict with" conscientious performance of official duties. Officers and employees of the Senate must inform their supervisors of *any* outside business or employment, and take action as the supervisor requires to avoid any conflict of interest or interference with duties in the Senate. Individual members and committees may determine whether an employee's outside services interfere with his or her duties to Congress.[26] Both conflicts of financial interest and conflicts of resources for the two employers are to be considered. The Senate ethics committee has found that, under this rule, it is inappropriate for a staff member to accept even an unpaid position with an organization actively interested in pending legislation due to the appearance of a conflict with staff responsibilities.[27]

The House places no parallel duty to report outside employment on its officers and employees, and is generally more liberal in permitting outside activities. House members, officers, and employees are simply required to give "a full day's labor for a full day's pay," which is interpreted as prohibiting outside employment which distracts the individual from his or her official duties.[28] More specifically, the House limits earned outside income of its members to 30 percent of their congressional salary, on the assumption that higher earnings would be at the expense of attention to official duties.[29] The Senate has no parallel provision for its members. House employees are prohibited from performing outside services during "official time," and may be further restricted by the committee or member for which they work.[30]

Representatives may also retain an interest in a law partnership[31] or other professional service business, but the income from that business is generally treated as earned income and limited by the 30 percent earned income rule.[32] In contrast, members, officers, and employees of the Senate paid more than $25,000 per year by the government may not affiliate with any firm, partnership, association, or corporation to provide professional services, permit their names to be used by such a business entity, or practice a profession for compensation to any extent during regular Senate working hours.[33]

A Senator, senatorial officer, or employee is also prohibited from serving as an officer or director of a publicly held or publicly regulated corporation or entity,[34] unless the official had continuously served as a director for at least two years before joining the Senate or Senate staff. Representatives are similarly restricted only to the extent that income for services to a regulated corporation or entity would bring their total outside earned income to greater than 30 percent of their congressional salary.[35]

Honoraria

In addition to the general prohibitions on outside sources of income, income attributable to honoraria is limited by rule and by statute. A member of the House or Senate may not receive honoraria which total more than 40 percent of base governmental salary.[36] Since honoraria are considered outside income, House Rule XLVII, which limits any outside noninvestment income to no more than 30 percent of a Representative's congressional salary, will more stringently limit total honoraria. The Senate does not have any parallel limit.

Each individual honorarium is limited as well as the annual total. The Federal Election Campaign Act does not permit any member, officer, or employee of the Senate to accept more than $2,000 for a speech, appearance, or article.[37]

Gifts

Senate Standing Rule XXXV and House Rule XLIII, clause 4, prohibit members, officers, and employees of the House and Senate, or their spouses and dependents,[38] from directly or indirectly accepting gifts with an aggregate value of more than $100 in any calendar year from any person with a direct interest in legislation before Congress[39] or from a foreign national.[40] Gifts of less than $35 (Senate) and $50 (House) are not included in the $100 aggregate. The rules also permit gifts from relatives and the personal hospitality of individuals.[41] The Senate rule permits gifts from foreign nationals who do not act for foreign governments, associations, or corporations.[42]

The term "gift" is defined to exclude legitimate loans and political contributions, bequests and inheritance, awards, meals, entertainment, mementos, and consumable products for office use contributed by home-state businesses.[43] The Senate also excludes things of value given to a spouse or dependent by his or her employer, in recognition of service provided by the spouse or dependent,[44] while the House excludes any "truly independent" gift to these individuals.[45] In addition, a member, officer, or employee may accept payment of necessary expenses, including travel and lodging, incurred to enable the member or employee to participate in functions within the scope of his or her official duties.[46]

Reimbursement of Expenses

Travel-related gift, lodging, and entertainment expenses are not considered gifts and thus may be reimbursed, provided that they are "necessary expenses" paid in compensation for value received.[47] The House committee has found that if a member or employee has "substantially participated" in a conference or other event, value has been given, and the expenses of participation may be reimbursed.[48] The participation must be "substantial," however, not merely perfunctory.[49] In addition, expenses for fact-finding trips may be reimbursed, even if no value is given, if the travel is "directly related to official duties."[50] The trip must be of an educational nature, offering information on matters "closely related to their official duties."[51]

The Senate ethics committee has interpreted Standing Rule XXXV to permit reimbursement of necessary expenses incurred in connection with any "officially related event."[52] Officially related events have been found to include participation in a meeting of a non-profit civic group,[53] speaking engagements,[54] and playing as a "celebrity" in a charitable golf-tennis tournament.[55]

These liberal policies permitting reimbursement of travel expenses do not extend to other types of expenses. A member may not accept private contributions to help defray office expenses. In addition to the general prohibition against accepting gifts from persons directly interested in legislation, Senate Standing Rule XXXVIII and House Rule XLV specifically prohibit such "unofficial office accounts" of funds donated by anyone. Funds or goods donated for these purposes are treated as campaign contributions which may be used for political, not personal, purposes.[56]

The Senate rule states that reimbursement of expenses incurred in connection with either official or political duties is not considered personal use of campaign funds. Thus office expenses and other legitimate expenses may be paid from donated funds, provided the contribution was made in compliance with the Federal Election Campaign Act and distributed to the Senator by a political committee. Otherwise, the only acceptable sources of funds are personal funds of the member, funds appropriated for senatorial expenses, and reimbursements of expenses incurred in providing a personal service to the organization making the reimbursement.

The House rule is more stringent. Funds offered to reimburse office expenses, like all campaign funds, may be used only for "bona fide campaign purposes." Expenses incurred in relation to "political" duties may be reimbursed, but not those related to "official" duties. Official expenses must be reimbursed from appropriated funds or the member's personal funds. No definitions are provided to aid in interpreting whether an expense is "official" or "political." The House ethics committee has given members considerable discretion in making that determination.[57]

Representational Activities

The representational activities of members, officers, and employees of the House and Senate are greatly limited by the restrictions placed on outside employment, as discussed above. In addition, several statutes further limit the practice of law by persons in the legislative branch.

The conflict of interest statutes limit the ability of members, officers, and employees of the House and Senate to represent the interests of others before federal courts and agencies. Legislative branch officers and employees are prohibited from representing other interests before any department, agency, or court in any proceeding in which the U.S. government is a party or has a direct or substantial interest,[58] and from receiving compensation for any of these services before a department or agency.[59] A narrow exception is provided for an employee who represents, without compensation, his or her parents, spouse, child, or acts as guardian, executor, administrator, trustee, or other fiduciary. The statute also contains exceptions for representation without compensation of fellow employees in certain personnel matters and provides a waiver if it is in the "national interest" to permit representation.[60]

Members of the House and Senate are far less stringently limited. Members may not accept fees for representing other interests in departmental or agency proceedings involving substantial interests of the United States.[61] They may, however, receive fees and represent the interests of any party adverse to the United States in any court except the U.S. Claims Court or the U.S. Court of Appeals for the Federal Circuit.[62] The restriction against accepting fees for representing clients with interests in federal agency actions has been narrowly interpreted to prohibit only representation *before* the agency, not merely advising a client on agency-related matters.[63]

Disqualification and Divestiture

There is no general statutory requirement that members, officers, or employees of Congress disqualify themselves from matters in which they have a personal financial interest.[64] Neither house places a blanket restriction on its members or employees. There are, however, a few limitations placed on legislative activities that affect the individual's interest.

Senate Standing Rule XXXVII prohibits members, officers, and employees from using their position to further the passage of any bill of which the *primary* purpose is to benefit the pecuniary interests of themselves, their families, or a limited class of which they or their families are members. Furthering the financial interests of a larger group to which the member or employee belongs is considered acceptable behavior.[65]

House Rule XLIII, clause 3, which broadly prohibits "beneficial interest from any source" accrued "by virtue of influence improperly exerted," has been interpreted to include a similar prohibition. The House ethics committee has found it an unethical use of influence to promote narrow legislation to specifically deal with a personal financial problem, or to seek benefits from or invest in an organization that the member had worked to establish in Congress.[66]

A common means of avoiding such financial conflicts of interest is to require divestiture of assets which may be affected by governmental duties. Because of the breadth of congressional responsibilities, the House of Representatives has no divestiture requirements.[67] Senators, officers of the Senate, and employees on Senators' staffs likewise need not divest themselves of assets to avoid conflicts of interest.[68] An employee on the staff of a Senate committee who is paid over $25,000 per year, however, must divest any substantial holdings which may be directly affected by actions of the committee. The employee's supervisor is permitted to make exceptions to this rule, or to arrange for the employee to work only on matters that will not create a conflict of interest.[69]

Future Employment

There is no statutory limitation placed on future employment of persons in the legislative branch.[70] The House also places no restrictions on its members or employees. Employment after leaving the Senate, however, is regulated under Senate Standing Rule XXXVII. A Senator who becomes a lobbyist or is employed or retained by a lobbying organization after leaving office may not lobby members, officers, or employees of the Senate for a period of one year. An employee who leaves the Senate and becomes a lobbyist, or is employed or retained by a lobbying organization, is prohibited for one year from lobbying the committee or member (and staff) for which the employee worked.

Financial Disclosure

Since members are not required to divest assets upon taking office or generally to abstain from voting on issues affecting their personal financial interests,[71] the principal means of deterring financial conflicts of interest is a comprehensive disclosure rule. Title I of the Ethics in Government Act of 1978 ("the Act") requires disclosure of assets by members of the House and Senate and high-ranking staff members.[72] Senate Standing Rule XXXIV adopts the provisions of Title I as a rule. Numerous Senate Interpretive Rulings clarify the requirements. The *House Ethics Manual* also includes a chapter of extensive interpretation of the Act.

Under the Act, members, officers, and employees compensated at a rate equal to or greater than grade GS-16 are required by law to file personal Financial Disclosure Statements by May 15 of each year detailing financial information concerning themselves, their spouses, and their dependent children.[73] The report must contain the following information:[74]

a. *Earned and unearned income.* The source, type, and amount of all income of greater than $100 must be reported.[75] If the source of the income is an investment, only the type of investment and indication of the range of income from it are required. The source of income of a qualified blind trust need not be reported.

b. *Gifts and travel-related reimbursements.* Gifts of food, lodging, transportation, entertainment, and reimbursements of expenses from one source which aggregate over $250 during the year must be disclosed. Other types of gifts aggregating over $100 must also be reported. Gifts from relatives, personal hospitality, and gifts values at $35 or less need not be aggregated or reported.

c. *Holdings.* All investment property such as stocks, bonds, and real estate with a fair market value over $1,000 must be reported.[76] Assets held in a qualified blind trust need not be disclosed.

d. *Debts*. Personal obligations owed to one creditor which exceed $10,000 must be disclosed.[77] Home mortgages and loans for the purchase of a car, furniture, or appliances need not be reported.

e. *Transactions*. Any purchase, sale, or exchange of investment property, such as real estate other than the personal residence and securities, with a value of over $1,000 must be reported.[78]

f. *Positions*. All positions held by the reporting individual must be disclosed except those in religious, social, fraternal or political groups, or positions of an honorary nature.

g. *Agreements*. Agreements involving the reporting individual which concern future employment, leaves of absence, continuation of payments from a private source, and continued participation in an employee benefit plan must be disclosed.

Administrative Officials

A working knowledge of government ethics is important for anyone who deals with the federal government in its administrative functions as well as in its legislative functions. There are obvious parallels between ethics rules for legislative officials and for administrative officials. But the law, regulations, and interpretations differ in significant respects. As with the rules for legislative officials, the rules for administrative officials are not intuitive. They must be studied and understood.

To compensate for the nonintuitive nature of government ethics rules for administrative employees, the federal government has established an elaborate system of ethics counseling. The system is directed by the Office of Government Ethics and "Designated Agency Ethics Officials" ("DAEOs") in every federal department and agency. These offices provide general and specific ethical advice that is generally consistent and reliable.[79] For this reason, the cardinal rule of government ethics is, "when in doubt, ask."

Background

The centerpiece of the law of government ethics for administrative officials is the federal conflict of interest statutes found at 18 U.S.C. §§202–209. With one exception, these statutes have their roots in legislation passed shortly before and after the Civil War in response to scandals and abuses involving contracts and fraudulent claims against the government.[80] In 1962, Congress amended and updated these conflict of interest laws.[81] The postemployment statute also was amended more recently by the Ethics in Government Act of 1978.[82] Thus the Civil War era statutes, as amended in 1962 and

1978, constitute the basic conflict of interest and ethics laws for administrative officials of the federal government. The 1978 Ethics in Government Act also instituted a system of public financial disclosure for high-level government employees and created the Office of Government Ethics.[83] The Office of Government Ethics has primary responsibility for administering the federal ethics program for departments and agencies, which includes as its essential elements, financial disclosure, counseling, and training.[84]

In addition to the conflict of interest statutes, there are other federal statutes that deal with related areas of government ethics for administrative employees. For purposes of this chapter, the most notable of these are the bribery statutes, 18 U.S.C. §201 (dealing with illegal payments to government officials), and the Hatch Act, 5 U.S.C. §§7321–7328 (dealing with government employee participation in partisan political activities).

To supplement the statutes, federal departments and agencies have regulations setting forth the standards of conduct for their own employees. These typically govern some areas, such as outside employment and gifts, that are not specifically addressed by the statutes. Federal employees are also expected to abide by relevant professional standards such as the rules of professional conduct for lawyers promulgated by the American and other Bar Associations. These standards address some of the same issues as the statutes and agency standards of conduct, but they may impose different or additional obligations in individual cases.

Enforcement of government ethics standards is accomplished in a variety of ways. Counseling, particularly in the context of review of financial disclosure forms, is the first and most prophylactic enforcement mechanism available. Federal departments and agencies have the authority to discipline their own employees for misconduct, and agency Inspectors General and their counterparts normally have broad investigative mandates with respect to allegations of misconduct.[85] The Department of Justice, (or, in the case of certain individuals, independent counsel) have authority to prosecute violations of the conflict of interest or other criminal laws. Courts and administrative agencies also have authority to disqualify individuals from participating in matters before them if they believe that misconduct has occurred or will occur.[86] Finally, but not insignificantly, the press and the Congress play powerful enforcement roles on selected matters of government ethics. Their influence can be considerable, not only on the agencies with official enforcement responsibilities, but also on the lives and reputations of the individuals involved in ethics matters.

Applicability

For the most part, government ethics rules are triggered by federal employment, that is, they apply to employees, former employees, and persons who deal with them.[87] For this reason, it is important as a preliminary matter to understand what constitutes government employment.

On one level, and in most cases, it is very easy to know whether or not an individual is a government employee. In some contexts, however, this distinction is blurred. For example, when an individual "volunteers" his services or advice to the government, his employment status is more difficult to discern for ethics purposes.[88] Similarly, independent contractors to the government are not government employees for purposes of the conflict of interest laws and standards of conduct, but the distinction between a bona fide independent contractor and an employee can be a difficult one.

Generally, the government looks to the Civil Service laws in defining whether an individual is a government employee for ethics purposes.[89] The Civil Service factors used in making this determination are (1) whether the person has been (or should have been) appointed by an officer or employee, (2) whether the person is engaged in the performance of federal functions, and (3) whether the person is subject to the supervision of a federal officer or employee while engaged in the duties of the position.[90] In any unclear situation, the relevant Designated Agency Ethics Official should be asked for an opinion concerning the employment status of the individual for government ethics purposes.

Among the class of individuals who are federal employees, there is a subset of employees whose work is of such a temporary or intermittent nature that Congress has determined that they should not be subject to the full array of government ethics rules. Instead these employees, called special government employees, are subject to a more limited set of ethics restrictions.[91]

Payments to Government Employees

As a general rule, payments to government employees are prohibited if they are from a source that does business with the employee's department or agency or if they otherwise relate to the government employment. Congress has provided that a government employee's salary must be paid by the U.S. government,[92] and has prohibited the payment of bribes and gratuities to public officials.[93] These standards were not designed to prevent outside income, but rather to prevent "linkage between the income and the performance of official duties."[94] Both the government employee and the payor are covered by these prohibitions which are criminal in nature.

In addition to the criminal prohibitions, each department and agency has promulgated regulations to govern the conduct of its employees in situations in which the linkage between income and employment may be less direct than that proscribed by the criminal statutes. These regulations typically deal with outside employment, gifts, honoraria, and travel reimbursement.

The Department of Justice standards of conduct[95] provide a good example of the type of regulations promulgated by a federal department. In most areas, other federal agencies have rules that correspond closely to the Justice Department rules, although they may differ in the precise wording or types of exceptions granted.

Gifts

With respect to gifts, the Justice Department regulations begin with a broad prohibition. A Department of Justice employee may not receive any "gift, gratuity, favor, entertainment, loan or any other thing of monetary value" from a person seeking to obtain contractual or business relations from the Department, a person conducting operations regulated by the Department, a person engaged as a principal or attorney before the Department proceedings, or any person who "has interests that may be substantially affected by the performance or nonperformance of the employee's official duty."[96]

The prohibition is followed by exceptions. A Department employee may accept gifts and items of monetary value from a parent, spouse, child, or other close relative if it is "clear" that the action was motivated by the personal or family relationship.[97] Additionally, food and refreshments of "nominal value" on "infrequent" occasions may be accepted if they are in the "ordinary course of a luncheon or dinner meeting or other meeting."[98] Loans from banks and financial institutions for proper and usual activities are permissible.[99] If the government employee receives unsolicited advertising materials, such as pens or calendars, they may be retained if they are of nominal intrinsic value.[100] Gifts from foreign governments may only be accepted as authorized by Congress in the Foreign Gifts Act[101]; and gifts for superiors must be voluntary, of nominal value, and made on a special occasion such as marriage or retirement.[102]

Awards

The rule regarding awards is different from that regarding gifts, although it is not always easy to distinguish an award from a gift. Employees may accept awards from organizations which are "charitable, religious, professional, social, fraternal, educational, recreational, public service or civic organizations," if acceptance does not create an appearance of impropriety.[103]

Honoraria

Acceptance of honorarium, royalties, or other fees for speeches, lectures, and publications is prohibited by the Justice Department if the activity was part of the employee's official duties. Similarly, employees may not accept compensation for speeches, lectures, or publications conducted on their own if they are substantially devoted to the responsibilities, programs, or operations of the Department or if they draw on nonpublic information.[104]

Reimbursement for Travel

Department of Justice employees are permitted to accept travel reimbursement only if the travel was not part of their official duties. There is a limited exception that permits the acceptance of travel reimbursement from organizations that are tax exempt pursuant to Section 501(c)(3) of the Internal Revenue Code (i.e., organizations that are tax exempt because they are charitable, religious, or educational). The Justice Department also has given employees limited permission to accept travel reimbursement for their spouses, but this rule deviates from that of most agencies and may have limited vitality in the future.[105]

Outside Employment

Federal agency regulations governing outside employment are not as uniform as many other standards of conduct. The Department of Justice has a relatively strict rule, prohibiting all outside professional practice, with limited exceptions: (1) for *pro bono* work, (2) for the representation of certain relatives, and (3) as granted by the Deputy Attorney General. Outside employment of a nonprofessional nature is permitted so long as it does not conflict with several principles set forth in the regulation.[106]

Representational Activities

The conflict of interest statutes prohibit government employees from representing interests in which the U.S. government is a party or has a direct and substantial interest,[107] and from receiving compensation for any of these services.[108] This means, for example, that an employee in the Department of Transportation may not represent his community association in an application for a grant before the Department of Health and Human Services.[109]

An exception to the restriction on representation is provided for an employee who represents, without compensation, his or her parents, spouse, child, or acts as guardian, executor, administrator, trustee, or personal fiduciary. However, the exception will not be applicable if the employee has participated in a matter personally and substantially as a government employee or if the matter is under the employee's official responsibility.[110] Applying the exception to an individual case, the Justice Department's Office of Legal Counsel held that a U.S. Attorney could appear on behalf of his daughter in an Internal Revenue Service office audit of her tax return.[111] Even though the U.S. Attorney's office could become the government's "collecting agent" if a civil or criminal judgment or fine had been imposed on the daughter, the Office of Legal Counsel concluded that the U.S. Attorney did not have any "official responsibility" for tax collection.[112]

The statute contains other exceptions for the representation, without compensation, of fellow employees in certain types of personnel matters. It provides for a "national interest" waiver in certain limited situations. In addition, it specifies that giving testimony under oath is not within the restriction of the statute.[113]

The restriction on accepting compensation for providing representation before federal agencies applies whether the representation was performed by the federal employee, or by another.[114] Because the provision applies to compensation for representation before a federal agency that occurred while the employee was in government service, it will bar an employee from receiving the compensation even after the employee leaves government service. This application of the statute can be a trap for the unwary. For example, a former government employee who joins a law or accounting firm as a partner may violate Section 203 inadvertently if his partnership draw in his early months at the firm includes compensation received by the firm for representation before federal agencies that occurred when the employee was still with the government. To avoid this dilemma, partners in these situations often arrange a fixed salary for services rendered for their early months at the firm. Alternatively, if the firm's business practices and accounting system permit it, the individual may arrange to delete any prohibited fees from partnership draw.

In addition to employees themselves, the partners of incumbent government employees are prohibited from representing anyone before a federal entity in matters in which the United States has an interest and in which the employee has participated personally and substantially or which are under the employee's official responsibility.[115] The Office of Government Ethics has opined that this restriction does not apply to limited partners of a government employee in a large limited partnership.[116] General partners or participants in small limited partnerships, however, should seek individual advice from the employee's DAEO before undertaking a representation that may be prohibited by this provision.

Government Disqualification

Disqualification for financial interest is governed by a conflict of interest statute. The statute provides that a government employee may not participate "personally and substantially" in a "particular" matter in which, to the employee's knowledge, he or she has a financial interest.[117] The government employee also is prohibited from participating in a particular matter if the financial interest in the matter is that of a "spouse, minor child, partner, organization in which he is serving as officer, director, trustee, partner or employee, or any person or organization with whom he is negotiating or has any arrangement concerning prospective employment."[118] The statute provides for general and case-by-case waivers of its restriction for remote or small interests;[119] but in the absence of a waiver by an appropriate official, the prohibition stands—no matter how small the financial interest.

Disqualification for reasons other than financial interest is not regulated as well or as clearly as financial disqualifications. Nonfinancial disqualification questions can arise, for example, with respect to the interests of friends or family or their employers, one's own former employer, or former clients. The Department of Justice has a regulation setting forth a procedure for resolving potential disqualification for personal or political reasons in criminal cases;[120] but the regulation is of limited applicability. Other federal agencies do not have comparable provisions in their standards of conduct.

The absence of guidance in the statutes and regulations does not mean that disqualification is not warranted or expected for other than financial reasons. Government employees are expected to exercise sound judgment to avoid the appearance of impropriety even when there is no statute or regulation to give them guidance. DAEOs are available to assist employees in resolving these questions; they should be consulted whenever a disqualification issue arises.

The Administrative Conference of the United States has published recommended guidelines for the disqualification of rulemaking officials[121] that are helpful in analyzing nonfinancial disqualification issues.[122] The guidelines aim to preclude the appearance of bias in judgments by federal decisionmakers. They propose, for example, that the federal official either abstain from a matter or be subject to a "cooling off" period during which the official must withdraw from a proceeding (1) which would affect the financial interest of an immediately prior employer or client; (2) where the immediately prior employer or client is a participant in the proceeding; or (3) where the official has participated in the proceeding before joining the government.[123] In applying these requirements, the guidelines attempt to balance various factors such as the nature, degree, and directness of the official's prior interest in the governmental matter, the nature and degree of the employee's connection to the interested party, the amount of time elapsed since the official's prior connection with the matter, and the government's need for the employee's services in the matter.[124] While these guidelines require the exercise of judgment in any individual case, they are helpful to employees and DAEOs in focusing attention on the pertinent issues.

Partisan Political Activities

Most government employees are limited by the Hatch Act in the extent to which they may participate in partisan political activities, although they retain a right to vote and to express opinions on political subjects and candidates. The Hatch Act[125] prohibits employees from taking an "active" part in political management or political campaigns. Regulations promulgated by the Special Counsel to the Merit Systems Protection Board, who enforces and interprets the statute, define the range of acceptable behavior by providing lists of "do's and don'ts."[126] For example, an employee may attend a political convention, but may not serve as a delegate to the convention. He may be a member of a political club or party, attend its meetings, and give it donations, but he may not be an officer of the club, solicit donations for it, or endorse a candidate. Guidance on the acceptability of activities not listed in the regulations may be obtained from the Special Counsel or the employee's DAEO.

In addition to the Hatch Act, certain other political activities are prohibited by criminal statutes.[127] The most notable, and perhaps surprising, of these is 18 U.S.C. §603, which prohibits employees from making political contributions to the campaign of their employer or employing authority.[128]

Postemployment Restrictions

The federal postemployment statute essentially proscribes three types of conduct.[129] First, former employees may never represent anyone, other than the United States, in any particular matter involving specific parties in which the employee participated "personally and substantially" while in the government.[130] Second, for a period of two years after leaving government, former employees may not represent anyone, other than the United States, in particular matters involving specific parties which were under their official responsibilities during their last year in government.[131] Finally, certain senior officials[132] may not have any contact regarding official business with their former department or agency for a one-year period after they leave government.[133] In some cases, this last ban on any contact with the agency may be limited to some part of the agency,[134] and there are limited exceptions for the representation of state and local governments and certain tax-exempt organizations.[135] The federal postemployment statute does not apply to the partners or associates of the former government employee, but bar association or other professional standards may reach them in certain cases.[136]

The Office of Government Ethics has published regulations to explain and implement the postemployment statute.[137] These regulations define such terms as "personally and substantially," "particular matter involving specific parties," and "official responsibility," and they give examples to illustrate the meaning and application of the statute. They are a valuable guide to the statute and should be consulted at the outset when any postemployment issue arises.

Financial Disclosure

Detailed public financial disclosure is required of all federal employees paid at the equivalent of a General Schedule (GS) 16 or above.[138] This includes all members of the Senior Executive Service and Executive Schedule employees. Other personnel below the GS-16 level may be required by their department or agency to fulfill similar reporting requirements, but their reports are not available for public inspection.[139]

Public financial disclosure reports are required from (1) new entrants to covered positions within 30 days of entry on duty (or within five days of nomination from nominees) and (2) incumbents annually on May 15, and within 30 days of terminating government service. While the items of disclosure vary for new employees and incumbents, generally employees must disclose income, assets, exchanges of property, gifts, reimbursements, liabilities, and certain positions held. The values of income and assets may generally be reported by category of value rather than exact amount. In many cases the subassets or contents of a fund such as a pension fund must be disclosed; but certain trusts and widely diversified mutual funds may be exempt from the reporting of subassets. The reporting requirements are set forth in detail on the financial disclosure forms themselves[140] and in regulations of the Office of Government Ethics.[141]

Every financial disclosure form must be signed and certified by an appropriate reviewing official.[142] A reviewing official accepts the employee's disclosures at "'face value' unless there is a patent omission or ambiguity or the official has independent knowledge of matters outside the report."[143] If the reviewing official determines that remedial steps must be taken, he or she must notify the reporting individual, allow an opportunity for personal consultation if practicable, choose the proper remedial action, and notify the reporting individual as to the type of remedial action and when it must be completed.[144] The available remedial steps are divestiture of the conflicting interest, restitution, establishment of a qualified trust, request for an exemption, recusal, or voluntary request for transfer, reassignment, limitation of duties, or resignation.[145] If the individual does not comply with the chosen remedial action, the reviewing official must notify the Office of Government Ethics and the supervising agency authority so that "appropriate action" can be taken, specifically including reassignment of duties or suspension of the employee for 14 days or less.[146]

A number of remedies, such as blind trusts and recusal policies, have specific and detailed requirements which must be followed. For example, trusts must be certified by the Office of Government Ethics to be deemed qualified and exempt from the usual requirement of public financial disclosure of subassets.[147]

Special Government Employees

Special government employees are subject to federal ethics rules to a more limited degree than other employees of the government. Special government employees are defined as those who, at the time of appointment, are expected to serve 130 days or less during the next 365 days.[148] Part of a day is to be counted as a whole day, and the determination made by the agency at the time of appointment will govern, even if the special government employee in fact serves more than 130 days.[149]

The rules applicable to special government employees may be summarized as follows:

1. The restrictions on outside representation, and related compensation, in certain matters involving the United States, apply to special government employees only with respect to matters: (a) in which the employee at any time participated personally and substantially while in the government; or (b) which are pending in the department or agency in which the special government employee is serving. Moreover, the latter restriction applies only to the special government employee once he or she has served in the government for more than 60 days of the preceding 365 days.[150]

2. While the bribery and gratuity statute applies with equal force to special government employees,[151] these employees are exempt from the prohibition on receiving supplementation of their salaries from outside sources.[152] The Department of Justice restrictions on outside professional practice similarly do not apply to special government employees.[153] On the other hand, if a special government employee elects to remain a partner in a law firm, his or her partners will face the same restrictions as those of a regular government employee.[154]

3. Rules regarding disqualification are the same for regular and special government employees.[155] With one small exception, the government's postemployment restrictions apply with equal force to special government employees.[156]

4. Rules regarding financial disclosure are the same for regular and special government employees, but employees may be relieved of filing an annual financial disclosure report for any calendar year in which they served less than 60 days.[157]

Notes

1. On October 21, 1988, Congress passed the Past Employment Restrictions Act, H.R. 5043, 100th Cong., 2d Sess. (1988). This bill would have placed additional constraints on future employment of persons in both the legislative and executive branches. President Reagan vetoed the bill on November 23, 1988. Because a similar measure could be revived under the next administration, the provisions of the bill that would have affected present rules and regulations are noted where appropriate in the discussion below.
2. SELECT COMM. ON ETHICS, U.S. SENATE, INTERPRETIVE RULINGS OF THE SELECT COMMITTEE ON ETHICS, 100th Cong., 2d Sess. (July 1988) (hereinafter cited as "SENATE INTERPRE-

TIVE RULINGS"); COMM. ON STANDARDS OF OFFICIAL CONDUCT, U.S. HOUSE OF REPRESEN-
TATIVES, ETHICS MANUAL FOR MEMBERS, OFFICERS, AND EMPLOYEES OF THE U.S. HOUSE
OF REPRESENTATIVES, 100th Cong., 1st Sess. (1987) (hereinafter "HOUSE MANUAL").

3. SENATE INTERPRETIVE RULINGS at III; HOUSE MANUAL at IV, 10.

4. Of the basic federal conflict of interest statutes, 18 U.S.C. §§203–209 (1982 & West Supp.
1988) (see Appendix E for text), Congress is exempt from: 18 U.S.C. §205 (1982) (prohibition against representational activities applies to legislative staff only); 18 U.S.C. §207
(West Supp. 1988) (limits on future employment apply to executive branch only); 18
U.S.C. §208 (West Supp. 1988) (disqualification requirements apply to executive branch
only); 18 U.S.C. §209 (1982 & West Supp. 1988) (prohibition against supplemental salaries
applies to executive branch only).

5. 18 U.S.C. §203 (West Supp. 1988).

6. 18 U.S.C. §204.

7. 18 U.S.C. §205.

8. See 2 U.S.C. §§701–709 (1982 & West Supp. 1988), *reprinted in* Appendix E.

9. The Federal Election Campaign Act and its implementing regulations are discussed only
to the extent they circumscribe behavior of members of Congress and their staffs. The full
panoply of rules and regulations governing campaign financing are beyond the scope of
this chapter.

10. SENATE INTERPRETIVE RULINGS at III.

11. Interpretive rulings which were subsequently overruled or which were based on rules that
have since been amended are not included in the volume. *Id.*

12. The volume focuses on the Standing Rules of the Senate, though some decisions also interpret statutes which circumscribe senatorial behavior, such as the Federal Election Campaign Act and the Foreign Gifts and Decorations Act.

13. HOUSE ETHICS MANUAL at 3; SELECT COMMITTEE ON ETHICS, U.S. SENATE, RULES OF PRO-
CEDURE, 99th Cong., 2d Sess. 2–3 (Jan. 1986) (hereinafter cited as "SENATE RULES OF
PROCEDURE").

14. U.S. CONST. art I, §5, cl. 2, *reprinted in* Appendix F.

15. HOUSE ETHICS MANUAL at 3.

16. SENATE RULES OF PROCEDURE at 3.

17. HOUSE ETHICS MANUAL at 3.

18. *Id.*

19. The wider applicability of 18 U.S.C. §201 (West Supp. 1988), the federal bribery statute, is
discussed *infra* in this chapter's section on bribery.

20. 18 U.S.C §201. Penalties vary depending on whether the thing given is a bribe or an illegal
gratuity. A bribe is given with the intent to influence an official act. A gratuity is given for
or because of an official act.

21. *See* Project, *Fourth Survey of White Collar Crime*, 24 AM. CRIM. L. REV. 405, 417–19
(1987) (discussing the "public official" element of the crime of bribery).

22. Persons acting "for or on behalf of" the United States or an agency or branch of the government has been interpreted to include officers of a private, nonprofit corporation that
administered and dispensed federal community development block grants. *Dixon v.
United States*, 465 U.S. 482, 490–97 (1984). Thus, it is likely that the statute reaches
bribes and illegal gratuities to persons such as contractors and unpaid volunteers who are
not clearly "employees" of the House or Senate.

23. HOUSE ETHICS MANUAL at 46.

24. 18 U.S.C. §209, which prohibits government employees from receiving private salary supplements to partially compensate them for performing official duties, applies only to the
executive branch.

25. HOUSE ETHICS MANUAL at 102–03; SENATE INTERPRETIVE RULINGS, INTERPRETIVE RUL-
ING Nos. 87, 183, at 38–39, 82.

26. E.g., SENATE INTERPRETIVE RULINGS, INTERPRETIVE RULING Nos. 39, 123, at 16, 52.

27. SENATE INTERPRETIVE RULINGS, INTERPRETIVE RULING No. 23, at 9. It must be noted that
financial conflicts of interest which exist when the individual enters the service of the
Senate are treated quite differently than conflicts created through subsequent outside
employment. See discussion, *infra*, of disqualification and divestiture.

28. HOUSE ETHICS MANUAL at 43, 195.

29. House Rule XVII.

30. HOUSE ETHICS MANUAL at 47, 57–58.

31. Further restrictions on the practice of law are discussed below as restrictions on representational activities.

32. HOUSE ETHICS MANUAL at 48.

33. This portion of the rule is generally intended to reach only the practice of professions
which involve clients and fiduciary relationships. Past committee rulings have prohibited

acceptance of an uncompensated "of counsel" position with a law firm and have prohibited selling real estate for a brokerage firm. Senate Interpretive Rulings, Interpretive Ruling Nos. 145, 166, at 63, 75.

34. Nonprofit, tax-exempt organizations are an exception to this rule, provided the Senator or staff member serves without compensation.

35. House Ethics Manual at 49.

36. 2 U.S.C. §31–1(b) (Supp. IV 1986), *reprinted in* Appendix E. Honoraria donated to charity are not included in calculating this total. *Id.* §31–1(c).

37. 2 U.S.C. §441i (1982), *reprinted in* Appendix E.

38. The Senate rule specifically prohibits these gifts. The House interprets the prohibition against "indirect" receipt of gifts to include gifts to the spouse and dependents. House Ethics Manual at 19.

39. People with a direct interest in legislation include registered lobbyists and the directors, officers, employees, and contractors of registered lobbying groups. Corporations, labor organizations, and other groups which maintain political action committees are also included in the definition, along with their officers, directors, and those of their employees and contractors who are involved in the political action committees' activities. Senate Standing Rule XXXV; House Ethics Manual at 19.

40. Gifts from foreign governments are further restricted by art. I, §9, cl. 8 of the U.S. Constitution (reprinted in Appendix F) and by the Foreign Gifts and Decorations Act, 5 U.S.C. §7342 (1982) (see Appendix E for text).

41. Senate Standing Rule XXXV; House Rule XLIII, cl. 4.

42. Senate Standing Rule XXXV.

43. Senate Standing Rule XXXV; House Ethics Manual at 16.

44. Senate Standing Rule XXXV.

45. House Ethics Manual at 19.

46. House Ethics Manual at 17. Senate Interpretive Rulings, Interpretive Ruling No. 1, at 1.

47. Senate Standing Rule XXXV; House Ethics Manual at 17.

48. House Ethics Manual at 17.

49. Addressing an audience, participating in a seminar, and actually playing in a pro-am golf tournament are examples of "substantial participation." Merely visiting a site is not sufficient. *Id.*

50. *Id.*

51. Examples of appropriate fact-finding events are a tour of an offshore oil rig, demonstrations of new logging techniques in a remote area, and foreign-sponsored programs "designed to promote better understanding and improve U.S. relations with that country." *Id.* at 17–18. Ship launchings and inaugural flights of airline routes are examples of nonreimbursable types of travel. *Id.* at 18.

52. Senate Interpretive Rulings, Interpretive Ruling No. 1, at 1.

53. *Id.*

54. Senate Interpretive Rulings, Interpretive Ruling Nos. 19, 202, at 7, 92.

55. Senate Interpretive Rulings, Interpretive Ruling No. 29, at 11.

56. Senate Standing Rule XXXVIII; House Ethics Manual at 97.

57. House Ethics Manual at 97–98.

58. 18 U.S.C. §205.

59. 18 U.S.C. §203.

60. 18 U.S.C. §205.

61. 18 U.S.C. §203.

62. 18 U.S.C. §204.

63. In *United States v. Myers,* 692 F.2d 823 (2d Cir. 1982), the Second Circuit ruled that a member of Congress who merely advises a client without appearing before an agency in a proceeding or without making any formal or informal contacts within the agency on behalf of the client has not violated 18 U.S.C. §203(a). *Id.* at 853–58.

64. 18 U.S.C. §208, which requires disqualification of government employees with a personal interest, applies only to officers and employees of the executive branch.

65. A Senate employee from a dairy state was permitted to work on dairy issues even though he owned a dairy farm since a far wider group than the employee and his family would be benefited by any bill passed. Senate Interpretive Rulings, Interpretive Ruling No. 36, at 14. Similarly, a Senator may support legislation beneficial to the profession practiced by his or her spouse, or may support legislation affecting the pensions of federally employed retired military personnel even though himself a retired military reservist. *Id.,* Interpretive Ruling Nos. 171, 63, at 77, 26.

66. House Ethics Manual at 116–17.

67. *Id.* at 118.

68. Although they are not required to do so, many members of the House and Senate establish "blind trusts" for their assets to avoid conflicts of interest. The requirements for establishing such a trust—which is not subject to the disclosure provisions described *infra*—are set out in 2 U.S.C. §702(e)(3) (1982). See HOUSE ETHICS MANUAL at 118.

69. Senate Standing Rule XXXVII.

70. 18 U.S.C. §207, which prohibits government employees from representing others in matters on which they worked as government employees for one year after leaving government service, applies only to the executive branch.

    The Past Employment Restrictions Act, H.R. 5043, vetoed by President Reagan on November 23, 1988, would have placed the following restrictions on future employment of members, officers, and employees of the legislative branch:

    1. Senators and Representatives would have been prohibited for one year from lobbying anyone in either body. *Id.* §2(e).

    2. Employees on the personal staff of a Senator or Representative, paid at a rate equal to or greater than a GS-17, would have been prohibited for one year from lobbying the Member by whom they were employed or the staff of that Member. *Id.*

    3. Committee employees paid at a rate equal to or greater than a GS-17 would have been prohibited for one year from lobbying any Member or employee of the committee by which they were employed. *Id.*

    4. Leadership staff paid at a rate equal to or greater than a GS-17 would have been prohibited for one year from lobbying any Member or employee of the leadership of the body by which they were employed. *Id.*

    5. Members and staff paid at a rate equal to or greater than a GS-17 would be prohibited for one year from representing the interests of a foreign entity to the government with the intent to influence a decision of the Government. A foreign entity is a foreign government, an instrumentality of a foreign government or an organization determined by OGE to be a foreign entity. *Id.* §2(f).

    These restrictions would not have applied to representations made as part of official duties as an official within the executive branch, and certain narrow exceptions were provided. *Id.* §2(e)(5)(B), (i), (k).

    The bill provided for enforcement by administrative debarment, civil penalties up to $50,000, and criminal penalties of imprisonment for up to two years with monetary fines. *Id.* §2(h), (n), (o).

71. See discussion of disqualification and divestiture, *supra.*

72. Pub. L. No. 95-521, Oct. 26, 1978, 92 Stat. 1864, Title I, *codified as amended at* 2 U.S.C. §§701-709.

73. 2 U.S.C. §701 (1982).

74. 2 U.S.C. §702(a) (1982).

75. The earned income of a spouse need only be reported if it exceeds $1,000 from any source. If the spouse is self-employed, only the nature of his or her business need be reported. 2 U.S.C. §702(d) (1982).

76. Holdings of the spouse or dependent need not be reported if: (1) the holdings are the sole interest of the spouse or dependent and the reporting individual has no knowledge of them; (2) they were not derived from the income, assets, or activities of the reporting individual; and (3) the reporting individual derives no benefit from them. 2 U.S.C. §702(d).

77. The debt of a spouse or dependent need not be disclosed if: (1) the debt is the sole liability of the dependent or spouse and the reporting individual has no knowledge of the debt; (2) the debt was not derived from the income, assets, or activities of the reporting individual; and (3) the reporting individual derives no benefits. 2 U.S.C. §702(d).

78. A transaction by the spouse or dependent of a reporting individual need not be reported if: (1) the transaction is the sole interest of the spouse or dependent and the reporting individual has no knowledge of the item; (2) the item was not derived from the income, assets, or activities of the reporting individual; and (3) the reporting individual derives no benefit from the item. 2 U.S.C. §702(d).

79. As a practical matter, an individual who seeks prospective advice through this system in good faith, will be protected even if the advice is later determined to have been incorrect. See, e.g., 5 C.F.R. §738.309 (1988) (regarding reliance upon formal advisory opinions of the Office of Government Ethics; there is no comparable regulation regarding the advice of Deputy DAEOs, but it is likely that the same principle would prevail).

80. These early statutes are discussed in Bayless Manning, *Federal Conflict of Interest Law* (1964), at pps. 15–16, 75–76, 110, and 182. The one exception, dealing with supplementation of government salaries, was enacted in 1914. *Id.* at 148.

81. Pub. L. No. 87-849, Oct. 23, 1962, 76 Stat. 1119.

82. Pub. L. No. 95-521, Oct. 26, 1978, 92 Stat. 1864.

83. *Id.* at Titles III and IV.

84. See generally *id.* at Title IV; 5 C.F.R. §733 (1988).

85. See, e.g., 5 U.S.C. App. 3 §4 (West Supp. 1988).

86. See, e.g., 18 U.S.C. §207(j).
87. The one notable exception is the bribery statute, 18 U.S.C. §201, which applies not only with respect to officers and employees of the government but also with respect to persons acting "for or on behalf of the United States." This latter category has been interpreted to reach as far as officers of a private, nonprofit corporation that administered and dispensed federal community development block grants. *Dixon v. United States,* 465 U.S. 482, 489–97 (1984).
88. While Congress has generally prohibited the acceptance of voluntary services by the government, 31 U.S.C. §1342 (1982) (see Appendix E for text), there are nonetheless a variety of circumstances in which persons are permitted to serve the government without compensation. See, e.g., J. Weinstein & W. Bonvillian, *A Part-Time Clerkship in the Federal Courts for Law Students,* 68 F.R.D. 265 (1975). Cf. 18 U.S.C. §209 (exempting from its own provision persons who serve without compensation).
89. See, e.g., U.S. Dept. of Justice, 10 Op. Off. Legal Counsel 20 (1977).
90. *Id.*
91. Most of the remainder of this chapter discusses the rules applicable to government employees who are not special government employees. In the last section of this chapter there is a description of the more limited application of the rules to special government employees.
92. 18 U.S.C. §209(a) (1982).
93. 18 U.S.C. §201. A bribe is a thing of value given with the intent to influence an official act. A gratuity is a thing of value given for or because of an official act.
94. Manning, *supra* note 80, at 146.
95. See generally 28 C.F.R. §45 (1987).
96. 28 C.F.R. §45.735–14(a) (1987).
97. 28 C.F.R. §45.735–14(c)(1) (1987).
98. 28 C.F.R. §45.735–14(c)(2) (1987). This exception has been discussed at considerable length in an opinion of the Office of Government Ethics dated October 23, 1987.
99. 28 C.F.R. §45.735–14(c)(3) (1987).
100. 28 C.F.R. §45.735–14(c)(4) (1987).
101. 28 C.F.R. §45.735–14(d) (1987).
102. 28 C.F.R. §45.735–14(e) (1987).
103. 28 C.F.R. §45.735–14a(d), (e) (1987).
104. 28 C.F.R. §45.735–12 (1987).
105. The Department of Justice rules regarding travel reimbursement are found at 28 C.F.R. §45.735–14a (1987).
106. See generally 28 C.F.R. §45.735–9.
107. 18 U.S.C. §205.
108. 18 U.S.C. §203.
109. There are also restrictions on postemployment representational activities of former government employees, but these will be discussed in a subsequent section of this chapter.
110. 18 U.S.C. §205 (1982). The government official responsible for appointment of the employee must approve of the representation. *Id.*
111. *Memorandum Opinion For The Director Of The Executive Office For United States Attorneys,* 1 Op. Off. Legal Counsel 148, 148 (Counsel Inf. Op. 1977).
112. *Id.*
113. See generally 18 U.S.C. §205.
114. See 18 U.S.C. §203.
115. 18 U.S.C. §207(g).
116. See Office of Government Ethics, Advisory Opinion No. 81–19 (1981).
117. 18 U.S.C. §208(a).
118. *Id.*
119. 18 U.S.C. §208(b).
120. 28 C.F.R. §45.735–4.
121. While the guidelines were established with rulemaking officials in mind, there is no reason that they should not be applied more generally to government employees.
122. Administrative Conference of the United States, 1980 Report, Recommendation 80–4: *Decisional Officials' Participation in Rulemaking Proceedings* (adopted June 5–6, 1980), at 51–55 (March 1981).
123. *Id.* at 53.
124. *Id.*
125. 5 U.S.C. §§7321–7328 (1982) (see Appendix E for text).

126. 5 C.F.R. §733.111–733.122 (1988).

127. See 18 U.S.C. §§591–607 (1982) (Chapter 29).

128. President Carter questioned the constitutionality of this provision when he signed this law. See Weekly Compilation of Presidential Documents, Vol. 16, Part 1, p. 38 (1980).

129. The Past Employment Restrictions Act, H.R. 5043, vetoed by President Reagan on November 23, 1988, would have added the following restrictions:
    1. All employees would have been prohibited for one year from representing, aiding, or advising on any trade negotiation where the United States is a party or has an interest and which the employee knows was pending under his or her official responsibility, or in which the employee participated, at any time within the last year of government employment. *Id.* §2(a)(3).
    2. The President, Vice-President, Executive Level I–V and comparable White House appointees, Military O-8 and above, and certain designated officials GS-17, SES and above, and Military O-7 and above would be prohibited for one year from representing the interests of a foreign entity to the government with the intent to influence a decision of the Government. A foreign entity is a foreign government, an instrumentality of a foreign government or an organization determined by OGE to be a foreign entity. *Id.* §2(f).

130. 18 U.S.C. §207(a). H.R. 5043, §2(a)(1), which was vetoed by President Reagan, would have strengthened this provision to prohibit "representing, aiding or advising" any other person on such a matter.

131. 18 U.S.C. §207(b). H.R. 5043, §2(a)(2), vetoed by President Reagan, would have limited the applicability of this section to matters which the employee *knows* were pending under his or her official responsibility.

132. All Executive Level officials, as well as some Senior Executive Service employees who are designated by the Office of Government Ethics, are subject to this provision. 18 U.S.C. §207(d). H.R. 5043, §2(b), (c), (d) would have imposed separate restrictions on (1) designated positions at GS-17, SES level, and Military O-7 and above; (2) Executive Level III, IV, V, and comparable White House appointees and above; (3) the President, Vice-President, Executive Level I, II, and comparable White House appointees, and Military O-9 and O-10.

133. 18 U.S.C. §207(c). H.R. 5043, vetoed by President Reagan, would have replaced this provision with the following prohibitions:
    1. Designated official GS-17, SES, Military O-7, and above would have been prohibited for one year from representing any person before his or her former agency on a matter pending before that agency or in which the agency has a direct interest. H.R. 5043 §2(b).
    2. Executive Level III-V and comparable White House appointees would have been prohibited for one year from representing any person before his or her former agency on a matter in which the United States is a party or has a direct interest. *Id.* §2(c).
    3. The President, Vice-President, Executive Levels I, II, and comparable White House appointees and Military O-9, O-10 would have been prohibited for one year from representing any person to his or her former agency or to any executive level appointee on a matter in which the United States is a party or has an interest. *Id.* §2(d).

134. See 18 U.S.C. §§207(d)(1)(c) and (e). Under H.R. 5043, vetoed by President Reagan, this limiting of the restrictions to components would not have been available to the President, Vice-President, Executive Level I–V, and comparable White House appointees, or Military O-9, O-10.

135. 18 U.S.C. §207(d)(2). There is a similar exemption for certain communications of a scientific nature. 18 U.S.C. §207(f).

136. See, e.g., Rule 1.11(c) of the Model Rules of Professional Conduct of the American Bar Association. The Model Rules have not been adopted in all jurisdictions. The earlier Model Code has no parallel provision. H.R. 5043 would have imposed restrictions directly on partners of former officers and employees of the executive branch, including the President and Vice-President. Partners would have been prohibited from representing any person before an agency or court in a matter in which the United States is a party and the partner knows that the former official participated personally and substantially. *Id.* §2(l).

137. The regulations can be found at 5 C.F.R. Part 737 (1988). See also Administrative Conference of the U.S., 1979 Report, Recommendation 79–7: *Appropriate Restrictions on Participation By a Government Agency Official in Matters Involving the Agency* (adopted Dec. 14 1979), at 67–69 (April 1980) (recommendation on limiting the scope of Sec. 207, and establishment of alternative administrative enforcement system).

138. 5 C.F.R. §734.201–734.304 (1988). There are limited exclusions and waivers available as described in the regulations.

139. 5 C.F.R. §734.104(a)(7) (1988).

140. Office of Government Ethics, Standard Form 278.

141. 5 C.F.R. §734 (1988).

142. 5 C.F.R. §734.602.

143. 5 C.F.R. §734.604(b)(1).

144. 5 C.F.R. §734.604(b)(4).
145. 5 C.F.R. §734.604(b)(5).
146. 5 C.F.R. §734.604(b)(6), (7).
147. 5 C.F.R. §734.405.
148. 18 U.S.C. §202 (West Supp. 1988).
149. See generally FEDERAL PERSONNEL MANUAL, Chapter 735, Appendix C, Conflicts of Interest Statutes and Their Effects on Special Government Employees.
150. 18 U.S.C. §§203, 205.
151. 18 U.S.C. §201.
152. 18 U.S.C. §209.
153. 28 C.F.R. §45.735-9.
154. 18 U.S.C. §207(g). See discussion *supra*.
155. See, e.g., 18 U.S.C. §208.
156. See 18 U.S.C. §207. The one exception is that the high-level "no-contact rule" of Sec. 207(c) does not apply to special government employees who serve less than 60 days in a calendar year. See 18 U.S.C. §207(c).
157. 5 C.F.R. §734.201.

4

Corporate Lobbying Communications

Christopher S. Vaden

The Federal Election Campaign Act of 1971 prohibits corporations and labor unions from making any contribution or expenditure from their general treasuries in connection with any federal election.[1] However, corporations have a right, guaranteed by the First Amendment to the U.S. Constitution, to engage in a wide range of nonpartisan or political speech independent of particular candidates or elections. Under exceptions to the FEC Act, they may also establish and pay the administrative expenses of "separate segregated funds," which are commonly called "political action committees." Money contributed to the separate segregated fund—under specific limitations on solicitation—by corporate stockholders, employees, and executives, may be used for election-related contributions and expenditures. Corporations are also permitted to engage in a range of nonpartisan activities with respect to federal elections.

The Right to Participate in Political Debate

Despite the specific restrictions on corporate expenditures related to elections and political candidates, corporations retain the right to participate in political debate independent of particular campaigns or candidates. In *First National Bank of Boston v. Bellotti*,[2] a divided (5–4) U.S. Supreme Court struck down a Massachusetts law making it a crime for a corporation to make any contributions or expenditures for the purpose of influencing the vote on any voter referendum, except one affecting the property, business, or assets of the corporation. The statute further specified that no referendum solely concerning the issue of an individual income tax would be deemed to affect corporate property, business, or assets.[3] The corporate parties wanted to spend money to oppose a proposed constitutional amendment that would have permitted the state legislature to impose a graduated individual income tax. The amendment was to be submitted to the voters as a ballot question at an upcoming general election. However, the state attorney general threatened prosecution, so the corporations sought a declaration that the expenditure ban was unconstitutional.[4]

The Supreme Judicial Court of Massachusetts upheld the law, reasoning that a corporation's First Amendment rights arise only as incident to its property rights under the Fourteenth Amendment. Therefore, the court ruled, corporate speech is protected only if it materially affects the corporation's property or assets.[5]

The Supreme Court majority adopted a different approach in addressing the question. The Court focused not on whether corporations "have" First Amendment rights to free speech, but on whether the expression in question is of a type that the First Amendment was intended to protect.[6] A major purpose of the First Amendment, according to the Court, is to protect the free discussion of governmental affairs. Speech such as that directed to the merits of the Massachusetts income tax is "indispensable to decisionmaking in a democracy," regardless of whether the speech comes from a corporation or an individual.[7] In other words, the First Amendment goes beyond protection of individual self-expression to prohibit government from limiting the stock of information from which the public may draw.[8]

In light of that purpose, the "inherent worth of the speech in terms of its capacity for informing the public does not depend on the identity of the source, whether corporation, association, union or individual."[9] Moreover, the Court stated, the institutional press has no monopoly on the ability to enlighten,[10] so First Amendment protections are not limited to media corporations.

In the area of protected speech, the legislature may not dictate the subjects about which persons may speak, or who may address a public issue.[11] Requiring corporations to demonstrate a material effect on their business or property before they may "speak" on political issues "amounts to an impermissible legislative prohibition of speech based on the identity of interests that spokesmen may represent in public debate over controversial issues."[12]

In addition to reaffirming that corporate political expression is constitutionally protected, the *Bellotti* case is an instructive example of the standard the Supreme Court applies in reviewing restraints on speech. A statute which restricts core political speech will be subjected to "exacting scrutiny."[13] The statute will be upheld only if the government shows the existence of a compelling interest within the sphere of governmental concern; even then, the statute must be closely drawn to avoid any unnecessary abridgement of the freedom of speech.[14] Massachusetts advanced two justifications for its prohibition of corporate speech: (1) the state's interest in sustaining the active role of the individual citizen in the electoral process, thereby preventing diminution of the citizens' confidence in government; and (2) the interest in protecting the rights of shareholders whose political views may differ from those expressed by management on behalf of the corporation.[15]

While the Court found these interests to be weighty, it determined that they were not served by the state's prohibition. First, there had been no showing that the relative voice of corporations was overwhelming or even significant in influencing referenda in Massachusetts, or that there was any threat to the confidence of the citizenry in their government.[16] Furthermore, the possible risk of corruption perceived in candidate elections (and used to justify prohibitions on corporate contributions to candidates) is not present in a popular vote on a public issue. While corporate advertising may influence the outcome of a vote, that is no reason to restrict it. The Constitution protects advocacy which is persuasive as well as that which is not. Moreover, government may not restrict the speech of some elements of society in order to enhance the relative voice of others.[17]

Second, the statute was not carefully drawn to protect the interests of dissenting shareholders. It was underinclusive because it did not restrict other forms of political activity that some shareholders might disagree with, such as direct lobbying of the legislature with respect to the defeat or passage of legislation. It was also overinclusive because it prevented certain corporate speech even if the unanimous consent of shareholders was obtained.[18] Thus, the statute failed to survive the Court's exacting scrutiny and was declared invalid.

The Court noted, however, that the government could require identification of the source of political advertising, so that the public could evaluate the credibility of the arguments to which they were being subjected.[19]

With this constitutional background, restrictions on corporate political activity related to federal elections can be considered.

Restrictions on Corporate Political Activity

Congress first outlawed corporate financial contributions to federal candidates in 1907 in the Tillman Act.[20] The statute was a response to the popular perception that aggregated capital had an undue influence on the nation's politics and threatened to "undermine the political integrity of the Republic."[21] It sprang from the same tide of reform protest against concentrated wealth that spawned the Sherman Act in 1890 and the income tax in 1894.[22] The influence of "big money" campaign contributions became an issue in the 1904 presidential elections, after which President Theodore Roosevelt responded to public pressure by calling on Congress to enact a ban on corporate contributions.[23]

Amendments in 1910 required political committees working to influence congressional elections in two or more states to report on contributions and expenditures; the following year Congress imposed reporting requirements and spending limitations on candidates themselves.[24] The Federal Corrupt Practices Act, enacted in 1925, prohibited corporate contributions of "anything of value" to a federal candidate, and made acceptance of a corporate contribution as well as the giving of such a contribution a crime.[25]

In 1943, the growing influence of labor unions prompted Congress to place the same limitations on union campaign contributions as those applicable to corporations.[26]

These early statutes were not considered particularly effective.[27] Congress strengthened and codified the campaign finance laws in the Federal Election Campaign Act of 1971,[28] with additional refinements in 1974,[29] 1976,[30] and 1980.[31]

The underlying rationale put forth in support of this kind of legislation in the early 1900s is still judged adequate today to support limitations on corporations' rights to engage in political speech. Writing for a unanimous Supreme Court in 1982, then-Associate Justice Rehnquist acknowledged that the statute reflects a legislative judgment that the special characteristics of the corporate structure require particularly careful regulation.[32] In upholding the specific regulations at issue in that case, the Court agreed with the Federal Election Commission that the regulations were justified by the two purposes of the FEC Act: (1) to ensure that substantial aggregations of wealth amassed due to the special advantages which go with the corporate form of organization would not be converted into political war chests which could be used to incur political debts from legislators who are aided by the contributions, and (2) to protect the individuals who have paid money into a corporation for purposes other than the support of candidates from having that money used to support political candidates to whom they may be opposed.[33]

The Federal Election Campaign Act

Limitations on Campaign Participation and Political Speech

The current version of the Federal Election Campaign Act forbids corporations from using general treasury funds to make any contribution or expenditure in connection with any federal election, or any primary, caucus, or political convention selecting candidates for federal office.[34] "Contribution or expenditure" is defined broadly to include any sort of transfer of money, services, or thing of value to a candidate, campaign committee, political party, or organization.[35]

A corporation may, however, make certain nonpartisan expenditures, and may establish a "separate segregated fund" to be utilized for political purposes.[36] Significantly, corporate treasury funds may be used for the establishment, administration, and solicitation of contributions to the separate segregated fund.[37] This gives a corporation the mechanism to direct and control campaign expenditures, and use such expenditures as a lobbying tool, while avoiding use of accumulated capital or sales revenues to influence federal elections.

A separate segregated fund established by a corporation falls within the definition of a "political committee," commonly referred to as a "political action committee" or "PAC," and is thus subject to the laws and regulations governing PAC fundraising and expenditures.[38] An overview of these detailed requirements and procedures is useful in understanding the limits on corporate activity.

Limitations on PAC Expenditures and Contributions

Most corporate PACs are permitted to contribute up to $5,000 per election to any candidate for federal office.[39] Such a political committee is also limited to giving $15,000 per calendar year to any national political party, and $5,000 per year to any other political committee.[40]

Contributions to a candidate's authorized political committees (including his or her principal campaign committee) count against the limit on contributions to the candidate.[41] Separate limits apply, however, to general elections on the one hand, and nominating primaries, caucuses, and conventions on the other.[42] Thus, a corporate PAC may contribute $5,000 to a presidential candidate during the primaries, and another $5,000 towards his or her general election campaign. A single limit applies to all presidential elections other than the general election in any calendar year.[43] In other words, contributions made to support a candidate's efforts in various state primaries and caucuses count against a single aggregate limit, regardless of the fact that the primaries take place on different dates.

Contributions in support of a nominee for Vice President are considered contributions for the benefit of his or her running mate.[44] Also, contributions made through an intermediary or in any way earmarked for a particular candidate are treated as contributions directly to that candidate.[45] In other words, a contribution by a PAC to a national political party, or by an individual to a PAC, if earmarked for a particular candidate, counts against the donor's limit on contributions to that candidate.

Where a corporation, together with its parent, subsidiaries, and divisions, controls or maintains more than one PAC fund, all such funds are treated as a single separate segregated fund for the purpose of the contribution limitations.[46]

All of these limitations apply to a corporate PAC that qualifies as a "multicandidate political committee." A "multicandidate political committee" is a PAC that has been registered with the FEC for at least six months,[47] has received contributions from more than 50 persons, and has made contributions to five or more candidates for federal office.[48] A PAC which fails to meet any of these three criteria is subject to the same contribution limits as individuals: $1,000 per candidate per election, $20,000 per calendar year to a national political party, and $5,000 per year to any other political committee.[49]

Limitations on Solicitation of Funds

Federal law limits the amount of money that may be contributed to a PAC by any person or entity to $5,000 per calendar year.[50] The constitutionality of this limitation was upheld by the Supreme Court in *California Medical Association v. Federal Election Commission.*[51]

A sponsoring corporation may not contribute its own general treasury funds to its affiliated PAC, but may, of course, pay for PAC administration and solicitation expenses.[52] There is no dollar limit on the payment of these expenses.[53]

The FEC Act also places limitations on the class of persons who may be solicited for contributions to the corporate PAC. A corporation and its affiliated PAC are prohibited from soliciting contributions to the PAC from anyone other than corporate stockholders, executives, administrative personnel, employees, or the families of those persons.[54]

Only two solicitations in each calendar year may be directed to corporate employees (other than stockholders, executives, and administrative personnel) and their families.[55] These twice-yearly solicitations must be in writing and sent to stockholders, executive or administrative personnel, and employees at their residences.[56] These solicitations must be designed so that the corporation or fund conducting the solicitation cannot determine the identity of persons making no contribution or contributions of $50 or less.[57]

The Act does not limit the number of solicitations to members of a "restricted class" made up of stockholders, executive or administrative personnel, and their families. For the purposes of the Act, "executive or administrative personnel" includes corporate employees who are paid a salary, rather than an hourly wage, and who exercise policymaking, managerial, professional, or supervisory responsibilities.[58]

Contributions may not be obtained through force, job discrimination, financial reprisal, or threats of any such acts; contribution to the separate segregated fund may not be required as a condition of employment.[59] Any person soliciting a corporate employee for a contribution must inform him, at the time of the solicitation, of the political purposes of the fund and of the employee's right to refuse to contribute without reprisal.[60]

Formal and Procedural Requirements for Operation of a Separate Segregated Fund

The FEC Act and Federal Election Commission regulations impose extensive recordkeeping and reporting requirements on separate segregated funds, or PACs. The following outline is intended to be illustrative, not exhaustive.

Forming a PAC—Initial Registration

A separate segregated fund must file a statement of organization with the FEC within 10 days after establishment.[61] The statement of organization is required to include:

1. The name, address, and type of committee;
2. The name, address, relationship, and type of any connected organization (e.g., the corporate sponsor of a corporation PAC) or affiliated committee;
3. The name, address, and position of the custodian of books and accounts of the committee;
4. The name and address of the treasurer of the PAC;
5. For a committee authorized by a particular candidate, the name, office sought, and party affiliation of the candidate; and
6. A list of all banks, safety deposit boxes, and other depositories used by the PAC.[62]

Any changes to the information reported in the statement of organization must be reported to the Commission within 10 days of the date of the change.[63] A PAC may be terminated with the filing of a written statement with the FEC that it will no longer receive any contributions or make any disbursements, and that it has no outstanding debts or obligations.[64]

Designated Bank Accounts

A PAC must designate as its campaign depository one or more depository institutions, and must maintain at least one checking account. All receipts received by the committee must be deposited in accounts at the designated depositories.[65] All disbursements must be made by check drawn on one of those accounts, except that the PAC may maintain a petty cash fund for disbursements of up to $100 per person per transaction. The treasurer must maintain a record of all petty cash disbursements.[66]

Duties of the PAC Treasurer

Every PAC is required to have a treasurer, and may not accept contributions or make expenditures while the post is vacant.[67] Every expenditure by the PAC must be authorized by the treasurer or his designated agent.[68] Any person who receives a contribution of over $50 for a PAC must forward the contribution, the name and address of the donor, and the date of receipt to the PAC treasurer within 10 days; contributions of $50 or less must be forwarded within 30 days.[69] The Act imposes on the PAC treasurer the obligation to maintain, and preserve for three years, the following records:

1. An account of all contributions received by or on behalf of the PAC;
2. The name, address, and date of contribution for each donor contributing over $50;
3. The identity of each person contributing an aggregate of more than $200 in a calendar year, with the date and amount of each contribution;
4. The identification of any other political committee contributing to the PAC, with the date and amount of the contribution;
5. An account of all disbursements, including
   a. the name and address of every person receiving a disbursement,
   b. the date, amount, and purpose of the disbursement,
   c. the name of the candidate, if any, for whom the disbursement was made, and the office sought by that candidate, and
   d. for disbursements over $200, a receipt, invoice, or cancelled check; and
6. Copies of all reports required to be filed with the FEC.[70]

A PAC treasurer's best effort to obtain and maintain the required information is sufficient to be deemed in compliance with the Act.[71]

Reports of Receipts and Disbursements

A PAC is required to file with the FEC detailed reports, signed by the treasurer, of receipts and disbursements.[72] The PAC may elect to file its reports either:

1. monthly (except that it must file pre and postgeneral election reports in lieu of November and December reports in any year in which a general election is held)[73]; or
2. semiannually in nonelection years, and quarterly in election years, with additional year end and pre and postgeneral election reports.[74]

The reports must be cumulative for the calendar year to which they relate.[75] The Act requires the reports to contain detailed information on receipts, expenditures, contributors, and recipients of PAC contributions or expenditures. The specific requirements for information that must be disclosed in reports filed by corporate PACs is set out in the footnote.[76]

Reports and statements filed with the FEC pursuant to the requirements of the Act must be filed at the same time with the appropriate state officers, generally the Secretary of State or other official charged by state law with the responsibility of maintaining state election campaign reports.[77] A corporate PAC that makes a contribution in connection with a presidential election must file reports in the states where the recipient and the PAC have their respective headquarters.[78] A PAC making independent expenditures relating to a person seeking nomination as a candidate for President or Vice President must file a copy of its report in the state where the PAC has its headquarters, and must report in each state in which such expenditures are made the transactions relating to that state.[79] Where a PAC makes contributions to, or independent expenditures in connection with, a primary or general election campaign for the office of Senator or Representative, the PAC must file in each state at least the portions of its report applicable to candidates seeking election in that state.[80]

Trade Associations

A trade association with corporate members is subject to the same general limitations on campaign contributions and expenditures as corporations. Thus, a trade association may not use general funds—raised at least in part from dues paid by corporate members—for contributions directly to a candidate's election campaign. Like a corporation, an association may use its assets to establish, administer, or solicit contributions to a separate segregated fund, or PAC.

Solicitation of funds by an association PAC is subject to special limitations not applicable to others. A trade association or its PAC may solicit contributions to the separate segregated fund from the stockholders, executive and administrative personnel, and families of stockholders and executive and administrative personnel, of member corporations. However, that solicitation is only permitted if the member corporation has separately and specifically approved the solicitation. Moreover, a corporation may not approve solicitations by more than one trade association of which it is a member for any calendar year.[81] Once solicitation is approved, the approved PAC is not limited in the number of times it may solicit contributions during the calendar year, unless the corporation in its approval imposes such a limitation.[82]

Of course, a trade association may not solicit contributions from the funds of its member corporations, because that would enable corporations to achieve indirectly what the law bars them from doing directly.[83] If an association has individual noncorporate members, it is permitted to solicit contributions to its PAC from those members.[84]

Enforcement of the FEC Act

The Federal Election Commission is empowered to initiate civil actions to enforce the provisions of the FEC Act;[85] an action by the Commission is the exclusive civil remedy for enforcement of the Act.[86] The Commission is also authorized to investigate apparent violations and report them to appropriate law enforcement authorities.[87] In addition, the Act provides a procedure for the Commission to hear and act upon sworn complaints.[88] Various criminal penalties are available for knowing and willful violations of the Act's requirements and limitations.[89]

Interpretation of the Federal Election Campaign Act by the Courts and the FEC

Court Decisions

In *Buckley v. Valeo*,[90] the Supreme Court upheld most aspects of the FEC Act against broad-based challenges, but declared some aspects of the Act unconstitutional. The Court first addressed the extent to which the restrictions on contributions and expenditures infringed on constitutionally protected activity. The Justices recognized that the First Amendment affords its broadest protection to political expression such as the discussion of public issues and debate on the qualifications of candidates for public office.[91] This protection extends as well to the right to associate with others for the common advancement of political beliefs and ideas.[92] Limitations on *expenditures* for political communication restrict the exercise of those freedoms because they reduce the quantity of expression by restricting the number of issues discussed, the depth of their exploration, and the size of the audience reached.[93] In contrast, limitations on *contributions* to a particular candidate by an individual or group only marginally restrict the contributor's ability to engage in free communication, because a contribution serves only as a general expression of support for a candidate and his views, but does not indicate the underlying basis for the support.[94] In the Supreme Court's view, the "quantity" of communication by the contributor does not increase perceptibly with the size of the contribution.

Absent evidence that the individual contribution limitations prevented candidates from amassing the resources necessary for effective advocacy, the Court upheld the limitation on contributions by individuals and groups.[95] It found the Act's primary purpose of limiting both the actuality and appearance of corruption resulting from large contributions constitutionally sufficient to justify the limitations on individual and PAC contributions.[96]

The government's interest in preventing corruption was not found adequate, however, to support the limitation on independent expenditures by individuals or groups relative to a clearly identified candidate. That restriction was found to be a direct restraint on the quantity of political speech.[97] The advocacy of the election or defeat of candidates for federal office is no less entitled to constitutional protection than the discussion of political policy generally or the advocacy of passage or defeat of legislation.[98] Restrictions on such core First Amendment rights are subject to exacting scrutiny. The Court found that independent advocacy does not pose the same danger of real or apparent corruption as large, direct campaign contributions.[99] Moreover, restriction of this speech cannot be justified by a desire to equalize the ability of different individuals to influence the outcome of elections; the government may not restrict the speech of some to enhance the relative voice of others.[100]

The Supreme Court also struck down limitations on the amount a candidate can spend from his or her own personal funds,[101] while upholding the reporting, disclosure, and record-keeping provisions of the Act.[102]

In later cases the Supreme Court has addressed much narrower aspects of the FEC Act. In *California Medical Association v. Federal Election Commission,*[103] the Court upheld the annual limitation on the amount individuals or unincorporated associations can contribute to a PAC, reasoning in part that the restriction prevents circumvention of the limitations on contributions directly to candidates.[104] *Federal Election Commission v. National Right to Work Committee*[105] dealt with the definition of "member" of nonstock corporations permitted to solicit PAC contributions from their members. While not defining "member," the Court held that the term must mean more than simply one who responds to an essentially random mass mailing. The Court noted that the statute reflects a legislative judgment that the special characteristics of the corporate structure require particularly careful regulation.[106]

In *Federal Election Commission v. National Conservative Political Action Committee,*[107] NCPAC, a well-known independent political action committee, brought a constitutional challenge against a particular statutory contribution limit. That statute made it a criminal offense for any PAC to expend more than $1,000 to further the election of a presidential candidate who had decided to utilize the public campaign financing option. Relying on *Buckley v. Valeo,* the Court found the expenditures in question to involve speech at the core of the First Amendment.[108] Preventing corruption or the appearance of corruption are the only legitimate and compelling government interests thus far identified that are sufficient to justify restrictions on campaign finances.[109] However, because the independent expenditures in question were not prearranged or coordinated with the candidate's campaign, the expenditures appeared to present a lesser danger of corruption.[110] Accordingly, the restriction of core First Amendment rights was not supportable.

While noting that a corporation's expenditures to propagate its views on issues of general public interest are of a different constitutional stature than corporate contributions to candidates, the Court declined to expressly reach the question whether a corporation can constitutionally be restricted in making independent expenditures to influence elections for public office.[111] The Court did, however, distinguish between traditional corporations organized for economic gain and corporations such as NCPAC, an incorporated political committee designed expressly to participate in political debate.[112] The Court's statement that the government has a greater interest in restricting the political influence of the former suggests that the holding of the *NCPAC* decision may not be applicable to traditional business corporations.

The Supreme Court again addressed application of restrictions on independent expenditures in *Federal Election Commission v. Massachusetts Citizens for Life, Inc.*[113] There, the Court first held that the statutory definition of a prohibited "expenditure" necessarily incorporates a requirement that a communication "expressly advocate" the election or defeat of clearly identified candidates.[114] Therefore, expenditures that do not constitute "express advocacy" are not prohibited. "Express advocacy" depends on the use of such language as "vote for," "elect," "support," and so on.[115] The Federal Election Commission, however, has taken the position that this portion of the Court's opinion is *dicta,* and thus does not represent a final resolution of the issue.[116] Therefore, there is still some doubt as to whether corporate independent expenditures that are intended to influence federal elections but do not constitute express advocacy for or against identifiable candidates are prohibited.

The Court also found that certain kinds of nonprofit corporations do not exhibit the characteristics that Congress legitimately perceived as exerting an undesirable influence on the electoral process. Consequently, application of the broad prohibition on independent expenditures by these nonprofit corporations was held unconstitutional. The Court again distinguished between traditional corporations and incorporated political associations:

> "Regulation of corporate political activity thus has reflected concern not about use of the corporate form *per se,* but about the potential for unfair deployment of wealth for political purposes. Groups such as [Massachusetts Citizens For Life], however, do not pose that danger of corruption. MCFL was formed to disseminate political ideas, not to amass capital. The resources it has available are not a function of its success in the economic marketplace, but its popularity in the political marketplace. While MCFL may derive some advantages from its corporate form, those are advantages that redound to its benefit as a political organization, not as a profit-making enterprise."[117]

In response to the *Massachusetts Citizens for Life* decision, the FEC has initiated a rulemaking to determine the applicability of an "express advocacy" test to independent expenditures, and to draft regulations that would spell out the qualifications for nonprofit corporations to be exempt from the Act's expenditure limitations.[118]

FEC Pronouncements

The Federal Election Commission is the independent federal agency vested with exclusive jurisdiction over civil enforcement of the Federal Election Campaign Act.[119] The FEC is authorized to render advisory opinions concerning application of the FEC Act or the Commission's rules and regulations to particular circumstances.[120] The Commission is required to respond to a request for an advisory opinion within 60 days.[121] Both the requesting party and persons involved in specific transactions indistinguishable from those at issue in an advisory opinion are entitled to rely on the opinion.[122]

Anyone unsure about the effect of the Act or FEC regulations on proposed political solicitations or expenditures should obtain an advisory opinion from the Commission.[123] Advisory opinion requests are part of the Commission's public record, and the Commission is required to accept written public comments from any interested party.[124]

Independent and Nonpartisan Political Communications by Corporations

Despite the broad prohibitions of the FEC Act, numerous types of political communications by corporations are either expressly excepted from the provisions of the Act or are not among the among the kinds of activities—contributions and expenditures in connection with a federal election—intended to be covered by the Act in the first instance. For example, the general prohibitions of the Act do not bar corporations from communicating with their stockholders, executive and administrative personnel, and families of stockholders and executive and administrative personnel, on any subject, including matters of political interest.[125] In addition, a corporation may also expend its own funds for nonpartisan registration and get-out-the-vote campaigns aimed at its stockholders, executive and administrative personnel, and their families.[126] There are specific rules governing those expenditures.

Partisan Communications to Restricted Class

A corporation may make partisan political communications to a "restricted class" made up of its stockholders, executive and administrative personnel, and their families.[127] If those communications expressly advocate the election or defeat of a clearly identified candidate, and the costs directly attributable to express-advocacy communications in any one election exceed $2,000, then those expenditures must be reported to the FEC.[128]

FEC regulations give several examples of the means by which partisan communications expressly advocating the election or defeat of a clearly identified candidate may be distributed:

a. Printed materials may be distributed if they are produced at the expense of the organization and constitute a communication of the views of the organization. The corporation may not simply republish or reproduce any broadcast, graphic, or campaign material prepared by the candidate or his campaign committee, although the corporate materials may use brief quotations from candidate materials that demonstrate the candidate's position on issues.[129]

b. A corporation may allow a candidate or party representative to address members of the restricted class at a meeting or convention of the corporation. Employees outside the restricted class who are necessary to administer the meeting, limited invited guests, and members of the news media may be present. At such an appearance, the candidate may solicit contributions to his campaign or party, and the incidental solicitation of persons outside the restricted class will not be deemed to be a violation of FEC regulations.[130]

c. A corporation may establish and operate partisan phone banks to urge members of its restricted class to register or to vote for specific candidates.[131]

d. A corporation may also conduct registration and get-out-the-vote drives aimed at members of the restricted class. These drives may be partisan in that individuals may be urged to register with a particular party or vote for particular candidates. These drives may include assistance in registering or voting and providing transportation to the polls, but that assistance or transportation may not be withheld or refused on a partisan basis.[132]

Nonpartisan Communications to Employees

A corporation may also sponsor nonpartisan candidate or party appearances at corporate meetings, conventions, or on corporate premises.[133] Corporate employees outside the restricted class, and their families, may attend if the following conditions are met:

a. If a candidate for the Senate or the House (or the representative of a candidate) is permitted to meet or address corporate employees, all candidates for the same seat who request to appear must be given the same opportunity to do so. If a candidate for President or Vice President (or the representative of a candidate) is given the opportunity to meet or address employees, then all major party candidates (or candidates who are on the general election ballot in enough states to win a majority of the electoral votes) who request to appear must be given the same opportunity. Finally, if representatives of a political party meet or address employees, all political parties that either had a candidate on the ballot for the last general election or will have a candidate on the ballot for the next general election must be given the same opportunity.[134]

b. The corporation, its PAC, and members of its restricted class may make no effort to solicit, direct, or control contributions by members of the audience in connection with any such candidate appearance.[135]

c. The corporation, its PAC, and members of its restricted class may not endorse, support, or oppose any candidate or party in connection with any such candidate or party representative appearance.[136]

Nonpartisan Communications to the General Public

A corporation may make the following kinds of nonpartisan political communications to members of the general public as well as to its employees and members of its restricted class. The company may include its logo or otherwise identify itself as the sponsor of the communication.

a. *Nonpartisan registration and get-out-the-vote communications.* These communications are considered nonpartisan if they name or depict no particular candidates, or name or depict all candidates for a particular office without favoring any. Nonpartisan communications in this category may not name political parties except for the purpose of identifying the party affiliation of all candidates named. These communications are limited to urging acts such as voting and registering, and to describing the hours and places of registration or voting.[137] Nonpartisan registration and get-out-the-vote communications may be made through billboards, broadcast media, newspapers, brochures, or other means of communicating with the general public.[138]

b. *Official registration and voting information.* A corporation may distribute, or reprint in whole and distribute, registration or voting information, such as instructional materials, produced by official election administrators. A company may also donate funds to state or local agencies responsible for the administration of elections to help defray the expense of printing or distributing registration and voting information. Any information distributed, or for which funds are donated, must be distributed in a nonpartisan manner. A corporation may not endorse or support a particular party or candidate in connection with the distribution.[139]

c. *Voting records.* It is permissible for a corporation to prepare and distribute the voting records of members of Congress, but not for the purpose of influencing a federal election.[140]

d. *Voter guides.* Nonpartisan voter guides consisting of

questions posed to candidates concerning campaign issues and the candidates' responses may be prepared and distributed by corporations. Several factors will determine whether a voter guide is nonpartisan:

"(i) The questions are directed to all candidates for a particular seat or office, and all candidates are given equal time to respond, except that questions to Presidential and Vice Presidential candidates need only be directed to major party candidates or candidates appearing on the general election ballot of enough states to win a majority of the electoral votes.

"(ii) The voter guide reprints verbatim the candidates' responses, without additional comment, editing or emphasis (although limitations on the number of words may be imposed).

"(iii) The wording of the questions does not suggest or favor any position on the issues covered.

"(iv) The voter guide presents no editorial position concerning the issues covered, and does not indicate support for or opposition to any candidate or party.

"(v) The voter guide may include biographical information asked of and received from the candidates.

"(vi) The guide must be made available to the public in the geographical area where the sponsoring organization normally operates."[141]

These guidelines need not be followed where the corporation distributes voter guides obtained from nonprofit, tax-exempt organizations which do not support, endorse, or oppose candidates or parties. However, those guides may not favor one candidate or party over others.[142]

Nonpartisan Registration and Get-Out-the-Vote Drives

Corporations may participate in a limited manner in voter registration and get-out-the-vote drives. The drives are not required to be limited to the restricted class if certain requirements are met. To participate in a drive, a corporation must jointly sponsor it with a nonprofit, tax-exempt organization that does not support, endorse, or oppose candidates or parties, or with the state or local agency responsible for administering elections. The services the drive provides must be made available without regard to the voter's political preference, and the activities of the drive must be conducted by the tax-exempt organization or the state or local agency. However, permitting the use of space on the corporate premises and providing employees to assist in the distribution of official registration or voting information is not considered "conducting" a registration or voting drive, and thus these activities are permitted of the corporate cosponsor.[143]

A corporation may also donate funds to be used for registration drives by nonprofit, tax-exempt organizations or by state or local agencies responsible for the administration of elections.[144] Such an organization or agency may utilize corporate employees or facilities in conducting a nonpartisan drive.[145] Any materials prepared for distribution to the general public in connection with a registration or voting drive must include the full names of all drive sponsors.[146]

Nonpartisan Candidate Debates

A corporation may donate funds to a qualified nonprofit organization for the purpose of staging nonpartisan candidate debates.[147]

Use of Corporate Facilities

FEC regulations also govern the extent to which corporate facilities may be used for individual volunteer activity by employees and stockholders. Subject to the rules and practices of the corporation, stockholders and employees may make "occasional, isolated, or incidental use" of corporate facilities for individual volunteer activity in connection with a federal election. They will only be required to reimburse the corporation to the extent that the overhead or operating costs of the corporation are increased. If the use is more than occasional, isolated, or incidental, the stockholder or employee must reimburse the corporation for the normal and usual rental charge for the facility.[148]

"Occasional, isolated, or incidental use" includes: (1) use by an employee during working hours that does not prevent the employee from completing his or her normal amount of work; (2) use by stockholders during working hours that does not interfere with the corporation's normal activities; and (3) any activity that does not exceed one hour per week or four hours per month, regardless of whether it takes place during or after working hours.[149]

Anyone who uses the facilities of a corporation to "produce materials" in connection with a federal election must reimburse the corporation for the normal and usual charge of producing those materials in the commercial market. If persons other than employees or stockholders make use of corporate facilities for activity in connection with a federal election, such as using telephones or typewriters or borrowing corporate office furniture, they must reimburse the corporation for the normal and usual rental charge.[150] A candidate or person traveling on behalf of a candidate who uses a corporate airplane for travel in connection with an election must reimburse the corporation in advance.[151]

Individual Employees' Time

As a general rule, corporations may not pay their employees to provide services to political committees without charge. In other words, employees may not be compensated for performing volunteer campaign activities on "company time." No compensation is deemed paid to the employee if (a) an employee paid on an hourly or salaried basis makes up the time spent on political activity; (b) an employee is paid on a commission or piecework basis, or is paid only for work performed and the employee's time is considered his or her own; or (c) the employee engages in political activity during bona fide vacation or earned leave time.[152] Similarly, while an employee may engage in political activity during an unpaid leave of absence, a corporation may not pay the employer's share of the cost of fringe benefits, such as insurance premiums and retirement plan contributions, for employees who participate in federal political campaigns while on leave without pay.[153]

Despite the general rule, a corporation may continue to pay the regular salary of lawyers or accountants who provide legal or accounting services to political committees in certain circumstances. Those services rendered to a political party do not constitute a contribution if the person paying for the services is the regular employer of the service provider and if the services are not attributable to activities which directly further the election of any designated candidate for federal office.[154] Legal or accounting services may be provided to a candidate's authorized committee or a PAC if the person paying for the services is the regular employer of the service provider and the services are provided solely to ensure compliance with the FEC Act.[155] These donations of professional services must be reported by the recipient committee.

Extension of Credit to Candidates

A corporation may extend credit to a candidate or political committee in the ordinary course of the corporation's business and on terms substantially similar to extensions of credit to nonpolitical debtors which are of similar risk and size of obligation.[156] A corporation may not forgive debts incurred by a candidate or political committee. However, a corporate creditor may settle the debt for less than the amount owed if the initial extension of credit was proper under FEC regulations, the debtor has taken all commercially reasonable steps to try to satisfy the outstanding debt, and the corporate creditor has pursued available remedies, including litigation, similar in intensity to the means employed to collect from nonpolitical debtors. The corporation and the debtor are required to file a statement of settlement with the FEC.[157]

Conclusion

Because of a perceived threat of corruption or appearance of corruption of the political process, Congress has severely restricted the extent to which business corporations may make contributions or expenditures in connection with federal elections. Those restrictions have been upheld as legitimate limitations on what would otherwise be protected activity under the First Amendment. However, corporations may engage in political activity in three major areas: (1) establishing and administering a separate segregated fund, or PAC; (2) engaging in political speech or conducting political affairs programs on issues not tied to federal election campaigns or federal candidates; and (3) engaging in nonpartisan activity with respect to federal elections. Thus, although corporations must navigate a considerable regulatory minefield to engage in political expression, they retain a number of mechanisms to express their political views to the public and their elected representatives.

Notes

1. See 2 U.S.C. §441b(a); 11 C.F.R. §114.2(b) (1988). The Federal Election Campaign Act is codified at 2 U.S.C. §§431 *et seq.* (See Appendix G for excerpts from the statute.) State laws affecting lobbying communications by corporations are beyond the scope of this discussion. However, federal law expressly supersedes any state laws dealing with contributions or expenditures in connection with federal elections, and the organization and registration of political committees supporting federal candidates. See 2 U.S.C. §453, 11 C.F.R. §108.7. For a survey of state statutes relating to political expenditures by corporations, see Note, *Corporate Speech on Political Issues: The First Amendment in Conflict with Democratic Ideals?* 1985 U. Ill. L. Rev. 445, 470–72.

2. 435 U.S. 765 (1978).

3. See *id.* at 768.

4. *Id.* at 769.

5. See *id.* at 771, 778, *quoting from* 371 Mass. 773, 784–85, 359 N.E.2d 1262, 1270 (1977).

6. 435 U.S. at 776.

7. *Id.* at 776–77.

8. *Id.* at 783.

9. *Id.* at 777.

10. *Id.* at 782.

11. *Id.* at 784–85.

12. *Id.* at 784.

13. *Id.* at 786 and n.23.

14. *Id.* at 786.

15. *Id.* at 787.

16. *Id.* at 789–90.

17. *Id.* at 790–91.

18. *Id.* at 793–94.

19. *Id.* at 792 n.32. More recent cases not specifically involving corporations have reaffirmed the right to make expenditures in connection with ballot measures submitted to popular vote. In *Citizens Against Rent Control v. City of Berkeley*, 454 U.S. 290 (1981), a local ordinance had placed a $250 limitation on contributions to committees formed to support or oppose ballot initiatives. The Supreme Court struck down the restriction as violative of both the right of association and the free speech guarantees of the First Amendment. The Supreme Court has also invalidated a Colorado statute that prohibited paying individuals to circulate petitions to have initiatives or referendums placed on the general election ballot. *Meyer v. Grant*, 486 U.S. _____ (1988). The Court held that the circulation of a referendum petition involves the type of interactive communication concerning political change that is core political speech. *Id.* at _____. Read in conjunction with *Bellotti*, these cases reinforce the ability of corporations to make expenditures to express their political views, at least where issues rather than candidates are involved.

20. Ch. 420, 34 Stat. 864.

21. *United States v. United Automobile Workers*, 352 U.S. 567, 570 (1957), *quoting from* 2 S. Morison and H. Commager, The Growth of the American Republic, 355 (4th ed. 1950).

22. 352 U.S. at 570.

23. *Id.* at 572–75.
24. See *id.* at 575–76.
25. 43 Stat. 1070.
26. Smith-Connally Act, 57 Stat. 163, 167; Taft-Hartley Act, ch. 120, §304, 61 Stat. 136, 159. While many of the provisions governing corporate political activity today also apply to labor organizations, a more detailed treatment of the limitations and restrictions affecting union lobbying and political activities is beyond the scope of this discussion.
27. See Nicholson, *The Supreme Court's Meandering Path in Campaign Finance Regulation and What It Portends for Future Reform,* 3 J.L. & POL'Y 509, 510 (1987).
28. 86 Stat. 3.
29. 88 Stat. 1263.
30. 90 Stat. 475.
31. 93 Stat. 1339.
32. *Federal Election Comm'n v. National Right to Work Comm.,* 459 U.S. 197, 209–10 (1982).
33. *Id.* at 207–08.
34. 2 U.S.C. §441b(a); 11 C.F.R. §114.2(b). National banks and federally chartered corporations are also barred from making contributions or expenditures in connection with state elections. 2 U.S.C. §441b(a). Separate provisions govern contributions by government contractors. See Chapter 7, *infra.*
35. 2 U.S.C. §441b(b)(2); 11 C.F.R. §114.1(a)(1).
36. 2 U.S.C. §441b(b)(2)(C). The separate segregated fund may be completely controlled by the sponsoring corporation. *Federal Election Comm'n v. National Right to Work Comm.,* 459 U.S. 197, 200 n.4 (1982). The "fund must be separate from the sponsoring [corporation] only in the sense that there must be a strict segregation of its monies" from the corporation's other assets. *Id.; Pipefitters v. United States,* 407 U.S. 385, 414–17 (1972).
37. 2 U.S.C. §441b(b)(2)(C).
38. See 2 U.S.C. §431(4)(B).
39. 2 U.S.C. §441a(a)(2)(A); 11 C.F.R. §110.2(b)(1).
40. 2 U.S.C. §441a(a)(2)(B)-(C); 11 C.F.R. §110.2(c)-(d).
41. 2 U.S.C. §§441a(a)(2)(A), 441a(a)(7)(A).
42. 2 U.S.C. §441a(a)(6).
43. *Id.*
44. 2 U.S.C. §441a(a)(7)(C).
45. 2 U.S.C. §441a(a)(8).
46. 2 U.S.C. §441a(a)(5).
47. See discussion at pp. 69–71, *infra.*
48. 2 U.S.C. §441a(a)(4).
49. 2 U.S.C. §441a(a)(1); 11 C.F.R. §110.1(b)-(d).
50. 2 U.S.C. §441a(a)(1)(C); 11 C.F.R. §110.1(d).
51. 453 U.S. 182 (1981). Although four justices dissented from the Court's judgment, they did so on jurisdictional grounds, and did not address the constitutional merits of the case. *See* 453 U.S. at 204 (opinion of Stewart, J., dissenting).
52. 2 U.S.C. §441b(a)-(b).
53. See 2 U.S.C. §431(8)(B)(vi); *California Medical Ass'n v. Federal Election Comm'n,* 453 U.S. at 200.
54. 2 U.S.C. §441b(b)(4), 11 C.F.R. §114.5(g)(1). Corporations without capital stock are permitted to solicit contributions from members of the corporation. 2 U.S.C. §441b(b)(4)(C). For a discussion of what constitutes "membership" in a nonstock corporation, see *Federal Election Comm'n v. National Right to Work Comm.,* 459 U.S. 197 (1982).
55. 2 U.S.C. §441b(b)(4)(B), 11 C.F.R. §114.6.
56. 2 U.S.C. §441b(b)(4)(B), 11 C.F.R. §114.6(c).
57. 2 U.S.C. §441b(b)(4)(B), 11 C.F.R. §114.6(d).
58. 2 U.S.C. §441b(b)(7); 11 C.F.R. §114.1(c).
59. 2 U.S.C. §441b(b)(3)(A); 11 C.F.R. §114.5(a)(1).
60. 2 U.S.C. §441b(b)(3)(B)-(C); 11 C.F.R. §114.5(a)(3)-(4).
61. 2 U.S.C. §§433(a), 432(g)(4); 11 C.F.R. §102.1(c).
62. 2 U.S.C. §433(b); 11 C.F.R. §102.2(a)(1).
63. 2 U.S.C. §433(c); 11 C.F.R. §102.2(a)(2).
64. 2 U.S.C. §433(d)(1); 11 C.F.R. §102.3(a).
65. 2 U.S.C. §432(h)(1); *see* 11 C.F.R. Part 103.
66. 2 U.S.C. §432(h)(1)-(2).

67. 2 U.S.C. §432(a).
68. *Id.*
69. 2 U.S.C. §432(b)(2). These requirements are more stringent for a candidate's principal campaign committee or other PAC authorized to receive contributions on his behalf. 2 U.S.C. §432(b)(1).
70. 2 U.S.C. §432(c)-(d); 11 C.F.R. §104.3(a)-(c).
71. 2 U.S.C. §432(i); 11 C.F.R. §104.7.
72. 2 U.S.C. §434(a)(1).
73. 2 U.S.C. §434(a)(4)(B); 11 C.F.R. §104.5(c).
74. 2 U.S.C. §434(a)(4)(A); 11 C.F.R. §104.5(c). The pre-election report need only be filed if the PAC makes a contribution or expenditure on behalf of a candidate in that election, and the requirement to file a report for the third quarter of the calendar year is waived if it would be due at approximately the same time as a preelection report required for that year. See 2 U.S.C. §434(a)(8).
75. 2 U.S.C. §434(a)(7).
76. The FEC Act, 2 U.S.C. §434(b), requires reports filed by corporate PACs to disclose the following information:
   1. the amount of cash on hand at the beginning of the reporting period;
   2. for the reporting period and the calendar year-to-date, total receipts and the total amount of receipts in the following categories:
      "a. contributions from persons other than political committees;
      "b. [omitted];
      "c. contributions from political party committees;
      "d. contributions from other political committees;
      "e. [omitted];
      "f. transfers from affiliated committees;
      "g. [omitted];
      "h. all loans;
      "i. rebates, refunds, and other offsets to operating expenditures;
      "j. dividends, interest, and other forms of receipts; and
      "k. [omitted];
   3. the identification of each of the following, along with the date and the amount of each contribution, loan or receipt:
      "a. person who makes a contribution during the reporting period whose total contributions during the calendar year have an aggregate amount or value over $200;
      "b. political committee making a contribution during the reporting period;
      "c. candidate-authorized committee which makes a transfer to the reporting committee;
      "d. affiliated committee which makes a transfer to the reporting committee during the reporting period;
      "e. person who makes a loan to the reporting committee, and any endorser or guarantor of the loan;
      "f. person who provides a rebate, refund or other offset in an aggregate amount over $200 in the calendar year;
      "g. person who provides any dividend, interest or other receipt with an aggregate value over $200 in the calendar year;
   4. for the reporting period and the calendar year-to-date, the total amount of disbursements, and all disbursements in the following categories:
      "a. expenditures for candidate or committee operating expenditures;
      "b. [omitted];
      "c. transfers to affiliated committees;
      "d. [omitted];
      "e. repayment of loans;
      "f. contribution, refunds, and other offsets to contributions;
      "g. [omitted];
      "h. contributions made to other political committees, loans made by the reporting committee, independent expenditures, and any other disbursements; and
      "i [omitted];
   5. the name and address of each of the following, along with the date and amount of the payment, transfer or expenditure:
      "a. person to whom expenditures aggregating more than $200 in the calendar year to meet a candidate or committee operating expense are made, along with the purpose of the operating expenditure;
      "b. authorized committee to which a transfer is made;
      "c. affiliated committee to which a transfer is made during the reporting period;
      "d. person who receives a loan repayment during the reporting period; and
      "e. person who receives a contribution refund or other offset to a contribution reported under the requirements of the Act;

6. the name and address of each of the following, along with the date and amount of the contribution or expenditure:
   "a. political committee which has received a contribution from the reporting committee during the reporting period;
   "b. person who has received a loan from the reporting committee during the reporting period;
   "c. person to whom disbursements aggregating more than $200 in the calendar year are made in connection with an independent expenditure by the reporting PAC, along with the purpose of the independent expenditure, a statement whether the independent expenditure is in support of or opposition to a candidate, the name and office sought by such candidate, and a certification under penalty of perjury whether the independent expenditure is made in cooperation or concert with any candidate or candidate-authorized committee;
   "d. [omitted]; and
   "e. any other person receiving any disbursement, not otherwise reported, aggregating more than $200 in the calendar year, along with the purpose of such disbursement;
7. the total sum of all contributions to the PAC, the total contributions less offsets, the total sum of all operating expenditures, the total operating expenditures less offsets, both for the reporting period and the calendar year; and
8. a statement of the amount and nature of outstanding debts owed by the PAC, and where such debts are settled for less than their reported value, a statement of the circumstances and conditions under which the debts were extinguished. (Requirements not relevant to corporation-affiliated PACs omitted.) See also 11 C.F.R. §104.3.

77. 2 U.S.C. §439(a)(1); 11 C.F.R. §§108.1, 108.5.
78. 11 C.F.R. §108.4.
79. 2 U.S.C. §439(a)(2)(A); 11 C.F.R. §108.2.
80. 2 U.S.C. §439(a)(2)(B); 11 C.F.R. §108.3.
81. 2 U.S.C. §441b(b)(4)(D); 11 C.F.R. §114.8(c)-(d).
82. 11 C.F.R. §114.8(e).
83. See 2 U.S.C. §441b(a); 11 C.F.R. §114.8(b).
84. 2 U.S.C. §441b(b)(4)(D).
85. 2 U.S.C. §437d(a)(6).
86. 2 U.S.C. §437d(e).
87. 2 U.S.C. §437d(a)(9).
88. 2 U.S.C. §437g(a).
89. 2 U.S.C. §437g(d).
90. 424 U.S. 1 (1976) (per curiam).
91. 424 U.S. at 14.
92. *Id.* at 15.
93. *Id.* at 19.
94. *Id.* at 20–21.
95. *Id.* at 21–22, 29.
96. *Id.* at 26, 35.
97. *Id.* at 39.
98. *Id.* at 48.
99. *Id.* at 46.
100. *Id.* at 48–49.
101. *Id.* at 53–54.
102. *Id.* at 60–84.
103. 453 U.S. 182 (1981).
104. *Id.* at 197–98.
105. 459 U.S. 197 (1982).
106. *Id.* at 209–10.
107. 470 U.S. 480 (1985).
108. *Id.* at 493–94.
109. *Id.* at 496–97.
110. *Id.* at 497–98.
111. *Id.* at 496.
112. *Id.* at 500.
113. 479 U.S. 238 (1986).
114. *Id.* at 249.

115. *Id.*
116. Advance Notice of Proposed Rulemaking, 53 Fed. Reg. 416 (Jan, 7, 1988).
117. *Id.* at 628.
118. Advance Notice of Proposed Rulemaking, 53 Fed. Reg. 416 (Jan. 7, 1988).
119. 2 U.S.C. §§437c(b)(1), 437d(a), (e).
120. 2 U.S.C. §437f(a).
121. 2 U.S.C. §437f(a).
122. 2 U.S.C. §437f(c).
123. FEC regulations governing the submission of requests for advisory opinions are found at 11 C.F.R. Part 112. The text of Part 112 is reproduced in Appendix H.
124. 2 U.S.C. §437f(d).
125. 2 U.S.C. §441b(b)(2)(A).
126. 2 U.S.C. §441b(b)(2)(B).
127. 11 C.F.R. §114.3(a)(1).
128. 11 C.F.R. §§100.8(b)(4), 104.6, 114.3(b).
129. 11 C.F.R. §114.3(c)(1).
130. 11 C.F.R. §114.3(c)(2).
131. 11 C.F.R. §114.3(c)(3).
132. 11 C.F.R. §114.3(c)(4).
133. 11 C.F.R. §114.4(a)(2).
134. 11 C.F.R. §114.4(a)(2)(i)-(iii).
135. 11 C.F.R. §114.4(a)(2)(iv).
136. 11 C.F.R. §114.4(a)(2)(v).
137. 11 C.F.R. §114.4(b)(2)(i).
138. 11 C.F.R. §114.4(b)(2)(i).
139. 11 C.F.R. §114.4(b)(3).
140. 11 C.F.R. §114.4(b)(4).
141. 11 C.F.R. §114.4(b)(5)(i).
142. 11 C.F.R. §114.4(b)(5)(ii).
143. 11 C.F.R. §114.4(c)(1).
144. 11 C.F.R. §114.4(c)(2).
145. 11 C.F.R. §114.4(c)(3).
146. 11 C.F.R. §114.4(c)(5).
147. 11 C.F.R. §114.4(e); see 11 C.F.R. §110.13.
148. 11 C.F.R. §114.9(a).
149. 11 C.F.R. §114.9(a)(1).
150. 11 C.F.R. §114.9(c)-(d).
151. 11 C.F.R. §114.9(e).
152. 11 C.F.R. §100.7(a)(3).
153. 11 C.F.R. §114.12(c)(1).
154. 11 C.F.R. §100.7(b)(13).
155. 11 C.F.R. §100.7(b)(14).
156. 11 C.F.R. §114.10(a). Note that the Federal Aviation Administration, Federal Communications Commission, and Interstate Commerce Commission may apply specific restrictions to corporations operating within the industries they regulate.
157. 11 C.F.R. §114.10(c).

5

Lobbying and Antitrust

*Anthony C. Epstein, Carl S. Nadler, and
David E. Zerhusen*

Lobbying, in a very real sense, is a competitive enterprise. Whatever the market involved, be it for goods or services or even ideas,
lobbying at its essence involves the promotion of particular alternatives at the expense of others. The federal antitrust statutes, for their
part, are designed principally to curb certain competitive conduct.
Thus among the questions that repeatedly confront lobbyists are
whether, and under what circumstances, their essentially competitive conduct violates the nation's antitrust laws.[1]

The shorthand answer to these questions is that, generally
speaking, genuine efforts to influence governmental conduct are *immunized* from federal antitrust scrutiny. This is the *"Noerr-Pennington"* doctrine, so named in honor of the Supreme Court cases
that first recognized the immunity.[2] As with most general principles,
however, *Noerr-Pennington* has important doctrinal limitations and
admits to several important exceptions. This chapter is intended to
provide a basic understanding of that doctrine and a sensitivity to
those limitations.

Lobbying Immunity: The *Noerr-Pennington* Doctrine

The *Noerr-Pennington* doctrine shields from federal antitrust liability "[c]oncerted efforts to restrain or monopolize trade by petitioning government officials."[3] The primary rationale underlying *Noerr-
Pennington* is one of public policy: the antitrust laws were not
designed or intended to interfere with citizens' petitioning conduct in
furtherance of the governmental process.[4] Thus, bona fide efforts to
influence public action are protected from antitrust scrutiny, regardless of the anticompetitive consequences of the actor's conduct.

The antitrust immunity afforded by *Noerr-Pennington* applies, although in varying degrees, to lobbying efforts directed at the legislative, executive, and judicial branches of government.[5] In the legislative context, the principle was first articulated in *Noerr* itself.[6] There, a particular trucking firm (Noerr) filed suit against 24 railroads, an association of railroad presidents, and a public relations firm, charging that those entities had conspired to manipulate public opinion against the trucking industry during the post-World War II competition over long-haul freight.[7] The specific manipulation about which Noerr complained was a publicity campaign that involved a number of deceitful and unethical practices,[8] while the specific damage allegedly suffered was that the railroads succeeded in persuading the Governor of Pennsylvania to veto a bill that would have allowed truckers to carry heavier loads through the state.[9] The railroad defendants freely admitted conducting the "lobbying/publicity" campaign in question.[10] They argued, however, that they were simply educating the public to the harms caused by the trucking industry, and seeking legislation to restrict the industry's growth.[11]

The Supreme Court, in an opinion by Justice Black, unanimously held that the railroads' petitioning activities were beyond the scope of the antitrust laws: "[N]o violation of the [Sherman Antitrust] Act can be predicated upon mere attempts to influence the passage or enforcement of laws."[12] The Court rested its holding on two grounds. First, it stated that because *legislatures* can restrain trade or create monopolies with impunity (the so-called state-action doctrine), private individuals and associations are free to encourage legislative restraints-of-trade without risking antitrust liability.[13] Second, the Court emphasized that the legislative process would be severely hampered by restrictions imposed upon the types of information available to representatives from the public, restrictions not intended by the nation's antitrust laws.[14] Indeed, the Court further suggested, although refrained from specifically holding, that the right to petition the government for redress of grievances guaranteed by the First Amendment of the U.S. Constitution might itself independently compel an immunity from antitrust prosecution, on the facts presented in *Noerr*.[15] The Court's opinion expressly found the defendants' intent to restrain competition to be legally irrelevant to the existence of an immunity from antitrust suit.[16]

The Supreme Court next considered the issue of antitrust immunity for petitioning conduct in *United Mine Workers v. Pennington,* an "executive branch" petitioning case.[17] There a plaintiff labor union sued several owners of a small coal company for royalty payments under a certain federal statute.[18] Those small coal companies counterclaimed against the union, arguing that the industry's minimum wage as set by the Secretary of Labor (at the union's behest, among others) resulted from an illegal agreement between the union and certain large producers of coal.[19] That agreement, the counterclaimants charged, was intended to reduce industry production and increase profits for large coal producers by driving up costs to small and intermediate coal producers, forcing them out of business.[20] Ratifying and expanding *Noerr,* the Supreme Court held in *Pennington* that antitrust immunity extends to attempts to influence the executive branch (i.e., the Secretary of Labor) as well as the legislative branch of government. The Court once again stressed that the union's purpose in seeking the government action in question was legally irrelevant to the immunity issue.[21]

Seven years later, the Supreme Court was called upon to consider the applicability of *Noerr-Pennington* antitrust immunity to the "judicial" petitioning context. In *California Motor Transport Co. v. Trucking Unlimited,*[22] a plaintiff alleged that the defendant routinely used various judicial processes to "resist and defeat [the plaintiff's] applications * * * to acquire operating rights or to transfer or register those rights."[23] In response, the Supreme Court announced that attempts to influence government action through judicial petitioning directly implicate the First Amendment, and that immunity from antitrust liability for legitimate "First Amendment" petitioning extends to efforts to influence the judicial—as well as the legislative and executive—branch of government.[24] The Court went on to hold, however, that the specific petitioning engaged in by the *California Motor* defendant was illegitimate or a "sham" under the peculiar circumstances of that case, and thus refused to extend *Noerr-Pennington* immunity to that particular party, on those particular facts.[25]

The net result of the *Noerr-Pennington-California Motors* trilogy is that lobbying or other petitioning activity, legitimately designed to influence governmental action, is beyond the reach of the nation's antitrust legislation. Among the specific lobbying/petitioning activities immunized by the courts from antitrust attack consistent with the *Noerr-Pennington* protection include the hiring of a public relations firm and the "staging" of public dissatisfaction with a competitor;[26] institution of a statewide legislative initiative to outlaw a competitive product;[27] face-to-face meetings with the Secretary of Agriculture to influence milk price supports;[28] testimony before a local assembly regarding a zoning ordinance;[29] a meeting with administrative officials to insure a competitor will not receive authorization to market a product;[30] private meetings with a city mayor to secure a city license, at least where the court was satisfied that the license was not exchanged for an illegal gratuity[31] and a meeting to advise the police about a competitor's activities.[32]

While *Noerr-Pennington* protection extends to legitimate petitioning conduct directed at the legislature, the executive, and the judiciary, it does *not* extend to lobbying activities designed to influence "quasi-public, quasi-private" organizations (such as associations of fire chiefs or attorneys general). That is so even where the quasi-public/quasi-private organizations promulgate codes of conduct that subsequently are incorporated into federal or state laws or regulations.

This conclusion was reached by the Supreme Court in 1988 in a decision reversing the prevailing trend of several lower federal courts. In *Allied Tube & Conduit Corp. v. Indian Head, Inc.*,[33] the petitioners had manipulated the election process of a private standards-setting group (the Association of Western Fire Chiefs) in order to exclude the respondent's product from a national electrical code. Rejecting petitioners' argument that *Noerr-Pennington* protection immunized their conduct from subsequent antitrust challenge, the Supreme Court announced that the *type* of forum as well as the *nature* and *context* of the challenged activity collectively determine when *Noerr-Pennington* protections should attach. On the *Allied Tube* facts, the non-political environment of the Fire Chiefs Association, combined with the essentially commercial character of the "petitioning" involved, dictated the absence of antitrust immunity. After *Allied Tube*, efforts to influence nongovernmental rate or standards-setting bodies can be subjected to the full panoply of federal and state antitrust laws.

Allied Tube nowhere purports to overrule or to limit the application of *Noerr-Pennington* protection in the legislative, judicial, or executive contexts. The structure of the *Allied Tube* lead opinion (written by Justice Brennan), however, when combined with its emphasis on the political versus commercial impact of the petitioning activity in question, suggests that the Court may be willing to rethink certain aspects of *Noerr-Pennington* should an appropriate case present itself in the future. Still, for now, those who petition governments can take comfort in the fact that *Noerr-Pennington* protection continues to apply to their legitimate advocacy efforts carried out in the course of petitioning the three branches of government for public action.

Exceptions to the *Noerr-Pennington* Doctrine

The protection afforded by the *Noerr-Pennington* doctrine is not absolute. In many situations, courts will deem conduct that appears to involve petitioning the government unworthy of *Noerr-Pennington* protection and, for this reason, subject to full antitrust scrutiny. In general, exceptions to the doctrine arise when a person's petitioning is found to have been in bad faith or to have involved misconduct. Some courts have also refused to immunize petitioning that may be characterized as "commercial" or "conspiratorial." The extent to which exceptions to the *Noerr-Pennington* doctrine will be recognized depends on the type of petitioning activity involved. Courts are most reluctant to find the doctrine inapplicable in traditional lobbying or publicity campaigns. When the petitioning involves administrative or judicial litigation, however, courts are more willing to recognize exceptions.[34]

The Sham Exception

The *Noerr-Pennington* doctrine protects only genuine efforts to influence the government. "[P]rivate action that is not genuinely aimed at procuring favorable government action is a mere sham that cannot be deemed a valid effort to influence government action,"[35] and that action is unprotected by the doctrine.

The existence of a sham exception was first noted by the Court in *Noerr* itself:

"There may be situations in which a publicity campaign, ostensibly directed toward influencing governmental action, is a mere sham to cover what is actually nothing more than an attempt to interfere directly with the business relationships of a competitor and the application of the Sherman Act would be justified."[36]

The Court, however, found the sham exception inapplicable in *Noerr,* because there was no dispute that the railroads were "making a genuine effort to influence legislation and law enforcement practices."[37]

Legislative Lobbying

Application of the sham exception depends heavily on the type of governmental petitioning involved. In the almost 30 years since *Noerr* was decided, no court has applied the sham exception to subject legislative lobbying to antitrust scrutiny.[38] Indeed, one court has ruled that the sham exception does not even apply to "direct lobbying efforts," but only to the indirect publicity campaign involved in *Noerr.*[39] Most courts would likely apply the sham exception if they found that a legislative lobbying effort was intended solely to injure a competitor with no real desire to achieve its stated legislative goals. Absent such a showing, however, legislative lobbying is well protected by the *Noerr-Pennington* doctrine.

The sham exception will not be applied simply because a lobbying effort seeks passage of legislation that is unconstitutional or otherwise invalid. As the Fifth Circuit has explained "[a] contrary rule would unduly chill petitioning conduct because it would 'require an advocate to predict whether the desired legislation would withstand a * * * challenge in the courts and to expose itself to a potential treble damage antitrust action based on that prediction.'"[40] Thus, *Noerr-Pennington* shields lobbying even if the legislation being sought is invalid.

Administrative and Judicial Litigation

Lobbying activities frequently take place in conjunction with litigation on related matters. Moreover, it is in the litigation area that courts have given the clearest definition to the sham exception. Thus, those who lobby must be familiar with the application of the sham doctrine to litigation petitioning.

Courts have been much more willing to find the sham exception applicable with respect to petitioning before courts and administrative tribunals.[41] Indeed, the Supreme Court first found that a plaintiff had alleged a proper case for application of the sham exception in a litigation case, *California Motor Transport Co. v. Trucking Unlimited.*[42] In *California Motor,* as discussed earlier, the plaintiffs alleged that a group of California truckers had conspired to delay or prevent their competitors from securing new trucking routes by routinely opposing the potential competitors' applications for regulatory approval of the routes. Justice Douglas' opinion announced that such an agreement would not be condoned:

> "One claim, which a court or agency may think baseless, may go unnoticed; but a pattern of baseless, repetitive claims may emerge which leads the factfinder to conclude that the administrative and judicial processes have been abused. That may be a difficult line to discern and draw. But once it is drawn, the case is established that abuse of those processes produced an illegal result, viz., effectively barring respondents from access to the agencies and courts. Insofar as the administrative or judicial processes are involved, actions of that kind cannot acquire immunity by seeking refuge under the umbrella of 'political expression.'"[43]

Cases involving litigation provide the best insight into exactly what courts will considered a sham.[44] For example, some courts have focused on the litigant's motivation to bring suit, finding a sham only when there is no genuine desire for judicial or administrative relief:

> "A litigant should enjoy petitioning immunity from the antitrust laws so long as a genuine desire for judicial relief is a significant motivating factor underlying the suit. This criterion takes account of the mixed motives that usually actuate human conduct, yet requires that good faith in seeking the protection of the courts be a substantial factor."[45]

Other courts have placed more emphasis on determining whether the harm complained of in the lawsuit derives from the process of litigation or from the results of the litigation:

> "[I]t is important to identify the source of the injury to competition. If the injury is caused by persuading the government, then the antitrust laws do not apply to the * * * persuasion * * *. If the injury flows directly from the 'petitioning'—if the injury occurs no matter how the government responds to the request for aid, then we have an antitrust case. When private parties help themselves to a reduction in competition, the antitrust laws apply."[46]

This analysis, however, would allow application of the sham exception even in cases where the petitioner genuinely sought judicial relief but happened to injure a competitor through the process of bringing suit. Such a result is difficult to square with the *Noerr-Pennington* doctrine's basic protection of those who seek the government's aid in good faith.

Still other courts focus on the merits of the claim presented:

"We hold that when a lawsuit raises a legal issue of genuine substance, it raises a rebuttable presumption that it is a serious attempt to obtain a judgment on the merits instead of a mere sham or harassment. The first amendment interests concerned and the case law discussed earlier support placing the evidentiary burden on the antitrust plaintiff to prove that the action of the defendant comes within the sham exception to *Noerr-Pennington* in this kind of case."[47]

Most courts and commentators recognize that a litigant's success on the merits presents at most a strong presumption that the litigation was a genuine effort to obtain judicial relief—a presumption that may be overcome by other evidence that the plaintiff's sole motivation was anticompetitive.[48] Conversely, the fact that a litigant's position is ultimately rejected by the court or administrative agency is not, in itself, evidence that the suit was a sham.[49]

Some early cases suggested that no sham could be found unless the antitrust plaintiff demonstrated, in the words of *California Motor*, a "pattern of baseless, repetitive claims."[50] It appears firmly established, however, that a single lawsuit—if not motivated by a desire for judicial relief—can establish the sham exception and thus be subject to the antitrust laws.[51] Similarly, early cases which required that the sham litigation prevent the injured parties' access to the courts or the administrative process[52] have given way to recognition that this is only one factor to take into account in determining the existence of a sham.[53] And at least one court has found that the baseless defense of a lawsuit may qualify for sham treatment.[54]

Finally, the courts have addressed several issues relating to litigation but not involving direct lawsuits. If bringing litigation is protected by the *Noerr-Pennington* doctrine, for example, what of threatening to bring a suit? Most, but not all, courts have ruled that litigation warnings, if made in good faith, are immune from antitrust review.[55] On the other hand, one court refused to extend *Noerr-Pennington* immunity to a party that, lacking standing to bring suit directly, financed and encouraged another party to sue.[56]

Executive Branch

Good faith efforts to lobby or otherwise influence the executive branch are, of course, fully protected by *Noerr-Pennington*.[57] However, the sham exception is applicable to these activities. For example, one court found the sham exception applicable based on allegations that a party had submitted bids to a city's park district, not intending that the bids would be accepted, but hoping instead that the bids would drive their competitors into unfavorable contracts with the park district.[58]

Abuses of the Petitioning Process

Even a good faith effort to secure governmental assistance may lose its *Noerr-Pennington* protection if the petitioner engages in conduct that is sufficiently egregious:

> "[T]here are other instances of sham petitioning in which the defendant genuinely seeks to achieve his governmental result, but does so through *improper means* * * *. In such cases, the defendant may well succeed in procuring the desired governmental action, but has nonetheless misused his petitioning privilege."[59]

Once again, however, the scope of the exception to *Noerr-Pennington* varies with the type of petitioning activity.

Misrepresentations and Unethical Conduct

With respect to legislative lobbying and publicity campaigns directed at the general public, immunity is not lost even if the "campaign employs unethical and deceptive methods * * *."[60] In *Noerr* itself, the publicity campaign conducted by the railroads involved "unethical business conduct" and "was aptly characterized * * * as involving 'deception of the public, manufacture of bogus sources of reference, [and] distortion of public sources of information.'"[61] Notwithstanding the Supreme Court's conclusion that the railroads' conduct fell "far short of the ethical standards generally approved in this country,"[62] the Court held that *Noerr-Pennington* immunity would still apply:

> "It does not follow, however, that the use of [unethical conduct] in a publicity campaign designed to influence governmental action constitutes a violation of the Sherman Act. Insofar as that Act sets up a code of ethics at all, it is a code that condemns trade restraints, not political activity * * *."[63]

Following *Noerr,* courts have held that in the legislative lobbying field, *Noerr-Pennington* immunity is unaffected by claims of *ex parte* meetings[64] and misrepresentations.[65]

By contrast, misrepresentations made in litigation will not be protected by the *Noerr-Pennington* doctrine:

> "[T]he adjudicatory sphere is much different from the political sphere. There is an emphasis on debate in the political sphere, which could accommodate false statements and reveal their falsity. In the adjudicatory sphere, however, information supplied by the parties is relied on as accurate for decision making and dispute resolving. The supplying of fraudulent information thus threatens the fair and impartial functioning of these agencies and does not deserve immunity from the antitrust laws."[66]

Thus, courts will apply the full force of the antitrust laws to misrepresentations made in adjudication before courts or executive agencies.[67]

The *Noerr-Pennington* treatment of misrepresentations made to members of the executive branch presents a more difficult question. The executive branch performs a broad range of functions, ranging from quasi-judicial to quasi-legislative in nature. Whether or not the sham exception will be applicable to misrepresentations in this context depends on where the executive action in question falls on this continuum:

> "Executive officials may administer the law, adjudicate claims under the law, or, by framing policy, make law. The lines between the executive, legislative, and judicial functions are often quite indistinct. Careful case-by-case analysis is necessary. Where the executive action sought was more a matter of administering than of making law, misrepresentations inducing the governmental decision will be actionable in antitrust despite the *Noerr-Pennington* doctrine."[68]

Threats, Duress, and Coercion

Regardless of the governmental context, courts generally will not extend *Noerr-Pennington* immunity to illegal threats, duress, and coercion. As one court concluded:

> "The allegations are basically that due to threats, duress, and other coercive measures exercised by the defendants upon the California State Fair officials, these officials issued a directive forbidding the sale of any Coca-Cola upon the fairgrounds during the 1966 State Fair * * *. [I]t does not seem to this Court that the doctrines of *Noerr* and *Pennington* were intended to protect those who employ illegal means to influence their representatives in governments."[69]

However, this rule only applies to threats that are in some way unlawful or improper. Other "threats" may be deemed a normal part of the political process and, as such, protected by *Noerr-Pennington*.

In the U.S. Football League's antitrust suit against the National Football League, for example, the trial court refused to allow the USFL to call a witness to testify that the NFL had attempted to influence members of Congress with threats to move football franchises from the states of uncooperative members. The court held the sham exception inapplicable to these efforts to "persuade government officials simply by appealing to their political interests."[70]

Payments to Public Officials

"Campaign contributions are, whether we like it or not, a part of the political process,"[71] the Seventh Circuit wrote in 1975. Recognizing this fact, the courts have refused to allow *Noerr-Pennington* immunity to be affected by allegations of such contributions.[72] Similarly, courts have refused to limit *Noerr-Pennington* protection simply because lobbyists gave public officials "promotional gifts,"[73] or hired former members of the governmental unit being lobbied.[74] On the other hand, courts have uniformly held that the *Noerr-Pennington* doctrine will not protect the payment of bribes to government officials.[75]

The Commercial Exception

The courts have engaged in a spirited debate as to whether the *Noerr-Pennington* doctrine, created in the context of political efforts to influence government, should extend to situations where parties deal with the government on purely commercial terms. Should a vendor who secures an exclusive franchise for sales at a government-owned airport be protected by the doctrine? Early on, some courts expressed doubt that it should.

> "*Noerr* stressed the importance of full access to public officials vested with significant policy-making discretion. We doubt whether the Court, without expressing additional rationale, would have extended the *Noerr* umbrella to public officials engaged in purely commercial dealings when the case dealt with other issues."[76]

Other courts have ruled squarely that "[t]here is no commercial exception to the *Noerr-Pennington* doctrine."[77] As the Fifth Circuit has explained:

> "*Noerr-Pennington* extends to situations where the government enters into a contractual relationship with a private entity, at least in situations 'where the government engages in a policy decision and at the same time acts as a participant in the marketplace.'"[78]

The Supreme Court's recent decision in *Allied Tube* cites a leading treatise which argues that *Noerr-Pennington* ought not apply to commercial dealings with the government.[79] In rejecting application of the doctrine to efforts to influence an industry standards-setting organization, moreover, the Court observed that "[j]ust as the antitrust laws should not regulate political activities 'simply because those activities have a commercial impact,' * * * so the antitrust laws should not necessarily immunize what are in essence commercial activities simply because they have a political impact."[80] Although *Allied Tube* does not decide the issue, these passages may suggest that the Court would recognize the existence of a commercial exception to *Noerr-Pennington*.

The Coconspirator Exception

Courts have also divided over the existence and scope of a "coconspirator" exception to the *Noerr-Pennington* doctrine. The theory of this exception is that *Noerr* extends to private efforts to influence government, not to anticompetitive schemes carried out jointly by government and private parties.

"Both *Noerr* and *Pennington* involved suits against *private parties* who had allegedly conspired to influence governmental action. In neither case was it alleged that the governmental entity had collaborated to promote the conspiracy. Where the complaint goes beyond mere allegations of official persuasion by anticompetitive *lobbying* and claims official participation with private individuals in a scheme to restrain trade, the *Noerr-Pennington* doctrine is inapplicable."[81]

Other courts have rejected the coconspirator exception, especially where there was little evidence of "conspiracy" beyond the public officials' agreement with the position of those attempting to lobby him.[82]

Antitrust Liability

Conduct covered by the *Noerr-Pennington* doctrine is immune from antitrust liability, but the converse is not true: the absence of *Noerr-Pennington* immunity does not mean that antitrust liability exists. Even if an antitrust defendant's *Noerr-Pennington* claim is rejected (because, for example, it falls within the sham or coconspirator exception), the plaintiff must still prove that the defendant violated the antitrust laws, and the defendant is still free to assert other defenses.

This section discusses when lobbying activity unprotected by *Noerr-Pennington* violates the antitrust laws. A detailed analysis of the antitrust laws is far beyond the scope of this book—and far beyond the needs of most who conduct lobbying or counsel lobbyists. The following discussion summarizes some of the basic principles which ought to be understood so that one knows when antitrust issues may exist. If and when a lobbyist perceives potential antitrust issues, expert advice should be obtained. Antitrust law is a complex and changing set of rules, and judges frequently disagree both about the content of those rules and about how those rules ought to be applied to specific facts. The following discussion, therefore, is no substitute for thorough scrutiny of potentially problematic conduct by experienced antitrust counsel.

This section does not purport to analyze whether the federal action sought by the lobbyist violates the antitrust laws or whether private action taken under color of that federal action is illegal. Antitrust immunity for most lobbying activity does not necessarily mean that the lobbied-for action is also immune: lobbying is protected because, and to the extent that, it does not directly cause any competitive injury. If the governmental action sought favors some competitors at the expense of others, that action may or may not violate any number of federal laws and regulations, including but not limited to the antitrust laws. There is no attempt to address these issues except in a very limited, general way.

General Principles

To put this discussion in perspective, a brief overview of the antitrust laws is useful. The principal antitrust law of concern in the area of lobbying is Section 1 of the Sherman Act. What follows is a brief description of the scope of Section 1 and its application to the federal government.

Section 1 of Sherman Act

Section 1 of the Sherman Act states that "every contract, combination in the form of trust or otherwise, or conspiracy, in restraint of trade or commerce among the several States, or with foreign nations, is declared to be illegal."[83]

In the words of the Supreme Court: "The Sherman Act was designed to be a comprehensive charter of economic liberty aimed at preserving free and unfettered competition as the rule of trade."[84] The literal language of Section 1 would prohibit all concerted activity that restricts the freedom of participants throughout the economy. Because the Supreme Court has recognized that *every* contract or agreement restrains competition to some degree, it has long interpreted Section 1 to prohibit only *unreasonable* restraints of trade.[85]

Agreements raising antitrust issues fall into two general categories. In the first category are restraints that are always, automatically illegal—often called *per se* violations of the antitrust laws. *Per se* violations include price-fixing agreements,[86] divisions of markets or customers,[87] group boycotts,[88] and certain tying arrangements.[89] These agreements are illegal even if motivated by the best of intentions or even if the agreed-upon restrictions are beneficial.

In the second category of restrictions are those that may violate the antitrust laws depending on the circumstances. Common examples of these agreements include exclusive dealing contracts,[90] requirements contracts,[91] and restrictions imposed by manufacturers on distributors.[92] These kinds of agreements may have legitimate, procompetitive justifications; but they may also reduce competition, particularly in markets where there are few competitors. Accordingly, they are analyzed under the so-called rule of reason to determine whether the procompetitive benefits exceed the anticompetitive risks.[93] The rule of reason is an open-ended test under which judges and juries consider the competitiveness and structure of the market, the actual or probable impact of the restraint on competition, and the reasons why the restraint was adopted.[94]

Antitrust and the Federal Government

Although the antitrust laws make the preservation and protection of competition an important national policy, that policy must on occasion give way to other important national policies. The antitrust laws prohibit any private association that is "in reality an extra-governmental agency, which prescribes rules for the regulation and restraint of interstate commerce," because such an entity "'trenches upon the power of the national legislature.'"[95] These concerns about usurpation of the governmental regulatory function are absent when the government acts through its elected and appointed public officials. Indeed, the federal government needs the flexibility to pursue national goals that require competition to give way.

Accordingly, "the United States, its agencies and officials, remain outside the reach of the Sherman Act," and the Sherman Act "does not expose United States instrumentalities to liability * * * for conduct alleged to violate antitrust constraints."[96] This antitrust exemption for the federal government applies even when government instrumentalities are acting not as regulators but as direct competitors against private entities.[97]

In a case involving the applicability of the antitrust laws to the actions of state governments, the Supreme Court suggested that state governments might lose their antitrust exemption if their officials act as coconspirators of private parties.[98] As one influential treatise puts it, "[t]he conspiracy claim often does double duty: to deprive the private antitrust defendant of *Noerr* protection for his dealings with the governmental body and to supply the illegal conspiracy allegedly violating Sherman Act §1."[99] The scope of any coconspirator exception is unclear, and no reported case has applied that exception to federal officials. The exception may be limited to situations involving the actions of federal officials who have been bribed or who have close personal or financial ties to private parties benefiting from governmental action.[100]

Although the federal government is generally exempt from the operation of the antitrust laws, state and in particular local governments have more limited (but still significant) immunity. Consequently, the antitrust laws have potentially broader application to private conduct in which state or local governments participate than to private conduct related to the federal government. State and local governments may violate the antitrust laws, depending in part on whether their conduct is authorized by state law.[101] Private parties, in turn, may derive immunity from state and local governments provided that the governmental body not only directs or authorizes the private conduct but also actively supervises it.[102] The scope of antitrust exposure for state and local governments and for private parties acting pursuant to their authority is outside the scope of this discussion.

Antitrust Exposure of Activities of Federal Lobbyists Not Covered by *Noerr-Pennington*

Federal lobbyists benefit from the broad antitrust exemption available to federal officials. Federal immunity complements and reinforces *Noerr-Pennington* immunity. If governmental action is immune, the private efforts to obtain that action must be immune as well. "First Amendment petitioning privileges would indeed be hollow if upon achieving a petitioned-for end the petitioner were then subjected to antitrust liability for his success."[103]

Furthermore, in antitrust cases challenging joint governmental and private conduct, the result must be the same whether the plaintiff sues private or governmental defendants. "The success of an antitrust action should depend upon the nature of the activity challenged, rather than on the identity of the defendant."[104] Otherwise, a person "could frustrate any [governmental] program merely by filing suit against the regulated private parties, rather than the [governmental] officials who implement the plan."[105] Therefore, private parties who engage in conduct that a lobbyist persuaded the federal government to direct or authorize should not incur antitrust liability. Antitrust liability not only would thwart the purpose of the governmental program but would unfairly impose legal penalties on a party that relied upon governmental authorization.

Although the exemption for federal governmental action means that efforts to persuade the federal government to take action ought to be immune, the converse is not necessarily true. Even if federal governmental action is not immune from antitrust scrutiny, lobbying to obtain that action may still be protected. Petitioning for lawful governmental action would be inhibited if the petitioner had to predict on penalty of antitrust damages whether or not a court would ultimately conclude that the governmental action being sought is lawful or not. Consequently, courts have held that joint action which succeeds in persuading a public body to make an erroneous decision cannot give rise to a federal antitrust claim.[106]

The presumption that lobbying should not lose its antitrust immunity because of its success applies with particular force to legislative lobbying. Suppose a private company persuades Congress to take action that confers competitive benefits—for example, a tax break not available to competing firms. It would make no sense to argue that one congressional enactment (a tax law) violates another (the antitrust laws). Congress must be presumed to have taken the competitive impact of its laws into account and determined that any such impact is outweighed by other benefits of the law.

One instance in which dealings with the federal government are *not* protected is when the government is the victim of private conduct that violates the Sherman Act. For example, if private companies engage in a price-fixing conspiracy that causes the government to pay higher prices, the conspiracy is not insulated from antitrust liability merely because the government was involved. To the contrary, Congress specifically authorized the federal government to sue under the antitrust laws to obtain damages when it is injured by an antitrust violation.[107]

Private conduct may also be subject to antitrust liability if the government's involvement is passive or if the conspiracy has consequences regardless of government involvement. In one Supreme Court case, even though a principal coconspirator was a purchasing agent appointed by the Canadian government, a conspiracy was found to be illegal because the purchasing agent was not a public official and there was no indication that any public official approved or would have approved the anticompetitive conduct.[108]

By the same token, "[t]he national policy in favor of competition cannot be thwarted by casting * * * a gauzy cloak of [governmental] involvement over what is essentially a private price-fixing arrangement."[109] If the government does not actively supervise private conduct (for example, by establishing prices or reviewing the reasonableness of prices established by private parties), the private parties who engage in the conduct may be liable under the antitrust laws notwithstanding general authorization of the conduct by a federal agency. As the Supreme Court has stated in connection with state governmental action, "a state does not give immunity to those who violate the Sherman Act by authorizing them to violate it, or by declaring that their action is lawful * * *."[110]

If for some reason the participation of the federal government does not confer antitrust immunity, it is still important to ask whether the government's conduct would violate the antitrust laws if performed by a private party. The antitrust issues primarily involve government contracting and other circumstances that would arguably fall within any commercial exception to the *Noerr-Pennington* doctrine.[111] In other words, dealings with the executive branch, outside the formal agency rule-making context, may be the most likely source of antitrust complaints. Although the distinction may make sense in theory, it may in practice be difficult, if not impossible, to distinguish between actions taken by the government as a policymaker in the commercial context and actions taken by the government as a participant in the marketplace.[112]

For example, a disappointed competitor might challenge on antitrust grounds an exclusive contract that a lobbyist persuaded the government to award. Even if that decision is not absolutely immune because the basic challenge is to a decision of the federal government, the government would not have greater antitrust exposure than a private party. Exclusive contracts are not *per se* illegal, and their legality depends on the amount of business that they cover and the reasons why the purchaser decided to award an exclusive contract.[113] If a private party had awarded the contract and would not be liable under traditional antitrust rules, then neither would the government be liable.

Similarly, a potential bidder for government business may complain that the government adopted specifications that its competitors can meet more easily and that its competitors persuaded the government to adopt. In some circumstances, agreements to adopt unreasonable specifications may violate the antitrust laws.[114] The antitrust laws do not restrict efforts to persuade the government to adopt specifications that may have incidental effects on competition any more severely than efforts to persuade private purchasers to adopt the specifications. However, false statements to the government that lead to the adoption of those specifications may not only cause the lobbying to fall within the sham exception to the *Noerr-Pennington* doctrine but may also strip the specifications of their legitimacy.[115]

Determining whether allegedly sham judicial or administrative litigation violates the antitrust laws may pose vexing problems. Malicious prosecution and abuse of process are prohibited by general state tort law principles.[116] However, not all malicious prosecution or abuse of process cases in the commercial context violate the antitrust laws.

Similarly, misrepresentations in obtaining patents or in seeking government franchises or contracts may not violate the antitrust laws even if they fall within the sham exception to the *Noerr-Pennington* doctrine. The antitrust laws do not prohibit all business torts that are illegal under state law.[117] Section 5 of the Federal Trade Commission Act generally prohibits unfair methods of competition,[118] but only the Federal Trade Commission, and not private parties, can sue for violations of that section.[119] Although unfair methods of competition to obtain a lucrative contract from a private company may violate other laws, they do not necessarily violate the Sherman Act, and those methods may also not constitute antitrust violations when the federal government is involved. One should recall, however, that when the federal government is victimized by anticompetitive conduct, it has remedies not only under the antitrust laws but under other provisions of federal law.[120]

Antitrust Remedies

The penalties for Sherman Act violations are severe. Companies injured by antitrust violations are not limited to the damages caused by the violations, and if they prove damages, they are automatically entitled to recover three times their actual damages, i.e., "treble damages."[121] In addition, victims of antitrust violations have the right to recover their legal fees in any lawsuit to vindicate their rights under the Sherman Act.[122]

Violations also have the potential to carry criminal penalties, including up to three years imprisonment and $100,000 in fines for individuals and up to $1,000,000 in fines for corporations.[123] However, it is significantly more difficult to prove criminal violations than it is to pursue civil violations of the antitrust laws. In a criminal case, the prosecution must prove guilt beyond a reasonable doubt, and it must prove that the defendant's action were knowing and willful.[124] In contrast, the plaintiff in a civil case need prove the case only by a preponderance of the evidence (that is, that it is more likely than not that the defendant violated the antitrust laws), and willfulness is generally not an element of a civil case. As a practical matter, the federal government prosecutes criminally only in hard-core cases involving *per se* violations of the antitrust laws such as price-fixing,[125] and the likelihood of a criminal antitrust prosecution involving lobbying activity is remote.

Protected Lobbying Activity as Evidence of Anticompetitive Intent

One final word of caution. Even if lobbying activity does not itself violate the antitrust laws, it may be used as evidence in a challenge that related conduct directed against competitors was undertaken with anticompetitive intent.[126] This issue usually arises where a company accuses a competitor of trying to destroy it in a variety of ways, including the pursuit of lobbying. Although the plaintiff may not be able to recover damages caused by the lobbying activity, he may be able to use that activity as evidence that the rest of the defendant's alleged campaign was intended to destroy him as a viable participant in the marketplace.

Use of lobbying activity as evidence of anticompetitive intent is not unfettered.[127] However, the possibility that statements and actions in the lobbying arena may be used to prove antitrust violations outside that arena suggests the desirability of exercising restraint in the kind of statements that lobbyists make. Particularly if the individual or entity responsible for lobbying is engaged in other conduct that may expose the client to the risk of antitrust litigation, the lobbyist should avoid unnecessarily inflammatory or dramatic language that might be used in an antitrust case.

Notes

1. The principal antitrust law of concern to lobbyists is discussed *infra*.
2. Actually, the term *"Noerr-Pennington"* ordinarily refers to legal principles arising from a trilogy of Supreme Court cases: *Eastern Railroad Presidents Conference v. Noerr Motor Freight, Inc.*, 365 U.S. 127 (1961); *United Mine Workers v. Pennington*, 381 U.S. 657 (1965); and *California Motor Transp. Co. v. Trucking Unlimited*, 404 U.S. 508 (1972).
3. *Allied Tube & Conduit Corp. v. Indian Head, Inc.*, 486 U.S.____ (1988).
4. *Noerr*, 365 U.S. at 136–40.
5. At least one court has interpreted the doctrine to apply to attempts by lobbyists to influence foreign governments. *Coastal States Mktg., Inc. v. Hunt*, 694 F.2d 1358, 1364–66 (5th Cir. 1983) (applying *Noerr* to lobbying foreign governments); contra *Occidental Petroleum Corp. v. Buttes Gas & Oil Co.*, 331 F. Supp. 92, 107–08 (C.D. Cal. 1971), *aff'd on other grounds*, 461 F.2d 1261 (9th Cir.) (per curiam), *cert. denied*, 409 U.S. 950 (1972). For a general discussion, see Note, *Coastal States v. Hunt: Noerr-Pennington Goes Abroad*, 8 DEL. J. CORP. L. 525 (1983). Other courts have applied *Noerr-Pennington* in nonantitrust contexts. See generally Note, *The Misapplication of the Noerr-Pennington Doctrine in Non-Antitrust Right to Petition Cases*, 36 STAN. L. REV. 1243 (1984).
6. *Noerr*, 365 U.S. at 127.
7. *Id.* at 129–30.

8. *Id.* at 144–45.

9. *Id.* at 130.

10. *Id.* at 131.

11. *Id.*

12. *Id.* at 135.

13. *Id.* at 136–37.

14. *Id.* at 137–39.

15. *Id.* at 132 n.6, 137, 139.

16. *Id.* at 140, 142, 143, 144–45.

17. 381 U.S. 657 (1965).

18. *Id.* at 659.

19. *Id.*

20. *Id.*

21. *Id.* at 669–70.

22. *California Motor Transp. Co. v. Trucking Unlimited,* 404 U.S. 508 (1972).

23. *Id.* at 509.

24. *Id.* at 510.

25. The "sham" and other exceptions to the *Noerr-Pennington* doctrine are discussed *infra.*

26. *Noerr,* 365 U.S. at 129–30

27. *Subscription Television, Inc. v. Southern Cal. Theatre Owners Ass'n,* 576 F.2d 230, 232 (1978).

28. *George Benz & Sons, Inc. v. Twin City Milk Producers Ass'n,* 299 F. Supp. 679, 682–84 (D. Minn. 1969).

29. *Manego v. Orleans Bd. of Trade,* 598 F. Supp. 231, 235–40 (D. Ma. 1984), *aff'd,* 773 F.2d 1, 7 (1st Cir. 1985), *cert. denied,* 475 U.S. 1084 (1986).

30. *Alexander v. National Farmers Org.,* 687 F.2d 1173, 1195 (8th Cir. 1982), *cert. denied,* 461 U.S. 937 (1983).

31. *Metro Cable Co. v. CATV of Rockford, Inc.,* 516 F.2d 220, 230 (D.C. Cir. 1975).

32. *Ottensmeyer v. Chesapeake & Potomac Tel. Co.,* 756 F.2d 986, 993–94 (4th Cir. 1985); *Forro Precision, Inc. v. International Business Mach. Corp.,* 673 F.2d 1045, 1059–60 (9th Cir. 1982).

33. *Allied Tube & Conduit Corp. v. Indian Head, Inc.,* 486 U.S.____ (1988).

34. See generally Hurwitz, *Abuse of Governmental Processes, the First Amendment, and the Boundaries of Noerr,* 76 Geo. L.J. 65, 82–90 (1985).

35. 486 U.S.____, ____ n.4 (1988).

36. *Eastern R.R. Presidents Conference v. Noerr Motor Freight, Inc.,* 365 U.S. 127, 144 (1961).

37. *Id.*

38. See Handler & DeSovo, *The Noerr Doctrine and Its Sham Exception,* 6 Cardozo L. Rev. 1, 18 (1984).

39. *Franchise Realty Interstate Corp. v. San Francisco Local Joint Executive Bd. of Culinary Workers,* 542 F.2d 1076, 1080 (9th Cir. 1976), *cert. denied,* 430 U.S. 940 (1977).

40. *Greenwood Utils. Comm'n v. Mississippi Power Co.,* 751 F.2d 1484, 1499–500 (5th Cir. 1985); see also *Subscription Television, Inc. v. Southern Cal. Theatre Owners,* 576 F.2d 230, 233 (9th Cir. 1978).

41. See Handler & DeSovo, *supra* note 38, at 20–30.

42. *California Motor Transp. Co. v. Trucking Unlimited,* 404 U.S. 508 (1972)

43. 404 U.S. at 513.

44. For an excellent discussion of the various formulations courts have used in defining a sham, see Hurwitz, *Abuse of Governmental Processes, the First Amendment, and the Boundaries of Noerr,* 74 Geo. L.J. 65, 94–108 (1985).

45. *Coastal States Mktg. v. Hunt,* 694 F.2d 1358, 1372 (5th Cir. 1983). *See also Grip-Pak, Inc. v. Illinois Tool Works, Inc.,* 694 F.2d 466, 472 (7th Cir. 1982) ("The line is crossed when his purpose is not to win a favorable judgment against a competitor but to harass him, and deter others, in the process itself—regardless of the outcome—of litigating"), *cert. denied,* 461 U.S. 958 (1983); *Winterland Concession Co. v. Trela,* 735 F.2d 257 (7th Cir. 1984) (applying *Grip-Pak* analysis); *In re IBP Confidential Business Documents Litig.,* 755 F.2d 1300, 1313 (8th Cir.) ("Sham activities 'are activities which, although 'ostensibly directed toward influencing governmental action,' are actually nothing more than an attempt to harm another"), *adhered to, In re IBP Confidential Business Documents Litig.,* 800 F.2d 787 (8th Cir. 1986); *Assigned Container Ship Claims v. American President Lines, Inc.,* 784 F.2d 1420, 1423 (9th Cir. 1986) ("a 'sham petition' has been defined as a petition 'un-

dertaken solely to interfere with free competition and without the legitimate expectation that such efforts will in fact induce lawful government action'"), *cert. denied,* 479 U.S. 915 (1986).

46. *Campbell v. City of Chicago,* 823 F.2d 1182, 1186 (7th Cir. 1987).

47. *Westmac, Inc. v. Smith,* 797 F.2d 313, 318 (6th Cir. 1986), *cert. denied,* 479 U.S. 1035 (1987).

48. *In re Burlington N., Inc.,* 822 F.2d 518, 527-28 (5th Cir. 1987):

> "The determinative inquiry is not whether the suit was won or lost, but whether it was significantly motivated by a genuine desire for judicial relief. Of course, the success of the claim presented is persuasive evidence that the litigant in fact wanted the relief. It is highly unlikely that a party with a meritorious claim will not be significantly motivated by a desire to obtain relief on that claim. Thus, an antitrust plaintiff attempting to base liability on successful petitioning must overcome a strong inference that *Noerr-Pennington* applies and in many cases may be unable to do so."

Accord Kinter & Bauer, *Antitrust Exemptions From Private Requests for Governmental Action: A Critical Analysis of the Noerr-Pennington Doctrine,* 17 U.C. DAVIS L. REV. 599, 576 (1984). Handler & Desoto, on the other hand, argue that successful petitioning may never be found a sham. Handler & Desoto, *supra* note 38, at 30-31.

49. *Potters Medical Center v. City Hosp. Ass'n,* 800 F.2d 568, 579 (6th Cir. 1986); *Greenwood Utils. Comm'n v. Mississippi Power Co.,* 751 F.2d 1484, 1500 (5th Cir. 1985).

50. See *City of Cleveland v. The Cleveland Elec. Illuminating Co.,* 734 F.2d 1157, 1162-63 (6th Cir.) ("Whether a single legal proceeding, even if found to be meritless, may be considered a basis of a 'sham' exception is not altogether clear."), *cert. denied,* 469 U.S. 884 (1984); *Hydro-Tech Corp. v. Sundstrand Corp.,* 673 F.2d 1171, 1175-76 (10th Cir. 1982); *Omni Resources Dev. Corp. v. Conoco,* 739 F.2d 1412, 1413-14 (9th Cir. 1984); *Hospital Bldg. Co. v. Trustees of Rex Hosp.,* 691 F.2d 678, 688 (4th Cir. 1982), *cert. denied,* 464 U.S. 890, 904 (1983); *Huron Valley Hosp., Inc. v. City of Pontiac,* 466 F. Supp. 1301, 1314 (E.D. Mich. 1979), *vacated on other grounds,* 666 F.2d 1029 (6th Cir. 1981); *Mountain Grove Cemetery Ass'n v. Norwalk Vault Co.,* 428 F. Supp. 951, 955-56 (D. Conn. 1977); *Central Bank of Clayton v. Clayton Bank,* 424 F. Supp. 163, 167 (E.D. Mo. 1976), *aff'd mem.,* 553 F.2d 102 (8th Cir.), *cert. denied,* 433 U.S. 910 (1977).

51. "If the activity is not genuine petitioning activity, the antitrust laws are not suspended and continue to prohibit the violating activities. Because application of the antitrust laws is not suspended, it will prohibit sham activity, whether that activity consists of single or multiple sham suits."

Clipper Express v. Rocky Mountain Motor Tariff Bureau, 690 F.2d 1240, 1255 (9th Cir. 1982), *cert. denied,* 459 U.S. 1227 (1983); accord *Feminist Women's Health Center v. Mohammad,* 586 F.2d 530, 543 n.6 (5th Cir. 1978), *cert. denied,* 444 U.S. 924 (1979); *MCI Communications Corp. v. AT&T,* 708 F.2d 1081, 1154 (7th Cir.), *cert. denied,* 464 U.S. 891 (1983); *Grip-Pak, Inc. v. Illinois Tool Works, Inc.,* 694 F.2d 466, 472 (7th Cir. 1982), *cert. denied,* 461 U.S. 958 (1983); *Razorback Ready Mix Concrete Co. v. Weaver,* 761 F.2d 484, 487 (8th Cir. 1985); *Omni Resource Dev. Corp. v. Conoco, Inc.,* 739 F.2d 1412, 1414 (9th Cir. 1984); *Energy Conservation v. Heliodyne, Inc.,* 698 F.2d 386, 389 (9th Cir. 1983); *Colorado Petroleum Marketers Ass'n v. Southland Corp.,* 476 F. Supp. 373, 378 (D. Colo. 1979); *Technicon Medical Information Sys. Corp. v. Green Bay Packaging, Inc.,* 480 F. Supp. 124, 126-28 (E.D. Wis. 1979); *First Nat'l Bank of Omaha v. Marquette Nat'l Bank,* 482 F. Supp. 514, 520 (D. Minn. 1979), *aff'd,* 636 F.2d 195 (8th Cir. 1980), *cert. denied,* 450 U.S. 1042 (1981); *Associated Radio Serv. v. Page Airways, Inc.,* 414 F. Supp. 1088, 1096 (N.D. Tex. 1976); *Cyborg Sys., Inc. v. Management Science Am., Inc.,* 1978 Trade Cas. ¶61, 927, at ¶73, 918 (N.D. Ill. 1978).

52. See *Miracle Mile Assocs. v. City of Rochester,* 617 F.2d 18, 21 (2d Cir. 1980); *Central Bank of Clayton v. Clayton Bank,* 424 F. Supp. 163, 167 (E.D. Mo. 1976), *aff'd mem.,* 553 F.2d 102 (8th Cir.), *cert. denied,* 433 U.S. 910 (1977); *Wilmorite v. Egan Real Estate,* 454 F. Supp. 1124, 1133-35 (N.D.N.Y. 1977), *aff'd,* 578 F.2d 1372 (2d Cir.), *cert. denied,* 439 U.S. 983 (1978).

53. See *Clipper Express,* 690 F.2d at 1255-56; *Ernest W. Hahn v. Codding,* 615 F.2d 830, 841 n.14 (9th Cir. 1980); *Outboard Marine Corp. v. Pezetel,* 474 F. Supp. 168, 178 (D. Del. 1979). See also Hurwitz, *supra* note 44, at 101-02.

54. *In re Burlington N., Inc.,* 822 F.2d 518, 532 (5th Cir. 1987) ("We perceive no reason to apply a different standard to defending lawsuits than to initiating them").

55. See *Coastal States Mktg. v. Hunt,* 694 F.2d 1358 (5th Cir. 1983); *Zenith Radio Corp. v. Matsushita Elec. Indus.,* 513 F. Supp. 1100, 1155-57 (E.D. Pa. 1981), *aff'd in part, rev'd in part sub nom. In re Japanese Elec. Prods. Antitrust Litig.,* 723 F.2d 238 (3d Cir. 1983); *Outboard Marine Corp. v. Pezetel,* 474 F. Supp. 168, 174 (D. Del. 1979). At least two courts, however, have ruled that threats of litigation are not protected by the *Noerr-Pennington* doctrine. See *Alexander v. National Farmers Org.,* 687 F.2d 1173, 1200-03 (8th Cir. 1982), *cert. denied,* 461 U.S. 937 (1983); *Oahu Gas Serv. v. Pacific Resources, Inc.,* 460 F. Supp. 1359, 1386 (D. Hawaii 1978).

56. See *In re Burlington N., Inc.*, 822 F.2d 518, 530 (5th Cir. 1987) ("our holding subjects to antitrust scrutiny only those persons whose interests are such that Congress or the Courts have independently determined not to be the proper parties to assert the claim in court. To the extent a party has an interest in a case sufficient to support a reasonable claim of standing, his efforts to directly or indirectly participate in the litigation are protected."), *cert. denied sub nom. Union Pacific RR. Co. v. Energy Transp. Sys., Inc.*, 484 U.S. 1007 (1988).

57. For example, efforts to influence the direction of police investigations are protected by the doctrine. See *Ottensmeyer v. Chesapeake & Potomac Tel. Co.*, 756 F.2d 986 (4th Cir. 1988); *Forro Precision, Inc. v. International Business Machs. Corp.*, 673 F.2d 1045 (9th Cir. 1982); *Midwest Constr. Co. v. Illinois Dep't of Labor*, 684 F. Supp. 991, 995 (N.D. Ill. 1988).

58. *Kurek v. Pleasure Driveway and Park Dist.*, 557 F.2d 580, 594 (7th Cir. 1977), *vacated on other grounds*, 435 U.S. 992 (1978), *reinstated*, 583 F.2d 378 (7th Cir.), *cert. denied*, 439 U.S. 1090 (1979).

59. *Sessions Tank Liners, Inc. v. Joor Mfg., Inc.*, 827 F.2d 458, 465 n.5 (9th Cir. 1987), *vacated on other grounds*, 487 U.S. ____ (1988).

60. *Allied Tube & Conduit Corp. v. Indian Head, Inc.*, 486 U.S. ____, ____ (1988).

61. *Noerr*, 365 U.S. at 140.

62. *Noerr*, 365 U.S. at 140.

63. *Noerr*, 365 U.S. at 140.

64. *In re Airport Car Rental Antitrust Litig.*, 766 F.2d 1292, 1295 (9th Cir. 1985), *cert. denied*, 476 U.S. 1141 (1986). But see *Central Telecommunications v. TCI Cablevision, Inc.*, 800 F.2d 711, 725 (8th Cir. 1986) (holding *Noerr-Pennington* inapplicable because, among other things, defendant coerced a city government into holding private negotiations in violation of the terms of a request for proposals and contrary to state "sunshine" laws requiring open meetings), *cert. denied*, 480 U.S. 910 (1987).

65. *Boone v. Redevelopment Agency*, 841 F.2d 886, 894 (9th Cir. 1988) ("While we do not condone misrepresentations, we trust that the council and agency, acting in the political sphere, can 'accommodate false statements and reveal their falsity.'") (citing *Clipper Express v. Rocky Mountain Motor Tariff Bureau*, 690 F.2d 1240, 1261 (9th Cir. 1980), *cert. denied*, 459 U.S. 1227 (1983)); see also *Sessions Tank Liners, Inc. v. Joor Mfg., Inc.*, 827 F.2d 458, 467 (9th Cir. 1987) (misrepresentations in the legislative field do not affect *Noerr-Pennington* immunity), *vacated on other grounds*, 487 U.S. ____ (1988); *First Am. Title Co. v. South Dakota Land Title Ass'n*, 714 F.2d 1439, 1447 (8th Cir. 1983) (same), *cert. denied*, 464 U.S. 1042 (1984).

In *McDonald v. Smith*, 472 U.S. 479 (1985), the Supreme Court found that Smith could maintain a libel action against McDonald for writing allegedly false letters to the executive and legislative branches opposing Smith's appointment as attorney general. One commentator has argued that *McDonald* may support limiting *Noerr-Pennington* protection for misstatements made to the legislative branch. See Hurwitz, *supra* note 44, at 83–84.

66. *Clipper Express*, 690 F.2d at 1261.

67. *Allied Tube & Conduit Corp. v. Indian Head, Inc.*, 486 U.S. ____, ____ (1988) ("But in less political arenas, unethical and deceptive practices can constitute abuses of administrative or judicial processes that may result in antitrust violations"); *In re IBP Confidential Business Documents Litig.*, 755 F.2d 1300 (8th Cir.) (misrepresentations to court not protected), *adhered to*, 800 F.2d 787 (8th Cir. 1986) (en banc), *cert. denied*, 479 U.S. 1088 (1987); *Razorback Ready Mix Concrete Co. v. Weaver*, 761 F.2d 484, 487 (8th Cir. 1985) (misrepresentation before court not protected); *St. Joseph's Hosp., Inc. v. Hospital Corp. of Am.*, 795 F.2d 948, 955 (11th Cir. 1986) (misrepresentations before agency acting judicially not protected); *Transkentucky Transp. R.R. v. Louisville & Nashville R.R.*, 581 F. Supp. 759-60 (E.D. Ky. 1983) ("the commission of fraud and the knowing submission of false information do not enjoy immunity under the *Noerr* doctrine * * *."); *Outboard Marine Corp. v. Pezetel*, 474 F. Supp. 1160, 1162 (S.D.N.Y. 1982) (litigation misrepresentations not protected).

At least one court, however, has held that the misrepresentations must be material if they are to strip away *Noerr-Pennington* protection. See *Interstate Properties v. Pyramid Co.*, 586 F. Supp. 1160, 1163 (S.D.N.Y. 1982) ("The deliberate misrepresentation is to be faulted, but that misrepresentation could not have been material to the [state agency's] conclusion that Pyramid had failed to establish an economic necessity warranting the wetlands' destruction.").

68. *Sessions Tank Liners, Inc. v. Joor Mfg., Inc.*, 827 F.2d 458, 468 (9th Cir. 1987), *vacated on other grounds*, 487 U.S. ____ (1988).

69. *Sacramento Coca-Cola Bottling Co. v. Chauffeurs, Teamsters, and Helpers Local No. 150*, 440 F.2d 1096, 1099 (9th Cir.), *cert. denied*, 404 U.S. 826 (1971). Accord *Central Telecommunications v. TCI Cablevision, Inc.*, 800 F.2d 711, 722 (8th Cir. 1986) (upholding jury instruction that "*Noerr-Pennington* protects all 'genuine' lobbying efforts but does not protect 'threats, intimidation, or other unlawful acts' which were 'not genuine efforts to

influence public officials'"), *cert. denied,* 480 U.S. 910 (1987); *In re IBP Confidential Business Documents Litig.,* 755 F.2d 1300, 1313 (8th Cir.) (*Noerr-Pennington* does not protect illegal acts); *adhered to,* 800 F.2d 787 (8th Cir. 1986), *cert. denied,* 479 U.S. 1088 (1987).

70. *United States Football League v. National Football League,* 842 F.2d 1335, 1374 (2d Cir. 1988).

71. *Metro Cable Co. v. CATV of Rockford, Inc.,* 516 F.2d 220, 230-31 (7th Cir. 1975).

72. *Id.;* see also *Boone v. Redevelopment Agency,* 841 F.2d 886, 894 (9th Cir. 1988).

73. See *Sessions Tank Liners, Inc. v. Joor Mfg., Inc.,* 827 F.2d 458, 466 (9th Cir. 1987), *vacated on other grounds,* 487 U.S. ____ (1988).

74. See *Boone v. Redevelopment Agency,* 841 F.2d 886, 894 (9th Cir. 1988).

75. See *Instructional Sys. Dev. Corp. v. Aetna Cas. & Sur. Co.,* 817 F.2d 639, 649-50 (10th Cir. 1987) ("ISDC presented evidence that Doron bribed purchasing officials, * * *. [B]ribery, or misuse or corruption of governmental processes are outside the protection of the *Noerr-Pennington* doctrine and may give rise to an antitrust claim"); *Razorback Ready Mix Concrete Co. v. Weaver,* 761 F.2d 484, 487 (8th Cir. 1985) (same); *Westborough Mall, Inc. v. City of Cape Girardeau,* 693 F.2d 733, 756 (8th Cir. 1982) (same), *cert. denied,* 461 U.S. 945 (1983); *Gorman Towers v. Bogoslavsky,* 626 F.2d 607, 615 (8th Cir. 1980) (same); *Cipollone v. Ligget Group, Inc.,* 668 F. Supp. 408, 410 (D.N.J. 1987) (same). But see *Cow Palace, Ltd. v. Associated Milk Producers, Inc.,* 390 F. Supp. 696, 699 (D. Colo. 1975) (applying *Noerr* to dismiss complaint alleging that defendant "made illegal campaign contributions and paid bribes" to members of Congress).

76. *George R. Whitten, Jr., Inc. v. Paddock Pool Builders, Inc.,* 424 F.2d 25, 33 (1st Cir.), *cert. denied,* 400 U.S. 850 (1970). Accord *Israel v. Baxter Laboratories,* 466 F.2d 272, 257-77 (D.C. Cir. 1972)(same); *Hecht v. Pro-Football, Inc.,* 444 F.2d 931 (D.C. Cir.)(same), *cert. denied,* 404 U.S. 1047 (1971); *Sacramento Coca-Cola Bottling Co. v. Chauffeurs, Teamsters, and Helpers Local No. 150,* 440 F.2d 1096, 1099 (9th Cir.) (same), *cert. denied,* 404 U.S. 826 (1971); *Hill Aircraft & Leasing Corp. v. Fulton County, Georgia,* 561 F. Supp. 667, 675 (N.D. Ga. 1982) ("Thus, *Noerr* applies to insure access to policy makers, where action is designed to influence policy. * * * It is not a defense for parties who seek to influence officials acting in a purely commercial, or proprietary, rather than 'governmental' capacity"), *aff'd mem.,* 729 F.2d 1467 (11th Cir. 1984); *Cincinnati Riverfront Coliseum Inc. v. City of Cincinnati,* 556 F. Supp. 664, 665 (S.D. Ohio 1983) (same); *F. Buddie Contracting, Inc. v. Seawright,* 595 F. Supp. 422, 433 (N.D. Ohio 1984) (same); *COMPACT v. Metropolitan Gov't of Nashville,* 594 F. Supp. 1567, 1573 (M.D. Tenn. 1984), *remanded on other grounds,* 786 F.2d 227 (6th Cir. 1987) (same); *City of Atlanta v. Ashland Warren, Inc.,* 1982 Trade Cas. −64, 537 (N.D. Ga. 1981) (same). See also *Federal Prescription Serv., Inc. v. American Pharmaceutical Ass'n,* 663 F.2d 253, 263 (D.C. Cir. 1981) (recognizing, but not applying "commercial exception" to *Noerr-Pennington*), *cert. denied,* 455 U.S. 928 (1982); *Kurek v. Pleasure Driveway and Park Dist.,* 557 F.2d 580, 594 (7th Cir. 1977), *vacated,* 435 U.S. 992, *reinstated,* 583 F.2d 378 (7th Cir. 1978) (same).

77. *In re Airport Car Rental Antitrust Litig.,* 693 F.2d 84, 85 (9th Cir. 1982), *cert. denied,* 462 U.S. 1133 (1983).

78. *Independent Taxicab Drivers' Employees v. Greater Houston Transp. Co.,* 760 F.2d 607, 613, (5th Cir.), *cert. denied,* 474 U.S. 903 (1985); see also *Greenwood Utils. Comm'n v. Mississippi Power Co.,* 751 F.2d 1484, 1498-99 (5th Cir. 1985); *Bright v. Ogden City,* 635 F. Supp. 31, 35 (D. Utah), *aff'd,* 824 F.2d 819 (10th Cir. 1987); *Sakamoto v. Duty Free Shoppers, Ltd.,* 613 F. Supp. 381, 388-89 (D. Guam 1984), *aff'd,* 764 F.2d 1285 (9th Cir. 1985), *cert. denied,* 475 U.S. 1081 (1986); *Rural Elec. Co. v. Cheyenne Light, Fuel, & Power Co.,* 762 F.2d 847 (10th Cir. 1985) (applying *Noerr-Pennington* to efforts to secure power franchise).

79. *Allied Tube,* 486 U.S. ____, *citing* 1 P. AREEDA & D. TURNER, ANTITRUST LAW ¶206 (1978). The cited passage explains that:

> "Defendants selling to a government agency or renting from it under exclusive terms sometimes claim that their arrangements are immunized by the *Noerr* principle from antitrust scrutiny. Such claims are usually unsound. In the absence of legislation or a valid quasi-legislative ruling, a private person dealing with the government as buyer, seller, lessor, lessee, or franchisee has no greater antitrust privilege or immunity that in similar dealings with non-governmental parties."

80. *Allied Tube,* 486 U.S. at ____ (citation and footnote omitted).

81. *Duke & Co. v. Foerster,* 521 F.2d 1277, 1282 (3d Cir. 1975). Accord *Affiliated Capital Corp. v. City of Houston,* 735 F.2d 1555, 1566-67 (5th Cir. 1984) (en banc), *cert. denied,* 474 U.S. 1053 (1986); *Federal Prescription Serv., Inc. v. American Pharmaceutical Ass'n,* 663 F.2d 253, 264 & n.11 (D.C. Cir. 1981) *cert. denied,* 455 U.S. 928 (1982); *Kurek v. Pleasure Driveway and Park Distr.,* 557 F.2d 580, 594 (7th Cir. 1977), *vacated on other grounds,* 435 U.S. 992, *reinstated,* 583 F.2d 378 (7th Cir. 1978); *Mercy-Peninsula Ambulance, Inc. v. City of San Mateo,* 592 F. Supp. 956, 917 (N.D. Cal. 1984), *aff'd,* 791 F.2d 755 (9th Cir. 1986); *Richard Hoffman Corp. v. Integrated Bldg. Sys., Inc.,* 581 F. Supp. 367, 374 (N.D. Ill. 1984); *Czajkowski v. State of Illinois,* 460 F. Supp. 1265, 1281 (N.D. Ill. 1977), *aff'd mem.,*

588 F.2d 839 (7th Cir. 1987); *Sessions Tank Liners, Inc. v. Joor Mfg., Inc.*, 827 F.2d 458, 466 (9th Cir. 1987), *vacated on other grounds*, 487 U.S. ____ (1988); *Razorback Ready Mix Concrete Co. v. Weaver*, 761 F.2d 484, 487 (8th Cir. 1985).

In *Allied Tube*, the Supreme Court cited approvingly to *Pennington's* holding that *Noerr* immunity applied given that "the trade restraint at issue 'was the act of a public official who is not claimed to be a co-conspirator * * *.'" 486 U.S. ____ n.7.

82. See *First Am. Title Co. v. South Dakota Land Title Ass'n*, 714 F.2d 1439, 1446 n.6 (9th Cir. 1983), *cert. denied*, 464 U.S. 1042 (1984); *Metro Cable, Inc. v. CATV of Rockford, Inc.*, 516 F.2d 220, 230 (7th Cir. 1975); *Boone v. Redevelopment Agency*, 841 F.2d 886, 897 (9th Cir. 1988); *Savage v. Waste Management, Inc.*, 623 F. Supp. 1505, 1515 (D.S.C. 1985); *Sakamoto v. Duty Free Shoppers, Ltd.*, 613 F. Supp. 381 (D. Guam), *aff'd*, 764 F.2d 1285 (9th Cir. 1985), *cert. denied*, 475 U.S. 1081 (1986). See generally Fischel, *Antitrust Liability for Attempts to Influence Government Action: The Basis and Limits of the Noerr-Pennington Doctrine*, 45 U. CHI. L. REV. 80, 115 (1977) ("in most cases the conspirator exception is unworkable and should not be recognized").

83. 5 U.S.C. §1. Section 2 of the Sherman Act prohibits monopolization and attempted monopolization of any line of commerce. 15 U.S.C. §2. Because antitrust cases involving lobbyists are most likely to involve claims of conspiracy among companies engaged in an industry lobbying campaign or between the company engaged in lobbying and the federal government, this discussion focuses on §1 rather than §2. "The offense of monopoly under §2 of the Sherman Act has two elements: (1) the possession of monopoly power in the relevant market and (2) the willful acquisition or maintenance of that power as distinguished from growth or development as a consequence of a superior product, business acumen, or historic accident." *United States v. Grinnell Corp.*, 384 U.S. 563, 570–71 (1966). Monopolists and near-monopolists may be prohibited from engaging in competitive practices that are lawful when performed by nonmonopolists. *Greyhound Computer v. IBM*, 559 F.2d 488, 498 (9th Cir.), *cert. denied*, 434 U.S. 1040 (1978); *United States v. Aluminum Co. of America*, 148 F.2d 416 (2d Cir. 1945).

84. *Northern Pac. Ry. v. United States*, 356 U.S. 1, 4 (1958).

85. *Chicago Bd. of Trade v. United States*, 246 U.S. 231, 238 (1918); *National Soc'y of Professional Eng'rs v. United States*, 435 U.S. 679, 687–90 (1978).

86. *Arizona v. Maricopa County Medical Soc'y*, 457 U.S. 332 (1982); *United States v. Trenton Potteries Co.*, 273 U.S. 392 (1927).

87. *United States v. Topco Assocs.*, 405 U.S. 596 (1979).

88. *Eastern States Retail Lumber Dealers' Ass'n v. United States*, 234 U.S. 600 (1914); *Klor's, Inc. v. Broadway-Hale Stores*, 359 U.S. 207 (1959).

89. *Northern Pac. Ry. v. United States*, 356 U.S. 1 (1958); *Fortner Enters., Inc. v. United States Steel Corp.*, 394 U.S. 495 (1969).

90. *Standard Oil Co. v. United States (Standard Stations)*, 337 U.S. 293 (1949).

91. *Tampa Elec. Co. v. Nashville Coal Co.*, 365 U.S. 320 (1961).

92. *Continental T.V., Inc. v. GTE Sylvania, Inc.*, 433 U.S. 36 (1977).

93. *Id.* at 49.

94. *Chicago Bd. of Trade v. United States*, 246 U.S. 231, 238 (1918); *Continental T.V., Inc. v. GTE Sylvania, Inc.*, 433 U.S. 36, 49 (1977); *National Soc'y of Professional Eng'rs v. United States*, 435 U.S. 679, 690–92 (1978).

95. *Fashion Originators' Guild v. FTC*, 312 U.S. 457, 465 (1941) (citation omitted).

96. *Sea-Land Serv., Inc. v. Alaska R.R.*, 659 F.2d 243 (D.C. Cir. 1981), *cert. denied*, 455 U.S. 919 (1982); *Rex Sys., Inc. v. Holiday*, 814 F.2d 994, 997 (4th Cir. 1987); *Sakamoto v. Duty Free Shoppers, Ltd.*, 764 F.2d 1285, 1289 (9th Cir. 1985), *cert. denied*, 475 U.S. 1081 (1986); *Greenwood Utils. v. Mississippi Power Co.*, 751 F.2d 1484, 1504 (5th Cir. 1985); *Jet Courier Servs. v. Federal Reserve Bank*, 713 F.2d 1221, 1228 (6th Cir. 1983).

97. *Sea-Land Serv., Inc. v. Alaska R.R.*, 659 F.2d at 247.

98. *Parker v. Brown*, 317 U.S. 341, 352 (1943); *Affiliated Capital Corp. v. City of Houston*, 735 F.2d 1555 (5th Cir. 1984) (en banc), *cert. denied sub nom. Gulf Coast Cable Television Co. v. Affiliated Capital Corp.*, 474 U.S. 1053 (1986).

99. P. AREEDA & H. HOVENKAMP, ANTITRUST LAW at 37 (1987 Supp.).

100. *Id.* at 33. However, in *Affiliated Capital Corp.*, 735 F.2d 1555, no such bias on behalf of the municipal officials was present.

101. See generally *Parker v. Brown*, 317 U.S. 341; *California Retail Liquor Dealers Ass'n v. Midcal Aluminum, Inc.*, 445 U.S. 97 (1980); *Town of Hallie v. City of Eau Claire*, 471 U.S. 34 (1985).

102. *California Retail Liquor Dealers Ass'n v. Midcal Aluminum, Inc.*, 445 U.S. at 105; *Southern Motor Carriers Rate Conference v. United States*, 471 U.S. 48, 58–59 (1985).

103. *Greenwood Utils. v. Mississippi Power Co.*, 751 F.2d at 1505.

104. *Southern Motor Carriers Rate Conference v. United States*, 471 U.S. 48, 58–59 (1985).

105. *Id.* at 56.

106. *Subscription Television, Inc. v. Southern California Theatre Owners Ass'n,* 576 F.2d 230, 232–33 (9th Cir. 1978).

107. 15 U.S.C. §15a.

108. *Continental Ore Co. v. Union Carbide & Carbon Corp.,* 370 U.S. 690 (1962); see *United Mine Workers v. Pennington,* 381 U.S. 657, 671 n.4.

109. *California Retail Liquor Dealers Ass'n v. Midcal Aluminum, Inc.,* 445 U.S. 97, 106 (1980).

110. *Parker v. Brown,* 317 U.S. 341, 351 (1943); *California Retail Liquor Dealers Ass'n v. Midcal Aluminum, Inc.,* 445 U.S. at 105–06.

111. See text at notes 76–80, *supra.*

112. See text at notes 81–82, *supra.* See *Greenwood Utils. v. Mississippi Power Co.,* 751 F.2d at 1505.

113. See text at notes 95–102, *supra.*

114. *George R. Whitten, Jr. Inc. v. Paddock Pool Builders, Inc.,* 508 F.2d 547 (1st Cir. 1974), *cert. denied,* 421 U.S. 1004 (1975); *F. Buddie Contracting, Inc. v. Seawright,* 595 F. Supp. 422, 436–38 (N.D. Ohio 1984).

115. In *General Aircraft Corp. v. Air Am., Inc.,* 482 F. Supp. 3, 8 (D.D.C. 1979), the court held that the government's decision not to purchase the plaintiff's products and services was outside the protection of the *Noerr-Pennington* doctrine, and the defendants' alleged misrepresentations and false disparagements concerning the plaintiff might subject them to antitrust liability.

116. W. PROSSER, THE LAW OF TORTS, chs. 119 and 121 (4th ed. 1977).

117. *A.D.M. Corp. v. Sigma Instruments,* 628 F.2d 753, 754 (1st Cir. 1980) (per curiam); *Larry R. George Sales v. Cool Attic Corp.,* 587 F.2d 266, 272 (5th Cir. 1979).

118. 15 U.S.C. §45(a)(1).

119. *Holloway v. Bristol-Myers Corp.,* 485 F.2d 986, 997 (D.C. Cir. 1973).

120. See discussion, *supra.*

121. 15 U.S.C. §15.

122. *Id.*

123. 15 U.S.C. §1.

124. *United States v. United States Gypsum Co.,* 438 U.S. 422, 435 (1978).

125. Assistant Attorney General R. Rule, *Criminal Enforcement of the Antitrust Laws: Targeting Naked Cartel Restraints,* 57 ANTITRUST L.J. 257, 268–70 (1988).

126. Although conduct sufficient to invoke the sham exception may not be prosecuted criminally as an antitrust violation, it may be prosecuted under other federal criminal statutes. For example, making false statements to federal officials may violate 18 U.S.C. §1001 (which generally prohibits false statements), 18 U.S.C. §287 (which prohibits false claims against the United States), or 18 U.S.C. §§1341, 1343 (which prohibits use of the U.S. mails or interstate telephone calls as part of a fraudulent scheme).

127. *United Mine Workers v. Pennington,* 381 U.S. at 670 n.3. A judge may exclude the evidence if the connection between the immune lobbying conduct and the potentially unlawful other conduct is weak or if use of that evidence would be confusing to the jury. *Id.*

6

Lobbying and Defamation

Anthony C. Epstein

The First Amendment to the U.S. Constitution recognizes free speech as one of our most highly prized rights. And no speech is more valuable to our democracy than vigorous debate on political issues. Lobbying is at the heart of the free flow of information and ideas necessary to make our political process work. To achieve the goal of influencing governmental action, the lobbyist relies on one principal tool—speech.

From a practical perspective, participants in the rough-and-tumble of the political process need to be able to accept criticism and even hostile attack. In addition, the volatility of political debate often leaves little time for reflective consideration of each and every statement. Accordingly, the law of defamation has responded to the necessity of free-wheeling debate by allowing maximum freedom from liability for statements made as part of the political process.

Statements made by lobbyists to legislators and staff in the course of lobbying activities have effective protection from defamation liability, even if the statements are defamatory and inaccurate. Indeed, testimony as a witness at legislative hearings is absolutely protected, no matter how grossly or deliberately inaccurate the statement may be. Although statements outside the hearing room concerning political figures and matters of public concern do not enjoy absolute immunity, they are protected by safeguards designed to provide a reasonable margin for error.

None of this means that lobbyists run no risk of liability for defamation under current law. This chapter will serve as a guide around the remaining pitfalls. One need not consult this chapter every time a communication is made in the course of lobbying activities. Instead, this guide can be of assistance when treading upon the inevitable gray areas involving statements that reflect badly upon individuals, businesses, and products or services.

Before beginning, a bit of advice—you do not need a guide if you

109

already know where you're going. If one engaged in lobbying habitually investigates the sources and checks the accuracy of information received and disseminated, the likelihood of a successful challenge for defamation is remote. The kind of thoroughness that makes one an effective lobbyist also provides a legal defense to defamation liability. In other words, careful professional research that first safeguards a lobbyist's credibility also provides protection against defamation claims and liability.

Basic Principles

Defamation liability is principally a product of state law, and the law varies widely among the states. In recent years, however, the U.S. Supreme Court has applied federal constitutional principles to the state laws on defamation. The result of these decisions has been more national uniformity in defamation law. Since this chapter explores defamation liability for lobbying at the federal level, the focus here will be on federal constitutional principles of defamation law.

Defamation historically has included both libel—the written, printed, or broadcast word—and slander—the spoken word. While substantial differences between the two types of defamation used to exist, these differences have largely disappeared.[1] Thus, "defamation" in this chapter includes both libel and slander.

If a statement made in the course of federal lobbying is challenged by an individual or corporation claiming to have been defamed by the statement, the challenge could bring a lawsuit against those responsible for the statement. From the plaintiff's side, a defamation suit involves four elements. The plaintiff must prove (1) that a factual statement was defamatory, (2) that it was false, (3) that the defendant was at fault in making the statement, and (4) that the statement injured the plaintiff. If these elements are proven, the defendant may still assert a defense or privilege to avoid liability for defamation.

Before discussing the specifics of these rules, it may be useful to address a common misconception. The rules governing the defamation liability of the media—newspaper, television, or radio reporters—normally are the same as the rules for everyone else. Generally speaking, media defendants enjoy no greater or lesser protection under the law of defamation than nonmedia defendants.

Defamatory and Untrue Statements

There is obviously no liability unless there is a defamatory statement. Any statement that imputes deceit, fraud, immorality, unethical behavior, or criminal conduct to an individual or corporation is defamatory.[2] Statements are also defamatory if they imply lack of knowledge or skill in the conduct of an individual's or corporation's business,[3] or if they suggest that a product is not as good as it is touted to be.[4]

True statements are always protected—there is no defamation liability for statements that are factually accurate. In the past, truth was only a defense to a defamation action. The law has since changed. The modern rule is that the plaintiff generally must prove that the statement is false.[5] This approach makes it more difficult for plaintiffs to succeed in defamation suits where it is difficult to prove the truth or falsity of the statement.

Generally, defamatory statements must be an assertion of fact. "Under our Constitution, there is no such thing as a false idea."[6] The truth or falsity of an idea must be determined in the free marketplace of ideas, not in the courtroom. Thus, there is no liability for expressing an opinion about a person or a product.[7] Ridicule and parody are viewed as opinion and do not create defamation liability no matter how vicious or cruel.[8] As long as parody is not intended to be factual, there is no liability even if the parody was intended to hurt someone.

The distinction between fact and opinion can be a fine one indeed. If the statement is indefinite and ambiguous, cannot be objectively characterized as true or false, and does not influence the audience to believe the statement is based on facts, then the statement will be considered opinion, and there will be no defamation liability.[9] If the opinion does not state those facts, and leaves the audience of the statement to supply the rationale for the statement, there may be potential for defamation liability.[10] In other words, if the innuendo contained in an opinion leads the audience to believe that some false fact is true, there may be trouble.

Liability for defamatory statements is not limited to the person who first uttered the defamatory statement: people who repeat a defamatory statement of another can be just as liable as the person who originally made the statement.[11] Previous defamations may mean that the last repetition causes less incremental damage, and it may be more reasonable to trust the facts contained in a much-repeated story than in a rumor with limited circulation. But the fact that a statement has been made before does not make it any less defamatory or untrue or actionable.

If an organization employs staff to help in its lobbying activities, remember that defamatory statements made by staff can lead to "vicarious" liability for the employer. For this reason, it is important to make sure that staff uses that same high degree of care in checking the accuracy of its statements as discussed earlier.

Fault

The plaintiff in a defamation suit must prove that the defendant was at fault in making the defamatory statement. Before 1964, defendants could be found liable for defamatory statements even if the defendant acted in complete good faith and simply made an honest mistake, or at least it was up to the defendant to prove his lack of fault. In 1964, the landmark case of *New York Times v. Sullivan*[12] permanently altered the defamation landscape. In that case, the Supreme Court interpreted the First Amendment to place a heavy burden on defamation plaintiffs. It is not enough that the defendant simply made an untrue and defamatory statement: the plaintiff must also prove that the defendant was irresponsible, or even malicious, in making that statement.

The degree of fault that the plaintiff must prove depends on two principal factors. First, is the plaintiff a public official or public figure? Second, does the statement address a matter of public or private concern? In theory, a public figure is any person involved in a public controversy, particularly if the person sought out the limelight.[13] A public figure is generally expected to take the bitter with the sweet, and is presumed to have more access to the media to tell his or her side of the story. Politicians and consumer activists are usually viewed as "all-purpose" public figures—they are public figures for virtually all aspects of their lives. Others are viewed as "limited-purpose" public figures—not public figures for all aspects of their lives, but only for the particular controversy in which their actions are known to the public.[14]

The line between public and private matters is more difficult to draw. Private matters are those that are of no concern to the general public. That is not to say private matters cannot be interesting. For example, one may find the credit reports on a neighbor to be interesting, but that does not make the report a matter of public concern.[15] Fortunately, the distinction between public and private matters may not be critical to lobbyists since the daily concerns of lobbyists—legislative and regulatory issues generally involving products or services—are almost by definition matters of public concern.

The definitions of public figures and public matters all relate to the degree of fault defamation plaintiffs must prove. Public figures must show *actual malice* to recover for injuries, regardless of whether the statement was about a public or private matter. Actual malice means that the defendant knew the statement was false, or that the defendant made the statement in reckless disregard for its truth or falsity.[16] In other words, if a speaker suspects that a defamatory statement is untrue but simply does not care whether it is true or not, the speaker can be liable even though the statement concerns a public figure. A corporation or business whose products or services have been defamed may, depending on the circumstances, also have to prove *actual malice* to recover damages for the defamatory statement. Defamatory statements relating to matters of public concern and concerning private figures, on the other hand, may create liability if the defendant was merely *negligent* in making a statement.[17] The greatest exposure to defamation liability arises when a statement concerns private figures and private matters. In that instance, a defendant is *strictly liable* for a defamatory statement which turns out to be false even if the statement was innocently made and the accuracy of the statement was carefully checked.

The definitions of public figures and public concerns are difficult enough for lawyers and judges, let alone lobbyists who have little time to fine-tune their statements in their daily work. Some practical guidelines: the more well-known the individual, the more he or she seeks the public eye, the more access he or she has to the media and legislative forums, then the more likely the person is a public figure. Thus, the more complete the celebrity or notoriety of the person, the more latitude a lobbyist has to discuss matters concerning that person as an "all-purpose" public figure. Similarly, the more publicized and controversial a legislative issue, the greater likelihood that the issue is of public concern. A company's products or services often may be matters of public concern, but statements about lesser known businesses may not fit into this more protected category.

Of course, the best way to prevent defamation liability is to check the accuracy of the information and the reliability of its source. Because it is easier for private persons to win defamation cases, careful and thorough investigation is especially important when the statement concerns a private figure.

Injury

The individual or corporation must be injured to recover for a defamatory statement. That means that the statement must have a provable effect on the person's reputation among his family, friends, and coworkers. A statement that is patently defamatory but does not injure anyone is generally not actionable. One important caveat: with speech involving private figures and matters of private concern, a plaintiff's damages from defamatory statements may be presumed if the statement was made negligently,[18] and damages may also be presumed if a public figure proves that a false and defamatory statement was made with actual malice. The simple fact that the defamatory statement was made with the required degree of fault means that the plaintiff can recover presumed damages without proof of actual injury or loss to his reputation, and depending on the circumstances, presumed damages can be awarded in any amount the jury decides is appropriate.

Punitive damages may also be recoverable in defamation cases. A small award of presumed damages or even nominal damages (nominal damages can be as little as $1) can support a punitive damage award of significant proportions. Usually, an "evil motive" must be shown to support an award of punitive damages. An evil motive is present when the statement is made to deliberately hurt someone.

The intent that a defendant must have to support a punitive damage recovery is sometimes called malice, but confusingly, the kind of "malice" needed to recover punitive damages is not the same as the "malice" that a public figure must prove to recover anything at all under the First Amendment.[19] Constitutional malice does not require an intent or desire to injure the subject of the defamatory statement. Conversely, even if a speaker makes an untrue and defamatory statement to hurt a public figure's reputation, the speaker will not be liable unless he or she knew the statement was untrue or recklessly disregarded its falsity.

One possible way to reduce a potential plaintiff's recovery is to retract a defamatory statement that turns out to be untrue. Retractions may not, however, eliminate the injury completely, either because they do not reach all those who heard or read the initial statement or because they cannot undo the damage altogether.[20] Although retractions may affect damages, they are not likely to affect liability; a retraction or correction does not prevent a plaintiff from filing a lawsuit about the retracted statement.

Privileges

Privileges come in two self-descriptive forms: absolute and qualified. Absolute privileges protect the speaker regardless of any fault or motive in making the statement. In contrast, qualified privileges provide immunity from liability conditioned upon publication of the defamatory statement in a reasonable manner and for a proper purpose.

Absolute Privileges

There are two principal absolute privileges—the legislative privilege and the "fair reporting" privilege.

The legislative privilege extends to members of legislative bodies and their staffs and to witnesses in legislative hearings.[21] The privilege protects legislators and their staffs only in the performance of their official duties during legislative sessions.[22] Activities that go beyond those duties are not protected by the privilege.[23]

The legislative privilege also protects lobbyists—but only with respect to statements made while they are testifying at legislative hearings. Testimony given by lobbyists at legislative hearings is absolutely protected from defamation liability.[24] Statements made outside of the hearing room, including press releases summarizing the content of the testimony, lose the protection of this particular privilege.

Statements that are a fair report of a legislative proceeding are also absolutely privileged. The privilege applies only to reporting that is fair, complete, and balanced.[25] In other words, this privilege will not insulate from liability an incomplete account of a hearing that singles out for emphasis a defamatory statement, particularly if the account does not include contrary statements or denials at the hearing.[26]

Qualified Privileges

Qualified privileges protect against defamation liability when publication of the statement is done in a reasonable manner and for a proper purpose. The First Amendment requirement that defamation plaintiffs prove fault protects speakers in the same way that qualified privileges do, and indeed, the First Amendment limitations on liability have sometimes been called a constitutional privilege. This section, however, describes more traditional qualified privileges, which are defenses for the defendant to prove rather than hurdles the plaintiff must overcome. There are several types of qualified privileges.

Communications to one who acts in the public interest are entitled to a qualified privilege.[27] These communications are protected only to the extent they are reasonable. An example of a statement covered by this privilege would be a statement to a legislative aide intended to provide information that would assist the aide in performing official duties.

A related qualified privilege protects statements addressed to an entity that can help protect one's interests.[28] The privilege will not apply unless the person to whom the statement was addressed actually has the power to protect the speaker's interest.[29] This privilege may apply to legislative staff or to a government agency with jurisdiction over the matter presented to its representative.

Statements made in furtherance of a common interest are also entitled to a qualified privilege.[30] For example, statements made during discussions among members of a lobbying coalition would be covered to the extent they are intended to facilitate the goals of the coalition. This privilege gives members of a group more breathing room to express their views candidly to a limited audience with a common objective. Such statements are protected, as are all qualified privileges, only to the extent that the statements were published in a reasonable manner and for a proper purpose. And this privilege does not cover statements outside the group, even if those statements merely repeat privileged statements made within the group.

Other Types of Legal Liability Involving False Statements in Lobbying

As if defamation liability were not enough, false statements in lobbying activities can also create both civil and criminal liability in other areas of the law.

Civil Liability

False statements can create several other types of civil liability. Liability under the antitrust laws for false statements in lobbying activities are addressed in Chapter 5 of this book.

Other claims of liability for false statements may be characterized not as defamation, but rather as invasion of privacy or intentional infliction of emotional distress. Invasion of privacy is a separate basis of liability where the statement is true, but the statement exposes to the public private matters unrelated to any legitimate public interest.[31] The tort of intentional infliction of emotional distress arises when the defendant engages in *outrageous* conduct to intentionally harass the plaintiff.[32] When publication of an allegedly defamatory statement is claimed to constitute intentional infliction of emotional distress, constitutional safeguards of free speech, for example, those protecting statements of opinion, apply.[33]

As with the tort of defamation, plaintiffs in cases involving these two other torts may be able to recover based on a single statement by the defendant. Accordingly, this broader potential for liability places an even greater premium on prudence in making statements about other people and companies.

Criminal Liability

False statements to federal officials and at least some congressional departments are crimes.[34] Obstruction of a congressional investigation through false statements also exposes one to criminal liability.[35] Conviction requires proof that the defendant acted knowingly and willfully; honest or even careless mistakes cannot support a criminal conviction. All of the special protections for defendants in criminal cases (for example, proof beyond a reasonable doubt) apply in prosecutions for these offenses.

Notes

1. One remaining distinction between libel and slander is that the plaintiff in a slander suit must prove "special" damages —actual monetary loss—unless the slanderous remarks suggest that a person committed a crime involving moral turpitude, has a loathsome (usually veneral) disease, is incompetent in his or her business, trade or profession, or that a woman is unchaste. See generally W. PROSSER, LAW OF TORTS 750-66 (4th ed. 1971). In a libel case, damages may be presumed. See discussion, *infra*.
2. See *Peck v. Tribune Co.*, 214 U.S. 185 (1909).
3. RESTATEMENT (SECOND) OF TORTS §573 (1977).
4. See *Bose Corp. v. Consumers Union of United States*, 466 U.S. 485 (1984).
5. *Philadelphia Newspapers, Inc. v. Hepps*, 475 U.S. 767 (1986).
6. *Bose Corp. v. Consumers Union of United States*, 466 U.S. 485, 504 (1984).
7. *Ollman v. Evans*, 750 F.2d 970, 975 (D.C. Cir. 1984), *cert. denied*, 471 U.S. 1127 (1985). A related common law concept, the "fair comment" doctrine, also provides protection for

opinions concerning public persons and matters of public interest. See *Gertz v. Robert Welch, Inc.,* 418 U.S. 323, 339 (1974).

8. *Hustler Magazine, Inc. v. Falwell,* 485 U.S. 46 (1988); RESTATEMENT (SECOND) OF TORTS §566 comment d (1977).

9. *Ollman v. Evans,* 750 F.2d 970, 979 (D.C. Cir. 1984), *cert. denied,* 471 U.S. 1127 (1985).

10. *Lewis v. Time, Inc.,* 710 F.2d 549 (9th Cir. 1983).

11. See, e.g., *Schiavone Constr. Co. v. Time, Inc.,* 735 F.2d 94 (3d Cir. 1984).

12. 376 U.S. 254 (1964).

13. R. SMOLLA, LAW OF DEFAMATION §2.09[2] at 2–30 (1986).

14. *Time, Inc. v. Firestone,* 424 U.S. 448 (1976).

15. See *Dun & Bradstreet, Inc. v. Greenmoss,* 472 U.S. 749, (1985).

16. *New York Times v. Sullivan,* 376 U.S. at 279–80.

17. *Curtis Publishing Co. v. Butz,* 388 U.S. 130 (1967).

18. *Dun & Bradstreet, Inc. v. Greenmoss,* 472 U.S. 749 (1985).

19. *Dun & Bradstreet, Inc. v. Greenmoss,* 472 U.S. 749, 753–55 (1985).

20. See R. SMOLLA, LAW OF DEFAMATION §9.12[2][c] (1986).

21. *Gravel v. United States,* 408 U.S. 606 (1972).

22. *Chastain v. Sundquist,* 833 F.2d 311, 314 (1987), *cert. denied,* 487 U.S. ____ (1988).

23. *Hutchinson v. Proxmire,* 443 U.S. 111, 123–33 (1979).

24. See, e.g., *Webster v. Sun Co.,* 790 F.2d 157 (D.C. Cir. 1986).

25. See *Time, Inc. v. Pape,* 401 U.S. 279 (1971).

26. See, e.g., *Associated Press v. Walker,* 388 U.S. 130 (1967).

27. RESTATEMENT (SECOND) OF TORTS §598 (1977).

28. See *British Am. & E. Co. v. Wirth, Ltd.,* 592 F.2d 75 (2d Cir. 1979); RESTATEMENT (SECOND) OF TORTS §594 (1977).

29. See *Avins v. White,* 627 F.2d 637, 645 (2d Cir.), *cert. denied,* 449 U.S. 982 (1980).

30. See *Roland v. d'Arazien,* 685 F.2d 653 (D.C. Cir. 1982); RESTATEMENT (SECOND) OF TORTS §596 (1977).

31. RESTATEMENT (SECOND) OF TORTS §652D comment d (1977).

32. See, e.g., *State Rubbish Collectors Ass'n v. Siliznoff,* 38 Cal. 2d 330 (1952). Only private figures can recover for injuries resulting from the intentional infliction of emotional distress if the injury was caused by the publication of a defamatory statement.

33. See *Hustler Magazine, Inc. v. Falwell,* 485 U.S. 46 (1988).

34. 18 U.S.C. §1001.

35. 18 U.S.C. §1505.

7

Lobbying by Government Contractors

Leland J. Badger

Those who receive federal funds as contractors or grantees are restricted from using those funds for lobbying.

The restrictions are relatively recent, but they have historical and public policy bases. As a general proposition, both business and nonprofit organizations that receive federal funds should avoid spending those funds on lobbying. As with any general rule, however, important exceptions also exist. The applicable statutes and regulations have grown to constitute a complicated and often confusing business and legal environment for the recipient of federal funds which lobbies, even if the recipient uses only nonfederal funds for its lobbying.

General

To begin with, certain very specific federal fund-use prohibitions exist, but they do not apply in all circumstances. Whether these specific fund-use prohibitions apply in a particular case will depend on a number of factors, including the time of the award of the federal funds, the nature of the awardee, the vehicle through which the funds are awarded, the specific lobbying use contemplated, and, in some cases, the identity of the awarding agency.

If these specific prohibitions do not apply, the recipient faces the perhaps more difficult task of determining whether more general federal fund-use and lobbying prohibitions apply. This can be difficult because the very process of awarding and administering federal funds inherently involves negotiations between the recipient and the awarding agency (certain aspects of which might be viewed by some as lobbying) and, because the recipients generally hesitate to "bite the hand that feeds them," these issues are seldom adjudicated to the point of a reported decision. Thus, great care should be used in reaching a conclusion as to whether, or to what extent, any federal prohibitions will limit the recovery of lobbying expenses or the use of federal funds, already disbursed, to engage in lobbying activities.

Public Policy Considerations

In 1984, the Office of Management and Budget of the Executive Office of the President, which coordinated the development of the newer specific prohibitions against using federal funds for most types of lobbying, stated the rationale underpinning the prohibitions: "It would not be appropriate or cost-efficient to permit Federal tax dollars to be used [for *lobbying,* advertising, fund-raising, and entertainment] on grounds of public policy."[1] OMB stated that it "seeks to avoid the appearance that, by awarding Federal grants, contracts, or other agreements to organizations engaged in political advocacy on particular sides of public issues, the government has endorsed, fostered, or 'prescribe[d] [as] orthodox' a particular view on such issues."[2]

History of the Regulations

In 1975, before there were specific regulations prohibiting the use of federal funds for lobbying, Congress required the Defense Contract Audit Agency to audit certain defense contractors.[3] These audits uncovered many "questioned costs," including costs for alleged entertainment and lobbying of government officials.[4] In late 1981, after much study and comment by contractors and others, the Department of Defense revised its procurement regulations to specifically disallow lobbying costs.[5] These provisions were seen as very harsh, disallowing "virtually any and every relationship between the citizenry represented by defense contractors and their legislative representatives, regardless of the nature and regardless of who initiated the action."[6] The two other major procurement regulations incorporated similar provisions.[7]

In January 1983, OMB proposed specific, more widely applicable regulations governing the use of federal funds which would bar recovery of money spent on "political advocacy."[8] After receiving tens of thousands of comments, OMB limited and more specifically defined unallowable lobbying costs.[9] The final version of the regulations was published on April 27, 1984, to become effective May 29, 1984.[10] It covered most nonprofit recipients of federal funds,[11] and nearly identical amendments to the procurement regulations immediately followed.[12]

Uncertain Scope of Statutory Prohibition

At least one commentator has suggested that Section 1913 of Title 18 of the U.S. Code generally prohibits the use of federal funds for lobbying.[13] Although the plain language of the statute seems to confirm this suggestion, such a broad statutory interpretation has not been clearly accepted. On the one hand, one court has explicitly stated that the statute may be enforced criminally and against only government officials.[14] Further, courts generally discussing the issue have held that the statute provides no private cause of action.[15] On the other hand, another commentator has suggested that the statute may make it a crime for a government official to reimburse a government contractor for its lobbying expenses.[16] This issue apparently has not been litigated.

Overview

Application of the Various Regulations

To determine the applicable set of regulations, one must consider the time of the award, the nature of the awardee, the type of the award, and, in some cases, the identity of the awarding agency.

Time of the Award

The specific prohibitions against recovery of lobbying costs apply only prospectively.[17]

Nature of the Awardee

Business organizations are generally awarded procurement contracts rather than other funding arrangements. The FAR governs these awards.[18] Cost recovery for most nonprofit organizations is generally governed by OMB Circular A-122.[19] Cost recovery for educational institutions is governed by OMB Circular A-21.[20] Cost recovery for state and local governments is governed by OMB Circular A-87.[21] Cost recovery for hospitals is governed by Section 74 of Title 45 of the Code of Federal Regulations.[22] These provisions do not overlap.[23] To illustrate, a nonprofit educational institution is governed by OMB Circular A-21 because it is an educational institution and not by A-122, which applies to most other nonprofit organizations.[24]

Subawardees are governed largely depending on the nature of the subawardee and not by the regulations which govern the prime awardee.[25] For example, suppose the federal government grants money to a state government for some purpose. Suppose further that the state government awards a subcontract under the federal grant to an institution of higher education. OMB Circular A-87 applies to

the costs incurred by the state, whereas OMB Circular A-21 applies
to the costs incurred by the educational institution.[26]

Type of Award

Because most federal fund recipients think of themselves first
not simply as a "business," "nonprofit," or "educational entity," but
rather as a "contractor," "grantee," or "awardee" of a cooperative
agreement, and because federal procurement contracts are now uniformly regulated, some discussion of the type of federal funds award
is necessary to an understanding of the total regulatory scheme.

Procurement Contracts. Virtually all the paths through which
the federal government dispenses money involve contracts. However, the government enters into many different kinds of contracts.
A procurement contract is the appropriate means by which the government obtains goods, services, and leases of realty.[27] Procurement
contracts are governed by the FAR or its predecessors.[28] The FAR
provides specific regulations regarding the recovery of costs for certain specified items including lobbying costs.[29] Because the government obtains much of its goods, services, and leases from for-profit
business organizations, these regulations were designed to cover contracts with business entities. Thus, the FAR exempts from these general cost-recovery provisions contracts with educational institutions,
state and local governments, nonprofit organizations, and hospitals.
In these instances, the FAR incorporates by reference the provisions
of the applicable OMB Circulars.[30]

Grants. Federal grants, though the name brings to mind the concept of gifts, are actually contracts.[31] Grants differ from gifts in that
the awardee obligates itself, among other things, to use the money in
the agreed-upon way.[32] Grants are the proper instrument through
which the government may spend money when the goal is something
other than the acquisition of property or services for direct benefit of
the federal government and the nature of the relationship is such that
the government is not substantially involved beyond the payment of
the money.[33]

Unlike procurement contracts and the FAR, there is no single
regulation covering grants. Which regulations apply to a specific
grant depends largely on the nature of the grantee and the identity of
the awarding agency.[34] Likewise, there are no general rules regarding
the recovery of costs in grants; these rules depend upon the nature of
the grantee[35] and the particular grant or granting agency.[36] Grantees
must also remain aware of the terms of the grant, as these can provide additional rules.

Cooperative Arrangements. Cooperative arrangements are similar to grants except that the government expects to involve itself
substantially in the performance of the objectives of the arrangement.[37] The regulatory scheme which applies to grants applies similarly to cooperative arrangements.[38]

Other Contracts. The government enters into other contracts in which the problems of spending federal funds on lobbying are not particularly acute. These include employment contracts, in which the employee is generally free to spend his or her government paycheck in any lawful way a nongovernmental employee might.[39] Also included are contracts for the purchase or sale of real property, the value of which generally does not depend upon anything other than the land itself; thus the contracts are not subject to attempts to recover costs.[40]

For-Profit and Nonprofit Contractors

General Principles of Allowability

No cost, including a lobbying cost, will be allowed unless it is reasonable, allocable to performance of the contract, computed in accordance with appropriate accounting standards, and not in conflict with the terms of the contract.[41]

These principles support the disallowance of otherwise expressly allowed lobbying costs which are, for example, excessive or unrelated to the purposes of the contract. Upon a determination that lobbying costs are generally unreasonable or that they cannot properly be allocated to the performance of a contract, these general provisions could conceivably support disallowing lobbying costs not otherwise explicitly covered by statutes or regulations.

Specific Prohibitions

Procurement Contracts Effective Prior to May 29, 1984

The older regulatory scheme of the ASPR/FPR/NASAPR did not specially prohibit recovery of lobbying costs.[42] Contracts entered into under that scheme are subject to no specific regulations regarding lobbying costs.[43]

In late 1981, after years of debate, the Defense Department added a specific lobbying prohibition to its procurement regulations.[44] Seen as very harsh,[45] this regulation precludes recovery for costs incurred directly or indirectly for the purposes of influencing any legislative body or any of the legislative body's employees to take any legislative action.[46] The corresponding provisions of the FPR and NASAPR mandate disallowing the same costs, excepting, however, the costs of certain "legislative liaison activity" including attendance at legislative sessions, gathering information regarding legislation, and some communications with legislators or legislatures,[47] all of which may properly be recoverable costs.

Procurement Contracts Effective on or After May 29, 1984

The general scheme embodied in OMB Circular A-122 governs the allowability of lobbying costs in government contracts effective on or after May 29, 1984.[48] In OMB's own words, the costs of the following activities are unallowable:

"(1) Federal, state or local electioneering and support of such entities as campaign organizations and political action committees;

"(2) Most direct lobbying of Congress and, with the exceptions noted below, state legislatures, to influence legislation [sic];

"(3) Lobbying of the Executive Branch in connection with decisions to sign or veto enrolled legislation;

"(4) Efforts to utilize state or local officials to lobby Congress or state legislatures;

"(5) Grassroots lobbying concerning either Federal or state legislation; and

"(6) Legislative liaison activities in support of unallowable lobbying activities."[49]

Contracting agencies may implement or supplement these provisions with regulations of their own.[50] As of early 1989, only the Department of Energy has done so.[51]

Other Contracts

Contracts with nonprofit organizations are governed generally by the corresponding provision of OMB A-122, which is essentially identical to the above-quoted section of the FAR.[52] Contracts with educational institutions,[53] state and local governments,[54] and hospitals[55] are treated elsewhere in this chapter.

Exceptions

Certain lobbying costs are not expressly prohibited by the new regulations.[56] OMB considers the following excepted from the specific provisions regarding unallowable costs:

(1) Lobbying at the local level;

(2) Lobbying to influence state legislation, in order to directly reduce the cost of performing the grant or contract, or to avoid impairing the organization's authority to do so;

(3) Lobbying in the form of a technical and factual presentation to Congress or state legislatures, at their request;

(4) Contacts with executive branch officials other than lobbying for the veto or signing of enrolled bills; and

(5) Lobbying on regulatory actions.[57]

Executive Branch Lobbying

Although the "legislative lobbying" cost principles cover the lobbying of executive branch officials regarding their signing or vetoing of legislation,[58] the FAR separately prohibits recovery of costs associated with other methods of lobbying executive branch officials, including, apparently, the recovery of costs incurred influencing regulatory actions.[59] This rule, however, effective April 7, 1986, simply and rather vaguely prohibits recovery of costs incurred to "improperly" influence an officer or employee of the executive branch of the federal government regarding regulations or contracts "on any basis other than the merits of the matter."[60] Furthermore, OMB has not prohibited similar behavior by nonprofits in OMB Circular A-122.

Reporting and Record Keeping

The federal government requires contractors to submit certain records kept in certain ways as a condition to reimbursement for the contractor's costs.[61] Further, the government requires some specific records supporting reimbursement for any costs when the contractor engages in lobbying.[62] Generally, a lobbying contractor seeking reimbursement for any indirect costs must:

(1) Separately identify lobbying costs from other indirect costs[63];

(2) Certify that the contractor has complied with the rules regarding the recovery of legislative lobbying costs[64];

(3) Maintain adequate records to show that it has in fact complied with the rules[65];

(4) Keep time logs or similar records for employees if the employee spends more than 25 percent of his work time lobbying or if the contractor has "materially misstated" its costs within the last five years.[66]

Nearly identical provisions govern nonprofit institutions with which the government has contracts.[67]

Enforcement and Sanctions

The government relies primarily upon the voluntary compliance of the individual contractor.[68] To facilitate this, the rules provide a mechanism to encourage a contractor to seek advance agreements concerning recovery of its lobbying costs.[69] Failing the voluntary compliance by the contractor, several other enforcement techniques exist. The audit provisions[70] and the accounting standards[71] give the contract officer the tools required to fulfill his duty to review for unallowable costs for which the contractor requests payment.[72] The FAR provides procedures for a contract officer to disallow costs,[73] as well as "appeals" procedures for use when the contractor disputes the contract officer's determination.[74] Further lines of defense against noncompliance include the federal contract audit organizations, especially the Defense Contract Audit Agency.[75] A final line remains in the federal inspectors general and the Comptroller General.[76]

The primary sanction for violations is recovery of the misspent money.[77] Gross or continued violations may warrant suspension or termination of the contract.[78] Even worse misconduct may result in debarment.[79] The OMB expressly rejected as inappropriate any financial penalties for attempts to recover unallowable costs.[80] A publicized example of an enforcement action being taken in this regard was the 1985 withholding by the Defense Department of over $400 million from General Dynamics Corporation on grounds including suspicions that lobbying costs had been charged to one or more contracts.[81]

Additional enforcement means may exist through prosecuting offenders for perjury.[82] In certain instances the contractor must certify that it has complied with the cost principles in his request for payment.[83] If the certifying officer does so falsely, he or she may be guilty of perjury. The government also retains all its other means to enforce its laws, for example, prosecuting an offender for fraud.

Grantees and Awardees of Cooperative Arrangements

General Principles of Allowability

The principles of allowability which apply to business and nonprofit contractors also generally apply to grantees and awardees of cooperative arrangements,[84] the chief difference being the source to which the recipient looks for regulation.[85] Instead of the FAR, grantees and cooperative awardees are governed based on the nature of the recipient, and, to a lesser extent, the identity of the awarding organization. All these regulations provide the same essentials: the cost must be reasonable, allocable to fulfillment of the award's purpose, computed in accordance with appropriate accounting standards, not conflicting with the terms of the award.[86] Additionally, general provisions restrict the use of federal funds to meet fund-sharing or matching requirements of other funding programs and require that costs be treated consistently.[87]

Specific Prohibitions

Although it does not state its reasons for this conclusion, OMB felt that lobbying costs were unrecoverable prior to the OMB Circular A-122 revision specifically disallowing lobbying costs.[88] It nevertheless "clarified" that prohibition in its amendment to the Circular.[89] These specific prohibitions are word-for-word identical to those in FAR,[90] except that where reference is made in the FAR to "contracts" or "contractors," it is replaced in A-122 with more general reference to "contracts, grants, or other agreement." Because A-122 specifically exempts from its operation the following groups, noncontractual awards to educational institutions,[91] state and local governments,[92] and hospitals[93] are treated elsewhere in this chapter.

Awardees must also remain aware of the statutes and regulations governing the award and the awarding agency.[94] Although these generally either simply adopt the principles of the OMB Circulars or promote other socially desirable goals, one cannot ignore the possibility that an agency will implement special lobbying rules.

Exceptions

The exceptions to the lobbying costs prohibitions applicable to noncontractual awardees are the same as those which apply to contractors.[95] Again, the text is identical except for the language regarding the nature of the relationship between the parties.[96]

Reporting and Record Keeping

Likewise, the reporting requirements for businesses and nonprofits are functionally equivalent.[97] However, certain awardees believe there are serious First Amendment problems with these requirements, in that to recover any indirect cost the awardee must disclose the extent of its expenditures for lobbying even when it does not attempt to recover any of those lobbying expenses.[98]

Enforcement and Sanctions

Except to the extent that procurement contract administration differs from the administration of other awards, the enforcement policies and mechanisms for grants and cooperative agreements are identical to that for contracts discussed elsewhere in this chapter.[99]

Educational Institutions

The cost principles governing the use of federal funds by educational institutions are contained in OMB Circular A-21. While there is no specific prohibition in the cost principles for educational institutions against the recovery of lobbying costs from the federal government, a prohibition may exist under more general cost principles. First, general principles of allowability applying to educational institutions are very similar to those applying to nonprofit organizations.[100] These general principles may provide a basis on which agencies may disallow lobbying costs.[101] Second, a commentator noted earlier that it may be a crime for the government to reimburse lobbying costs.[102]

State and Local Governments

The cost principles governing the use of federal funds by state and local governments are contained in OMB Circular A-87.[103] While there is no specific prohibition in the cost principles for state and local governments against the recovery of lobbying costs, that recovery may be prohibited in much the same manner as discussed elsewhere in this chapter concerning educational institutions.[104]

Hospitals

The cost principles governing the use of federal funds by hospitals are contained in Section 74 of Title 45 of the Code of Federal Regulations. While there is no specific prohibition in these regulations against the recovery of lobbying costs, that recovery may be prohibited in much the same manner as discussed elsewhere in this chapter concerning educational institutions.[105]

Notes

1. 49 Fed. Reg. 18,260, 18,260 (1984) (OMB Circular A-122 Cost Principles for Nonprofit Organizations; "Lobbying" Revision, Preamble, §I) (hereinafter cited as "A-122" and included, with original 1980 Circular A-122 and revisions to the 1984 Circular A-122, in Appendix I).
2. *Id.* at 18,263 (quoting *West Va. Bd. of Educ. v. Barnette*, 319 U.S. 624, 645 (1943) (violates First Amendment for state to require school children to salute the U.S. flag)).
3. See P. Trueger, Accounting Guide for Government Contracts 568 (1988).
4. *Id.*
5. *Id.* The then-current regulation is known as the Defense Acquisition Regulations, codified at Title 32 of the Code of Federal Regulations and hereinafter cited as "DAR." The DAR succeeded the Armed Services Procurement Regulations, hereinafter "ASPR," which applied at the time of the 1975 inquiries. For the specific prohibition, see *infra* note 46.
6. P. Trueger, *supra* note 3, at 568.
7. These were the Federal Procurement Regulations, hereinafter "FPR," codified at Title 41 of the Code of Federal Regulations, and the National Aeronautics and Space Administration Procurement Regulations, hereinafter "NASAPR," codified at Chapter 18 of Title 41 of the Code of Federal Regulations. For the text of the lobbying provisions contained in these regulations, see 41 C.F.R. §1–15.205-52 (FPR); *id.* §1815.205–51 (NASAPR).
8. See 48 Fed. Reg. 3,348–51 (1983).
9. 49 Fed. Reg. 18,260, 18,261–62. The term was changed from "political advocacy" to "lobbying and related activities" and then simply to "lobbying." *Id.* For the text of the current version, see *infra* notes 48 and 56.
10. 49 Fed. Reg. 18,260 (A-122—"Lobbying" Revision, Preamble).

11. See *infra* notes 18–26 and accompanying text.
12. See 49 Fed. Reg. 18,260, 18,278. The then-applicable procurement regulation was the Federal Acquisition Regulation, hereinafter "FAR," which succeeded the FPR, DAR, and NASAPR as a uniform regulation for procurements. The lobbying amendment to the FAR immediately followed the lobbying revision to A-122 in the *Federal Register*. See 49 Fed. Reg. 18,260. The Department of Defense issued a harsher regulation as part of its FAR supplement, but on July 1, 1984, adopted the provision in the FAR. P. Trueger, *supra* note 3, at 569.
13. T. Boggs, Jr., & K. Boyce, Corporate Political Activity §6.04 at 6–9 (1986). The statute provides:

> "No part of the money appropriated by any enactment of Congress shall, in the absence of express authorization by Congress, be used directly or indirectly to pay for any personal service, advertisement, telegram, telephone, letter, printed or written matter, or other device, intended or designed to influence in any manner a Member of Congress, to favor or oppose, by vote or otherwise, any legislation or appropriation by Congress, whether before or after the introduction of any bill or resolution proposing such legislation or appropriation; but this shall not prevent officers or employees of the United States or of its departments or agencies from communicating to Members of Congress on the request of any Member or to Congress, through the proper official channels, requests for legislation or appropriations which they deem necessary for the efficient conduct of public business.
> "Whoever, being an officer or employee of the United States or of any department or agency thereof, violates or attempts to violate this section, shall be fined not more than $500 or imprisoned not more than one year, or both; and after notice and hearing by the superior officer vested with the power of removing him, shall be removed from office or employment."

18 U.S.C. §1913.
14. See *Grassley v. Legal Servs. Corp.*, 535 F. Supp. 818, 826 n.6 (D. Iowa 1982) (Members of Congress had no private cause of action under 18 U.S.C. §1913 to enjoin alleged lobbying with federal funds by Legal Services Corp.).
15. *National Treasury Employees Union v. Campbell*, 654 F.2d 784, 789–90 (D.C. Cir. 1981) (labor union had no private cause of action under 18 U.S.C. §1913 to enjoin the director of the Office of Personal Management, a member of the Executive Branch, from using federal funds to urge the passage of legislation in Congress).
16. See R. Smith, *Should Government Contracts Subsidize Industry Lobbying?* 23 Air Force L. Rev. 408, 422 (1982–83).
17. 49 Fed. Reg. 18,260, 18,260. ("The revision will affect only grants, contracts, and other agreements entered into after the effective date [of this revision to A-122]. Existing grants, contracts, and other agreements will not be affected.").
18. See 48 C.F.R. §§1 to 199 (1987).
19. See 45 Fed. Reg. 46,022, 46,023 (1980), *amended* 49 Fed. Reg. 18,260 (1984), *amended* 49 Fed. Reg. 19,588 (1984), *amended* 52 Fed. Reg. 19,788 (1987). Attachment C to A-122 is a list of nonprofit organizations specifically exempted from A-122 because of the organizations' similarity to for-profit institutions. See 45 Fed. Reg. 46,022, 46,034. These organizations are covered by the regulations governing for-profit institutions, largely the FAR. *Id.* at 46,023.
20. See infra notes 100–02 and accompanying text.
21. See infra notes 103–04 and accompanying text.
22. See infra note 105 and accompanying text.
23. 48 C.F.R. §§31.302 to .703 (1987) (FAR statements concerning the applications of the various regulations to the various types of awardee); 45 Fed. Reg. 46,022, 46,023 (1980) (A-122 statements concerning the applications of the various regulations to the various types of awardee).
24. See, e.g., 45 C.F.R. §74.176 (1987) (describing this scheme).
25. 45 Fed. Reg. 46,022, 46,023 (A-122 §3b). Note however, that procurements by awardees charged to the award are generally governed only indirectly by the costs principles of the FAR. See, e.g., 45 C.F.R. §74.160 (1987) (procurement regulations for HHS awardees).
26. 45 C.F.R. §74.176 (1987) (example given in HHS regulations).
27. 31 U.S.C. §6303.
28. See *supra* notes 5, 7, and 12 for a discussion of the FAR's predecessors.
29. See 48 C.F.R. §31 (1987).
30. See 48 C.F.R. §§31.301 to .303 (educational institutions, referring to OMB A-21); *id.* §§31.601 to .603 (state and local governments, referring to OMB A-87; *id.* §§31.701 to .703 (nonprofit organizations, referring to OMB A-122).
31. J. Cibinic, Jr., & R. Nash, Jr., Cost Reimbursement Contracting 5–8 (1981).

32. *Id.*

33. 31 U.S.C. §6304.

34. See, e.g., OMB Circular A-110 (uniform administrative requirements for grants and other agreements with institutions of higher education, hospitals, and other nonprofit organizations); OMB Circular A-102 (uniform administrative requirements for grants-in-aid to state and local government).

35. See *supra* notes 18–26 and accompanying text.

36. See, e.g., 7 C.F.R. §3015.190 (1988) (cost principles for Department of Agriculture grants).

37. 31 U.S.C. §6305.

38. For a discussion of the application of the various regulations, see *supra* notes 18–26 and accompanying text.

39. Contrast the employer/employee relationship with a contract for personal services which is governed generally by the FAR. This distinction is treated at 5 U.S.C. §2101.

40. See 41 U.S.C. §405(a)(1) (explicit statement that FAR does not apply to purchase and sale of real property).

41. 48 C.F.R. §31.201-2 (1987); see also OMB Circular A-21 (Cost principles for educational institutions), §C.2 (similar provision governing educational institutions); 45 C.F.R. §74 App. E, subsection III.B (similar provision governing hospitals). Older contracts are governed by similar provisions in the procurement regulations. See 32 C.F.R. §15-201.2 (1984) (DAR); 41 C.F.R. §1-15.201-2 (1984) (FPR); *id.* §1815.201-2 (1984) (NASAPR).

    Certain additional general restrictions apply to nonprofit organizations, see 45 Fed. Reg. 46,022, 46,024 (1980) (A-122, Attachment A, §A.2) (Costs may not be included if used to meet fund sharing or matching requirements of other federal programs; costs must be adequately documented), and to state and local governments, see 46 Fed. Reg. 9,548, 9,549 (1981) (OMB Circular A-87, §C.1) (Costs may not be general expenses of the government; costs must either be authorized or not prohibited by state or local law or regulation; costs cannot be included if included or properly includable in another federally funded program; costs must include applicable credits).

    Further, reasonableness and allocability are defined in the allowability regulations. See 48 C.F.R. §31.201-3 (FAR definition of reasonableness); *id.* §31.201-4 (FAR definition of allocability); 45 Fed. Reg. 46,022, 46,024 (A-122, §A.3) (definition of reasonableness regarding nonprofit organizations); *id.* (A-122, §A.4) (definition of allocability regarding nonprofit organizations); 46 Fed. Reg. 9,548, 9,549 (OMB A-87, §C.2) (definition of allocability regarding state and local governments; there is no corresponding definition of reasonableness); OMB Circular A-21 (Cost principles for educational institutions), §C.3 (reasonableness for educational institutions); *id.* §C.4 (allocability for educational institutions); 45 C.F.R. §74 App. E, subsection III.D (allocability and hospitals). These terms are defined for older contracts at 32 C.F.R. §15-201.3 and .4 (DAR), 41 C.F.R. §1-15.201-3 and -4 (FPR), and *id.* §1815.201-3 and -4 (NASAPR).

42. P. TRUEGER, *Accounting Guide for Government Contracts* 568 (1988).

43. See *id.*

44. See 32 C.F.R. §15-205.51 (1984). Costs for the following activities, potentially related to lobbying, are governed by separate regulations:
    Advertising. A-122 Attachment B §1; 48 C.F.R. §31.205-1.
    Alcoholic beverages. 48 C.F.R. §31.205-51.
    Entertainment. A-122 Attachment B §12; 48 C.F.R. §31.205-14.
    Meetings, conferences. A-122 Attachment B §§24, 25; 48 C.F.R. §31.205-43.
    Preaward/precontract costs. A-122 Attachment B §33; 48 C.F.R. §31.205-32.
    Professional services (consultants). A-122 Attachment B §34; 48 C.F.R. §31.205-33.
    Public information/Public relations. A-122 Attachment B §36; 48 C.F.R. §31.205-1.
    Publication and printing. A-122 Attachment B §37; 48 C.F.R. §31.205-1.
    Selling. 48 C.F.R. §31.205-38 (no comparable A-122 provision).
    Travel. A-122 Attachment B §50; 48 C.F.R. §31.205-46.

45. See P. TRUEGER, *supra* note 42 at 568.

46. 32 C.F.R. §15-205.51 (1984). The rule provides:

    "(a) For the purpose of this section, lobbying is defined as any activity, including legislative liaison, or communication which is intended or designed to influence, directly or indirectly, or to engage in any campaign to encourage others to influence members of any legislative body, their staffs, or the staffs of their committees to favor or oppose legislation, appropriations or other actions of the legislative body, its members, or its committees. Lobbying activity includes, but is not limited to, all forms of communications for the above-mentioned purposes by the contractor, its employees, or its agents with the legislative body, its members, and staffs of members and committees.

    "(b) The costs of lobbying as defined herein, including the applicable portion of the salaries of the contractor's employees and the fees of individuals or firms engaged in lobbying, on behalf of the contractor (whether or not the individuals or firms are registered as lobbyists under the applicable law) are unallowable. In addition, the directly associated costs (see [rule regarding the accounting for unallowable costs]) of lobbying are unallowable."

47. See 41 C.F.R. §1–15.205-52 (FPR); *id.* §1815.205–51 (NASAPR). Both the FPR and the NASAPR contain rules almost identical to the that in the DAR. The exception for "legislative liaison activity" varies slightly between the FPR and the NASAPR. The FPR provides:

> "Legislative liaison activities, such as attendance at committee hearings and gathering information regarding pending legislation, are not lobbying and are allowable. In addition, written or oral communications, appearances before legislative committees and subcommittees, and meetings with legislative representatives are allowable legislative liaison activities when such efforts are undertaken in conjunction with a legislative public hearing or meeting in response to a public notice, or a specific invitation or request from a legislative source, and the notice, invitation, or request is documented, the contractor shall maintain and make available to the Government, records and documentation sufficient to identify the costs and clearly establish the nature and purpose of the legislative liaison activity to which the costs relate."

Id. §1–15.205-52(c). The corresponding rule in the NASAPR provides:

> "Legislative liaison activities, such as attendance at committee hearings, gathering information regarding pending legislation, analysis of the effect of pending legislation, and the like are not lobbying and are allowable. In addition, communications that would be considered lobbying in accordance with [the definition section, *see supra* note 48] shall be allowable if they are performed after receipt of an invitation or request from a congressional or executive branch source."

Id. §1–15.205-51(c).

48. 49 Fed. Reg. 18,261, 18,261 (1984). See also *id.* at 18,278 (the parallel FAR provision). As codified in the FAR:

Costs associated with the following activities are unallowable:

(1) Attempts to influence the outcomes of any Federal, State, or local election, referendum, initiative, or similar procedure, through in kind or cash contributions, endorsements, publicity, or similar activities;

(2) Establishing, administering, contributing to, or paying the expenses of a political party, campaign, political action committee, or other organization established for the purpose of influencing the outcomes of elections;

(3) Any attempt to influence (i) the introduction of Federal or state legislation, or (ii) the enactment or modification or any pending Federal or state legislation through communication with any member or employee of the Congress or state legislature (including efforts to influence state or local officials to engage in similar lobbying activity), or with any government official or employee in connection with a decision to sign or veto enrolled legislation;

(4) Any attempt to influence (i) the introduction of Federal or state legislation, or (ii) the enactment or modification or any pending Federal of state legislation by preparing, distributing or using publicity or propaganda, or by urging members of the general public or any segment thereof to contribute to or participate in any mass demonstration, march, rally, fund raising drive, lobbying campaign or letter writing or telephone campaign; or

(5) Legislative liaison activities, including attendance at legislative sessions or committee hearings, gathering information regarding legislation, and analyzing the effect of legislation, when such activities are carried on in support of or in knowing preparation for an effort to engage in unallowable activities."

48 C.F.R. §31.205-22(a).

49. 49 Fed. Reg. 18,260, 18,261 (A-122—"Lobbying" Revision, Preamble, §III).

50. 48 C.F.R. §1.301(a)(1). They may issue implementing and supplementing regulations for any FAR provision. *Id.*

51. See 53 Fed. Reg. 21,648 (1988) (to be codified at 48 C.F.R. §970.5204–13, -14, and -17) (the latest version of the DOE regulations regarding the recovery of lobbying costs).

52. See 49 Fed. Reg. 18,260, 18,276 (A-122—"Lobbying" Revision, Attachment B, §B21, subsection 1.a).

53. See *infra* notes 100–02 and accompanying text.

54. See *infra* notes 103–04 and accompanying text.

55. See *infra* note 105 and accompanying text.

56. This is not the same as saying that these costs are definitively allowed, although that may be the practical effect. See *supra* notes 13–16 and accompanying text for other theories under which costs may be disallowed even though not specifically prohibited. The FAR excepts from the coverage of the regulation, *supra* note 48, the following:

> "(1) Providing a technical and factual presentation of information on a topic directly related to the performance of a contract through hearing testimony, statements or letters to the Congress or a state legislature, or subdivision, member, or cognizant staff member thereof, in response to a documented request (including a Congressional Record notice requesting testimony or statements for the record at a regularly scheduled hearing) made by the recipient member, legislative body or subdivision, or a cognizant staff member thereof; provided such information is readily obtainable and can be readily put in deliverable form, and further provided that costs under this section for transportation, lodging or meals are unallowable unless incurred for the purpose of offering testimony at a regularly scheduled Congressional hearing pursuant to a written request for such presentation made by the Chairman or Ranking Minority Member of the Committee or Subcommittee conducting such hearing."
>
> (2) Any lobbying made unallowable by [provision (3), *supra* note 48] to influence state legislation in order to directly reduce contract cost, or to avoid material impairment of the contractor's authority to perform the contract."
>
> (3) Any activity specifically authorized by statute to be undertaken with funds from the contract."

    48 C.F.R. §31.205–22(b).

57. 49 Fed. Reg. 18,260, 18,261 (A-122—"Lobbying" Revision, Preamble §III) (parentheticals regarding changes over prior regulations or prior proposed regulations omitted). The last two items, "Contacts with Executive Branch officials * * *" and "Lobbying on regulatory actions" are now covered by the "Executive Lobbying" provision. See *infra* notes 58–60 and accompanying text.

58. See *supra* notes 48–49 and accompanying text.

59. See *supra* text accompanying note 57.

60. 48 C.F.R. §31.205–50 (incorporating the quoted language from 48 C.F.R. §3.401).

61. See generally J. Cibinic, Jr., & R. Nash, Jr., Cost Reimbursement Contracting 551–601 (chapter on payment and audit).

62. See 48 C.F.R. §31.205–22(c) to (f).

63. *Id.* §31.205–22(c).

64. *Id.* §31.205–22(d).

65. *Id.* §31.205–22(e).

66. *Id.* §31.205–22(f).

67. See 49 Fed. Reg. 18,260, 18,276–77 (A-122—"Lobbying" Revision, Attachment B, −B21, §c), *amended* 52 Fed. Reg. 19,788 (1987).

68. 49 Fed. Reg. 18,260, 18,275 (A-122—"Lobbying" Revision, Preamble, §IX) ("The bedrock for enforcing these provisions is voluntary compliance by grantees and contractors.").

69. See 48 C.F.R. §31.205–22(g); 49 Fed. Reg. 18,260, 18,277 (A-122—"Lobbying" Revision, §c5).

70. See 48 C.F.R. §42.705 (Final indirect cost rates); see also OMB Circulars A-73 (Audits of Federal Operations and Programs); A-50 (Audit Follow-up); A-88 (Indirect cost rates, audit, and audit followup at educational institutions); A-110 (uniform administrative requirements for grants and other agreements with institutions of higher education, hospitals, and other nonprofit organizations); A-128 (audits of state and local governments); see generally P. Trueger, *supra* note 42, at 9–18 (discussing interaction of contracting officers and auditors).

71. See 48 C.F.R. §30.

72. 48 C.F.R. §42.302(a)(7).

73. See 48 C.F.R. §42.801 (disallowance before costs incurred); *id.* §42.803 (disallowance after costs incurred).

74. See id. §42.801(f) (disputes over disallowance before the cost is incurred); *id.* §42.803(b)(3) (disputes over disallowance after the cost is incurred).

75. See generally J. Cibinic, Jr., & R. Nash, Jr., *supra* note 61 at 551–601 (chapter on payment and audit); P. Trueger, *supra* note 42, at 9–60 (1988) (chapter devoted to contract audit organizations).

76. See generally P. Trueger, *supra* note 42, at 1091–1109 (chapter devoted to federal inspectors general); *id.* at 1149–1205 (chapter devoted to General Accounting Office).

77. See 48 C.F.R. §42.8; see also 49 Fed. Reg. 18,260, 18,275–76 (1984) (A-122—"Lobbying" Revision, Preamble, §IX) (discussing OMB's enforcement approaches).

78. See 48 C.F.R. §42.8.
79. See 48 C.F.R. §9.406-2 (causes for debarment).
80. 49 Fed. Reg. 18,260, 18,275 (1984) (A-122—"Lobbying" Revision, Preamble, §IX).
81. Associated Press, Dec. 3, 1985, Tuesday, PM cycle; Defense Resumes General Dynamics Payments, Aviation Week and Space Tech., Aug. 5, 1985, at 20.
82. See 18 U.S.C. §1621 (federal perjury statute).
83. See *supra* text accompanying note 64.
84. See *supra* note 41 and accompanying text.
85. See *supra* note 41 and accompanying text. Grantees and awardees of cooperative arrangements are by definition not participating in a procurement action (see *supra* notes 27, 33, and 37 and accompanying text); therefore, they are not subject to the FAR.
86. See *supra* note 41 and accompanying text. See also 45 Fed. Reg. 46,022, 46,024 (1980) (A-122, Attachment A, §A.2) (general principles applicable to nonprofit organizations as awardees).
87. See 45 Fed. Reg. 46,022, 46,024 (1980) (A-122, Attachment A, §A.2).
88. 49 Fed. Reg. 18,260, 18,260 (A-122—"Lobbying" Revision, Preamble §I).
89. *Id.*
90. See *supra* notes 48–49 and accompanying text.
91. See *infra* notes 100–02 and accompanying text.
92. See *infra* notes 103–04 and accompanying text.
93. See *infra* note 105 and accompanying text.
94. See, e.g., 7 U.S.C. §450i(b) (USDA Research Grant Program); 7 C.F.R. §3200 (1988) (USDA Research Grant Program).
95. For those exceptions, see *supra* notes 56–57 and accompanying text.
96. See *supra* text accompanying note 90.
97. For those requirements, see *supra* notes 61–67 and accompanying text.
98. 49 Fed. Reg. 18,260, 18,276 (A-122—"Lobbying" Revision, §c.(1)).
99. For those policies and procedures, see *supra* notes 68–83 and accompanying text.
100. See OMB Circular A-21, §C.2 (general allowability principles for educational institutions) see also *supra* note 41 for a discussion of the very similar provisions relating to for-profit institutions. Awards to educational institutions are regulated by OMB Circular A-110 generally and OMB Circular A-88 concerning audits.
101. See *supra* note 41 and accompanying text.
102. See *supra* note 16 and accompanying text.
103. Though not reflected in its title, OMB Circular A-87 also applies to federally recognized Indian tribal governments. 46 Fed. Reg. 9,548 (1981).
104. See *supra* notes 100–02 and accompanying text. General allowability principles for state and local governments are contained in OMB Circular A-87, §C.2. State and local governments are regulated by OMB Circular A-102 generally and OMB Circular A-128 concerning audits.
105. See *supra* notes 100–02 and accompanying text. Hospitals are governed generally by 45 C.F.R. §74 (1987), which incorporates various OMB Circulars.

8

Tax Deductibility of Lobbying Expenses

Benjamin Beiler, Toni Prestigiacomo

Lobbying activities call into consideration two tax issues: Are business expenditures for "lobbying activities," including contributions to organizations which engage in those activities, tax deductible? Does the activity itself, when conducted by a tax-exempt entity, jeopardize the exempt status of the entity or otherwise impose any financial burdens or other penalties on the entity? This chapter considers the subject of the tax deductibility of expenditures related to lobbying activities. A discussion of the second issue is found in Chapter 9.

Historical Perspective

Section 162 of the Internal Revenue Code permits deductions for all ordinary and necessary expenses incurred in carrying on a trade or business. Expenses of influencing legislation which directly affect a business can logically be considered expenses that are ordinary and necessary for that business. Nevertheless, prior to 1962, expenditures for all legislative activities, including lobbying, the promotion or defeat of legislation, and the exploitation of propaganda other than trade advertising, were nondeductible. Treasury Department regulations established in 1918 specifically barred the deductibility of expenditures for all lobbying activities. Because these regulations were not based on any specific statutory authority, there was considerable doubt as to whether the Treasury Department could legally limit the deductibility of lobbying expenses under a general statute whose only limitation on business expense deductions was that the expenses be "ordinary and necessary."

In *Cammarano v. United States,*[1] the U.S. Supreme Court held that the longstanding provision in the regulations regarding the non-deductibility of lobbying expenses had acquired the "force of law" by virtue of repeated congressional reenactments of the controlling statutory provisions and congressional inaction in revoking the regulations which prohibited the deductibility of any lobbying expenses.[2]

Subsequently, in 1962, Congress enacted Section 162(e) and, in doing so, consciously chose to permit the deduction of expenses related to direct lobbying (e.g., the expenses of communicating with legislators and appearing before legislative committees) as an "ordinary and necessary" business expense under Section 162(e). At the same time, however, Congress retained the prohibition on the deductibility of expenses incurred in connection with grass-roots campaigns.

Current Law

Section 162(e) permits business expense deductions for the direct lobbying of legislators on legislation or proposed legislation of "direct interest" to the taxpayer. This deduction extends to the payment of dues to trade associations, professional societies, and other organizations that engage in direct lobbying activities which are of direct interest to the taxpayer and the organization in which the taxpayer is a member.[3] However, Section 162(e)(2)(B) disallows a deduction for any expenditure in connection with an attempt to influence the general public with respect to legislative matters or referendums. Such activities are usually referred to as "grass-roots lobbying."

Related to the issue of deductibility of direct lobbying expenses is that of the deductibility of institutional or "goodwill" advertising. Section 162(e)(2)(B) permits the deduction of institutional or "goodwill" advertising as an ordinary and necessary business expense in carrying on a trade or business, but only if the purpose of the advertising activity is (1) to keep the taxpayer's name before the public and (2) related to patronage the taxpayer might reasonably expect in the future. For example, a deduction will ordinarily be allowed for the cost of advertising which keeps the taxpayer's name before the public in connection with encouraging contributions to the Red Cross, the purchase of U.S. savings bonds, or participation in similar causes. Also deductible are expenditures for advertising which sets forth views on economic, financial, social, or other subjects of a general nature, but which do not involve grass-roots campaigns aimed at influencing the general public with respect to legislative matters, elections, or referendums.[4]

The Deductibility of Direct Lobbying Expenses

General Rule

Section 162(e)(1)(A) provides that a taxpayer may deduct all "ordinary and necessary" expenses paid or incurred in connection with:

(1) appearances before, submission of statements to, or sending communications to any member or committee of Congress or other legislative body with respect to legislation or proposed legislation of direct interest to the taxpayer; or

(2) communication of information between the taxpayer and an organization in which the taxpayer is a member with respect to legislation or proposed legislation of direct interest to the taxpayer and to the organization.

"Legislation or Proposed Legislation"

The term "legislation or proposed legislation" includes bills and resolutions introduced by a member of Congress or other legislative body for consideration by the body. The term also includes oral or written proposals for legislative action submitted to the legislative body or to a committee or member of the body.[5]

"Direct Interest"

The Treasury regulations define legislation to be of "direct interest" to a taxpayer if the legislation or proposed legislation will, or may reasonably be expected to, affect the trade or business of the taxpayer.[6] It is immaterial whether the effect, or expected effect, on the trade or business will be beneficial or detrimental to the trade or business or whether it will be immediate. However, if the nature of the legislation or proposed legislation is such that the likelihood of its having an effect on the trade or business of the taxpayer is remote or speculative, the legislation or proposed legislation is not of direct interest to the taxpayer.[7]

Under the regulations, the direct interest test is met if the legislation or proposed legislation will affect the taxpayer's trade or business. It is irrelevant that it also will affect the trade or business of other taxpayers or business in general. Further, to meet the direct interest test, it is not necessary that all provisions of the legislation or proposed legislation have an effect on the taxpayer's trade or business. The test is met if one of the provisions of the legislation has the specified effect.[8] Legislation or proposed legislation is of direct interest to a membership organization, such as a trade association or professional society, if it is of direct interest to the organization, as such, or if it is of direct interest to one or more of its members.[9]

The regulations provide the following examples of items of direct interest to a taxpayer's trade or business:

1. Legislation which would increase or decrease the taxes applicable to the trade or business, increase or decrease the operating costs or earnings of the trade or business, or increase or decrease the administrative burdens connected with the trade or business.
2. Legislation which would increase or liberalize the right to Social Security benefits meets the direct interest test. Such changes in the Social Security benefits may reasonably be expected to increase the employer's taxes or affect the retirement benefits which the employer will be asked to provide his employees.
3. Legislation which would impose a retailer's sales tax is of direct interest to a retailer. Although the tax may be passed on to customers, collection of the tax will impose additional burdens on the retailer, and the increased cost of products to the consumer may reduce the demand for them.
4. Legislation which would provide an income tax credit for shareholders is of direct interest to a corporation because those tax benefits may increase the sources of capital available to the corporation.
5. Legislation which would favorably or adversely affect the business of a competitor so as to affect the taxpayer's competitive position is also of direct interest to the taxpayer.[10]

On the other hand, according to the regulations, legislation relating to presidential succession in the event of the death of the President has only a remote and speculative effect on any trade or business and therefore does not meet the direct interest test. Similarly, if a corporation opposes an appropriation bill merely because of a desire for increased government economy with the hope that such economy will eventually cause a reduction in federal income tax, the legislation does not meet the direct interest test. Any effect such legislation may have on the corporation's trade or business is highly speculative.[11] A taxpayer does not have a direct interest in matters such as nominations, appointments, or the operation of a legislation body.[12]

Types of Deductible Lobbying Expenses

The business expense deduction allowed under Section 162(e) is for the "ordinary and necessary business expenses" directly incurred in connection with the taxpayer's appearance before, submission of statements to, or sending communications to the committees or individual members of Congress or other legislative bodies. This includes salaries for personal services, rent, travel expenses, and the cost of preparing testimony.[13]

The Nondeductibility of Grass-Roots Lobbying Expenses

General Rule

The Internal Revenue Code prohibits the deduction of amounts paid in connection with grass-roots lobbying.

Specifically, Section 162(c)(2)(B) provides that any amount paid or incurred "in connection with an attempt to influence the general public, or segments thereof, with respect to legislative matters, elections, or referendums" is not deductible. Treasury regulation §1.162–20(c)(4) provides that no deduction will be allowed for expenses "incurred in connection with 'grassroot' campaigns or any other attempts to urge or encourage the public to contact members of a legislative body for the purpose of proposing, supporting, or opposing legislation."

Definition of "Grass-Roots Lobbying"

Grass-roots lobbying has been defined as a campaign intended to develop a point of view on a legislative matter among the general public, which in turn is directed towards legislators.[14] The lobbying campaign's encouragement to contact legislators does not have to be explicit; it may be implicit depending upon the nature of the audience. For example, a corporation may send communications to its stockholders that explicitly request them to contact their legislators in support of (or in opposition to) pending legislation, or it merely may distribute a pamphlet indicating support for (or opposition to) the legislation. In either case, the communications will be considered grass-roots lobbying because the shareholders are likely to be motivated to contact their legislators.[15] Accordingly, the expenses incurred by a business in printing and distributing these communications will be nondeductible as grass-roots lobbying expenses. The general rule in determining whether a certain communication on a legislative matter will constitute grass-roots lobbying is that the communication itself must be judged without regard to the taxpayer's intention in sending it.[16]

Interpretation of the Internal Revenue Code provisions prohibiting grass-roots lobbying has been limited to only a handful of cases dealing with the deductibility of lobbying expenses. The cases generally involved situations in which a taxpayer engaged in a brief and intensive publicity or advertising campaign directed at a specific pending legislative issue. The *Cammarano* case, for example, was typical of the cases in which deductions have been disallowed for grass-roots lobbying.[17] *Cammarano* involved a publicity campaign by a group of wholesale beer and liquor distributors who opposed specific government initiatives or referendums regarding proposed prohibition measures. The court held that the regulations prohibiting the deductibility of expenses to influence legislation also prohibited the deductibility of expenses for publicity directed at influencing the general public with regard to legislation, initiatives, and referendum.

Another early example is *Pickrick v. United States*.[18] In *Pickrick*, Lestor Maddox, the former governor of Georgia and well known Atlanta restaurateur, ran a series of newspaper advertisements which combined advertising for Mr. Maddox's restaurant with both specific attacks on pending legislative proposals and a generalized statement of conservative political policy. Deductions for one sixth of the cost of this advertising were disallowed on the ground that one sixth of the advertising was barred by the regulations. In view of the *Consumers Power* case (discussed below), it is questionable whether *Pickrick* case would be decided in the same manner today.

Limitation on Grass-Roots Advertising

The leading case on grass-roots advertising is *Consumers Power Co. v. United States*.[19] *Consumers Power* involved an advertising campaign that was highly critical of governmental subsidiaries which were competitors of the taxpayer. The taxpayer retained an opinion research company and an advertising agency to coordinate a program known as "Electric Companies' Advertising Program." The opinion research company conducted public opinion surveys on specific topics, which were later developed into television commercials and magazine advertisements, the cost of which the taxpayer later sought to deduct. Although the court affirmed the government's denial of the taxpayer's deduction, the court rejected the government's rationale for disallowing the deduction. The government had argued that it was the taxpayer's intent to influence legislation. Instead, the court held that

> "the yardstick for use here is the language, and its import, contained in the advertising, the expense for which is sought to be deducted by plaintiff as a necessary and business expense. The regulation refers to 'expenditures * * * for the promotion or defeat of legislation * * * or for carrying on propaganda (including advertising) related to any of the foregoing purposes * * *.' It also refers to 'the cost of advertising to promote or defeat legislation or to influence the public with respect to the desirability or undesirability of proposed legislation * * *.' The advertising itself must be judged. No matter what the intent of its promulgation may have been, if it is clear of the regulatory prohibition, we cannot brand it violative."[20]

The court further stated that a fair reading of the advertisements in question, both individually and collectively, compelled the conclusion that they belonged to the nondeductible category of expenses within the purview of Treas. Reg. §1.162–20. The court rejected the taxpayer's argument that the disallowance should be limited to the total lineage or total wordage which related to the regulatory prohibition. The court concluded that the advertising had to be judged *in toto* and in context, and it attached three of the advertisements to its opinion in order to illustrate its reasoning.[21]

In 1978, the IRS articulated further criteria for identifying non-deductible grass-roots advertising.[22] The revenue ruling held that an advertisement need not refer to specific legislation or request the public to contact their elected representatives. Instead, the prohibition would apply if an advertisement, through words or pictures, was an attempt to develop a grass-roots point of view by influencing the general public, or segments thereof, to propose, support, or oppose legislation.

"General Public, or Segments Thereof"

Corporate shareholders constitute a segment of the general public, and a corporation's communications sent to the shareholders concerning legislation have been held nondeductible.[23] In contrast, an association may contact its members about pending legislation and request that they contact their legislators about the legislation without jeopardizing the tax deductibility of the members' dues or payments to the association. This is based on the rationale that the association members do not constitute a segment of the general public. However, if the association contacts nonmembers or prospective members, or asks its members to contact their employees and customers to support or oppose certain legislation, these contacts will be viewed as being directed at segments of the general public and will likely be considered grass-roots lobbying.[24]

Guidelines

The Internal Revenue Service has not adopted any specific guidelines as to what particular activities constitute grass-roots lobbying. In 1980, however, the Internal Revenue Service issued proposed regulations attempting to clarify the definition of "grass-roots lobbying" by establishing a three-prong test for determining whether a communication constitutes an attempt to influence the general public, or a segment thereof, with respect to legislative matters.[25] The proposed regulations provide that a communication will be considered as an attempt at grass-roots lobbying only if the communication satisfies each of the following three tests:

1. It pertains to legislation being considered by, or likely in the immediate future to be proposed to, a legislative body, or seeks or opposes legislation;
2. It reflects a view with respect to the desirability of legislation (for this purpose, a communication that pertains to legislation

but expresses no explicit view on the legislation shall be deemed to reflect a view on legislation if the communication is selectively disseminated to persons likely to share a common view of the legislation); and

3. It is communicated in a form and distributed in a manner so as to reach individuals as members of the general public, that is, as voters or constituents, as opposed to a communication designed for academic, scientific, or similar purposes. A communication may meet this test even if it reaches the public only indirectly as in a news release submitted to the media.[26]

The proposed regulations also provide that no portion of an expenditure in connection with an advertisement is deductible if any part of the advertisement constitutes an attempt to influence the general public with respect to legislative matters.

The three-prong test set forth in the proposed regulations has never been finalized. Therefore, to provide guidelines as to what types of activities or communications constitute grass-roots lobbying, it is helpful to review situations in which the IRS has found grass-roots lobbying:

1. The expenses incurred by a corporation for preparing, printing, and distributing to its shareholders a pamphlet focusing on proposed legislation that would adversely affect the company's tax liability and suggesting that the shareholders contact their congressmen to make known their views concerning such proposed legislation were not deductible. The communication from the company to its shareholders was held to constitute grass-roots lobbying.[27]

2. The expenses incurred by a corporation in preparing and placing advertisements in major state newspapers and regional magazines setting forth objections to proposed legislation of direct interest to the corporation were not deductible because the corporation's media campaign was a clear attempt to influence the general public to oppose the proposed legislation.[28]

3. The expenses incurred by a corporation in printing and distributing to its shareholders its president's remarks given before a state legislature concerning the corporation's opposition to certain proposed legislation were not deductible. The text distributed to the shareholders was an attempt to influence the shareholders to oppose legislation that was of direct interest to the corporation.[29]

To constitute prohibited grass-roots lobbying there must generally be a legislative matter involved. Activities that merely encourage a viewpoint favorable to the taxpayer's concept and do not involve a discussion of proposed legislation or are focused on nonpartisan educational activities or private conduct will not constitute grass-roots lobbying.[30] For example, advertisements espousing the free enterprise system would not be considered a grass-roots campaign, while those that mentioned pending legislation such as depreciation reform or energy policy would.[31]

Any mention of the tax system or the need for tax reform appears to constitute grass-roots lobbying.[32] Solutions to tax problems are considered to be solely a legislative matter and, therefore, are construed to involve grass-roots lobbying. Accordingly, in one ruling, advertisements and booklets distributed by a trade association to the general public constituted grass-roots lobbying where the main theme of the trade association's advertising campaign was the adverse impact of state taxes on local businesses. Even though no legislation was pending at the time the advertisements ran, the advertisements and booklets were considered an attempt "to create a view or predisposition in the general public" with regard to a legislative matter (i.e., the need for tax reform).[33]

Public opinion surveys and other research materials obtained for gauging the opinions of the public on an issue should not constitute a grass-roots campaign.[34] However, if the surveys were conducted for the direct purpose of communicating with the public, the activity would probably constitute grass-roots lobbying.[35]

The Nondeductibility of Association Dues Spent for Grass-Roots Lobbying

General Rule

Membership dues paid to a trade association, professional society, or other business organization[36] are generally deductible in full by a corporate taxpayer as ordinary and necessary business expenses. If, however, a "substantial part" of the activities of an association consists of grass-roots lobbying, that portion of a taxpayer's dues or payments to the association which is attributable to the grass-roots lobbying expenditures will not be allowed as a business expense deduction. A deduction will be allowed only for the portion of the dues or other payments to the trade association that the taxpayer can clearly establish was spent for direct communications or appearances with respect to legislation or proposed legislation that is of direct interest to the taxpayer and to the association.[37]

Deductibility of Membership Dues

To determine the appropriate tax treatment of a member's dues, an association must use a three-part analysis: First, the association should identify its lobbying activities as direct or grass-roots lobbying. Second, the association must determine the amount of expenditures allocable to grass-roots lobbying. All costs directly related to grass-roots lobbying activities are nondeductible, including printing, mailing, and postage costs, salaries of individuals hired to engage in grass-roots lobbying, and similar expenses. Also nondeductible, but more difficult to ascertain, are the indirect costs of grass-roots lobbying activities, such as allocable portions of the salaries or overhead costs associated with the organization's employees who spend only a portion of their time on grass-roots activities.

Third, the association must determine whether the amount of expenditures allocable to grass-roots activities is a "substantial part" of the association's overall expenditures. Whether a substantial part of a trade association's activities involves grass-roots lobbying is based on all the facts and circumstances.[38] The regulations provide no definitive standards as to what constitutes "substantial" lobbying activities. At one time, the Treasury Department indicated a 5-percent test would be used to determine substantiality.[39] In the past, IRS field personnel have used a 15-percent test to determine substantiality. In 1978, however, the IRS instructed its field personal that the 15-percent test had been superseded by the "facts and circumstances" test to preclude *de minimis* assessments on individual members of an organization, and to eliminate a specific "safe harbor" applicable to all situations.[40] Despite this IRS pronouncement, it likely is safe to assume that grass-roots expenditures totaling less than 15 percent (especially those less than 5 percent) of an association's overall expenditures are not substantial. If the association's grass-roots expenditures are not substantial, the association's members may deduct the total amount of their dues.

Although not currently required, the association's management should perform this cost segregation analysis on an annual basis and provide its members with the proper percentage exclusion of the dues paid for grass-roots lobbying. Under the proposed regulations, exempt organizations such as trade associations and professional societies would be required to provide members or contributors who may deduct dues or contributions as business expenses under Section 162 with a statement showing what percentage of total expenditures during the calendar year was for grass-roots lobbying.[41] The statement would be required, according to the proposal, to be furnished on or before January 31 of the year following the year during which the organization is involved in grass-roots lobbying. However, the proposed regulations do not require statements if the portion of the member's payments to the organization allocable to grass-roots lobbying is: (a) less than $25 or (b) less than $50 and less than 5 percent of the total payments made by that person to the organization for the year.[42]

Conclusion

Businesses, associations, and other entities must be aware of the potential tax consequences of their communications. Based on the most recent IRS pronouncements in the area of grass-roots lobbying, it appears that if the subject matter is controversial and the taxpayer's communication may influence public opinion about that subject (even if specific legislation is not pending), the IRS may rule that the communication is grass-roots lobbying and, therefore, that related expenses are not tax deductible.

Notes

1. 358 U.S. 498 (1959).
2. 358 U.S. at 508–11.
3. I.R.C. §162(e)(1)(B) (1963) (see Appendix J for text).
4. Treas. Reg. §1.162–20(a)(2) (1965).
5. Treas. Reg. §1.162–20(c)(2)(ii)(a) (1965).
6. Treas. Reg. §1.162–20(c)(2)(ii)(b)(1)(i) (1965).
7. *Id.*
8. *Id.*
9. *Id.*
10. Treas. Reg. §1.162–20(c)(2)(ii)(b)(1)(ii) (1965).
11. *Id.*
12. Treas. Reg. §1.162–20(c)(2)(ii)(b)(3) (1965).
13. I.R.C. §162(a) (1982); I.R.C. §162(e) (1963).
14. H.R. REP. No. 1447, 87th Cong., 1st Sess. (1961); S. REP. No. 1881, 87th Cong., 2d Sess. (1962), *reprinted in* 1962 U.S. Code Cong. & Admin. News 3304, 3324–25.
15. Rev. Rul. 78–111, 1978–1 C.B. 41.
16. *Consumers Power Co. v. United States*, 299 F. Supp. 1180 (E.D. Mich. 1969), *aff'd*, 427 F.2d 78 (6th Cir.), *cert. denied*, 400 U.S. 925 (1970).
17. 358 U.S. 498 (1959).
18. 65–2 U.S. T.C. ¶9543 (N.D. Ga. 1965).
19. *Consumers Power Co. v. United States*, 299 F. Supp. 1180 (E.D. Mich. 1969), *aff'd*, 427 F.2d 78 (6th Cir.), *cert. denied*, 400 U.S. 925 (1970).
20. 299 F. Supp. at 1183.
21. 299 F. Supp. at 1183, 1214–16.
22. Rev. Rul. 78–112, 1978–1 C.B. 42.
23. Rev. Rul. 74–407, 1974–2 C.B. 45, Rev. Rul. 78–111, 1978–1 C.B. 41.
24. Rev. Rul. 78–113, 1978–1 C.B. 43, Rev. Rul. 78–114, 1978–1 C.B. 44.
25. There are three statutory provisions in the Internal Revenue Code that govern the taxability of grass-roots lobbying: (1) Sec. 162(e), which limits the deduction of grass-roots lobbying expenditures for business taxpayers (e.g., associations); (2) Sec. 4945, which imposes an excise tax on grass-roots lobbying by private foundations; and (3) Sec. 4911(d)(1)(A), which limits the expenditures for grass-roots lobbying by electing public charities. Because each of these provisions has a different tax policy objective, Congress has provided slightly different definitions of grass-roots lobbying under each provision. On December 23, 1988, the IRS published proposed regulations under Secs. 4911 and 4945 regarding lobbying expenditures by certain tax-exempt public charities and private foundations. 53 Fed. Reg. 51,826 (1988) (see Appendix K for text). These regulations propose to define grass-roots lobbying as a communication that (1) refers to specific legislation; (2) reflects a view on such legislation; and (3) encourages the recipients of the communication to take action with respect to such legislation. Prop. Treas. Reg. §56.4911–5(f)(6)(ii), 53 Fed. Reg. 51,826 (1988).
    Although there have been many questions concerning the scope of this definition, it appears to apply only for purposes of limiting expenditures for grass-roots lobbying by electing public charities. Jerome P. Walsh Skelley, the author of the 1988 regulations, informed the authors of this chapter that the definition of grass-roots lobbying contained in the new proposed regulations is not intended to supersede the definition of grass-roots lobbying contained in the proposed regulations under Sec. 162(e). Therefore, for guidance in determining the deductibility of grass-roots lobbying expenditures, trade associations should look to the definition of grass-roots lobbying in the 1980 proposed regulations under Sec. 162(e).

26. Prop. Treas. Reg. §1.162–20(c)(4)(i), 45 Fed. Reg. 78,767 (1980).

27. Rev. Rul. 74–407, 1974–2 C.B.45.

28. Rev. Rul. 78–112, 1978–1 C.B. 42.

29. Rev. Rul. 78–111, 1978–1 C.B. 41.

30. Treas. Reg. §1.162–20(a)(2) (1965), and Prop. Treas. Reg. §1.162–20(c)(4)(iii), Example (1), 45 Fed. Reg. 78,767 (1980). See Becken, *A Tax Practitioner's Primer On Grass-roots Lobbying,* 59 TAXES—THE TAX MAGAZINE 93, 95 (1981).

31. *Id.*

32. Prop. Treas. Reg. §1.162–20(c)(4)(iii), Example (2), 45 Fed. Reg. 78,767 (1980); see Becken, *A Tax Practitioner's Primer on Grass-roots Lobbying,* 59 TAXES—THE TAX MAGAZINE 93, 95 (1981).

33. Priv. Ltr. Rul. 79–51-012, Sept. 13, 1979.

34. See Becken, *A Tax Practitioner's Primer on Grass-roots Lobbying,* 59 TAXES—THE TAX MAGAZINE 93, 95 (1981).

35. Priv. Ltr. Rul. 80–14-002, Sept. 12, 1979. This letter ruling was subsequently withdrawn by Priv. Ltr. Rul. 80–30-102, Aug. 6, 1980, and superseded by Priv. Ltr. Rul. 81–15-024, Apr. 22, 1981. In Priv. Ltr. Rul. 81–15-024, the IRS disallowed deductions for advertisements and educational material used in a nuclear industry campaign to broaden public support for the development of nuclear power. Deductions for the following items were disallowed: four-page educational articles containing one or two sentences on legislative matters; the funding and distribution of an independent study that was favorable to the taxpayer's position (the expenses of the study alone would have been deductible, however, such expenses became nondeductible when the favorable results of the study were distributed to the general public); and certain locally and nationally placed advertisements which coincided with five state referendums on nuclear power.

36. Generally, these organizations are tax-exempt pursuant to I.R.C. §501(c)(6).

37. Treas. Reg. §1.162–20(c)(3) (1965).

38. *Id.*

39. *Hearings on H.R. 10650 Before the Senate Finance Comm.,* 87th Cong., 2d. Sess. pt. 10, at 4365–66 (1962).

40. Audit Survey of Grass-roots Lobbying and Certain Other Activities Conducted by I.R.C. §501(c)(5) and (c)(6) Organizations, IRM Supplement 4(11) 6–57 (Feb. 3, 1978), INT. REV. MANUAL (Administration) −22,651.

41. Prop. Treas. Reg. §1.6033–2(k)

42. *Id.*

9

Lobbying by Charitable Organizations

Paula Cozzi Goedert

The laws which restrain some tax-exempt organizations from participating in lobbying and political campaigning are among the most troublesome in the Internal Revenue Code. The laws are often viewed by these organizations as a violation of the constitutional rights of freedom of speech and to petition the government. Frequently, charitable ends can be best accomplished through a legislative means, and yet those means are foreclosed. The statutory provisions are seen as an attempt by Congress to seal itself off from what would surely be a torrent of entreaties for social improvements.

From another perspective, the law can be viewed as preventing all American citizens (or the tax-paying ones) from sharing the costs for each special interest group promoting its own view of how the country should be run. As the U.S. Supreme Court analyzed the law, Congress may not *penalize* lobbying, but it is not required by the First Amendment to *subsidize* it by extending tax-exempt status to organizations that do lobby.[1]

Restrictions on Section 501(c)(3) Organizations

Charitable, educational, and religious organizations which are exempt under Section 501(c)(3) of the Internal Revenue Code ("C-3" organizations) enjoy the most favorable tax treatment, as they are themselves exempt from tax and eligible to receive tax-deductible contributions. They are also subject to the most stringent prohibitions on political activity. Since 1934,[2] C-3 organizations have been subject to a lobbying restriction that has varied only slightly in intervening revenue acts: no substantial part of the activities of a C-3 organization may consist of carrying on "propaganda" or otherwise at-

145

tempting to influence legislation. A prohibition against campaign intervention, added in 1954, provides that a C-3 organization may not participate or intervene (including the publishing or distributing of statements) in any political campaign on behalf of or in opposition to any candidate for public office.[3]

The general lobbying and campaign intervention rules are of critical importance to C-3s because the penalty for transgression is revocation of tax-exempt status. The severity of the penalty, however, lessens the chance of its application. IRS auditors are sometimes very hesitant to apply a penalty which the C-3 would be likely to challenge in litigation in order to avoid extinction. The vagueness of some of the rules also gives the C-3 latitude to argue that its activities are not within the scope of the rules. On the other hand, a C-3 that engages in lobbying or campaign intervention must do so knowing that if its actions are found to be outside the rules, it will lose its tax-exempt status, which is usually among a C-3's most valued assets.

The Treasury regulations under Section 501(c)(3) explain the lobbying and campaign intervention rules.[4] They provide that an organization will be entitled to receive and maintain 501(c)(3) status only if it is "operated exclusively" for one or more tax-exempt purposes. An organization is not operated for one or more tax-exempt purposes it if is an "action" organization. An organization is deemed an "action" organization if it meets any one of three tests, which can be summarized as follows: (1) a substantial part of its activities consist of lobbying, (2) it participates in political campaigns, or (3) its primary purposes can be accomplished only through legislation.

Lobbying Activities

The regulations define "lobbying" broadly as "attempting to influence legislation by propaganda or otherwise."[5] An organization is attempting to influence legislation if it contacts, or urges the public to contact, members of a legislative body for the purpose of proposing, supporting, or opposing legislation, or if it advocates the adoption or rejection of legislation.[6] Legislation is defined to include any action by Congress, any state legislature, any local council or similar governing body, or by the public in a referendum, initiative, constitutional amendment, or similar procedure. The definition was intended to be all-encompassing with respect to the actions of legislative bodies but apparently was not intended to cover actions by the executive, judicial, or administrative branches or government. Related provisions in the Treasury regulations exclude school boards, housing authorities, sewer and water districts, zoning boards, and other similar federal, state, or local special-purpose bodies as well as executive or judicial bodies.[7]

A C-3 is not engaged in lobbying if it responds to a request of a legislative body to provide testimony on pending legislation. If the C-3 initiates the request, however, a different result applies.[8] The Revenue Ruling explaining this result states that "it is unlikely that Congress * * * intended to deny itself access to the best technical expertise available on any matter on which it concerns itself."[9] This position permits congressional committees to hear what they want to hear and to effectively exclude, by declining to invite, groups whose views might differ from their own.

Neither the statute nor the Treasury regulations place an absolute prohibition on lobbying activity. A C-3 violates the rules only if a "substantial" part of its activities constitutes lobbying. Neither the Internal Revenue Code nor the Treasury regulations define this crucial term. The courts have generally not adopted a flat dollar or percentage test for determining substantiality, on the theory that any across-the-board test would obscure the complexity of balancing an organization's activities in relation to its objectives and circumstances.[10]

For example, in one case,[11] the court reviewed the circumstances of a Christian publisher and broadcaster which held tax-exempt status as a religious organization. The court cited 22 examples of politically oriented articles that the organization had published, but did not mention the total number of articles in the pool from which the sample was taken. Rejecting a percentage test, the court found that the numerous exhibited articles indicated that an "essential part" of the program of Christian Echoes was to promote desirable governmental policies consistent with its objectives through legislation. The court was apparently influenced by the fact that politically oriented articles were published regularly and continuously, and found this more persuasive than evidence of the relative number of such articles compared to all articles published.

The courts have not, however, uniformly equated "substantial" activities with regular or continuous activities, regardless of proportion. In another case,[12] for example, the plaintiff claimed that Section 501(c)(3) is unconstitutionally discriminatory in that it permits wealthier organizations to engage in numerous instances of lobbying while poorer organizations could lose their tax-exempt status for engaging in the same activities, because their politically oriented expenditures would be substantial in relation to their total budget. The court found sufficient merit in this argument to reverse and remand, although the case was ultimately disposed of on procedural grounds.

The judicial confusion and lack of statutory guidance as to the meaning of "substantial" activity led Congress to provide a "safe harbor" election for C-3s desiring to engage in some lobbying activity.[13] A C-3 need not, however, make the election to engage in lobbying. In the absence of an election, the "substantial" standard will continue to apply.

Campaign Intervention

The second type of activity that may qualify a C-3 as an "action" organization is intervention in political campaigns. The Treasury regulations state that a C-3 is an action organization if it participates or intervenes, directly or indirectly, in any political campaign on behalf or in opposition to any candidate for public office.[14] A "candidate for public office" is one who offers himself or herself, or is proposed by others, as a contestant for an elective public office, whether the office is national, state, or local. Intervention includes, but is not limited to, the publication or distribution of written or printed statements or the making of oral statements.

The rule against campaign intervention is not governed by the "substantial" test applicable to lobbying. C-3s are subject to an absolute prohibition against campaign intervention. C-3s must carefully monitor all activities, including all written documents and all oral addresses by representatives, to insure compliance. C-3s would be well advised to include an explanation of these rules in material distributed to new officers and directors so as to prevent inadvertent violations due to ignorance of the rules. The likely complainant to the IRS would be the criticized candidate or the opponent of the praised candidate.

As an example of how easily the rule is violated, a federal court found that a C-3 medical society had engaged in electioneering because it mentioned in its newsletter the names of certain political candidates who happened to be members of the society.[15] The newsletter stated that the candidates supported the fight against socialized medicine. Presumably, the mere mention of their candidacy would not have been found to be a violation, but the favorable comment on their position on an issue made the activity impermissible.

The IRS has agreed that certain voter education activities do not constitute campaign intervention, but has severely limited the scope of this exception. An organization that annually publishes the voting records of members of Congress on legislative issues on a wide range of subjects is engaged in voter education as opposed to campaign intervention.[16] An organization that solicits answers to a questionnaire from all candidates for an office, and publishes the responses without comment or bias, is also engaged in voter education.[17] If the questions reflect a bias on any issues, however, the activity will be considered campaign intervention.[18] In addition, if distribution by the C-3 of information about candidates' views by the C-3 is limited to issues with respect to which the C-3 has a particular interest, the IRS takes the position that the activity is not being undertaken to further voter education, but rather to influence voters to support candidates favorable to the C-3. The activity is therefore prohibited.[19]

This last position is particularly harsh and was softened somewhat by the IRS in a later pronouncement. If the C-3 publishes the voting record of all congressional incumbents on a particular issue without highlighting those of candidates, and points out the inherent limitations of judging candidates by their stand on isolated issues, the activity will not be deemed campaign intervention. The information must be distributed in a manner so that it is unlikely to have an impact on any campaign outcome. The example given by the IRS describes a C-3 that distributes nationwide a few thousand copies of this kind of publication to its members not concentrated in any particular state or congressional district.[20] The ruling makes a fine distinction between permitted and prohibited activities and should be followed with caution.

The IRS has been slow to apply the prohibition against campaign activities in traditional educational settings. For example, a university does not jeopardize its tax-exempt status where, as a part of a political science course, it requires students to participate in political campaigns of their choice.[21] Similarly, the fact that a university newspaper publishes editorials supporting political candidates does not jeopardize its tax-exempt status if the editorial policy is determined by the students, rather than representatives of the university.[22]

Legislation Necessary to the Organization's Purpose

An organization will be considered to be an action organization and ineligible for C-3 status if its main or primary objectives (as distinguished from incidental or secondary objectives) can be attained only by legislation or the defeat of proposed legislation and the organization advocates or campaigns for the attainment of those objectives.[23] The term "legislation" includes foreign as well as domestic laws. Thus a nonprofit organization formed to influence the laws of a foreign government was ineligible for exemption as a C-3 because its goals could only be attained through legislation.[24]

This section of the Treasury regulations was also applied to prohibit the exemption of an educational institution formed to research the impact of property taxes on land values for the purpose of advocating their abolition. Because the abolition of real property taxes could only be achieved through legislative means, and the organization encouraged that result, the organization was deemed to be an action organization ineligible for C-3 status.[25]

Excise Taxes on Political and Lobbying Expenditures

To discourage a perceived abuse by C-3s of the laws which limit lobbying and prohibit electioneering, Congress imposed two new excise taxes in the Revenue Act of 1987. To add extra force to the discouragement, Congress pronounced that managers of C-3s could be personally liable for an excise tax in certain circumstances.

With respect to lobbying expenditures, new Section 4912 imposes an excise tax of 5 percent on the "lobbying expenditures" incurred by a C-3 during a year for which it loses its C-3 status because its lobbying expenditures were substantial. The tax applies only to organizations that did not elect to come under the "safe harbor" rules of Section 501(h) for the year. As discussed later in this chapter, more severe penalties are imposed on C-3s which do elect to be governed by the Section 501(h) rules and then transgress them. For purposes of the excise tax, the "lobbying expenditures" on which the tax is imposed are defined as amounts paid to carry on propaganda or attempt to influence legislation.

This tax by itself would most likely have little impact on an organization contemplating a lobbying expenditure. The loss of tax-exempt status alone is usually seen as a severe penalty, not only because the net income for the year becomes taxable, but also because of the adverse publicity. The imposition of a 5 percent excise tax to accompany revocation of tax-exempt status could be compared to the imposition of an excise tax to accompany capital punishment. In contrast, most persons responsible for C-3s would pay attention to a potential penalty, no matter how small, which might be assessed against them personally.

If a C-3 is liable for the 5 percent excise tax, any manager of the C-3 may also be liable for an additional 5 percent excise tax on the same lobbying expenditures if he or she agreed to the making of the expenditure knowing that the expenditure was likely to result in loss of C-3 status. The manager is excused from such liability if the agreement was not willful and was due to reasonable cause. If more than one person qualifies as a manager, they will be jointly and severally liable for the tax. The conditions for liability for the tax should give managers room to maneuver around it in all but the most flagrant cases. As a starting point for a defense, a manager might point to the legislative history of Section 501(h), which confirms that the "substantial" standard of Section 501(c)(3) is vague.[26] The uncertainty of the standard may well have prevented the manager from knowing that the expenditure would have caused the C-3 to violate it.

Another excise tax is imposed on electioneering expenses of C-3s, regardless of whether the political expenditure resulted in loss of exempt status. Section 4955 imposes a 10 percent excise tax on any "political expenditure," defined as any amount paid by a C-3 to participate or intervene in any political campaign on behalf of or in opposition to any candidate for public office, including the publication or distribution of any statements.

If an expenditure is made, the C-3 not only is automatically liable for the 10 percent tax, but it must take action to correct the transgression or it will become liable for an additional tax equal to 100 percent of the expenditures. The correction required by Section 4955 is the recovery of part or all of the expenditure, to the extent recovery is possible and, where not possible, future regulations will prescribe a suitable alternative. In addition, the C-3 must establish safeguards to prevent future political expenditures. The correction must be made before the earlier of the date the excise tax is assessed or the date of any notice of deficiency with respect to the excise tax.

The provision contains special rules for C-3s that are found to have been formed primarily for promoting a candidacy or are controlled by a candidate or prospective candidate and are used for these purposes. Political expenditures include amounts paid to the candidate for speeches, travel, polls, publicity, or any other actions that promote the candidate's public recognition or accrue to his or her benefit. These rules would seem to address abusive cases, as a C-3 cannot be formed primarily for such purposes. The C-3s to which these special rules would apply might have failed to disclose their true purposes on the application for tax-exempt status, or might have radically changed their purposes from the time of application.

The Section 501(h) Election

The vagueness of the rules governing lobbying and political activities of C-3s led Congress to enact a "safe harbor" election as a part of the Tax Reform Act of 1976.[27] Embodied in Section 501(h) of the Internal Revenue Code, the provision attempts to quantify the "substantial" standard applicable to lobbying activity by using expenditures as a measure of the activity. It permits certain C-3s to elect to be governed by its provisions, but those that do not or cannot make the election remain subject to the "substantial" standard.

Section 501(h) specifically provides that it shall not be construed to affect the interpretation of the "substantial standard" with respect to nonelecting C-3s, or C-3s that are not eligible to make the election. The legislative history of the provision shows that Congress was concerned that some C-3s might not want to comply with the disclosure requirements of the provision; Congress did not want to subject C-3s to the choice between disclosure and abandonment of all lobbying activity.[28]

It is important to note that Section 501(h) was intended by Congress to provide a "safe harbor" only with respect to the requirement in Section 501(c)(3) that no substantial part of the activities of a qualified organization consists of carrying on propaganda or influencing, or attempting to influence, legislation. It does not affect the question of whether an expenditure might cause the C-3 to lose its exempt status because it is not being operated "exclusively" for charitable, scientific, or educational purposes, which is a separate requirement in Section 501(c)(3). In other words, lobbying activity may violate two separate clauses of Section 501(c)(3), but Section 501(h) only provides a "safe harbor" with respect to one of them. This interpretation is set forth in a footnote in the House Report on the proposed language that became law, but may be open to challenge based on the actual wording of the statute.[29] Section 501(h) states that "exemption from taxation under subsection (a) shall be denied because a substantial part of the activities of such organization consists of carrying on propaganda, or otherwise attempting to influence legislation, but only if such organization normally" makes expenditures in excess of specified limits. The plain wording of the statute thus provides that lobbying activity will cause exemption to be denied only if expenditures exceed the limits. The use of the phrase "only if" would seem to preclude the position that lobbying activities could cause loss of exempt status for any reason other than violation of the expenditure limits.

The Section 501(h) election is generally available to publicly supported charities exempt under Section 501(c)(3). Private foundations are not eligible.[30] In addition, Section 501(h) prohibits church-related C-3s from making the election. This includes not only churches, but auxiliaries of churches, associations or conventions of churches, and members of affiliated groups of organizations if one or more members are such church-related C-3s.

In general, Section 501(h) provides for a dollar limitation on permissible lobbying expenditures each year. If an electing C-3 exceeds the permitted limit, it will be subject to an excise tax of 25 percent of its excess expenditures. If the average lobbying expenditures over a four-year period exceed 150 percent of those permitted, the organization will be stripped of its exempt status.

Covered Lobbying Activities

Section 501(h) provides a "safe harbor" only for political activities that come under the headings of direct lobbying or grass-roots lobbying. No electioneering or campaign activities are covered; these remain prohibited activities that could cause a C-3 to lose its exempt status if engaged in to any extent.[31]

Direct lobbying includes any attempt to influence legislation through communication with any member or employee of a legislative body or with any government official or employee who may participate in the formulation of legislation.[32] Certain activities are excluded from the type of direct lobbying activities that must be accounted for by electing C-3s. These are the dissemination of the results of nonpartisan research, study, or analysis, and the provision of technical advice or assistance to a governmental unit in response to a written request. In addition, the statute excludes so-called defensive lobbying—i.e., appearances before, or communications to, any legislative body with respect to proposed or enacted legislation affecting the powers, duties, tax-exempt status, or deductibility of contributions of or to the C-3.[33] The exclusion of these activities is apparently intended to permit electing C-3s to engage in the activities without limitation.

The second type of lobbying covered by a Section 501(h) election, grass-roots lobbying, is defined as efforts to influence legislation through an attempt to affect the opinions of the general public or any segment of it. Communications between a C-3 and its members with respect to proposed or enacted legislation of direct interest to the organization and its members is not included in the definition of grass-roots lobbying, and is thus protected. If, however, the communication urges the member to contact the legislature or other government representative, or urges members to urge nonmembers to do so, the activity is considered grass-roots lobbying.[34]

The statute exempts only communications with "bona fide" members. To be a bona fide member, the person must have more than a nominal connection with the C-3 and should have affirmatively requested membership.[35] By this limitation, Congress intended to prevent a C-3 from unilaterally proclaiming whole classes of persons (e.g., all residents of a particular city or state) to be "members" of the organization on the theory that this would permit the C-3 to communicate with these members on legislative topics without limitation. The legislative history further provides that a payment of dues or a contribution of time in more than a nominal amount, or selection as a "life" or honorary member for valid reasons, will be additional factors considered in determining whether members are bona fide. These factors are not intended, however, to be exclusive. A C-3 with different membership requirements may be eligible to treat its members as "bona fide" if it can convince the Internal Revenue Service that its membership qualifications do not serve as a subterfuge for grassroots lobbying.[36]

A communication with bona fide members will not be disqualified simply because an insubstantial number of copies are sent to nonmembers. The fact that a C-3 sends copies of its newsletter or magazine to libraries or other nonmember subscribers will not cause any portion of the communication to be considered grass-roots lobbying unless the copies distributed to nonmembers exceeds 50 percent of the total distribution.[37]

Proposed Treasury regulations define the term "grass-roots lobbying communication" to include only those communications that: (1) refer to specific legislation; (2) reflect a view on such legislation; and (3) encourage the recipient of the communication to take action with respect to such legislation.[38]

Importantly, a communication is not a grass-roots lobbying communication unless the communication's reference to legislation is to "specific legislation." This term includes both legislation that has already been introduced in a legislative body and a specific legislative proposal that the organization either supports or opposes.[39]

The rules also indicate that a communication is not a grass-roots lobbying communication unless it encourages its recipients to take action with respect to the specific legislation. A communication encourages its recipients to take action only if the communication:

(1) states that the recipient should contact a legislator or an employee of a legislative body, or should contact any other government official or employee who may participate in the formulation of legislation (but only if the principal purpose of

    urging contact with the government official or employee is to influence legislation);

(2) states the address, telephone number, or similar information of a legislator or an employee of a legislative body;

(3) provides a petition, tear-off postcard, or similar material for the recipient to communicate his or her views to a legislator or an employee of a legislative body, or to any other government official or employee who may participate in the formulation of legislation (but only if the principal purpose of so facilitating contact with the government official or employee is to influence legislation); or

(4) specifically identifies one or more legislators who will vote on the legislation as: (a) opposing the communication's view with respect to the legislation; (b) being undecided with respect to legislation; (c) being the recipient's representative in the legislature; (d) being a member of the legislative committee that will consider the legislation. Encouraging the recipient to take action under this fourth category does not include naming the main sponsor(s) of the legislation for purposes of identifying the legislation.[40]

Communications that are described in categories (1) through (3) above are deemed not only to encourage action with respect to legislation, but also to "directly encourage" action with respect to legislation. This distinction is important because only communications in category (4), which encourage the recipient to take action with respect to legislation without "directly encouraging" such action, may be within the exception for nonpartisan analysis, study, or research and, as a result, not be grass-roots lobbying communication.[41]

The one exception to the above three-part definition of lobbying is a special rule for certain mass media communications. If within two weeks before a vote by a legislative body, or committee thereof, on a highly publicized piece of legislation, an organization makes a communication in the mass media that reflects a view on the general subject of such legislation and either (1) refers to the highly publicized legislation or (2) encourages the public to communicate with their legislators on the general subject of such legislation, then the communication will be presumed to be a grass-roots lobbying communication.[42] An organization can rebut this presumption by demonstrating that the communication is a type of communication regularly made by the organization in the mass media without regard to the timing of legislation (that is, a customary course of business exception) or that the timing of the communication was for reasons unrelated to the upcoming legislative action.[43] For purposes of this special rule, the term "mass media" means television, radio, and certain general-circulation newspapers and magazines. Any mass media communication that is not made within two weeks before a legislative vote on a highly publicized piece of legislation will be tested by the general three-part test for grass-roots lobbying.

Excess Lobbying Expenditures

A C-3 that elects to be governed by Section 501(h) will incur tax if it has "excess lobbying expenditures." A C-3's excess lobbying expenditures are the greater of its total lobbying expenditures in excess of the permitted level, or its grass-roots lobbying expenditures in excess of the permitted level.[44]

Nontaxable levels of direct and grass-roots lobbying expenditures are measured as a percentage of "exempt purpose expenditures."[45] These are the total amounts paid or incurred by the C-3 to further the charitable, educational, scientific, or other exempt purpose for which it was organized.[46] The larger a C-3's exempt purpose expenditures, the larger will be the amount it can spend on lobbying without incurring a tax.

The computation of exempt purpose expenditures requires some adjustment from a simple total of cash outlay. Expenditures for assets with a useful life, exceeding one year, or other capital items must be capitalized rather than counted as a lump sum in the year spent. An allowance for depreciation on the capital assets may, however, be included in the yearly total of exempt purpose expenditures over the assets' lives. Expenditures related to an unrelated business are also excluded from the total. Amounts paid to a unit of the C-3 which engages primarily in fundraising, or amounts paid to nonemployee fundraisers, are also excluded from exempt purpose expenditures.[47] Amounts paid for administrative expenses are includable in exempt purpose expenditures, provided that they are incurred for exempt purposes.[48] The wording of the proviso implies that administrative expenses allocable to other purposes, such as an unrelated business, must be excluded from exempt purpose expenditures. Amounts provided for lobbying are also included in the total, whether or not they are incurred in furtherance of the organization's exempt purpose. Amounts paid to other C-3s will also generally be included in exempt purpose expenditures, unless the donor C-3 earmarks the contribution to be used for a nonqualified purpose.[49]

The percentage of exempt purpose expenditures that an electing C-3 can spend on lobbying varies based on the following scale:

If the exempt purpose expenditures are	*The nontaxable amount is*
Not over $500,000	20% of the exempt purpose expenditures
Over $500,000 but not over $1,000,000	$100,000 plus 15% of the excess of the exempt purpose expenditures over $500,000
Over $1,000,000 but not over $1,500,000	$175,000 plus 10% of the exempt purpose expenditures over $1,000,000

Over $1,500,000 $225,000 plus 5% of the excess of the exempt purpose expenditures over $1,500,000

In no event, however, can total direct lobbying expenditures exceed $1,000,000.[50]

The amount that an organization can spend on grass-roots lobbying during any taxable year equals 25 percent of the amount it can spend on direct lobbying for the same year.[51] Note that grass-roots lobbying expenditures are counted in total lobbying expenditures, which are measured against the sliding scale, and are then subjected to the separate test for grass-roots lobbying expenditures. The excess lobbying expenditures for the year will be the greater of (a) the excess of total lobbying expenditures over the permitted nontaxable amounts or (b) the excess of the grass-roots lobbying expenditures for the year over the permitted nontaxable amounts.[52]

Total lobbying expenditures include all "direct lobbying expenditures" and "grass-roots lobbying expenditures." Direct lobbying expenditures are any amounts paid or incurred for, or in connection with, lobbying.[53] They include the allocable portion of administrative, overhead, and other general expenditures attributable to direct lobbying.[54] "Grass-roots lobbying expenditures" are any amounts paid or incurred for, or in connection with, grass-roots lobbying, including allocable portions of administrative, overhead, and other general expenditures.[55]

A mixed grass-roots and direct lobbying expenditure is to be treated as a grass-roots expenditure, except to the extent that the organization demonstrates that the expenditure was incurred primarily for direct lobbying purposes, in which case a reasonable allocation must be made between the direct and grass-roots lobbying purposes served by the communication.[56]

For lobbying communications that also serve a bona fide nonlobbying purposes, such as fund raising, there are two different allocation rules. Which rule is used depends upon whether the communication is sent primarily to members or nonmembers.[57]

For communications that are sent primarily to bona fide members (that is, for communications sent to more members than nonmembers), an organization must make a reasonable allocation between the amount expended for the lobbying purpose and the amount spend for the nonlobbying purpose. Including as a lobbying expenditure only the amount expended for the specific sentence or sentences that encourage the recipient to action is not considered a reasonable allocation.[58]

For lobbying communications that are not sent primarily to bona fide members, all costs attributable to those parts of the communication that are on the same specific subject as the lobbying message must be included as lobbying expenditures for allocation purposes.[59] The costs attributable to parts of a lobbying communication that are not on the same specific subject as the lobbying message are not considered a lobbying expenditures. Whether or not a portion of a communication is on the same specific subject as the lobbying message will depend on the surrounding facts and circumstances. In general, a portion of a communication will be on the same specific subject as the lobbying message if that portion discusses an activity that would be directly affected by the proposed legislation that is the subject of the lobbying message. Moreover, discussion of the background or consequences of either the proposed legislation or of an activity directly affected by the proposed legislation will also be considered to be on the same specific subject as the lobbying communication.[60]

As part of the same legislation which enacted Section 501(h), Congress also added a provision to the Internal Revenue Code that prohibits deductions for out-of-pocket lobbying expenditures made on behalf of C-3s eligible to make a Section 501(h) election.[61] Congress was concerned that C-3s with a Section 501(h) election would attempt to reduce their lobbying expenditures by having individuals pay them directly on the theory that the individuals would then be eligible for a charitable contribution deduction.[62] In closing this possible loophole, Congress prohibited charitable deductions for lobbying expenditures, whether or not the C-3 has made a Section 501(h) election; to do otherwise would have penalized C-3s for electing what Congress perceived to be a relief provision.

Affiliated Groups

If a C-3 is a member of an affiliated group, the lobbying rules are generally expanded to cover actions or expenditures by another member of the group.[63] "Affiliation" is given a unique definition for this purpose. Two organizations will be considered affiliated if the governing instrument of one organization requires it to be bound by the decisions of the other organization on legislative matters. In addition, they will be considered affiliated if one organization has representatives on the governing body of the other organization who, by pooling their votes, have sufficient voting power to cause or prevent action on legislative issues.[64]

For example, a national association, state council, and local chapter each has a nine-member board of directors and each is a C-3. The articles of incorporation of the state council require that five members of its board shall be board members of the national association. The articles of incorporation of the local chapter require that five members of its board shall be members of the board of directors of the state council. The three C-3s form an affiliate group for purposes of Section 501(h).[65]

The legislative history indicates the concern of Congress that

C-3s would create numerous related organizations to circumvent the decreasing percentage test applied to exempt purpose expenditures and the $1 million ceiling on total lobbying expenditures.[66] To prevent this possibility, the law requires the calculation of excess lobbying expenditures to be made as if the affiliated group constituted one entity.

This means that if any member of an affiliated group has a Section 501(h) election in effect, the lobbying expenditures of all C-3 members of the group will be counted to determine whether the group has excess lobbying expenditures. The same percentage tests will be applied to the exempt purpose expenditures of the entire group, no matter how many C-3s are included. The liability for any excise tax on excess lobbying expenditures will be apportioned among the C-3 members of the group with a Section 501(h) election in effect for the year.[67] If the excess lobbying expenditures for the group exceed the absolute limits imposed by Section 501(h), each C-3 member of the group with a Section 501(h) election status in effect will lose its tax-exempt status.[68]

Status as a member of an affiliated group confers some benefits as well as burdens. Expenditures excluded from consideration as direct lobbying because they are "self- defense" lobbying expenditures are deemed to include expenses for legislative activity with respect to the existence, powers, duties, or tax status of an affiliated group member. Similarly, expenditures excluded from grass-roots lobbying expenditures as communications with members are deemed to include communications with members of the other organizations included in the affiliated group.[69]

For purposes of making affiliated group computations, the taxable year of the group will be presumed to be a calendar year. The only permitted exception to this rule is for group members that all have the same noncalendar fiscal years: that fiscal year will be used to determine the various expenditures in deciding whether an excise tax is due.[70]

The affiliation rules are further complicated by special provisions which provide limited relief from the group calculation in those rare instances in which members meet the definition of an affiliated group only because governing instruments provide for control on issues with respect to national legislation. In general, the controlling organization need only count the national lobbying expenditures of the controlled organization in its Section 501(h) computations, and the controlled organization is not treated as a member of the affiliated group.[71]

The legislative history dealing with the affiliation provisions acknowledges that they may have a significant impact on the liability of C-3 for an excise tax or possible loss of exemption. Because of the complex nature of the rules, Congress charged the Internal Revenue Service with the duty to issue ruling letters to requesting C-3s on the question of affiliation. As with any ruling requests, however, C-3s should proceed with caution. The Internal Revenue Service can usually be expected to make a conservative interpretation of the law. A request for a ruling might focus attention on political activities that would be better unnoticed. The invitation of Congress does serve the useful purpose of reminding C-3s to consider all possible ramifications of the affiliation rules before rushing into a Section 501(h) election.

Loss of Exemption

As a part of its 1987 examination of permissible and impermissible C-3 lobbying, Congress focused on the fate of C-3s that became disqualified due to lobbying activity. Congress was concerned that disqualified C-3s could retain tax-exempt status (but not the ability to accept tax-deductible contributions) by claiming exemption as a social welfare organization under Section 501(c)(4). This not only lessened the severity of the punishment inflicted on C-3s for excessive lobbying, but it also gave rise to a possible loophole. A C-3 could build a large war chest from tax deductible contributions, and later lobby with impunity, counting on ultimate qualification as a social welfare organization to save it from income taxes.

To prevent this possibility, Congress enacted Section 504 of the Internal Revenue Code, which states that if a C-3 eligible to make a 501(h) election becomes disqualified as a C-3 by reason of excessive lobbying activities, it may not later qualify under Section 501(c)(4) as a social welfare organization. The provision is not intended to preclude the disqualified C-3 from mending its ways and qualifying for C-3 status in a later tax year. Once it is disqualified due to lobbying, however, Section 501(c)(4) status is forever foreclosed.

Excise Taxes on Private Foundations

Private foundations are a subcategory of Section 501(c)(3) organizations. Private foundations are generally those C-3s that receive their financial support from a small number of donors rather than from the public at large. For example, a family may make a large donation to establish an endowment fund to carry on some charitable activity. The fund would qualify as a C-3 on the basis of its charitable purpose; it would also be classified as a private foundation because of its limited source of financial support. Congress has subjected private foundations to stricter rules than those applied to other C-3s on the theory that a privately controlled C-3 is more likely to abuse its tax-exempt status than a C-3 accountable to a large donor base.

Among the special restrictions on private foundations are excise taxes on certain political activities. Although they were enacted almost 20 years earlier than the excise taxes on political activities of other C-3s, the statutory schemes are roughly equivalent, and both are intended to act as a strong deterrent against the prohibited activity.

The excise tax is imposed on "taxable expenditures," i.e., expenditures which further prohibited political activity and are thus subject to the excise tax.[72] Of the various types of taxable expenditures which a private foundation might incur, two focus on political activity:[73]

> "(a) any expenditure to carry on propaganda or otherwise attempt to influence legislations; and
> "(b) any expenditure to influence the outcome of any public election or carry on any voter registration drive (unless certain requirements are met)."

Propaganda and Legislative Influence

The definition of the first category of taxable expenditure contains familiar language: the phrase "carry on propaganda or attempt to influence legislation" is borrowed directly from Section 501(c)(3), which states that these activities can not be a "substantial" part of the activities of a C-3. The activities that will be deemed to result in taxable expenditures are thus generally the same as those that are subject to the test of substantiality already discussed with respect to public C-3s. Such activities include communications with members or employees of legislative bodies or with other government officials or employees, or attempts to influence public opinion on legislative matters.

One special situation bears note. Because other C-3s can lobby within prescribed limits, the IRS plugged a perceived loophole created by the ability of private foundations to make grants to other C-3s. The Treasury regulations provide that if a private foundation makes a grant to a public C-3 which is earmarked for lobbying purposes, the grant will be a "taxable expenditure" and subject to the excise tax.[74]

The regulations contain an example of "safe" grants to public C-3s. In the example, the regulations appear to impose on a private foundation the duty to determine whether the lobbying activity being carried on by the recipient constitutes a "substantial part" of its activities.

> "Example 1: M, a private foundation, makes a general purpose grant to Z, a public charity (an organization described in §509(a)(1)). As an 'insubstantial' portion of its activities, Z makes some attempts to influence the state legislature with regard to changes in the mental health laws. The use of the grant is not earmarked by M to be used in a manner which would violate §4945(d). In addition, there is no oral or written agreement which may influence the choice by Z of the activity or recipient to which the grant is to be devoted. Even if the grant is subsequently devoted by Z to its legislative activities, the grant by M is not a taxable expenditure under §4945(d)."[75]

The first example, however, is not an oversight or aberration. In a private letter ruling, the IRS reiterated the obligation to determine whether the recipient engages in lobbying, and set forth several examples of situations in which a private foundation can make a grant to a public charity without making a "taxable expenditure."[76]

Example 1: A request for a general support grant comes from a public charity which has been, or currently is, lobbying. To the best of the knowledge of the foundation's staff, such lobbying has been, and is, 'insubstantial' as defined in §501(c)(3).

Example 2: A request for a general support grant comes from a charity which has notified the foundation that it has, or will, elect to lobby within the percentage limitations of §501(h).

Example 3: A request for a general support grant comes from a public charity which has recently engaged in lobbying, has elected or will elect to lobby under §501(h), and whose proposed annual budget allocates funds for lobbying.

Example 4: Requests for specific project grants (containing no reference to lobbying) come from a public charity previously or currently engaged in lobbying, which has elected or will elect to lobby under §501(h).

Example 5: A public charity requests partial funding of a specific project containing a budget line for lobbying. However, the amounts in the nonlobbying budget lines exceed the amount of the foundation's grant.

The obligations imposed on private foundations by the Treasury regulation, as clarified by the private letter ruling, have important implications. Making grants and donations to public C-3s are among the most common activities of private foundations. To avoid having the transferred funds recharacterized as "taxable expenditures," the private foundation should request, and keep in its permanent records, a statement signed by the recipient that certifies to specific facts necessary to bring the private foundation within one of the "safe harbors" set forth in the private letter ruling. The extra paperwork is worth the effort, in view of the fact that the private foundation, in most cases, will have no actual control over the C-3's activities for the year, but could be liable if the C-3 violates the rules.

Alternatively, the private foundation could consider making a revocable gift to the public C-3. A written agreement could require the return of the gift if a finding is made by the IRS that the gift constitutes a taxable expenditure due to the lobbying activities of the public C-3. This procedure could give the private foundation a double benefit. A return of the funds before a preliminary audited report is finalized could mitigate against taxability. In addition, the public C-3 will have more incentive to monitor its lobbying expenditures, and lessen the likelihood that the donation will become a "taxable expenditure."

Public Elections and Voter Education

Taxable expenditures also include amounts paid by private foundations to influence the outcome of public elections or to carry on voter registration drives, with certain exceptions. The imposition of an excise tax on electioneering is a logical extension of the prohibition on those activities for all C-3s. The deterrent to voter registration drives, however, requires a look at the legislative history to see the logic.

The legislative history of the Tax Reform Act of 1969 indicates a strong suspicion that private foundation funds were being broadly used to support political campaigns. This was being done overtly, as well as covertly, under the guise of voter registration campaigns. Congress apparently believed that voter registration campaigns were being targeted at specific geographic areas where the majority of new voters were likely to hold the same political beliefs as the foundation sponsors. The Senate Finance Committee report states:

"The committee believes that it is impossible to give assurances in all cases that voter registration drives would be conducted in a way that does not influence the outcome of public elections. In fact, the usual motivation of those who conduct such drives is to influence the outcome of public elections."[77]

The solution to this problem was to permit foundation support for voter registration drives only if the sponsor is nonpartisan and the registration activities cover a broad geographic area. The special rules contained in Section 4945(f) permit registration activities if:

"(1) The organization is described in §501(c)(3) and is exempt from taxation under §501(a).
"(2) The activities of the organization are nonpartisan, are not confined to one specific election period, and are carried on in five or more states.
"(3) The organization spends at least 85 percent of its income directly for the 'active conduct' of the activities constituting the purpose or function for which it is organized and operated.
"(4) The organization receives at least 85 percent of its support (other than gross investment income) from exempt organizations, the general public, governmental units, or any combination of the foregoing; it does not receive more than 25 percent of its support (other than gross investment income) from any one exempt organization; and not more than half of its funds comes from gross investment income.
"(5) Contributions to the organization for voter registration drives are not subject to conditions that they must be used in specified states, possessions of the United States, or political subdivisions or other areas of any of the foregoing, or in the District of Columbia, or that they must be used in a specified election period."

An organization meeting these requirements is referred to as "4945(f) organization." A private foundation may qualify as a 4945(f) organization, or it may donate funds earmarked for voter registration drives to 4945(f) organizations without incurring taxable expenditures.

As a small mercy, the IRS has lifted from the shoulders of private foundations the burden of determining whether or not a grant recipient qualifies under Section 4945(f). The IRS will issue a ruling based on the application for 4945(f) status, and a private foundation can simply request a copy of the recipient organization's ruling letter before making the grant. A list of qualified organizations is also published in the Internal Revenue Bulletin.

Notes

1. *Secretary of the Treasury v. Taxation With Representation of Washington,* 461 U.S. 540 (1983).

2. Currently embodied in I.R.C. §501(c)(3), similar language was first included in the Revenue Act of 1934. The 1934 statute was passed to bolster the IRS's position in *Slee v. Commissioner of Internal Revenue,* 42 F.2d 184 (1930), in which the court refused to recognize the tax-exempt status of the Birth Control League because it disseminated propaganda to legislators and the public aimed at the repeal of laws preventing birth control. See *Christian Echoes Nat'l Ministry v. United States,* 470 F.2d 849 (10th Cir. 1972), *cert. denied,* 414 U.S. 864 (1973).

3. The campaign intervention prohibition was added as a floor amendment to the Internal Revenue Code of 1954. The sponsor of the amendment, Sen. Lyndon B. Johnson, remarked that "this amendment seeks to extend the provisions of section 501 * * * denying tax-exempt status to not only those people who influence legislation but also to those who intervene in any political campaign on behalf of any candidate for public office." 100 CONG. REC. 9604 (1954). The prohibition against campaigning "in opposition to" any candidate for public office was added by the Omnibus Budget Reconciliation Act of 1987 §10711(a)(2).

4. Treas. Reg. §1.501(c)(3)-1(c).

5. Treas. Reg. §1.501(c)(3)-1(c)(3)(ii).

6. Treas. Reg. §1.501(c)(3)-1(c)(3)(ii)(a)(b).

7. Treas. Reg. §1.4945-2(a)(2).

8. Rev. Rul. 70-449, 1970-2 C.B. 111.

9. *Id.*

10. *Christian Echoes Nat'l Ministry v. United States,* 470 F.2d 849 (10th Cir. 1972), *cert. denied,* 414 U.S. 864 (1973).

11. *Id.*

12. *Americans United, Inc. v. Commissioner,* 477 F.2d 169 (D.C. Cir. 1973), *rev'd on other grounds,* 416 U.S. 752 (1974).

13. 26 U.S.C. §501(h). See below.

14. Treas. Reg. §1.501(c)(3)-1(c)(3)(iii).

15. *Hammerstein v. Kelly,* 235 F. Supp 60 (E.D. Mo. 1964).

16. Rev. Rul. 78-248, 1978-1 C.B. 154.

17. *Id.*

18. *Id.*

19. *Id.*

20. Rev. Rul. 80-282, 1980-2 C.B. 178.

21. Rev. Rul. 72-512, 1972-2 C.B. 246.

22. Rev. Rul. 72-513, 1972-2 C.B. 246.

23. Treas. Reg. §1.501(c)(3)-1(c)(3)(iv).

24. Rev. Rul. 73-440, 1973-2 C.B. 177.

25. Rev. Rul. 62-71, 1962-1 C.B. 85.

26. H. REP. No. 94-1210 (on H.R. 13500), 94th Cong, 2d Sess. 8 (June 2, 1976).

27. *Id.*

28. *Id.*

29. *Id.* at 11.

30. *Id.* at 8.

31. *Id.* at 11 n.6.

32. I.R.C. §4911(d); I.R.C. §501(h)(2)(A).

33. I.R.C. §4911(d)(2). A footnote in the legislative history states that nonpartisan activities and responses to legislative requests were previously determined under IRS rulings to be excluded from the type of lobbying exempt status. The legislative history does not com-

ment on any inference to be drawn with respect to self-defense lobbying when carried on by nonelecting or ineligible C-3s. H. REP. No. 94-1210 (on H.R. 13500), 94th Cong., 2d Sess. 70 (June 2, 1976).

34. I.R.C. §4911(d)(2), (3).
35. H. REP. No. 94-1210 (on H.R. 13500), 94th Cong., 2d Sess. 10 (June 2, 1976).
36. *Id.*
37. Prop. Treas. Reg. §56.4911-5(e)(1), 53 Fed. Reg. 51,826 (1988) (see Appendix K for text).
38. Prop. Treas. Reg. §56.4911-2(b)(2), 53 Fed. Reg. 51,826 (1988).
39. 53 Fed. Reg. 51,826 (1988).
40. Prop. Treas. Reg. §56.4911-2(b)(2)(iii), 53 Fed. Reg. 51,826 (1988).
41. 53 Fed. Reg. 51,826 (1988).
42. Prop. Treas. Reg. §56-4911-2(b)(5), 53 Fed. Reg. 51,826 (1988).
43. *Id.*
44. I.R.C. §4911 (b).
45. I.R.C. §4911(c).
46. I.R.C. §4911(e)(1).
47. I.R.C. §4911(e)(1)(C).
48. I.R.C. §4911(e)(1)(B).
49. Prop. Treas. Reg. §56.4911-4(d), 53 Fed. Reg. 51,826 (1988).
50. I.R.C. §4911(c)(2).
51. I.R.C. §4911(c)(4).
52. I.R.C. §4911(b).
53. Prop. Treas. Reg. §56.4911-2(a) and (b), 53 Fed. Reg. 51,826 (1988).
54. Prop. Treas. Reg. §56.4911-3, 53 Fed. Reg. 51,826 (1988).
55. *Id.*
56. Prop. Treas. Reg. §56.4911-3(a)(3), 53 Fed. Reg. 51,826 (1988).
57. Prop. Treas. Reg. §56.4911-3(a)(2), 53 Fed. Reg. 51,826 (1988).
58. Prop. Treas. Reg. §56.4911-3(a)(2)(ii), 53 Fed. Reg. 51,826 (1988).
59. Prop. Treas. Reg. §56.4911-3(a)(2)(i), 53 Fed. Reg. 51,826 (1988).
60. *Id.*
61. I.R.C. §170(f)(6).
62. H. REP. No. 94-1210 (on H.R. 13500), 94th Cong., 2d Sess. 13 (June 2, 1976).
63. I.R.C. §4911(f)(1).
64. I.R.C. §4911(f)(2).
65. Prop. Treas. Reg. §56.4911-7(f), Example 1, 53 Fed. Reg. 51,826 (1988).
66. S. REP. No. 94-938, Part 2, 94th Cong., 2d Sess. 82 (July 20, 1976), 1976 U.S. CODE & CONG. ADMIN. NEWS 4030.
67. I.R.C. §4911(f)(1)(B).
68. I.R.C. §4911(f)(1)(C).
69. I.R.C. §4911(f)(1)(D).
70. I.R.C. §4911(f)(3); Prop. Treas. Reg. §56.4911-7(e)(3).
71. I.R.C. §4911(f)(4).
72. I.R.C. §4945.
73. *Id.*
74. Treas. Reg. §1.53.4945-2(a)(5).
75. Treas. Reg. §1.53.4945-2(a)(5)(iii).
76. Priv. Ltr. Rul. 78-10-041 (1978)
77. S. REP. No. 91-552, 91st Cong., 1st Sess. 2077 (1969).

Appendix A

Federal Regulation of Lobbying Act, 2 U.S.C. §§261–270

§ 261. Definitions

When used in this chapter—

(a) The term "contribution" includes a gift, subscription, loan, advance, or deposit of money or anything of value and includes a contract, promise, or agreement, whether or not legally enforceable, to make a contribution.

(b) The term "expenditure" includes a payment, distribution, loan, advance, deposit, or gift of money or anything of value, and includes a contract, promise, or agreement, whether or not legally enforceable, to make an expenditure.

(c) The term "person" includes an individual, partnership, committee, association, corporation, and any other organization or group of persons.

(d) The term "Clerk" means the Clerk of the House of Representatives of the United States.

(e) The term "legislation" means bills, resolutions, amendments, nominations, and other matters pending or proposed in either House of Congress, and includes any other matter which may be the subject of action by either House.

§ 262. Detailed accounts of contributions; retention of receipted bills of expenditures

(a) It shall be the duty of every person who shall in any manner solicit or receive a contribution to any organization or fund for the purposes hereinafter designated to keep a detailed and exact account of—

(1) all contributions of any amount or of any value whatsoever;

(2) the name and address of every person making any such contribution of $500 or more and the date thereof;

(3) all expenditures made by or on behalf of such organization or fund; and

(4) the name and address of every person to whom any such expenditure is made and the date thereof.

(b) It shall be the duty of such person to obtain and keep a receipted bill, stating the particulars, for every expenditure of such funds exceeding $10 in amount, and to preserve all receipted bills and accounts required to be kept by this section for a period of at least two years from the date of the filing of the statement containing such items.

§ 263. Receipts for contributions

Every individual who receives a contribution of $500 or more for any of the purposes hereinafter designated shall within five days after receipt thereof rendered [1] to the person or organization for which such contribution was received a detailed account thereof, including the name and address of the person making such contribution and the date on which received.

§ 264. Statements of accounts filed with Clerk of House

(a) Every person receiving any contributions or expending any money for the purposes designated in subparagraph (a) or (b) of section 266 of this title shall file with the Clerk between the first and tenth day of each calendar quarter, a statement containing complete as of the day next preceding the date of filing—

(1) the name and address of each person who has made a contribution of $500 or more not mentioned in the preceding report; except that the first report filed pursuant to this chapter shall contain the name and address of each person who has made any contribution of $500 or more to such person since August 2, 1946;

(2) the total sum of the contributions made to or for such person during the calendar year and not stated under paragraph (1) of this subsection;

(3) the total sum of all contributions made to or for such person during the calendar year;

(4) the name and address of each person to whom an expenditure in one or more items of the aggregate amount or value, within the calendar year, of $10 or more has been made by or on behalf of such person, and the amount, date, and purpose of such expenditure;

(5) the total sum of all expenditures made

---

[1] So in original. Probably should read "render".

by or on behalf of such person during the calendar year and not stated under paragraph (4) of this subsection;

(6) the total sum of expenditures made by or on behalf of such person during the calendar year.

(b) The statements required to be filed by subsection (a) of this section shall be cumulative during the calendar year to which they relate, but where there has been no change in an item reported in a previous statement only the amount need be carried forward.

§ 265. Preservation of statements

A statement required by this chapter to be filed with the Clerk—

(a) shall be deemed properly filed when deposited in an established post office within the prescribed time, duly stamped, registered, and directed to the Clerk of the House of Representatives of the United States, Washington, District of Columbia, but in the event it is not received, a duplicate of such statement shall be promptly filed upon notice by the Clerk of its nonreceipt;

(b) shall be preserved by the Clerk for a period of two years from the date of filing, shall constitute part of the public records of his office, and shall be open to public inspection.

§ 266. Persons to whom chapter is applicable

The provisions of this chapter shall apply to any person (except a political committee as defined in the Federal Corrupt Practices Act, and duly organized State or local committees of a political party), who by himself, or through any agent or employee or other persons in any manner whatsoever, directly or indirectly, solicits, collects, or receives money or any other thing of value to be used principally to aid, or the principal purpose of which person is to aid, in the accomplishment of any of the following purposes:

(a) The passage or defeat of any legislation by the Congress of the United States.

(b) To influence, directly or indirectly, the passage or defeat of any legislation by the Congress of the United States.

§ 267. Registration of lobbyists with Secretary of the Senate and Clerk of House; compilation of information

(a) Any person who shall engage himself for pay or for any consideration for the purpose of attempting to influence the passage or defeat of any legislation by the Congress of the United States shall, before doing anything in furtherance of such object, register with the Clerk of the House of Representatives and the Secretary of the Senate and shall give to those officers in writing and under oath, his name and business address, the name and address of the person by whom he is employed, and in whose interest he appears or works, the duration of such employment, how much he is paid and is to receive, by whom he is paid or is to be paid, how much he is to be paid for expenses, and what expenses are to be included. Each such person so registering shall, between the first and tenth day of each calendar quarter, so long as his activity

continues, file with the Clerk and Secretary a detailed report under oath of all money received and expended by him during the preceding calendar quarter in carrying on his work; to whom paid; for what purposes; and the names of any papers, periodicals, magazines, or other publications in which he has caused to be published any articles or editorials; and the proposed legislation he is employed to support or oppose. The provisions of this section shall not apply to any person who merely appears before a committee of the Congress of the United States in support of or opposition to legislation; nor to any public official acting in his official capacity; nor in the case of any newspaper or other regularly published periodical (including any individual who owns, publishes, or is employed by any such newspaper or periodical) which in the ordinary course of business publishes news items, editorials, or other comments, or paid advertisements, which directly or indirectly urge the passage or defeat of legislation, if such newspaper, periodical, or individual, engages in no further or other activities in connection with the passage or defeat of such legislation, other than to appear before a committee of the Congress of the United States in support of or in opposition to such legislation.

(b) All information required to be filed under the provisions of this section with the Clerk of the House of Representatives and the Secretary of the Senate shall be compiled by said Clerk and Secretary, acting jointly, as soon as practicable after the close of the calendar quarter with respect to which such information is filed and shall be printed in the Congressional Record.

§ 268. Reports and statements under oath

All reports and statements required under this chapter shall be made under oath, before an officer authorized by law to administer oaths.

§ 269. Penalties and prohibitions

(a) Any person who violates any of the provisions of this chapter, shall, upon conviction, be guilty of a misdemeanor, and shall be punished by a fine of not more than $5,000 or imprisonment for not more than twelve months, or by both such fine and imprisonment.

(b) In addition to the penalties provided for in subsection (a) of this section, any person convicted of the misdemeanor specified therein is prohibited, for a period of three years from the date of such conviction, from attempting to influence, directly or indirectly, the passage or defeat of any proposed legislation or from appearing before a committee of the Congress in support of or opposition to proposed legislation; and any person who violates any provision of this subsection shall, upon conviction thereof, be guilty of a felony, and shall be punished by a fine of not more than $10,000, or imprisonment for not more than five years, or by both such fine and imprisonment.

§ 270. Exemptions from chapter

The provisions of this chapter shall not apply to practices or activities regulated by the Federal Corrupt Practices Act nor be construed as repealing any portion of said Federal Corrupt Practices Act.

Appendix B

Report Pursuant to Federal Regulation of Lobbying Act

PLEASE RETURN 1 ORIGINAL TO: THE CLERK OF THE HOUSE OF REPRESENTATIVES, OFFICE OF RECORDS AND REGISTRATION, 1036 LONGWORTH HOUSE OFFICE BUILDING, WASHINGTON, D.C. 20515

PLEASE RETURN 1 ORIGINAL TO: THE SECRETARY OF THE SENATE, OFFICE OF PUBLIC RECORDS, 232 HART SENATE OFFICE BUILDING, WASHINGTON, D.C. 20510

PLACE AN "X" BELOW THE APPROPRIATE LETTER OR FIGURE IN THE BOX AT THE RIGHT OF THE "REPORT" HEADING BELOW:

"PRELIMINARY" REPORT ("Registration"): To "register," place an "X" below the letter "P" and fill out page 1 only.

"QUARTERLY" REPORT: To indicate which one of the four calendar quarters is covered by this Report, place an "X" below the appropriate figure. Fill out both page 1 and page 2 and as many additional pages as may be required. The first additional page should be numbered as page "3," and the rest of such pages should be "4," "5," "6," etc. Preparation and filing in accordance with instructions will accomplish compliance with all quarterly reporting requirements of the Act.

Year: 19...... ←	**R E P O R T** PURSUANT TO FEDERAL REGULATION OF LOBBYING ACT	P	QUARTER			
			1st	2d	3d	4th
			(Mark one square only)			

IDENTIFICATION NUMBER _____

Is this an Amendment?   ☐ YES   ☐ NO

NOTE on ITEM "A."– (a) IN GENERAL. This "Report" form may be used by either an organization or an individual, as follows:

(i) "Employee."–To file as an "employee," state (in Item "B") the name, address, and nature of business of the "employer." (If the "employee" is a firm [such as a law firm or public relations firm], partners and salaried staff members of such firm may join in filing a Report as an "employee.")

(ii) "Employer".–To file as an "employer," write "None" in answer to Item "B."

(b) SEPARATE REPORTS. An agent or employee should not attempt to combine his Report with the employer's Report:

(i) Employers subject to the Act must file separate Reports and are not relieved of this requirement merely because Reports are filed by their agents or employees.

(ii) Employees subject to the Act must file separate Reports and are not relieved of this requirement merely because Reports are filed by their employers.

A. ORGANIZATION OR INDIVIDUAL FILING

1. State name, address, and nature of business.
   ☐ CHECK IF ADDRESS IS DIFFERENT THAN PREVIOUSLY REPORTED

2. If this Report is for an Employer, list names of agents or employees who will file Reports for this Quarter.

NOTE on ITEM "B."– *Reports by Agents or Employees.* An employee is to file, each quarter, as many Reports as he has employers; except that: (a) If a particular undertaking is jointly financed by a group of employers, the group is to be considered as one employer, but all members of the group are to be named, and the contribution of each member is to be specified; (b) if the work is done in the interest of one person but payment therefor is made by another, a single Report–naming both persons as "employers"–is to be filed each quarter.

B. EMPLOYER – State name, address, and nature of business. If there is no employer, write "None."

NOTE ON ITEM "C."—(a) The expression "in connection with legislative interests," as used in this Report, means "in connection with attempting, directly or indirectly, to influence the passage or defeat of legislation." "The term 'legislation' means bills, resolutions, amendments, nominations, and other matters pending or proposed in either House of Congress, and includes any other matter which may be the subject of action by either House"— § 302(e).

(b) Before undertaking any activities in connection with legislative interests, organizations and individuals subject to the Lobbying Act are required to file a "Preliminary" Report (Registration).

(c) After beginning such activities, they must file a "Quarterly" Report at the end of each calendar quarter in which they have either received or expended anything of value in connection with legislative interests.

C. LEGISLATIVE INTERESTS AND PUBLICATIONS in connection therewith:

1. State approximately how long legislative interests are to continue. If receipts and expenditures in connection with legislative interests have terminated, place an "X" in the ☐ box at the left, so that this Office will no longer expect to receive Reports.

2. State the general legislative interests of the person filing and set forth the specific legislative interests by reciting: (a) Short titles of statutes and bills; (b) House and Senate numbers of bills, where known; (c) citations of statutes, where known; (d) whether for or against such statutes and bills.

3. In the case of those publications which the person filing has caused to be issued or distributed, in connection with legislative interests, set forth: (a) description, (b) quantity distributed, (c) date of distribution, (d) name of printer or publisher (if publications were paid for by person filing) or name of donor (if publications were received as a gift).

(Answer items 1, 2, and 3 in the space below. Attach additional pages if more space is needed.)

4. *If* this is a "Preliminary" Report (Registration) rather than a "Quarterly" Report, state below what the nature and amount of anticipated expenses will be; and, if for an agent or employee, state also what the daily, monthly, or annual rate of compensation is to be. *If this is a "Quarterly" Report, disregard this Item "C 4" and fill out Items "D" and "E" on the back of this page.* Do not attempt to combine a "Preliminary" Report (Registration) with a "Quarterly Report."←

STATEMENT OF VERIFICATION

I declare under penalty of perjury that the information contained herein is true and correct.

Check ONE of the following boxes:

    ☐ I am reporting AS AN INDIVIDUAL.

    ☐ I am _____ of the above-named organization and I am authorized to make this verification on behalf of such organization.

Executed on _____   (Signature) _____
                (date)   (Typed)

NOTE on ITEM "D."–(a) IN GENERAL. The term "contribution" includes *anything of value.* When an organization or individual uses printed or duplicated matter in a campaign attempting to influence legislation, money received by such organization or individual – for such printed or duplicated matter – is a "contribution." "The term 'contribution' includes a gift, subscription, loan, advance, or deposit of money, or anything of value and includes a contract, promise, or agreement, whether or not legally enforceable, to make a contribution"– § 302(a) of the Lobbying Act.

(b) IF THIS REPORT IS FOR AN EMPLOYER. – (i) *In General.* Item "D" is designed for the reporting of all receipts from which expenditures are made, or will be made, in connection with legislative interests.

(ii) *Receipts of Business Firms and Individuals.* – A business firm (or individual) which is subject to the Lobbying Act by reason of expenditures which it makes in attempting to influence legislation – but which has no funds to expend except those which are available in the ordinary course of operating a business not connected in any way with the influencing of legislation – will have no receipts to report, even though it does have expenditures to report.

(iii) *Receipts of Multi-purpose Organizations.* – Some organizations do not receive any funds which are to be expended solely for the purpose of attempting to influence legislation. Such, organizations make such expenditures out of a general fund raised by dues, assessments, or other contributions. The percentage of the general fund which is used for such expenditures indicates the percentage of dues, assessments, or other contributions which may be considered to have been paid for that purpose. Therefore, in reporting receipts, such organizations may specify what that percentage is, and report their dues, assessments, and other contributions on that basis. However, each contributor of $500 or more is to be listed, regardless of whether the contribution was made solely for legislative purposes.

(c) IF THIS REPORT IS FOR AN AGENT OR EMPLOYEE. – (i) *In general.* In the case of many employees, all receipts will come under Items "D 5" (received for services) and "D 12" (expense money and reimbursements). In the absence of a clear statement to the contrary, it will be presumed that your employer is to reimburse you for all expenditures which you make in connection with legislative interests.

(ii) *Employer as Contributor of $500 or More.* – When your contribution from your employer (in the form of salary, fee, etc.) amounts to $500 or more, it is not necessary to report such contributions under "D 13" and "D 14," since the amount has already been reported under "D 5," and the name of the "employer" has been given under Item "B" on page 1 of this report.

D. RECEIPTS (INCLUDING CONTRIBUTIONS AND LOANS):

Fill in every blank. If the answer to any numbered item is "None," write "NONE" in the space following the number.

Receipts (other than loans)

1. $----------------------- Dues and assessments

2. $----------------------- Gifts of money or anything of value

3. $----------------------- Printed or duplicated matter received as a gift

4. $----------------------- Receipts from sale of printed or duplicated matter

5. $----------------------- Received for services (e.g., salary, fee, etc.)

6. $----------------------- TOTAL for this Quarter (Add "1" through "5")

7. $----------------------- Received during previous Quarters of calendar year

8. $----------------------- TOTAL from Jan. 1 through this Quarter (Add "6" and "7")

Loans Received – "The term 'contribution' includes a . . . *loan* . . ." – § 302(a).

9. $----------------------- TOTAL now owed to others on account of loans

10. $----------------------- Borrowed from others during this Quarter

11. $----------------------- Repaid to others during this Quarter

12. $----------------------- "Expense Money" and Reimbursements received this quarter.

Contributors of $500 or More (from Jan. 1 through this Quarter)

13. Have there been such contributors?
    Please answer "yes" or "no": . . . . ←

14. In the case of each contributor whose contributions (including loans) during the "period" from January 1 through the last day of this Quarter, total $500 or more:

Attach hereto plain sheets of paper, approximately the size of this page, tabulate data under the headings "Amount" and "Name and Address of Contributor"; and indicate whether the last day of the period is March 31, June 30, September 30, or December 31. Prepare such tabulation in accordance with the following example:

Amount	Name and Address of Contributor
	("Period" from Jan. 1 through . . . ., 19. . . .)
$1,500.00	John Doe, 1621 Blank Bldg., New York, N.Y.
1,785.00	The Roe Corporation, 2511 Doe Bldg., Chicago, Ill.
$3,285.00	TOTAL

NOTE on ITEM "E".—(*a*) IN GENERAL. "The term 'expenditure' includes a payment, distribution, loan, advance, deposit, or gift of money or anything of value and includes a contract, promise, or agreement, whether or not legally enforceable, to make an expenditure"—§ 302(b) of the Lobbying Act.

(*b*) IF THIS REPORT IS FOR AN AGENT OR EMPLOYEE. In the case of many employees, all expenditures will come under telephone and telegraph (Item "E 6) and travel, food, lodging, and entertainment (Item "E 7").

E. EXPENDITURES (INCLUDING LOANS) in connection with legislative interests:

Fill in every blank. If the answer to any numbered item is "None," write "NONE" in the space following the number.

Expenditures (other than loans)

1. $----------------------- Public relations and advertising services

2. $----------------------- Wages, salaries, fees, commissions (other than Item "1")

3. $----------------------- Gifts or contributions made during Quarter

4. $----------------------- Printed or duplicated matter, including distribution cost

5. $----------------------- Office overhead (rent, supplies, utilities, etc.)

6. $----------------------- Telephone and telegraph

7. $----------------------- Travel, food, lodging, and entertainment

8. $----------------------- All other expenditures

9. $----------------------- TOTAL for this Quarter (Add "1" through "8")

10. $----------------------- Expended during previous Quarters of calendar year

11. $----------------------- TOTAL from Jan. 1 through this Quarter (Add "9" and "10")

Loans Made to Others—"The term 'expenditure' includes a . . . loan . . ."—§ 302(b).

12. $----------------------- TOTAL now owed to person filing

13. $----------------------- Lent to others during this Quarter

14. $----------------------- Repayments received during this Quarter

15. *Recipients of Expenditures of $10 or More* _____

If there were no single expenditures of $10 or more, please so indicate by using the word "NONE".

In the case of expenditures made during this Quarter by, or on behalf of, the person filing: Attach plain sheets of paper approximately the size of this page and tabulate data as to expenditures under the following headings: "Amount," "Date or Dates," "Name and Address of Recipient," "Purpose." Prepare such tabulation in accordance with the following example:

Amount	Date or Dates—Name and Address of Recipient—Purpose
$1,750.00	7-11:　Roe Printing Co., 3214 Blank Ave., St. Louis, Mo.—Printing and mailing circulars on the "Marshbanks Bill."
$2,400.00	7-15, 8-15, 9-15:　Britten & Blatten, 3127 Gremlin Bldg., Washington, D.C.—Public relations service at $800.00 per month.
$4,150.00	TOTAL

GPO: 1988 O—81-176(m)

Appendix C

Foreign Agent Registration Act, 22 U.S.C. §§611–621

§ 611. Definitions

As used in and for the purposes of this subchapter—

(a) The term "person" includes an individual, partnership, association, corporation, organization, or any other combination of individuals;

(b) The term "foreign principal" includes—

(1) a government of a foreign country and a foreign political party;

(2) a person outside of the United States, unless it is established that such person is an individual and a citizen of and domiciled within the United States, or that such person is not an individual and is organized under or created by the laws of the United States or of any State or other place subject to the jurisdiction of the United States and has its principal place of business within the United States; and

(3) a partnership, association, corporation, organization, or other combination of persons organized under the laws of or having its principal place of business in a foreign country.

(c) Expect [1] as provided in subsection (d) of this section, the term "agent of a foreign principal" means—

(1) any person who acts as an agent, representative, employee, or servant, or any person who acts in any other capacity at the order, request, or under the direction or control, of a foreign principal or of a person any of whose activities are directly or indirectly supervised, directed, controlled, financed, or subsidized in whole or in major part by a foreign principal, and who directly or through any other person—

(i) engages within the United States in political activities for or in the interests of such foreign principal;

(ii) acts within the United States as a public relations counsel, publicity agent, information-service employee or political consultant for or in the interests of such foreign principal;

(iii) within the United States solicits, collects, disburses, or dispenses contributions, loans, money, or other things of value for or in the interest of such foreign principal; or

(iv) within the United States represents the interests of such foreign principal before any agency or official of the Government of the United States; and

(2) any person who agrees, consents, assumes or purports to act as, or who is or holds himself out to be, whether or not pursuant to contractual relationship, an agent of a foreign principal as defined in clause (1) of this subsection.

(d) The term "agent of a foreign principal" does not include any news or press service or association organized under the laws of the United States or of any State or other place subject to the jurisdiction of the United States, or any newspaper, magazine, periodical, or other publication for which there is on file with the United States Postal Service information in compliance with section 3611 [2] of title 39, published in the United States, solely by virtue of any bona fide news or journalistic activities, including the solicitation or acceptance of advertisements, subscriptions, or other compensation therefor, so long as it is at least 80 per centum beneficially owned by, and its officers and directors, if any, are citizens of the United States, and such news or press service or association, newspaper, magazine, periodical, or other publication, is not owned, directed, supervised, controlled, subsidized, or financed, and none of its policies are determined by any foreign principal defined in subsection (b) of this section, or by any agent of a foreign principal required to register under this subchapter;

(e) The term "government of a foreign country" includes any person or groups of persons exercising sovereign de facto or de jure political jurisdiction over any country, other than the United States, or over any part of such country, and includes any subdivision of any such group and any group or agency to which such sovereign de facto or de jure authority or functions are directly or indirectly delegated. Such term shall include any faction or body of insurgents within a country assuming to exercise govern-

---

[1] So in original. Probably should be "except".

[2] So in original. Probably should be "section 3685".

mental authority whether such faction or body of insurgents has or has not been recognized by the United States;

(f) The term "foreign political party" includes any organization or any other combination of individuals in a country other than the United States, or any unit or branch thereof, having for an aim or purpose, or which is engaged in any activity devoted in whole or in part to, the establishment, administration, control, or acquisition of administration or control, of a government of a foreign country or a subdivision thereof, or the furtherance or influencing of the political or public interests, policies, or relations of a government of a foreign country or a subdivision thereof;

(g) The term "public-relations counsel" includes any person who engages directly or indirectly in informing, advising, or in any way representing a principal in any public relations matter pertaining to political or public interests, policies, or relations of such principal;

(h) The term "publicity agent" includes any person who engages directly or indirectly in the publication or dissemination of oral, visual, graphic, written, or pictorial information or matter of any kind, including publication by means of advertising, books, periodicals, newspapers, lectures, broadcasts, motion pictures, or otherwise;

(i) The term "information-service employee" includes any person who is engaged in furnishing, disseminating, or publishing accounts, descriptions, information, or data with respect to the political, industrial, employment, economic, social, cultural, or other benefits, advantages, facts, or conditions of any country other than the United States or of any government of a foreign country or of a foreign political party or of a partnership, association, corporation, organization, or other combination of individuals organized under the laws of, or having its principal place of business in, a foreign country;

(j) The term "political propaganda" includes any oral, visual, graphic, written, pictorial, or other communication or expression by any person (1) which is reasonably adapted to, or which the person disseminating the same believes will, or which he intends to, prevail upon, indoctrinate, convert, induce, or in any other way influence a recipient or any section of the public within the United States with reference to the political or public interests, policies, or relations of a government of a foreign country or a foreign political party or with reference to the foreign policies of the United States or promote in the United States racial, religious, or social dissensions, or (2) which advocates, advises, instigates, or promotes any racial, social, political, or religious disorder, civil riot, or other conflict involving the use of force or violence in any other American republic or the overthrow of any government or political subdivision of any other American republic by any means involving the use of force or violence. As used in this subsection the term "disseminating" includes transmitting or causing to be transmitted in the United States mails or by any means or instrumentality of interstate or foreign commerce or offering or causing to be offered in the United States mails;

(k) The term "registration statement" means the registration statement required to be filed with the Attorney General under section 612(a) of this title, and any supplements thereto required to be filed under section 612(b) of this title, and includes all documents and papers required to be filed therewith or amendatory thereof or supplemental thereto, whether attached thereto or incorporated therein by reference;

(l) The term "American republic" includes any of the states which were signatory to the Final Act of the Second Meeting of the Ministers of Foreign Affairs of the American Republics at Habana, Cuba, July 30, 1940;

(m) The term "United States", when used in a geographical sense, includes the several States, the District of Columbia, the Territories, the Canal Zone, the insular possessions, and all other places now or hereafter subject to the civil or military jurisdiction of the United States;

(n) The term "prints" means newspapers and periodicals, books, pamphlets, sheet music, visiting cards, address cards, printing proofs, engravings, photographs, pictures, drawings, plans, maps, patterns to be cut out, catalogs, prospectuses, advertisements, and printed, engraved, lithographed, or autographed notices of various kinds, and, in general, all impressions or reproductions obtained on paper or other material assimilable to paper, on parchment or on cardboard, by means of printing, engraving, lithography, autography, or any other easily recognizable mechanical process, with the exception of the copying press, stamps with movable or immovable type, and the typewriter;

(o) The term "political activities" means the dissemination of political propaganda and any other activity which the person engaging therein believes will, or which he intends to, prevail upon, indoctrinate, convert, induce, persuade, or in any other way influence any agency or official of the Government of the United States or any section of the public within the United States with reference to formulating, adopting, or changing the domestic or foreign policies of the United States or with reference to the political or public interests, policies, or relations of a government of a foreign country or a foreign political party;

(p) The term "political consultant" means any person who engages in informing or advising any other person with reference to the domestic or foreign policies of the United States or the political or public interest, policies, or relations of a foreign country or of a foreign political party;

(q) For the purpose of section 613(d) of this title, activities in furtherance of the bona fide commercial, industrial or financial interests of a domestic person engaged in substantial commercial, industrial or financial operations in the United States shall not be deemed to serve predominantly a foreign interest because such activities also benefit the interests of a foreign person engaged in bona fide trade or commerce which is owned or controlled by, or which owns or controls, such domestic person: *Provided*, That (i) such foreign person is not, and such activities are not directly or indirectly supervised, directed, controlled, financed or subsidized in whole or in substantial part by, a government of a foreign country or a foreign political party, (ii) the identity of such foreign person is disclosed to the agency or official of the United States with whom such activities are conducted, and (iii) whenever such foreign person owns or controls such domestic person, such activities are substantially in furtherance of the bona fide commercial, industrial or financial interests of such domestic person.

§ 612. Registration statement

(a) Filing; contents

No person shall act as an agent of a foreign principal unless he has filed with the Attorney General a true and complete registration statement and supplements thereto as required by subsections (a) and (b) of this section or unless he is exempt from registration under the provisions of this subchapter. Except as hereinafter provided, every person who becomes an agent of a foreign principal shall, within ten days thereafter, file with the Attorney General, in duplicate, a registration statement, under oath on a form prescribed by the Attorney General. The obligation of an agent of a foreign principal to file a registration statement shall, after the tenth day of his becoming such agent, continue from day to day, and termination of such status shall not relieve such agent from his obligation to file a registration statement for the period during which he was an agent of a foreign principal. The registration statement shall include the following, which shall be regarded as material for the purposes of this subchapter:

(1) Registrant's name, principal business address, and all other business addresses in the United States or elsewhere, and all residence addresses, if any;

(2) Status of the registrant; if an individual, nationality; if a partnership, name, residence addresses, and nationality of each partner and a true and complete copy of its articles of copartnership; if an association, corporation, or organization, or any other combination of individuals, the name, residence addresses, and nationality of each director and officer and of each person performing the functions of a director or officer and a true and complete copy of its charter, articles of incorporation, association, constitution, and bylaws, and amendments thereto; a copy of every other instrument or document and a statement of the terms and conditions of every oral agreement relating to its organization, powers, and purposes; and a statement of its ownership and control;

(3) A comprehensive statement of the nature of registrant's business; a complete list of registrant's employees and a statement of the nature of the work of each; the name and address of every foreign principal for whom the registrant is acting, assuming or purporting to act or has agreed to act; the character of the business or other activities of every such foreign principal, and, if any such foreign principal be other than a natural person, a statement of the ownership and control of each; and the extent, if any, to which each such foreign principal is supervised, directed, owned, controlled, financed, or subsidized, in whole or in part, by any government of a foreign country or foreign political party, or by any other foreign principal;

(4) Copies of each written agreement and the terms and conditions of each oral agreement, including all modifications of such agreements, or, where no contract exists, a full statement of all the circumstances, by reason of which the registrant is an agent of a foreign principal; a comprehensive statement of the nature and method of performance of each such contract, and of the existing and proposed activity or activities engaged in or to be engaged in by the registrant as agent of a foreign principal for each such foreign principal, including a detailed statement of any such activity which is a political activity;

(5) The nature and amount of contributions, income, money, or thing of value, if any, that the registrant has received within the preceding sixty days from each such foreign principal, either as compensation or for disbursement or otherwise, and the form and time of each such payment and from whom received;

(6) A detailed statement of every activity which the registrant is performing or is assuming or purporting or has agreed to perform for himself or any other person other than a foreign principal and which requires his registration hereunder, including a detailed statement of any such activity which is a political activity;

(7) The name, business, and residence addresses, and if an individual, the nationality, of any person other than a foreign principal for whom the registrant is acting, assuming or purporting to act or has agreed to act under such circumstances as require his registration hereunder; the extent to which each such person is supervised, directed, owned, controlled, financed, or subsidized, in whole or in part, by any government of a foreign country or foreign political party or by any other foreign principal; and the nature and amount of contributions, income, money, or thing of value, if any, that the registrant has received during the preceding sixty days from each such person in connection with any of the activities referred to in clause (6) of this subsection, either as compensation or for disbursement or otherwise, and the form and time of each such payment and from whom received;

(8) A detailed statement of the money and other things of value spent or disposed of by the registrant during the preceding sixty days in furtherance of or in connection with activities which require his registration hereunder and which have been undertaken by him either as an agent of a foreign principal or for himself or any other person or in conection[3] with any activities relating to his becoming an agent of such principal, and a detailed statement of any contributions of money or other things of value made by him during the preceding sixty days (other than contributions the making of which is prohibited under the terms of section 613 of title 18) in connection with an election to any political office or in connection with any primary election, convention, or caucus held to select candidates for any political office;

(9) Copies of each written agreement and the terms and conditions of each oral agreement, including all modifications of such agreements, or, where no contract exists, a full statement of all the circumstances, by reason of which the registrant is performing or assuming or purporting or has agreed to perform for himself or for a foreign principal or for any person other than a foreign principal any activities which require his registration hereunder;

(10) Such other statements, information, or documents pertinent to the purposes of this subchapter as the Attorney General, having due regard for the national security and the

---

[3] So in original. Probably should be "connection".

public interest, may from time to time require;

(11) Such further statements and such further copies of documents as are necessary to make the statements made in the registration statement and supplements thereto, and the copies of documents furnished therewith, not misleading.

(b) Supplements; filing period

Every agent of a foreign principal who has filed a registration statement required by subsection (a) of this section shall, within thirty days after the expiration of each period of six months succeeding such filing, file with the Attorney General a supplement thereto under oath, on a form prescribed by the Attorney General, which shall set forth with respect to such preceding six months' period such facts as the Attorney General, having due regard for the national security and the public interest, may deem necessary to make the information required under this section accurate, complete, and current with respect to such period. In connection with the information furnished under clauses (3), (4), (6), and (9) of subsection (a) of this section, the registrant shall give notice to the Attorney General of any changes therein within ten days after such changes occur. If the Attorney General, having due regard for the national security and the public interest, determines that it is necessary to carry out the purposes of this subchapter, he may, in any particular case, require supplements to the registration statement to be filed at more frequent intervals in respect to all or particular items of information to be furnished.

(c) Execution of statement under oath

The registration statement and supplements thereto shall be executed under oath as follows: If the registrant is an individual, by him; if the registrant is a partnership, by the majority of the members thereof; if the registrant is a person other than an individual or a partnership, by a majority of the officers thereof or persons performing the functions of officers or by a majority of the board of directors thereof or persons performing the functions of directors, if any.

(d) Filing of statement not deemed full compliance nor as preclusion from prosecution

The fact that a registration statement or supplement thereto has been filed shall not necessarily be deemed a full compliance with this subchapter and the regulations thereunder on the part of the registrant; nor shall it indicate that the Attorney General has in any way passed upon the merits of such registration statement or supplement thereto; nor shall it preclude prosecution, as provided for in this subchapter, for willful failure to file a registration statement or supplement thereto when due or for a willful false statement of a material fact therein or the willful omission of a material fact required to be stated therein or the willful omission of a material fact or copy of a material document necessary to make the statements made in a registration statement and supplements thereto, and the copies of documents furnished therewith, not misleading.

(e) Incorporation of previous statement by reference

If any agent of a foreign principal, required to register under the provisions of this subchapter, has previously thereto registered with the Attorney General under the provisions of section 2386 of title 18, the Attorney General, in order to eliminate inappropriate duplication, may permit the incorporation by reference in the registration statement or supplements thereto filed hereunder of any information or documents previously filed by such agent of a foreign principal under the provisions of said section.

(f) Exemption by Attorney General

The Attorney General may, by regulation provide for the exemption—

(1) from registration, or from the requirement of furnishing any of the information required by this section, of any person who is listed as a partner, officer, director, or employee in the registration statement filed by an agent of a foreign principal under this subchapter, and

(2) from the requirement of furnishing any of the information required by this section of any agent of a foreign principal.

where by reason of the nature of the functions or activities of such person the Attorney General, having due regard for the national security and the public interest, determines that such registration, or the furnishing of such information, as the case may be, is not necessary to carry out the purposes of this subchapter.

§ 613. Exemptions

The requirements of section 612(a) of this title shall not apply to the following agents of foreign principals:

(a) Diplomatic or consular officers

A duly accredited diplomatic or consular officer of a foreign government who is so recognized by the Department of State, while said officer is engaged exclusively in activities which are recognized by the Department of State as being within the scope of the functions of such officer;

(b) Officials of foreign government

Any official of a foreign government, if such government is recognized by the United States, who is not a public-relations counsel, publicity agent, information-service employee, or a citizen of the United States, whose name and status and the character of whose duties as such official are of public record in the Department of State, while said official is engaged exclusively in activities which are recognized by the Department of State as being within the scope of the functions of such official;

(c) Staff members of diplomatic or consular officers

Any member of the staff of, or any person employed by, a duly accredited diplomatic or consular officer of a foreign government who is so recognized by the Department of State, other than a public-relations counsel, publicity agent, or information-service employee, whose name and status and the character of whose duties as such member or employee are of public record in the Department of State, while said member or employee is engaged exclusively in the performance of activities which are recognized by the Department of State as being within the scope of the functions of such member or employee;

(d) Private and nonpolitical activities; solicitation of funds

Any person engaging or agreeing to engage only (1) in private and nonpolitical activities in furtherance of the bona fide trade or commerce of such foreign principal; or (2) in other activities not serving predominantly a foreign interest; or (3) in the soliciting or collecting of funds and contributions within the United States to be used only for medical aid and assistance, or for food and clothing to relieve human suffering, if such solicitation or collection of funds and contributions is in accordance with and subject to the provisions of subchapter II of chapter 9 of this title, and such rules and regulations as may be prescribed thereunder;

(e) Religious, scholastic, or scientific pursuits

Any person engaging or agreeing to engage only in activities in furtherance of bona fide religious, scholastic, academic, or scientific pursuit or of the fine arts;

(f) Defense of foreign government vital to United States defense

Any person, or employee of such person, whose foreign principal is a government of a foreign country the defense of which the President deems vital to the defense of the United States while, (1) such person or employee engages only in activities which are in furtherance of the policies, public interest, or national defense both of such government and of the Government of the United States, and are not intended to conflict with any of the domestic or foreign policies of the Government of the United States, (2) each communication or expression by such person or employee which he intends to, or has reason to believe will, be published, disseminated, or circulated among any section of the public, or portion thereof, within the United States, is a part of such activities and is believed by such person to be truthful and accurate and the identity of such person as an agent of such foreign principal is disclosed therein, and (3) such government of a foreign country furnishes to the Secretary of State for transmittal to, and retention for the duration of this subchapter by, the Attorney General such information as to the identity and activities of such person or employee at such times as the Attorney General may require. Upon notice to the Government of which such person is an agent or to such person or employee, the Attorney General, having due regard for the public interest and national defense, may, with the approval of the Secretary of State, and shall, at the request of the Secretary of State, terminate in whole or in part the exemption herein of any such person or employee;

(g) Persons qualified to practice law

Any person qualified to practice law, insofar as he engages or agrees to engage in the legal representation of a disclosed foreign principal before any court of law or any agency of the Government of the United States: *Provided,* That for the purposes of this subsection legal representation does not include attempts to influence or persuade agency personnel or officials other than in the course of established agency proceedings, whether formal or informal.

§ 614. Filing and labeling of political propaganda

(a) Copies to Attorney General; statement as to places, times, and extent of transmission

Every person within the United States who is an agent of a foreign principal and required to register under the provisions of this subchapter and who transmits or causes to be transmitted in the United States mails or by any means or instrumentality of interstate or foreign commerce any political propaganda for or in the interests of such foreign principal (i) in the form of prints, or (ii) in any other form which is reasonably adapted to being or which he believes will be, or which he intends to be, disseminated or circulated among two or more persons shall, not later than forty-eight hours after the beginning of the transmittal thereof, file with the Attorney General two copies thereof and a statement, duly signed by or on behalf of such agent, setting forth full information as to the places, times, and extent of such transmittal.

(b) Identification statement

It shall be unlawful for any person within the United States who is an agent of a foreign principal and required to register under the provisions of this subchapter to transmit or cause to be transmitted in the United States mails or by any means or instrumentality of interstate or foreign commerce any political propaganda for or in the interests of such foreign principal (i) in the form of prints, or (ii) in any other form which is reasonably adapted to being, or which he believes will be or which he intends to be, disseminated or circulated among two or more persons, unless such political propaganda is conspicuously marked at its beginning with, or prefaced or accompanied by, a true and accurate statement, in the language or languages used in such political propaganda, setting forth the relationship or connection between the person transmitting the political propaganda or causing it to be transmitted and such propaganda; that the person transmitting such political propaganda or causing it to be transmitted is registered under this subchapter with the Department of Justice, Washington, District of Columbia, as an agent of a foreign principal, together with the name and address of such agent of a foreign principal and of such foreign principal; that, as required by this subchapter, his registration statement is available for inspection at and copies of such political propaganda are being filed with the Department of Justice; and that registration of agents of foreign principals required by the subchapter does not indicate approval by the United States Government of the contents of their political propaganda. The Attorney General, having due regard for the national security and the public interest, may by regulation prescribe the language or languages and the manner and form in which such statement shall be made and require the inclusion of such other information contained in the registration statement identifying such agent of a foreign principal and such political propaganda and its sources as may be appropriate.

(c) Public inspection

The copies of political propaganda required by this subchapter to be filed with the Attorney General shall be available for public inspection under such regulations as he may prescribe.

(d) Library of Congress

For purposes of the Library of Congress, other than for public distribution, the Secretary of the Treasury and the United States Postal Service are authorized, upon the request of the Librarian of Congress, to forward to the Library of Congress fifty copies, or as many fewer thereof as are available, of all foreign prints determined to be prohibited entry under the provisions of section 1305 of title 19 and of all foreign prints excluded from the mails under authority of section 1717 of title 18.

Notwithstanding the provisions of section 1305 of title 19 and of section 1717 of title 18, the Secretary of the Treasury is authorized to permit the entry and the United States Postal Service is authorized to permit the transmittal in the mails of foreign prints imported for governmental purposes by authority or for the use of the United States or for the use of the Library of Congress.

(e) Information furnished to agency or official of United States Government

It shall be unlawful for any person within the United States who is an agent of a foreign principal required to register under the provisions of this subchapter to transmit, convey, or otherwise furnish to any agency or official of the Government (including a Member or committee of either House of Congress) for or in the interests of such foreign principal any political propaganda or to request from any such agency or official for or in the interests of such foreign principal any information or advice with respect to any matter pertaining to the political or public interest, policies or relations of a foreign country or of a political party or pertaining to the foreign or domestic policies of the United States unless the propaganda or the request is prefaced or accompanied by a true and accurate statement to the effect that such person is registered as an agent of such foreign principal under this subchapter.

(f) Appearances before Congressional committees

Whenever any agent of a foreign principal required to register under this subchapter appears before any committee of Congress to testify for or in the interests of such foreign principal, he shall, at the time of such appearance, furnish the committee with a copy of his most recent registration statement filed with the Department of Justice as an agent of such foreign principal for inclusion in the records of the committee as part of his testimony.

§ 615. Books and records

Every agent of a foreign principal registered under this subchapter shall keep and preserve while he is an agent of a foreign principal such books of account and other records with respect to all his activities, the disclosure of which is required under the provisions of this subchapter, in accordance with such business and accounting practices, as the Attorney General, having due regard for the national security and the public interest, may by regulation prescribe as necessary or appropriate for the enforcement of the provisions of this subchapter and shall preserve the same for a period of three years following the termination of such status. Until regulations are in effect under this section every agent of a foreign principal shall keep books of account and shall preserve all written records with respect to his activities.

Such books and records shall be open at all reasonable times to the inspection of any official charged with the enforcement of this subchapter. It shall be unlawful for any person willfully to conceal, destroy, obliterate, mutilate, or falsify, or to attempt to conceal, destroy, obliterate, mutilate, or falsify, or to cause to be concealed, destroyed, obliterated, mutilated, or falsified, any books or records required to be kept under the provisions of this section.

§ 616. Public examination of official records; transmittal of records and information

(a) Permanent copy of statement; inspection; withdrawal

The Attorney General shall retain in permanent form one copy of all registration statements and all statements concerning the distribution of political propaganda furnished under this subchapter, and the same shall be public records and open to public examination and inspection at such reasonable hours, under such regulations, as the Attorney General may prescribe, and copies of the same shall be furnished to every applicant at such reasonable fee as the Attorney General may prescribe. The Attorney General may withdraw from public examination the registration statement and other statements of any agent of a foreign principal whose activities have ceased to be of a character which requires registration under the provisions of this subchapter.

(b) Secretary of State

The Attorney General shall, promptly upon receipt, transmit one copy of every registration statement filed hereunder and one copy of every amendment or supplement thereto, and one copy of every item of political propaganda filed hereunder, to the Secretary of State for such comment and use as the Secretary of State may determine to be appropriate from the point of view of the foreign relations of the United States. Failure of the Attorney General so to transmit such copy shall not be a bar to prosecution under this subchapter.

(c) Executive departments and agencies; Congressional committees

The Attorney General is authorized to furnish to departments and agencies in the executive branch and committees of the Congress such information obtained by him in the administration of this subchapter, including the names of registrants under this subchapter, copies of registration statements, or parts thereof, copies of political propaganda, or other documents or information filed under this subchapter, as may be appropriate in the light of the purposes of this subchapter.

§ 617. Liability of officers

Each officer, or person performing the functions of an officer, and each director, or person performing the functions of a director, of an agent of a foreign principal which is not an individual shall be under obligation to cause such agent to execute and file a registration statement and supplements thereto as and when such filing is required under subsections (a) and (b) of section 612 of this title and shall also be under obligation to cause such agent to comply with all the requirements of sections 614(a) and (b) and 615 of this title and all other requirements of this subchapter. Dissolution of any organization acting as an agent of a foreign principal shall not relieve any officer, or person performing the functions of an officer, or any director, or person performing the functions of a director, from complying with the provisions of this section. In case of failure of any such agent of a foreign principal to comply with any of the requirements of this subchapter, each of its officers, or persons performing the functions of officers, and each of its directors, or persons performing the functions of directors, shall be subject to prosecution therefor.

§ 618. Enforcement and penalties

(a) Violations; false statements and willful omissions

Any person who—

(1) willfully violates any provision of this subchapter or any regulation thereunder, or

(2) in any registration statement or supplement thereto or in any statement under section 614(a) of this title concerning the distribution of political propaganda or in any other document filed with or furnished to the Attorney General under the provisions of this subchapter willfully makes a false statement of a material fact or willfully omits any material fact required to be stated therein or willfully omits a material fact or a copy of a material document necessary to make the statements therein and the copies of documents furnished therewith not misleading, shall, upon conviction thereof be punished by a fine of not more than $10,000 or by imprisonment for not more than five years, or both, except that in the case of a violation of subsection (b), (e), or (f) of section 614 of this title or of subsection (g) or (h) of this section the punishment shall be a fine of not more than $5,000 or imprisonment for not more than six months, or both.

(b) Proof of identity of foreign principal

In any proceeding under this subchapter in which it is charged that a person is an agent of a foreign principal with respect to a foreign principal outside of the United States, proof of the specific identity of the foreign principal shall be permissible but not necessary.

(c) Deportation

Any alien who shall be convicted of a violation of, or a conspiracy to violate, any provision of this subchapter or any regulation thereunder shall be subject to deportation in the manner provided by sections 1251 to 1253 of title 8.

(d) Nonmailable matter

The United States Postal Service may declare to be nonmailable any communication or expression falling within clause (2) of section 611(j) of this title in the form of prints or in any other form reasonably adapted to, or reasonably appearing to be intended for, dissemination or circulation among two or more persons, which is offered or caused to be offered for transmittal in the United States mails to any person or persons in any other American republic by any agent of a foreign principal, if the United States Postal Service is informed in writing by the Secretary of State that the duly accredited diplomatic representative of such American republic has made written representation to the Department of State that the admission or circulation of such communication or expression in such American republic is prohibited by the laws thereof and has requested in writing that its transmittal thereto be stopped.

(e) Continuing offense

Failure to file any such registration statement or supplements thereto as is required by either section 612(a) or section 612(b) of this title shall be considered a continuing offense for as long as such failure exists, notwithstanding any statute of limitation or other statute to the contrary.

(f) Injunctive remedy; jurisdiction of district court; expedition of proceedings

Whenever in the judgment of the Attorney General any person is engaged in or about to engage in any acts which constitute or will constitute a violation of any provision of this subchapter, or regulations issued thereunder, or whenever any agent of a foreign principal fails to comply with any of the provisions of this subchapter or the regulations issued thereunder, or otherwise is in violation of the subchapter, the Attorney General may make application to the appropriate United States district court for an order enjoining such acts or enjoining such person from continuing to act as an agent of such foreign principal, or for an order requiring compliance with any appropriate provision of the subchapter or regulation thereunder. The district court shall have jurisdiction and authority to issue a temporary or permanent injunction, restraining order or such other order which it may deem proper. The proceedings shall be made a preferred cause and shall be expedited in every way.

(g) Deficient registration statement

If the Attorney General determines that a registration statement does not comply with the requirements of this subchapter or the regulations issued thereunder, he shall so notify the registrant in writing, specifying in what respects the statement is deficient. It shall be unlawful for any person to act as an agent of a foreign principal at any time ten days or more after receipt of such notification without filing an amended registration statement in full compliance with the requirements of this subchapter and the regulations issued thereunder.

(h) Contingent fee arrangement

It shall be unlawful for any agent of a foreign principal required to register under this subchapter to be a party to any contract, agreement, or understanding, either express or implied, with such foreign principal pursuant to which the amount or payment of the compensation, fee, or other remuneration of such agent is contingent in whole or in part upon the success of any political activities carried on by such agent.

§ 619. Territorial applicability of subchapter

This subchapter shall be applicable in the several States, the District of Columbia, the Territories, the Canal Zone, the insular possessions, and all other places now or hereafter subject to the civil or military jurisdiction of the United States.

§ 620. Rules and regulations

The Attorney General may at any time make, prescribe, amend, and rescind such rules, regulations, and forms as he may deem necessary to carry out the provisions of this subchapter.

§ 621. Reports to Congress

The Attorney General shall, from time to time, make a report to the Congress concerning the administration of this subchapter, including the nature, sources, and content of political propaganda disseminated or distributed.

Appendix D

Regulations Pursuant to Federal Agent Registration Act, 28 C.F.R. Part 5

§ 5.1 Administration and enforcement of the Act.

(a) The administration and enforcement of the Foreign Agents Registration Act of 1938, as amended (22 U.S.C. 611–621), is subject to the general supervision and direction of the Attorney General, assigned to, conducted, handled, and supervised by the Assistant Attorney General in charge of the Criminal Division (§ 0.60(b) of this chapter).

(b) The Assistant Attorney General is authorized to prescribe such forms, in addition to or in lieu of those specified in the regulations in this part, as may be necessary to carry out the purposes of this part.

(c) Copies of the Act, and of the rules, regulations, and forms prescribed pursuant to the Act, and information concerning the foregoing may be obtained upon request without charge from the Registration Unit, Criminal Division, Department of Justice, Washington, D.C. 20530.

§ 5.2 Inquiries concerning application of the Act.

Any inquiry concerning the application of the Act to any person should be addressed to the Registration Unit and should be accompanied by a detailed statement containing the following information:

(a) The identity of the agent and the foreign principal involved;

(b) The nature of the agent's activities for or in the interest of the foreign principal;

(c) A copy of the existing or proposed written contract with the foreign principal, or a full description of the terms and conditions of each existing or proposed oral agreement.

§ 5.3 Filing of a registration statement.

All statements, exhibits, amendments, and other documents and papers required to be filed under the Act or under this part shall be submitted in duplicate to the Registration Unit. Filing of such documents may be made in person or by mail, and they shall be deemed to be filed upon their receipt by the Registration Unit.

§ 5.4 Computation of time.

Sundays and holidays shall be counted in computing any period of time prescribed in the Act or in the rules and regulations in this part.

§ 5.100 Definition of terms.

(a) As used in this part:

(1) The term "Act" means the Foreign Agents Registration Act of 1938, as amended (22 U.S.C. 611–621).

(2) The term "Attorney General" means the Attorney General of the United States.

(3) The term "Assistant Attorney General" means the Assistant Attor-

ney General in charge of the Criminal Division, Department of Justice, Washington, D.C. 20530.

(4) The term "Secretary of State" means the Secretary of State of the United States.

(5) The term "Registration Unit" means the Registration Unit, Internal Security Section, Criminal Division, Department of Justice, Washington, D.C. 20530.

(6) The term "rules and regulations" includes the regulations in this part and all other rules and regulations prescribed by the Attorney General pursuant to the Act and all registration forms and instructions thereon which may be prescribed by the regulations in this part or by the Assistant Attorney General.

(7) The term "registrant" means any person who has filed a registration statement with the Registration Unit, pursuant to section 2(a) of the Act and § 5.3.

(8) Unless otherwise specified, the term "agent of a foreign principal" means an agent of a foreign principal required to register under the Act.

(9) The term "foreign principal" includes a person any of whose activities are directed or indirectly supervised, directed, controlled, financed, or subsidized in whole or in major part by a foreign principal as that term is defined in section 1(b) of the Act.

(10) The term "initial statement" means the statement required to be filed with the Attorney General under section 2(a) of the Act.

(11) The term "supplemental statement" means the supplement required to be filed with the Attorney General under section 2(b) of the Act at intervals of 6 months following the filing of the initial statement.

(12) The term "final statement" means the statement required to be filed with the Attorney General following the termination of the registrant's obligation to register.

(13) The term "short form registration statement" means the registration statement required to be filed by certain partners, officers, directors, associates, employees, and agents of a registrant.

(b) As used in the Act, the term "control" or any of its variants shall be deemed to include the possession or the exercise of the power, directly or indirectly, to determine the policies or the activities of a person, whether through the ownership of voting rights, by contract, or otherwise.

(c) The term "agency" as used in sections 1(c), 1(o), 1(q), 3(g), and 4(e) of the Act shall be deemed to refer to every unit in the executive and legislative branches of the Government of the United States, including committees of both Houses of Congress.

(d) The term "official" as used in sections 1(c), 1(o), 1(q), 3(g), and 4(e) of the Act shall be deemed to include Members and officers of both Houses of Congress as well as officials in the executive branch of the Government of the United States.

(e) The terms "formulating, adopting, or changing," as used in section 1(o) of the Act, shall be deemed to include any activity which seeks to maintain any existing domestic or foreign policy of the United States. They do not include making a routine inquiry of a Government official or employee concerning a current policy or seeking administrative action in a matter where such policy is not in question.

(f) The term "domestic or foreign policies of the United States," as used in sections 1 (o) and (p) of the Act, shall be deemed to relate to existing and proposed legislation, or legislative action generally; treaties; executive agreements, proclamations, and orders; decisions relating to or affecting departmental or agency policy, and the like.

§ 5.200 Registration.

(a) Registration under the Act is accomplished by the filing of an initial statement together with all the exhibits required by § 5.201 and the filing of a supplemental statement at intervals of 6 months for the duration of the principal-agent relationship requiring registration.

(b) The initial statement shall be filed on Form OBD-63.

§ 5.201 Exhibits.

(a) The following described exhibits are required to be filed for each foreign principal of the registrant:

(1) *Exhibit A.* This exhibit, which shall be filed on Form OBD-67, shall set forth the information required to be disclosed concerning each foreign principal.

(2) *Exhibit B.* This exhibit, which shall be filed on Form OBD-65, shall set forth the agreement or under-

standing between the registrant and each of his foreign principals as well as the nature and method of performance of such agreement or understanding and the existing or proposed activities engaged in or to be engaged in, including political activities, by the registrant for the foreign principal.

(b) Any change in the information furnished in Exhibit A or B shall be reported to the Registration Unit within 10 days of such change. The filing of a new exhibit may then be required by the Assistant Attorney General.

(c) Whenever the registrant is an association, corporation, organization, or any other combination of individuals, the following documents shall be filed as Exhibit C:

(1) A copy of the registrant's charter, articles of incorporation or association, or constitution, and a copy of its bylaws, and amendments thereto;

(2) A copy of every other instrument or document, and a statement of the terms and conditions of every oral agreement, relating to the organization, powers and purposes of the registrant.

(d) The requirement to file any of the documents described in paragraphs (c) (1) and (2) of this section may be wholly or partially waived upon written application by the registrant to the Assistant Attorney General setting forth fully the reasons why such waiver should be granted.

(e) Whenever a registrant, within the United States, receives or collects contributions, loans, money, or other things of value, as part of a fund-raising campaign, for or in the interests of his foreign principal, he shall file as Exhibit D a statement so captioned setting forth the amount of money or the value of the thing received or collected, the names and addresses of the persons from whom such money or thing of value was received or collected, and the amount of money or a description of the thing of value transmitted to the foreign principal as well as the manner and time of such transmission.

§ 5.202 Short form registration statement.

(a) Except as provided in paragraphs (b), (c), and (d) of this section, each partner, officer, director, associate, employee, and agent of a registrant is required to file a registration statement under the Act. Unless the Assist-

ant Attorney General specifically directs otherwise, this obligation may be satisfied by the filing of a short form registration statement.

(b) A partner, officer, director, associate, employee, or agent of a registrant who does not engage directly in activity in furtherance of the interests of the foreign principal is not required to file a short form registration statement.

(c) An employee or agent of a registrant whose services in furtherance of the interests of the foreign principal are rendered in a clerical, secretarial, or in a related or similar capacity, is not required to file a short form registration statement.

(d) Whenever the agent of a registrant is a partnership, association, corporation, or other combination of individuals, and such agent is not within the exemption of paragraph (b) of this section, only those partners, officers, directors, associates, and employees who engage directly in activity in furtherance of the interests of the registrant's foreign principal are required to file a short form registration statement.

(e) The short form registration statement shall be filed on Form OBD–66. Any change affecting the information furnished with respect to the nature of the services rendered by the person filing the statement, or the compensation he receives, shall require the filing of a new short form registration statement within 10 days after the occurrence of such change. There is no requirement to file exhibits or supplemental statements to a short form registration statement.

§ 5.203 Supplemental statement.

(a) Supplemental statements shall be filed on Form OBD–64.

(b) The obligation to file a supplemental statement at 6-month intervals during the agency relationship shall continue even though the registrant has not engaged during the period in any activity in the interests of his foreign principal.

(c) The time within which to file a supplemental statement may be extended for sufficient cause shown in a written application to the Assistant Attorney General.

§ 5.204 Amendments.

(a) An initial, supplemental, or final statement which is deemed deficient by the Assistant Attorney General must be amended upon his request. Such amendment shall be filed upon Form OBD–68 and shall identify the item of the statement to be amended.

(b) A change in the information furnished in an initial or supplemental statement under clauses (3), (4), (6), and (9) of section 2(a) of the Act shall be by amendment, unless the notice which is required to be given of such change under section 2(b) is deemed sufficient by the Assistant Attorney General.

§ 5.205   Termination of registration.

(a) A registrant shall, within 30 days after the termination of his obligation to register, file a final statement on Form OBD–64 with the Registration Unit for the final period of the agency relationship not covered by any previous statement.

(b) Registration under the Act shall be terminated upon the filing of a final statement, if the registrant has fully discharged all his obligations under the Act.

(c) A registrant whose activities on behalf of each of his foreign principals become confined to those for which an exemption under section 3 of the Act is available may file a final statement notwithstanding the continuance of the agency relationship with the foreign principals.

§ 5.206   Language and wording of registration statement.

(a) Except as provided in the next sentence, each statement, amendment, exhibit, or notice required to be filed under the Act shall be submitted in the English language. An exhibit may be filed even though it is in a foreign language if it is accompanied by an English translation certified under oath by the translator before a notary public, or other person authorized by law to administer oaths for general purposes, as a true and accurate translation.

(b) A statement, amendment, exhibit, or notice required to be filed under the Act should be typewritten, but will be accepted for filing if it is written legibly in ink.

(c) Copies of any document made by any of the duplicating processes may be filed pursuant to the Act if they are clear and legible.

(d) A response shall be made to every item on each pertinent form, unless a registrant is specifically instructed otherwise in the form. Whenever the item is inapplicable or the appropriate response to an item is "none," an express statement to that effect shall be made.

§ 5.207   Incorporation by reference.

(a) Each initial, supplemental, and final statement shall be complete in and of itself. Incorporation of information by reference to statements previously filed is not permissible.

(b) Whenever insufficient space is provided for response to any item in a form, reference shall be made in such space to a full insert page or pages on which the item number and inquiry shall be restated and a complete answer given. Inserts and riders of less than full page size should not be used.

§ 5.208   Disclosure of foreign principals.

A registrant who represents more than one foreign principal is required to list in the statements he files under the Act only those foreign principals for whom he is not entitled to claim exemption under section 3 of the Act.

§ 5.209   Information relating to employees.

A registrant shall list in the statements he files under the Act only those employees whose duties require them to engage directly in activities in furtherance of the interests of the foreign principal.

§ 5.210   Amount of detail required in information relating to registrant's activities and expenditures.

A statement is "detailed" within the meaning of clauses 6 and 8 of section 2 (a) of the Act when it has that degree of specificity necessary to permit meaningful public evaluation of each of the significant steps taken by a registrant to achieve the purposes of the agency relation.

§ 5.211   Sixty-day period to be covered in initial statement.

The 60-day period referred to in clauses 5, 7, and 8 of section 2(a) of the Act shall be measured from the time that a registrant has incurred an obligation to register and not from the time that he files his initial statement.

§ 5.300 Burden of establishing availability of exemption.

The burden of establishing the availability of an exemption from registration under the Act shall rest upon the person for whose benefit the exemption is claimed.

§ 5.301 Exemption under section 3(a) of the Act.

(a) A consular officer of a foreign government shall be considered duly accredited under section 3(a) of the Act whenever he has received formal recognition as such, whether provisionally or by exequatur, from the Secretary of State.

(b) The exemption provided by section 3(a) of the Act to a duly accredited diplomatic or consular officer is personal and does not include within its scope an office, bureau, or other entity.

§ 5.302 Exemptions under sections 3 (b) and (c) of the Act.

The exemptions provided by sections 3 (b) and (c) of the Act shall not be available to any person described therein unless he has filed with the Secretary of State a fully executed Notification of Status with a Foreign Government (Form D.S. 394).

§ 5.303 Exemption available to persons accredited to international organizations.

Persons designated by foreign governments as their representatives in or to an international organization, other than nationals of the United States, are exempt from registration under the Act in accordance with the provisions of the International Organizations Immunities Act, if they have been duly notified to and accepted by the Secretary of State as such representatives, officers, or employees, and if they engage exclusively in activities which are recognized as being within the scope of their official functions.

§ 5.304 Exemptions under sections 3 (d) and (e) of the Act.

(a) As used in section 3(d), the term "trade or commerce" shall include the exchange, transfer, purchase, or sale of commodities, services, or property of any kind.

(b) For the purpose of section 3(d) of the Act, activities of an agent of a foreign principal as defined in section 1(c) of the Act, in furtherance of the bona fide trade or commerce of such foreign principal, shall be considered "private," even though the foreign principal is owned or controlled by a foreign government, so long as the activities do not directly promote the public or political interests of the foreign government.

(c) For the purpose of section 3(d) of the Act, the disclosure of the identity of the foreign person that is required under section 1(q) of the Act shall be made to each official of the U.S. Government with whom the activities are conducted. This disclosure shall be made to the Government official prior to his taking any action upon the business transacted. The burden of establishing that the required disclosure was made shall lie upon the person claiming the exemption.

(d) The exemption provided by section 3(e) of the Act shall not be available to any person described therein if he engages in political activities as defined in section 1(o) of the Act for or in the interests of his foreign principal.

§ 5.305 Exemption under section 3(f) of the Act.

The exemption provided by section 3(f) of the Act shall not be available unless the President has, by publication in the FEDERAL REGISTER, designated for the purpose of this section the country the defense of which he deems vital to the defense of the United States.

§ 5.306 Exemption under section 3(g) of the Act.

For the purpose of section 3(g) of the Act—

(a) Attempts to influence or persuade agency personnel or officials other than in the course of established agency proceedings, whether formal or informal, shall include only such attempts to influence or persuade with reference to formulating, adopting, or changing the domestic or foreign policies of the United States or with reference to the political or public interests, policies, or relations of a government of a foreign country or a foreign political party; and

(b) If an attorney engaged in legal representation of a foreign principal before an agency of the U.S. Government is not otherwise required to disclose the identity of his principal as a matter of established agency procedure, he must make such disclosure, in conformity with this section of the Act, to each of the agency's personnel or officials before whom and at the time his legal representation is undertaken. The burden of establishing that the required disclosure was made shall like upon the person claiming the exemption.

§ 5.400 Filing of political propaganda.

(a) The two copies of each item of political propaganda required to be filed with the Attorney General under section 4(a) of the Act shall be filed with the Registration Unit.

(b) Whenever two copies of an item of political propaganda have been filed pursuant to section 4(a) of the Act, an agent of a foreign principal shall not be required, in the event of further dissemination of the same material, to forward additional copies thereof to the Registration Unit.

(c) Unless specifically directed to do so by the Assistant Attorney General, a registrant is not required to file two copies of a motion picture containing political propaganda which he disseminates on behalf of his foreign principal, so long as he files monthly reports on its dissemination. In each such case this registrant shall submit to the Registration Unit either a film strip showing the label required by section 4(b) of the Act or an affidavit certifying that the required label has been made a part of the film.

§ 5.401 Dissemination report.

(a) A Dissemination Report shall be filed with the Registration Unit for each item of political propaganda that is transmitted, or caused to be transmitted, in the U.S. mails, or by any means or instrumentality of interstate or foreign commerce, by an agent of a foreign principal for or in the interests of any of his foreign principals.

(b) The Dissemination Report shall be filed on Form OBD-69.

(c) Except as provided in paragraph (d) of this section, a Dissemination Report shall be filed no later than 48 hours after the beginning of the transmittal of the political propaganda.

(d) Whenever transmittals of the same political propaganda are made over a period of time, a Dissemination Report may be filed monthly for as long as such transmittals continue.

(e) A Dissemination Report shall be complete in and of itself. Incorporation of information by reference to reports previously filed is not permissible.

§ 5.402 Labeling political propaganda.

(a) Within the meaning of this part, political propaganda shall be deemed labeled whenever it has been marked or stamped conspicuously at its beginning with a statement setting forth such information as is required under section 4(b) of the Act.

(b) An item of political propaganda which is required to be labeled under section 4(b) of the Act and which is in the form of prints shall be marked or stamped conspicuously at the beginning of such item with a statement in the language or languages used therein, setting forth such information as is required under section 4(b) of the Act.

(c) An item of political propaganda which is required to be labeled under section 4(b) of the Act but which is not in the form of prints shall be accompanied by a statement setting forth such information as is required under section 4(b) of the Act.

(d) Political propaganda as defined in section 1(j) of the Act which is televised or broadcast, or which is caused to be televised or broadcast, by an agent of a foreign principal, shall be introduced by a statement which is reasonably adapted to convey to the viewers or listeners thereof such information as is required under section 4(b) of the Act.

(e) An agent of a foreign principal who transmits or causes to be transmitted in the U.S. mails or by any means or instrumentality of interstate or foreign commerce a still or motion picture film which contains political propaganda as defined in section 1(j) of the Act shall insert at the beginning of such film a statement which is reasonably adapted to convey to the viewers thereof such information as is required under section 4(b) of the Act.

(f) For the purpose of section 4(e) of the Act, the statement that must preface or accompany political propaganda or a request for information shall be in writing.

§ 5.500 Maintenance of books and records.

(a) A registrant shall keep and preserve in accordance with the provisions of section 5 of the Act the following books and records:

(1) All correspondence, memoranda, cables, telegrams, teletype messages,

and other written communications to and from all foreign principals and all other persons, relating to the registrant's activities on behalf of, or in the interest of any of his foreign principals.

(2) All correspondence, memoranda, cables, telegrams, teletype messages, and other written communications to and from all persons, other than foreign principals, relating to the registrant's political activity, or relating to political activity on the part of any of the registrant's foreign principals.

(3) Original copies of all written contracts between the registrant and any of his foreign principals.

(4) Records containing the names and addresses of persons to whom political propaganda has been transmitted.

(5) All bookkeeping and other financial records relating to the registrant's activities on behalf of any of his foreign principals, including canceled checks, bank statements, and records of income and disbursements, showing names and addresses of all persons who paid moneys to, or received moneys from, the registrant, the specific amounts so paid or received, and the date on which each item was paid or received.

(6) If the registrant is a corporation, partnership, association, or other combination of individuals, all minute books.

(7) Such books or records as will disclose the names and addresses of all employees and agents of the registrant, including persons no longer acting as such employees or agents.

(8) Such other books, records, and documents as are necessary properly to reflect the activities for which registration is required.

(b) The books and records listed in paragraph (a) of this section shall be kept and preserved in such manner as to render them readily accessible for inspection pursuant to section 5 of the Act.

(c) A registrant shall keep and preserve the books and records listed in paragraph (a) of this section for a period of 3 years following the termination of his registration under § 5.205.

(d) Upon good and sufficient cause shown in writing to the Assistant Attorney General, a registrant may be permitted to destroy books and records in support of the information furnished in an initial or supplemental statement which he filed 5 or more years prior to the date of his application to destroy.

§ 5.501 Inspection of books and records.

Officials of the Criminal Division and the Federal Bureau of Investigation are authorized under section 5 of the Act to inspect the books and records listed in § 5.500(a).

§ 5.600 Public examination of records.

Registration statements, Dissemination Reports, and copies of political propaganda filed under section 4(a) of the Act, shall be available for public examination at the Registration Unit on official business days, from 10 a.m. to 4 p.m.

§ 5.601 Copies of records available.

(a) Copies of registration statements and Dissemination Reports may be obtained from the Registration Unit upon payment of a fee at the rate of 10 cents per copy of each page of the material requested.

(b) Information as to the fee to be charged for copies of registration statements and Dissemination Reports and the time required for their preparation may be obtained upon request to the Registration Unit.

(c) Payment of the fee shall accompany an order for copies, and shall be made in cash, by U.S. postal money order, or by certified bank check made payable to the Treasurer of the United States. Postage stamps will not be accepted.

§ 5.800 Ten-day filing requirement.

The 10-day filing requirement provided by section 8(g) of the Act shall be deemed satisfied if the amendment to the registration statement is deposited in the U.S. mails no later than the 10th day of the period.

§ 5.801 Activity beyond 10-day period.

A registrant who has within the 10-day period filed an amendment to his registration statement pursuant to a Notice of Deficiency given under section 8(g) of the Act may continue to act as an agent of a foreign principal beyond this period unless he receives a Notice of Noncompliance from the Registration Unit.

Appendix E

Statutory Provisions Relating to Lobbying and Ethics of Federal Officials

Conflict of Interests, 18 U.S.C. §§201–209

§ 201. Bribery of public officials and witnesses

(a) For the purpose of this section—

(1) the term "public official" means Member of Congress, Delegate, or Resident Commissioner, either before or after such official has qualified, or an officer or employee or person acting for or on behalf of the United States, or any department, agency or branch of Government thereof, including the District of Columbia, in any official function, under or by authority of any such department, agency, or branch of Government, or a juror;

(2) the term "person who has been selected to be a public official" means any person who has been nominated or appointed to be a public official, or has been officially informed that such person will be so nominated or appointed; and

(3) the term "official act" means any decision or action on any question, matter, cause, suit, proceeding or controversy, which may at any time be pending, or which may by law be brought before any public official, in such official's official capacity, or in such official's place of trust or profit.

(b) Whoever—

(1) directly or indirectly, corruptly gives, offers or promises anything of value to any public official or person who has been selected to be a public official, or offers or promises any public official or any person who has been selected to be a public official to give anything of value to any other person or entity, with intent—

(A) to influence any official act; or

(B) to influence such public official or person who has been selected to be a public official to commit or aid in committing, or collude in, or allow, any fraud, or make opportunity for the commission of any fraud, on the United States; or

(C) to induce such public official or such person who has been selected to be a public official to do or omit to do any act in violation of the lawful duty of such official or person;

(2) being a public official or person selected to be a public official, directly or indirectly, corruptly demands, seeks, receives, accepts, or agrees to receive or accept anything of value personally or for any other person or entity, in return for:

(A) being influenced in the performance of any official act;

(B) being influenced to commit or aid in committing, or to collude in, or allow, any fraud, or make opportunity for the commission of any fraud on the United States; or

(C) being induced to do or omit to do any act in violation of the official duty of such official or person;

(3) directly or indirectly, corruptly gives, offers, or promises anything of value to any person, or offers or promises such person to give anything of value to any other person or entity, with intent to influence the testimony under oath or affirmation of such first-mentioned person as a witness upon a trial, hearing, or other proceeding, before any court, any committee of either House or both Houses of Congress, or any agency, commission, or officer authorized by the laws of the United States to hear evidence or take testimony, or with intent to influence such person to absent himself therefrom;

(4) directly or indirectly, corruptly demands, seeks, receives, accepts, or agrees to receive or accept anything of value personally or for any other person or entity in return for being influenced in testimony under oath or affirmation as a witness upon any such trial, hearing, or other proceeding, or in return for absenting himself therefrom;

185

shall be fined not more than three times the monetary equivalent of the thing of value, or imprisoned for not more than fifteen years, or both, and may be disqualified from holding any office of honor, trust, or profit under the United States.

(c) Whoever—

(1) otherwise than as provided by law for the proper discharge of official duty—

(A) directly or indirectly gives, offers, or promises anything of value to any public official, former public official, or person selected to be a public official, for or because of any official act performed or to be performed by such public official, former public official, or person selected to be a public official; or

(B) being a public official, former public official, or person selected to be a public official, otherwise than as provided by law for the proper discharge of official duty, directly or indirectly demands, seeks, receives, accepts, or agrees to receive or accept anything of value personally for or because of any official act performed or to be performed by such official or person;

(2) directly or indirectly, gives, offers, or promises anything of value to any person, for or because of the testimony under oath or affirmation given or to be given by such person as a witness upon a trial, hearing, or other proceeding, before any court, any committee of either House or both Houses of Congress, or any agency, commission, or officer authorized by the laws of the United States to hear evidence or take testimony, or for or because of such person's absence therefrom;

(3) directly or indirectly, demands, seeks, receives, accepts, or agrees to receive or accept anything of value personally for or because of the testimony under oath or affirmation given or to be given by such person as a witness upon any such trial, hearing, or other proceeding, or for or because of such person's absence therefrom;

shall be fined under this title or imprisoned for not more than two years, or both.

(d) Paragraphs (3) and (4) of subsection (b) and paragraphs (2) and (3) of subsection (c) shall not be construed to prohibit the payment or receipt of witness fees provided by law, or the payment, by the party upon whose behalf a witness is called and receipt by a witness, of the reasonable cost of travel and subsistence incurred and the reasonable value of time lost in attendance at any such trial, hearing, or proceeding, or in the case of expert witnesses, a reasonable fee for time spent in the preparation of such opinion, and in appearing and testifying.

(e) The offenses and penalties prescribed in this section are separate from and in addition to those prescribed in sections 1503, 1504, and 1505 of this title.

§ 202. Definitions

(a) For the purpose of sections 203, 205, 207, 208, and 209 of this title the term "special Government employee" shall mean an officer or employee of the executive or legislative branch of the United States Government, of any independent agency of the United States or of the District of Columbia, who is retained, designated, appointed, or employed to perform, with or without compensation, for not to exceed one hundred and thirty days during any period of three hundred and sixty-five consecutive days, temporary duties either on a full-time or intermittent basis, a part-time United States commissioner, a part-time United States magistrate, or, regardless of the number of days of appointment, an independent counsel appointed under chapter 40 of title 28 and any person appointed by that independent counsel under section 594(c) of title 28. Notwithstanding the next preceding sentence, every person serving as a part-time local representative of a Member of Congress in the Member's home district or State shall be classified as a special Government employee. Notwithstanding section 29(c) and (d) of the Act of August 10, 1956 (70A Stat. 632; 5 U.S.C. 30r(c) and (d)), a Reserve officer of the Armed Forces, or an officer of the National Guard of the United States, unless otherwise an officer or employee of the United States, shall be classified as a special Government employee while on active duty solely for training. A Reserve officer of the Armed Forces or an officer of the National Guard of the United States who is voluntarily serving a period of extended active duty in excess of one hundred and thirty days shall be classified as an officer of the United States within the meaning of section 203 and sections 205 through 209 and 218. A Reserve officer of the Armed Forces or an officer of the National Guard of the United States who is serving involuntarily shall be classified as a special Government employee. The terms "officer or employee" and "special Government employee" as used in sections 203, 205, 207 through 209, and 218, shall not include enlisted members of the Armed Forces.

(b) For the purposes of sections 205 and 207 of this title, the term "official responsibility" means the direct administrative or operating authority, whether intermediate or final, and either exercisable alone or with others, and either personally or through subordinates, to approve, disapprove, or otherwise direct Government action.

§ 203. Compensation to Members of Congress, officers, and others in matters affecting the Government

(a) Whoever, otherwise than as provided by law for the proper discharge of official duties, directly or indirectly—

(1) demands, seeks, receives, accepts, or agrees to receive or accept any compensation for any services rendered or to be rendered either personally or by another—

(A) at a time when such person is a Member of Congress, Member of Congress Elect, Delegate, Delegate Elect, Resident Commissioner, or Resident Commissioner Elect; or

(B) at a time when such person is an officer or employee of the United States in the executive, legislative, or judicial branch of the Government, or in any agency of the United States, including the District of Columbia,

in relation to any proceeding, application, request for a ruling or other determination, contract, claim, controversy, charge, accusation, arrest, or other particular matter in which the United States is a party or has a direct and substantial interest, before any department, agency, court-martial, officer, or any civil, military, or naval commission; or

(2) knowingly gives, promises, or offers any compensation for any such services rendered or to be rendered at a time when the person to whom the compensation is given, promised, or offered, is or was such a Member, Delegate, Commissioner, officer, or employee;

shall be fined under this title or imprisoned for not more than two years, or both; and shall be incapable of holding any office of honor, trust, or profit under the United States.

(b) A special Government employee shall be subject to subsection (a) only in relation to a particular matter involving a specific party or parties—

(1) in which such employee has at any time participated personally and substantially as a Government employee or as a special Government employee through decision, approval, disapproval, recommendation, the rendering of advice, investigation or otherwise; or

(2) which is pending in the department or agency of the Government in which such employee is serving except that paragraph (2) of this subsection shall not apply in the case of a special Government employee who has served in such department or agency no more than sixty days during the immediately preceding period of three hundred and sixty-five consecutive days.

§ 204. Practice in United States Claims Court or the United States Court of Appeals for the Federal Circuit by Members of Congress

Whoever, being a Member of Congress, Member of Congress Elect, Delegate from the District of Columbia, Delegate Elect from the District of Columbia, Resident Commissioner, or Resident Commissioner Elect, practices in the United States Claims Court or the United States Court of Appeals for the Federal Circuit, shall be fined not more than $10,000 or imprisoned for not more than two years, or both, and shall be incapable of holding any office of honor, trust, or profit under the United States.

§ 205. Activities of officers and employees in claims against and other matters affecting the Government

Whoever, being an officer or employee of the United States in the executive, legislative, or judicial branch of the Government or in any agency of the United States, including the District of Columbia, otherwise than in the proper discharge of his official duties—

(1) acts as agent or attorney for prosecuting any claim against the United States, or receives any gratuity, or any share of or interest in any such claim in consideration of assistance in the prosecution of such claim, or

(2) acts as agent or attorney for anyone before any department, agency, court, court-martial, officer, or any civil, military, or naval commission in connection with any proceeding, application, request for a ruling or other determination, contract, claim, controversy, charge, accusation, arrest, or other particular matter in which the United States is a party or has a direct and substantial interest—

Shall be fined not more than $10,000 or imprisoned for not more than two years, or both.

A special Government employee shall be subject to the preceding paragraphs only in relation to a particular matter involving a specific party or parties (1) in which he has at any time

participated personally and substantially as a Government employee or as a special Government employee through decision, approval, disapproval, recommendation, the rendering of advice, investigation or otherwise, or (2) which is pending in the department or agency of the Government in which he is serving: *Provided,* That clause (2) shall not apply in the case of a special Government employee who has served in such department or agency no more than sixty days during the immediately preceding period of three hundred and sixty-five consecutive days.

Nothing herein prevents an officer or employee, if not inconsistent with the faithful performance of his duties, from acting without compensation as agent or attorney for any person who is the subject of disciplinary, loyalty, or other personnel administration proceedings in connection with those proceedings.

Nothing herein or in section 203 prevents an officer or employee, including a special Government employee, from acting, with or without compensation, as agent or attorney for his parents, spouse, child, or any person for whom, or for any estate for which, he is serving as guardian, executor, administrator, trustee, or other personal fiduciary except in those matters in which he has participated personally and substantially as a Government employee, through decision, approval, disapproval, recommendation, the rendering of advice, investigation, or otherwise, or which are the subject of his official responsibility, provided that the Government official responsible for appointment to his position approves.

Nothing herein or in section 203 prevents a special Government employee from acting as agent or attorney for another person in the performance of work under a grant by, or a contract with or for the benefit of, the United States provided that the head of the department or agency concerned with the grant or contract shall certify in writing that the national interest so requires.

Such certification shall be published in the Federal Register.

Nothing herein prevents an officer or employee from giving testimony under oath or from making statements required to be made under penalty for perjury or contempt.

§ 206. Exemption of retired officers of the uniformed services

Sections 203 and 205 of this title shall not apply to a retired officer of the uniformed services of the United States while not on active duty and not otherwise an officer or employee of the United States, or to any person specially excepted by Act of Congress.

§ 207. Disqualification of former officers and employees; disqualification of partners of current officers and employees

(a) Whoever, having been an officer or employee of the executive branch of the United States Government, of any independent agency of the United States, or of the District of Columbia, including a special Government employee, after his employment has ceased, knowingly acts as agent or attorney for, or otherwise represents, any other person (except the United States), in any formal or informal appearance before, or, with the intent to influence, makes any oral or written communication on behalf of any other person (except the United States) to—

(1) any department, agency, court, court-martial, or any civil, military, or naval commission of the United States or the District of Columbia, or any officer or employee thereof, and

(2) in connection with any judicial or other proceeding, application, request for a ruling or other determination, contract, claim, controversy, investigation, charge, accusation, arrest, or other particular matter involving a specific party or parties in which the United States or the District of Columbia is a party or has a direct and substantial interest, and

(3) in which he participated personally and substantially as an officer or employee through decision, approval, disapproval, recommendation, the rendering of advice, investigation or otherwise, while so employed; or

(b) Whoever, (i) having been so employed, within two years after his employment has ceased, knowingly acts as agent or attorney for, or otherwise represents, any other person (except the United States), in any formal or informal appearance before, or, with the intent to influence, makes any oral or written communication on behalf of any other person (except the United States) to, or (ii) having been so employed and as specified in subsection (d) of this section, within two years after his employment has ceased, knowingly represents or aids, counsels, advises, consults, or assists in representing any other person (except the United States) by personal presence at any formal or informal appearance before—

(1) any department, agency, court, court-martial, or any civil, military or naval commission of the United States or the District of Columbia, or any officer or employee thereof, and

(2) in connection with any judicial or other proceeding, application, request for a ruling or other determination, contract, claim, controversy, investigation, charge, accusation, arrest or other particular matter involving a specific party or parties in which the United States or the District of Columbia is a party or has a direct and substantial interest, and

(3) as to (i), which was actually pending under his official responsibility as an officer or employee within a period of one year prior to the termination of such responsibility, or, as to (ii), in which he participated personally and substantially as an officer or employee; or

(c) Whoever, other than a special Government employee who serves for less than sixty days in a given calendar year, having been so employed as specified in subsection (d) of this section, within one year after such employment has ceased, knowingly acts as agent or attorney for, or otherwise represents, anyone other than the United States in any formal or informal appearance before, or, with the intent to influence, makes any oral or written communication on behalf of anyone other than the United States, to—

(1) the department or agency in which he served as an officer or employee, or any officer or employee thereof, and

(2) in connection with any judicial, rulemaking, or other proceeding, application, request for a ruling or other determination, contract, claim, controversy, investigation, charge, accusation, arrest, or other particular matter, and

(3) which is pending before such department or agency or in which such department

or agency has a direct and substantial interest—

shall be fined not more than $10,000 or imprisoned for not more than two years, or both.

(d)(1) Subsection (c) of this section shall apply to a person employed—

(A) at a rate of pay specified in or fixed according to subchapter II of chapter 53 of title 5, United States Code, or a comparable or greater rate of pay under other authority;

(B) on active duty as a commissioned officer of a uniformed service assigned to pay grade of O-9 or above as described in section 201 of title 37, United States Code; or

(C) in a position which involves significant decision-making or supervisory responsibility, as designated under this subparagraph by the Director of the Office of Government Ethics, in consultation with the department or agency concerned. Only positions which are not covered by subparagraphs (A) and (B) above, and for which the basic rate of pay is equal to or greater than the basic rate of pay for GS-17 of the General Schedule prescribed by section 5332 of title 5, United States Code, or positions which are established within the Senior Executive Service pursuant to the Civil Service Reform Act of 1978, or positions of active duty commissioned officers of the uniformed services assigned to pay O-7 or O-8, as described in section 201 of title 37, United States Code, may be designated. As to persons in positions designated under this subparagraph, the Director may limit the restrictions of subsection (c) to permit a former officer or employee, who served in a separate agency or bureau within a department or agency, to make appearances before or communications to persons in an unrelated agency or bureau, within the same department or agency, having separate and distinct subject matter jurisdiction, upon a determination by the Director that there exists no potential for use of undue influence or unfair advantage based on past government service. On an annual basis, the Director of the Office of Government Ethics shall review the designations and determinations made under this subparagraph and, in consultation with the department or agency concerned, make such additions and deletions as are necessary. Departments and agencies shall cooperate to the fullest extent with the Director of the Office of Government Ethics in the exercise of his responsibilities under this paragraph.

(2) The prohibition of subsection (c) shall not apply to appearances, communications, or representation by a former officer or employee, who is—

(A) an elected official of a State or local government, or

(B) whose principal occupation or employment is with (i) an agency or instrumentality of a State or local government, (ii) an accredited, degree-granting institution of higher education, as defined in section 1201(a) of the Higher Education Act of 1965, or (iii) a hospital or medical research organization, exempted and defined under section 501(c)(3) of the Internal Revenue Code of 1986, and the appearance, communication, or representation is on behalf of such government, institution, hospital, or organization.

(e) For the purposes of subsection (c), whenever the Director of the Office of Government Ethics determines that a separate statutory agency or bureau within a department or agency exercises functions which are distinct and separate from the remaining functions of the department or agency, the Director shall by rule designate such agency or bureau as a separate department or agency; except that such designation shall not apply to former heads of designated bureaus or agencies, or former officers and employees of the department or agency whose official responsibilities included supervision of said agency or bureau.

(f) The prohibitions of subsections (a), (b), and (c) shall not apply with respect to the making of communications solely for the purpose of furnishing scientific or technological information under procedures acceptable to the department or agency concerned, or if the head of the department or agency concerned with the particular matter, in consultation with the Director of the Office of Government Ethics, makes a certification, published in the Federal Register, that the former officer or employee has outstanding qualifications in a scientific, technological, or other technical discipline, and is acting with respect to a particular matter which requires such qualifications, and that the national interest would be served by the participation of the former officer or employee.

(g) Whoever, being a partner of an officer or employee of the executive branch of the United States Government, of any independent agency of the United States, or of the District of Columbia, including a special Government employee, acts as agent or attorney for anyone other than the United States before any department, agency, court, court-martial, or any civil, military, or naval commission of the United States or the District of Columbia, or any officer or employee thereof, in connection with any judicial or other proceeding, application, request for a ruling or other determination, contract, claim, controversy, investigation, charge, accusation, arrest, or other particular matter in which the United States or the District of Columbia is a party or has a direct and substantial interest and in which such officer or employee or special Government employee participates or has participated personally and substantially as an officer or employee through decision, approval, disapproval, recommendation, the rendering of advice, investigation, or otherwise, or which is the subject of his official responsibility, shall be fined not more than $5,000, or imprisoned for not more than one year, or both.

(h) Nothing in this section shall prevent a former officer or employee from giving testimony under oath, or from making statements required to be made under penalty of perjury.

(i) The prohibition contained in subsection (c) shall not apply to appearances or communications by a former officer or employee concerning matters of a personal and individual nature, such as personal income taxes or pension benefits; nor shall the prohibition of that subsection prevent a former officer or employee from making or providing a statement, which is based on the former officer's or employee's own special knowledge in the particular area that is the subject of the statement, provided that no compensation is thereby received, other than that regularly provided for by law or regulation for witnesses.

(j) If the head of the department or agency in which the former officer or employee served finds, after notice and opportunity for a hearing, that such former officer or employee violated subsection (a), (b), or (c) of this section, such department or agency head may prohibit

that person from making, on behalf of any other person (except the United States), any informal or formal appearance before, or, with the intent to influence, any oral or written communication to, such department or agency on a pending matter of business for a period not to exceed five years, or may take other appropriate disciplinary action. Such disciplinary action shall be subject to review in an appropriate United States district court. No later than six months after the effective date of this Act, departments and agencies shall, in consultation with the Director of the Office of Government Ethics, establish procedures to carry out this subsection.

§ 208. Acts affecting a personal financial interest

(a) Except as permitted by subsection (b) hereof, whoever, being an officer or employee of the executive branch of the United States Government, of any independent agency of the United States, a Federal Reserve bank director, officer, or employee, or of the District of Columbia, including a special Government employee, participates personally and substantially as a Government officer or employee, through decision, approval, disapproval, recommendation, the rendering of advice, investigation, or otherwise, in a judicial or other proceeding, application, request for a ruling or other determination, contract, claim, controversy, charge, accusation, arrest, or other particular matter in which, to his knowledge, he, his spouse, minor child, partner, organization in which he is serving as officer, director, trustee, partner or employee, or any person or organization with whom he is negotiating or has any arrangement concerning prospective employment, has a financial interest—

Shall be fined not more than $10,000, or imprisoned not more than two years, or both.

(b) Subsection (a) hereof shall not apply (1) if the officer or employee first advises the Government official responsible for appointment to his position of the nature and circumstances of the judicial or other proceeding, application, request for a ruling or other determination, contract, claim, controversy, charge, accusation, arrest, or other particular matter and makes full disclosure of the financial interest and receives in advance a written determination made by such official that the interest is not so substantial as to be deemed likely to affect the integrity of the services which the Government may expect from such officer or employee, or (2) if, by general rule or regulation published in the Federal Register, the financial interest has been exempted from the requirements of clause (1) hereof as being too remote or too inconsequential to affect the integrity of Government officers' or employees' services. In the case of class A and B directors of Federal Reserve banks, the Board of Governors of the Federal Reserve System shall be the Government official responsible for appointment.

§ 209. Salary of Government officials and employees payable only by United States

(a) Whoever receives any salary, or any contribution to or supplementation of salary, as compensation for his services as an officer or employee of the executive branch of the United States Government, of any independent agency of the United States, or of the District of Columbia, from any source other than the Government of the United States, except as may be contributed out of the treasury of any State, county, or municipality; or

Whoever, whether an individual, partnership, association, corporation, or other organization pays, or makes any contribution to, or in any way supplements the salary of, any such officer or employee under circumstances which would make its receipt a violation of this subsection—

Shall be fined not more than $5,000 or imprisoned not more than one year, or both.

(b) Nothing herein prevents an officer or employee of the executive branch of the United States Government, or of any independent agency of the United States, or of the District of Columbia, from continuing to participate in a bona fide pension, retirement, group life, health or accident insurance, profit-sharing, stock bonus, or other employee welfare or benefit plan maintained by a former employer.

(c) This section does not apply to a special Government employee or to an officer or employee of the Government serving without compensation, whether or not he is a special Government employee, or to any person paying, contributing to, or supplementing his salary as such.

(d) This section does not prohibit payment or acceptance of contributions, awards, or other expenses under the terms of the Government Employees Training Act (Public Law 85–507, 72 Stat. 327; 5 U.S.C. 2301–2319, July 7, 1958).

(e) This section does not prohibit the payment of actual relocation expenses incident to participation, or the acceptance of same by a participant in an executive exchange or fellowship program in an executive agency: *Provided,* That such program has been established by statute or Executive order of the President, offers appointments not to exceed three hundred and sixty-five days, and permits no extensions in excess of ninety additional days or, in the case of participants in overseas assignments, in excess of three hundred and sixty-five days.

(f) This section does not prohibit acceptance or receipt, by any officer or employee injured during the commission of an offense described in section 351 or 1751 of this title, of contributions or payments from an organization which is described in section 501(c)(3) of the Internal Revenue Code of 1986 and which is exempt from taxation under section 501(a) of such Code.

Ethics in Government Act, 18 U.S.C. §§701–709

§ 701. Legislative personnel financial disclosure

(a) Members of Congress

Each Member in office on May 15 of a calendar year shall file on or before May 15 of that calendar year a report containing the information as described in section 702(a) of this title.

(b) Officers and employees

(1) Any individual who is an officer or employee of the legislative branch described in subsection (e) of this section during any calendar year and performs the duties of his position or office for a period in excess of sixty days in that calendar year shall file on or before May 15 of the succeeding year a report containing the information described in section 702(a) of this title if such individual is or will be such an officer or employee on such May 15.

(2) Any individual whose employment as an officer or employee described in subsection (e) of this section is terminated in any calendar year may be required—

(A) under the rules of the House of Representatives, if such individual would, but for such termination, file a report with the Clerk pursuant to section 703(a) of this title, or

(B) under the rules of the Senate, if such individual would, but for such termination, file a report with the Secretary pursuant to section 703(b) of this title,

to file a financial disclosure report covering (i) that part of such calendar year during which such individual was employed as such an officer or employee, and (ii) the preceding calendar year if the report required by paragraph (1) covering that calendar year has not been filed.

(c) Non-legislative personnel; temporary employment; effective date

Within thirty days of assuming the position of an officer or employee described in subsection (e) of this section, an individual, other than an individual who was employed in the legislative branch immediately before he assumed such position, shall file a report containing the information as described in section 702(b) of this title unless the individual has left another position described in subsection (e) of this section within thirty days prior to assuming his new position. The provisions of the preceding sentence shall not apply to an individual who, as determined by the designated committee of the Senate or the designated committee of the House, as appropriate, is not reasonably expected to perform the duties of his office or position for more than sixty days in a calendar year, except that if he performs the duties of his office or position for more than sixty days in a calendar year, the report required by the preceding sentence shall be filed within fifteen days of the sixtieth day. This subsection shall take effect on January 1, 1979.

(d) Congressional candidates

Within thirty days of becoming a candidate in a calendar year for any election for the office of Member, or on or before May 15 of that calendar year, whichever is later, but in no event later than seven days prior to the election, and on or before May 15 of each successive year the individual continues to be a candidate, an individual shall file a report containing the information as described in section 702(b) of this title. Notwithstanding the preceding sentence, in any calendar year in which an individual continues to be a candidate for any office but all elections for such office relating to such candidacy were held in prior calendar years, such individual need not file a report unless he becomes a candidate for another vacancy in that office or another office during that year.

(e) Covered officers and employees; legislative branch

The officers and employees referred to in subsections (b) and (c) of this section are—

(1) each officer or employee of the legislative branch who is compensated at a rate

equal to or in excess of the annual rate of basic pay in effect for grade GS–16 of the General Schedule; and

(2) at least one principal assistant designated for purposes of this section by each Member who does not have an employee compensated at a rate equal to or in excess of the annual rate of basic pay in effect for grade GS–16 of the General Schedule.

For the purposes of this chapter, the legislative branch includes the Architect of the Capitol, the Botanic Gardens, the Congressional Budget Office, the Cost Accounting Standards Board, the General Accounting Office, the Government Printing Office, the Library of Congress, the Office of the Attending Physician, National Commission on Air Quality, and the Office of Technology Assessment.

(f) Extensions of time to file

Reasonable extensions of time for filing any report may be granted by the designated committee of the Senate with respect to those filing with the Secretary and by the designated committee of the House of Representatives with respect to those filing with the Clerk but in no event may the extension granted to a Member or candidate result in a required report being filed later than seven days prior to an election involving the Member or candidate. If the day on which a report is required to be filed falls on a weekend or holiday, the report may be filed on the next business day.

(g) Congressional candidates in 1978

Notwithstanding the dates specified in subsection (d) of this section, an individual who is a candidate in calendar year 1978 shall file the report required by such subsection not later than November 1, 1978, except that a candidate for the Senate who has filed a report as of such date pursuant to the Rules of the Senate need not file the report required by subsection (d) of this section.

(h) Temporary employment

The designated committee of the House of Representatives, or the designated committee of the Senate, as the case may be, may grant a publicly available request for a waiver of any reporting requirement under this section for an individual who is expected to perform or has performed the duties of his office or position for less than one hundred and thirty days in a calendar year, but only if such committee determines that—

(1) such individual is not a full-time employee of the Government,

(2) such individual is able to provide services specially needed by the Government,

(3) it is unlikely that the individual's outside employment or financial interests will create a conflict of interest, and

(4) public financial disclosure by such individual is not necessary in the circumstances.

§ 702. Contents of reports

(a) Members of Congress; legislative officers and employees

Each report filed pursuant to subsections (a) and (b) of section 701 of this title shall include a full and complete statement with respect to the following:

(1)(A) The source, type, and amount or value of income (other than income referred to in subparagraph (B)) from any source

(other than from current employment by the United States Government), and the source, date, and amount of honoraria from any source including speeches, appearances, articles, or other publications, received during the preceding calendar year, aggregating $100 or more in value.

(B) The source and type of income which consists of dividends, interest, rent, and capital gains, received during the preceding calendar year which exceeds $100 in amount or value, and an indication of which of the following categories the amount or value of such item of income is within:

(i) not more than $1,000,

(ii) greater than $1,000 but not more than $2,500,

(iii) greater than $2,500 but not more than $5,000,

(iv) greater than $5,000 but not more than $15,000,

(v) greater than $15,000 but not more than $50,000,

(vi) greater than $50,000 but not more than $100,000, or

(vii) greater than $100,000.

(2)(A) The identity of the source and a brief description of any gifts of transportation, lodging, food, or entertainment aggregating $250 or more in value received from any source other than a relative of the reporting individual during the preceding calendar year, except that any food, lodging, or entertainment received as personal hospitality of any individual need not be reported, and any gift with a fair market value of $35 or less need not be aggregated for purposes of this subparagraph.

(B) The identity of the source, a brief description, and the value of all gifts other than transportation, lodging, food, or entertainment aggregating $100 or more in value received from any source other than a relative of the reporting individual during the preceding calendar year, except that any gift with a fair market value of $35 or less need not be aggregated for purposes of this subparagraph.

(C) The identity of the source and a brief description of reimbursements received from any source aggregating $250 or more in value and received during the preceding calendar year.

(D) In an unusual case, a gift need not be aggregated under subparagraph (A) or (B) if a publicly available request for a waiver is granted.

(3) The identity and category of value of any interest in property held during the preceding calendar year in a trade or business, or for investment or the production of income, which has a fair market value which exceeds $1,000 as of the close of the preceding calendar year, excluding any personal liability owed to the reporting individual by a relative or any deposits aggregating $5,000 or less in a personal savings account. For purposes of this paragraph, a personal savings account shall include any certificate of deposit or any other form of deposit in a bank, savings and loan association, credit union, or similar financial institution.

(4) The identity and category of value of the total liabilities owed to any creditor other than a relative which exceed $10,000 at any time during the preceding calendar year, excluding—

(A) any mortgage secured by real property which is a personal residence of the reporting individual or his spouse;

(B) any loan secured by a personal motor vehicle, household furniture, or appliances, which loan does not exceed the purchase price of the item which secures it.

With respect to revolving charge accounts, only those with an outstanding liability which exceeds $10,000 as of the close of the preceding calendar year need be reported under this paragraph.

(5) Except as provided in this paragraph, a brief description, the date, and category of value of any purchase, sale, or exchange during the preceding calendar year which exceeds $1,000—

(A) in real property, other than property used solely as a personal residence of the reporting individual or his spouse; or

(B) in stocks, bonds, commodities futures, and other forms of securities.

Reporting is not required under this paragraph of any transaction solely by and between the reporting individual, his spouse, or dependent children.

(6) The identity of all positions held on or before the date of filing during the current calendar year as an officer, director, trustee, partner, proprietor, representative, employee, or consultant of any corporation, company, firm, partnership, or other business enterprise, any nonprofit organization, any labor organization, or any educational or other institution other than the United States. This paragraph shall not require the reporting of positions held in any religious, social, fraternal, or political entity and positions solely of an honorary nature.

(7) A description of the date, parties to, and terms of any agreement or arrangement with respect to (A) future employment; (B) a leave of absence during the period of the reporting individual's Government service; (C) continuation of payments by a former employer other than the United States Government; and (D) continuing participation in an employee welfare or benefit plan maintained by a former employer.

(b) **Non-legislative personnel; Congressional candidates**

Each report filed pursuant to subsections (c) and (d) of section 701 of this title shall include a full and complete statement with respect to the information required by—

(1) paragraph (1) of subsection (a) of this section for the year of filing and the preceding calendar year,

(2) paragraphs (3) and (4) of subsection (a) of this section as of the date specified in the report but which is less than thirty-one days before the filing date, and

(3) paragraph (6) and, in the case of reports filed under section 701(c) of this title, paragraph (7) of subsection (a) of this section as of the filing date but for periods described in such paragraphs.

(c) **Categories of value; interests in real property and other items needing appraisals**

(1) The categories for reporting the amount or value of the items covered in paragraphs (3), (4) and (5) of subsection (a) of this section are as follows:

(A) not more than $5,000;

(B) greater than $5,000 but not more than $15,000;

(C) greater than $15,000 but not more than $50,000;

(D) greater than $50,000 but not more than $100,000;

(E) greater than $100,000 but not more than $250,000; and

(F) greater than $250,000.

(2) For the purposes of paragraph (3) of subsection (a) of this section if the current value of an interest in real property (or an interest in a real estate partnership) is not ascertainable without an appraisal, an individual may list (A) the date of purchase and the purchase price of the interest in the real property, or (B) the assessed value of the real property for tax purposes, adjusted to reflect the market value of the property used for the assessment if the assessed value is computed at less than 100 percent of such market value, but such individual shall include in his report a full and complete description of the method used to determine such assessed value, instead of specifying a category of value pursuant to paragraph (1) of this subsection. If the current value of any other item required to be reported under paragraph (3) of subsection (a) of this section is not ascertainable without an appraisal, such individual may list the book value of a corporation whose stock is not publicly traded, the net worth of a business partnership, the equity value of an individually owned business, or with respect to other holdings, any recognized indication of value, but such individual shall include in his report a full and complete description of the method used in determining such value. In lieu of any value referred to in the preceding sentence, an individual may list the assessed value of the item for tax purposes, adjusted to reflect the market value of the item used for the assessment if the assessed value is computed at less than 100 percent of such market value, but a full and complete description of the method used in determining such assessed value shall be included in the report.

(d) **Information respecting spouses and dependent children**

(1) Except as provided in the last sentence of this paragraph, each report shall also contain information listed in paragraphs (1) through (5) of subsection (a) of this section respecting the spouse or dependent child of the reporting individual as follows:

(A) The source of items of earned income earned by a spouse from any person which exceed $1,000 and, with respect to a spouse or dependent child, all information required to be reported in subsection (a)(1)(B) of this section with respect to income derived from any asset held by the spouse or dependent child and reported pursuant to paragraph (3). With respect to earned income, if the spouse is self-employed in business or a profession, only the nature of such business or profession need be reported.

(B) In the case of any gifts received by a spouse which are not received totally independent of the spouse's relationship to the reporting individual, the identity of the source and a brief description of gifts of transportation, lodging, food, or entertainment and a brief description and the value of other gifts.

(C) In the case of any reimbursements received by a spouse which are not received totally independent of the spouse's relationship to the reporting individual, the identity of the source and a brief description of each such reimbursement.

(D) In the case of items described in paragraphs (3) through (5), all information required to be reported under these paragraphs other than items (i) which the reporting individual certifies represent the spouse's or dependent child's sole financial interest or responsibility and which the reporting individual has no knowledge of, (ii) which are not in any way, past or present, derived from the income, assets, or activities of the reporting individual, and (iii) from which the reporting individual neither derives, nor expects to derive, any financial or economic benefit.

Each report referred to in subsection (b) of this section shall, with respect to the spouse and dependent child of the reporting individual, only contain information listed in paragraphs (1), (3), and (4) of subsection (a) of this section, as specified in this paragraph.

(2) No report shall be required with respect to a spouse living separate and apart from the reporting individual with the intention of terminating the marriage or providing for permanent separation; or with respect to any income or obligations of an individual arising from the dissolution of his marriage or the permanent separation from his spouse.

(e) Trusts or other financial arrangements; qualified blind trust

(1) Except as provided in paragraph (2), each reporting individual shall report the information required to be reported pursuant to subsections (a) and (b) of this section with respect to the holdings of and the income from a trust or other financial arrangement from which income is received by, or with respect to which a beneficial interest in principal or income is held by, such individual, his spouse, or any dependent child.

(2) A reporting individual need not report the holdings of or the source of income from any of the holdings of—

(A) any qualified blind trust (as defined in paragraph (3)); or

(B) a trust—

(i) which was not created directly by such individual, his spouse, or any dependent child, and

(ii) the holdings or sources of income of which such individual, his spouse, and any dependent child have no knowledge of,

but such individual shall report the category of the amount of income received by him, his spouse, or any dependent child from the trust under subsection (a)(1)(B) of this section.

(3) For purposes of this subsection, the term "qualified blind trust" includes any trust in which a reporting individual, his spouse, or any dependent child has a beneficial interest in the principal or income, and which meets the following requirements:

(A) The trustee of the trust is a financial institution, an attorney, a certified public accountant, a broker, or an investment adviser, who (in the case of a financial institution or investment company, any officer or employee involved in the management or control of the trust who)—

(i) is independent of and unassociated with any interested party so that the trustee cannot be controlled or influenced in the administration of the trust by any interested party,

(ii) is not or has not been an employee of any interested party, or any organization affiliated with any interested party and is not a partner of, or involved in any joint venture or other investment with, any interested party, and

(iii) is not a relative of any interested party.

(B) Any asset transferred to the trust by an interested party is free of any restriction with respect to its transfer or sale unless such restriction is expressly approved by the supervising ethics office of the reporting individual.

(C) The trust instrument which establishes the trust provides that—

(i) except to the extent provided in subparagraph (B) of this paragraph, the trustee in the exercise of his authority and discretion to manage and control the assets of the trust shall not consult or notify any interested party;

(ii) the trust shall not contain any asset the holding of which by an interested party is prohibited by any law or regulation;

(iii) the trustee shall promptly notify the reporting individual and his supervising ethics office when the holdings of any particular asset transferred to the trust by any interested party are disposed of or when the value of such holding is less than $1,000;

(iv) the trust tax return shall be prepared by the trustee or his designee, and such return and any information relating thereto (other than the trust income summarized in appropriate categories necessary to complete an interested party's tax return), shall not be disclosed to any interested party;

(v) an interested party shall not receive any report on the holdings and sources of income of the trust, except a report at the end of each calendar quarter with respect to the total cash value of the interest of the interested party in the trust or the net income or loss of the trust or any reports necessary to enable the interested party to complete an individual tax return required by law or to provide the information required by subsection (a)(1)(B) of this section but such report shall not identify any asset or holding;

(vi) except for communications which solely consist of requests for distributions of cash or other unspecified assets of the trust, there shall be no direct or indirect communication between the trustee and an interested party with respect to the trust unless such communication is in writing and unless it relates only (I) to the general financial interest and needs of the interested party (including, but not limited to, an interest in maximizing income or long-term capital gain), (II) to the notification of the trustee of a law or regulation subsequently applicable to the reporting individual which prohibits the interested party from holding an asset, which notification directs that the asset not be held by the trust, or (III) to directions to the trustee to sell all of an asset initially placed in the trust by an interested party which in the determination of the reporting individual creates a conflict of interest or the appearance thereof due to the subsequent assumption of duties by the reporting individual (but nothing herein shall require any such direction); and

(vii) the interested parties shall make no effort to obtain information with respect to the holdings of the trust, including obtaining a copy of any trust tax return filed or any information relating thereto except as otherwise provided in this subsection.

(D) The proposed trust instrument and the proposed trustee is approved by the reporting individual's supervising ethics office.

For purposes of this subsection "interested party" means a reporting individual, his spouse, and any dependent child if the reporting individual, his spouse, or dependent child has a beneficial interest in the principal or income of a qualified blind trust; "broker" has the meaning set forth in section 78c(a)(4) of title 15; "investment adviser" includes any investment adviser who, as determined under regulations prescribed by the supervising ethics office, is generally involved in his role as such an adviser in the management or control of trusts; and "supervising ethics office" means the designated committee of the House of Representatives for those who file the reports required by this chapter with the Clerk and the designated committee of the Senate for those who file the reports required by this chapter with the Secretary.

(4) An asset placed in a trust by an interested party shall be considered a financial interest of the reporting individual, for the purposes of section 208 of title 18, and any other conflict of interest statutes or regulations of the Federal Government, until such time as the reporting individual is notified by the trustee that such asset has been disposed of, or has a value of less than $1,000.

(5)(A) The reporting individual shall, within thirty days after a qualified blind trust is approved by his supervising ethics office, file with such office a copy of—

(i) the executed trust instrument of such trust (other than those provisions which relate to the testamentary disposition of the trust assets), and

(ii) a list of the assets which were transferred to such trust, including the category of value of each asset as determined under subsection (c)(1) of this section.

This paragraph shall not apply with respect to a trust meeting the requirements for being considered a qualified blind trust under paragraph (7) of this subsection.

(B) The reporting individual shall, within thirty days of transferring an asset (other than cash) to a previously established qualified blind trust, notify his supervising ethics office of the identity of each such asset and the category of value of each asset as determined under subsection (c)(1) of this section.

(C) Within thirty days of the dissolution of a qualified blind trust, a reporting individual shall—

(i) notify his supervising ethics office of such dissolution, and

(ii) file with such office a copy of a list of the assets of the trust at the time of such dissolution and the category of value under subsection (c) of this section of each such asset.

(D) Documents filed under subparagraphs (A), (B), and (C) of this paragraph and the lists provided by the trustee of assets placed in the trust by an interested party which have been sold shall be made available to the public in the same manner as a report is made available under section 704 of this title, and the provisions of that section shall apply with respect to such documents and lists.

(E) A copy of each written communication with respect to the trust under paragraph (3)(C)(vi) shall be filed by the person initiating the communication with the reporting individual's supervising ethics office within five days of the date of the communication.

(6)(A) A trustee of a qualified blind trust shall not knowingly or negligently (i) disclose any information to an interested party with respect to such trust that may not be disclosed under paragraph (3) of this subsection; (ii) acquire any holding the ownership of which is prohibited by the trust instrument; (iii) solicit advice from any interested party with respect to such trust, which solicitation is prohibited by paragraph (3) of this subsection or the trust agreement; or (iv) fail to file any document required by this subsection.

(B) A reporting individual shall not knowingly or negligently (i) solicit or receive any information with respect to a qualified blind trust of which he is an interested party that may not be disclosed under paragraph (3)(C) of this subsection, or (ii) fail to file any document required by this subsection.

(C)(i) The Attorney General may bring a civil action in any appropriate United States District Court against any individual who knowingly and willfully violates the provisions of subparagraph (A) or (B) of this paragraph. The court in which such action is brought may assess against such individual a civil penalty in any amount not to exceed $5,000.

(ii) The Attorney General may bring a civil action in any appropriate United States District Court against any individual who negligently violates the provisions of subparagraph (A) or (B) of this paragraph. The court in which such action is brought may assess against such individual a civil penalty in any amount not to exceed $1,000.

(7) Any trust may be considered to be a qualified blind trust if—

(A) the trust instrument is amended to comply with the requirements of paragraph (3) or, in the case of a trust instrument which does not by its terms permit amendment, the trustee, the reporting individual, and any other interested party agree in writing that the trust shall be administered in accordance with the requirements of this subsection and the trustee of such trust meets the requirements of paragraph (3)(A); except that in the case of any interested party who is a dependent child, a parent or guardian of such child may execute the agreement referred to in this subparagraph;

(B) a copy of the trust instrument (except testamentary provisions) and a copy of the agreement referred to in subparagraph (A), and a list of the assets held by the trust at the time of approval by the supervising ethics office, including the category of value of each asset as determined under subsection (d) of this section, are filed with such office and made available to the public as provided under paragraph (5)(D) of this subsection; and

(C) the supervising ethics office determines that approval of the trust arrangement as a qualified blind trust is in the particular case appropriate to assure compliance with applicable laws and regulations.

(f) Political campaign funds

Political campaign funds, including campaign receipts and expenditures, need not be included in any report filed pursuant to this chapter.

(g) Gifts and reimbursements

A report filed pursuant to subsection (a) or (b) of section 701 of this title need not contain the information described in subparagraphs (A), (B), and (C) of subsection (a)(2) of this section with respect to gifts and reimbursements received in a period when the reporting individual was not a Member or an officer or employee of the Federal Government.

§ 703. Filing of reports

(a) Persons filing with the Clerk

The reports required by section 701 of this title of Representatives, Delegates to Congress, the Resident Commissioner from Puerto Rico, officers and employees of the House, candidates seeking election to the House, and officers and employees of the Architect of the Capitol, the Botanic Gardens, the Congressional Budget Office, the Government Printing Office, and the Library of Congress shall be filed with the Clerk.

(b) Persons filing with the Secretary

The reports required by section 701 of this title of Senators, officers and employees of the Senate, candidates seeking election to the Senate, and officers and employees of the General Accounting Office, the Cost Accounting Standards Board, the Office of Technology Assessment, National Commission on Air Quality, and the Office of the Attending Physician shall be filed with the Secretary.

(c) State copies

A copy of each report filed by a Member or an individual who is a candidate for the office of Member shall be sent by the Clerk or Secretary, as the case may be, to the appropriate State officer as designated in accordance with section 439(a) of this title of the State represented by the Member or in which the individual is a candidate, as the case may be, within the seven-day period beginning the day that the report is filed with the Clerk or Secretary.

(d) Committee copies

(1) A copy of each report filed under this chapter with the Clerk shall be sent by the Clerk to the designated committee of the House of Representatives within the seven-day period beginning the day that the report is filed.

(2) A copy of each report filed with the Secretary shall be sent by the Secretary to the designated committee of the Senate.

(e) Federal Election Commission assistance

In carrying out their responsibilities under this chapter, the Clerk and the Secretary shall avail themselves of the assistance of the Federal Election Commission. The Commission shall make available to the Clerk and the Secretary on a regular basis a complete list of names and addresses of all candidates registered with the Commission, and shall cooperate and coordinate its candidate information and notification program with the Clerk and the Secretary to the greatest extent possible.

(f) Reporting forms; rules and regulations

In order to carry out their responsibilities under this chapter, the designated committee of the House of Representatives, and the designated committee of the Senate, shall develop reporting forms and may promulgate rules and regulations.

§ 704. Accessibility of reports

(a) Duty of Clerk

Except as provided in the second sentence of this subsection, within fifteen calendar days after a report is filed with the Clerk under this chapter, the Clerk shall make such report available for public inspection at reasonable hours. With respect to reports required to be filed by May 15 of any year, such reports shall be made available for public inspection within fifteen calendar days after May 15 of such year. A copy of any such report shall be provided by the Clerk to any person upon request.

(b) Duty of Secretary

Except as provided in the second sentence of this subsection, within fifteen days after a report is filed with the Secretary under this chapter, the Secretary shall make such report available for public inspection at reasonable hours. With respect to reports required to be filed by May 15 of any year, such reports shall be made available for public inspection within fifteen calendar days after May 15 of such year. A copy of any such report shall be provided by the Secretary to any person upon request.

(c) Application for inspection of reports; copies; fees

(1) Notwithstanding subsections (a) and (b) of this section, a report may not be made available under this section to any person nor may any copy thereof be provided under this section to any person except upon a written application by such person stating—

(A) that person's name, occupation, and address;

(B) the name and address of any other person or organization on whose behalf the inspection or copy is requested; and

(C) that such person is aware of the prohibitions on the obtaining or use of the report.

Any such application shall be made available to the public throughout the period during which the report is made available to the public.

(2) Any person requesting a copy of a report may be required to pay a reasonable fee to cover the cost of reproduction or mailing of such report, excluding any salary of any employee involved in such reproduction or mailing. A copy of such report may be furnished without charge or at a reduced charge if it is determined by the Clerk or Secretary that waiver or reduction of the fee is in the public interest because furnishing the information may be considered as primarily benefiting the public.

(d) Duration

Any report filed under this chapter with the Clerk or Secretary shall be available to the public for a period of six years after receipt of the report. After such six-year period the report shall be destroyed unless needed in an ongoing investigation, except that in the case of an individual who filed the report pursuant to section 701(d) of this title and was not subsequently elected, such reports shall be destroyed one year after the individual is no longer a candidate for election to the office of Member unless needed in an ongoing investigation.

(e) Unlawful uses; civil action; penalty

(1) It shall be unlawful for any person to obtain or use a report—

(A) for any unlawful purpose;

(B) for any commercial purpose other than by news and communications media for dissemination to the general public;

(C) for determining or establishing the credit rating of any individual; or

(D) for use, directly or indirectly, in the solicitation of money for any political, charitable, or other purpose.

(2) The Attorney General may bring a civil action against any person who obtains or uses a report for any purpose prohibited in paragraph (1). The court in which such action is brought may assess against such person a penalty in any amount not to exceed $5,000. Such remedy shall be in addition to any other remedy available under statutory or common law.

§ 705. Review and compliance procedures

(a) The designated committee of the House of Representatives and the designated committee of the Senate shall establish procedures for the review of reports sent to them under section 703(d)(1) of this title and section 703(d)(2) of this title to determine whether the reports are filed in a timely manner, are complete, and are in proper form. In the event a determination is made that a report is not so filed, the appropriate committee shall so inform the reporting individual and direct him to take all necessary corrective action.

(b) In order to carry out their responsibilities under this chapter the designated committee of the House of Representatives and the designated committee of the Senate, have power, within their respective jurisdictions, to render any advisory opinion interpreting this chapter, in writing, to persons covered by this chapter. Notwithstanding any other provisions of law, the individual to whom a public advisory opinion is rendered in accordance with this subsection, and any other individual covered by this chapter who is involved in a fact situation which is indistinguishable in all material aspects, and who, after the issuance of the advisory opinion, acts in good faith in accordance with the provisions and findings of such advisory opinion shall not, as a result of such act, be subject to any sanction provided in this chapter.

§ 706. Failure to file or filing false reports

The Attorney General may bring a civil action in any appropriate United States district court against any individual who knowingly and willfully falsifies or who knowingly and willfully fails to file or report any information that such individual is required to report pursuant to section 702 of this title. The court in which such action is brought may assess against such individual a civil penalty in any amount not to exceed $5,000. No action may be brought under this section against any individual with respect to a report filed by such individual in calendar year 1978 pursuant to section 701(d) of this title.

(Pub. L. 95-521, title I, § 106, Oct. 26, 1978, 92 Stat. 1833.)

§ 707. Definitions

For the purposes of this chapter, the term—

(1) "income" means all income from whatever source derived, including but not limited to the following items: compensation for services, including fees, commissions, and similar items; gross income derived from business (and net income if the individual elects to include it); gains derived from dealings in property; interest; rents; royalties; dividends; annuities; income from life insurance and endowment contracts; pensions; income from discharge of indebtedness; distributive share of partnership income; and income from an interest in an estate or trust;

(2) "relative" means an individual who is related to the reporting individual, as father, mother, son, daughter, brother, sister, uncle, aunt, great aunt, great uncle, first cousin, nephew, niece, husband, wife, grandfather, grandmother, grandson, granddaughter, father-in-law, mother-in-law, son-in-law,[1] daughter-in-law, brother-in-law, sister-in-law, stepfather, stepmother, stepson, stepdaughter, stepbrother, stepsister, half brother, half sister, or who is the grandfather or grandmother of the spouse of the reporting individual, and shall be deemed to include the fiance or fiancee of the reporting individual;

(3) "gift" means a payment, advance, forbearance, rendering, or deposit of money, or any thing of value, unless consideration of equal or greater value is received by the donor, but does not include—

(A) bequest and other forms of inheritance;

(B) suitable mementos of a function honoring the reporting individual;

(C) food, lodging, transportation, and entertainment provided by State and local governments, or political subdivisions thereof, by a foreign government within a foreign country, or by the United States Government;[2]

(D) food and beverages consumed at banquets, receptions, or similar events;

(E) consumable products provided by home-State businesses to a Member's office for distribution; or

(F) communications to the offices of a reporting individual including subscriptions to newspapers and periodicals;

(4) "honoraria" has the meaning given such term in the Federal Election Campaign Act of 1971 [2 U.S.C. 431 et seq.];

(5) "value" means a good faith estimate of the dollar value if the exact value is neither known nor easily obtainable by the reporting individual;

(6) "personal hospitality of any individual" means hospitality extended for a nonbusiness purpose by an individual, not a corporation or organization, at the personal residence of that individual or his family or on property or facilities owned by that individual or his family;

(7) "dependent child" means, when used with respect to any reporting individual, any individual who is a son, daughter, stepson, or stepdaughter and who—

(A) is unmarried and under age 21 and is living in the household of such reporting individual; or

(B) is a dependent of such reporting individual within the meaning of section 152 of title 26;

(8) "reimbursement" means any payment or other thing of value received by the reporting individual, other than gifts, to cover travel-related expenses of such individual other than those which are—

(A) provided by the United States Government, the District of Columbia, or any State or political subdivision thereof;

(B) required to be reported by the reporting individual under section 7342 of title 5; or

(C) required to be reported under section

---

[1] Comma inserted editorially.
[2] Semicolon substituted for period editorially.

304 of the Federal Election Campaign Act of 1971 (2 U.S.C. 434);

(9) "candidate" means an individual, other than a Member, who seeks nomination for election, or election, to the Congress whether or not such individual is elected, and for purposes of this paragraph, an individual shall be deemed to seek nomination for election, or election, (A) if he has taken the action necessary under the law of a State to qualify himself for nomination for election, or election, or (B) if he or his principal campaign committee has taken action to register or file campaign reports required by section 304(a) of the Federal Election Campaign Act of 1971 (2 U.S.C. 434(a));

(10) "Clerk" means the Clerk of the House of Representatives;

(11) "Secretary" means the Secretary of the Senate;

(12) "Member" means a United States Senator, a Representative in Congress, a Delegate to Congress, or the Resident Commissioner from Puerto Rico;

(13) "election" means (A) a general, special, primary, or runoff election, or (B) a convention or caucus of a political party which has authority to nominate a candidate;

(14) "officer or employee of the House" means any individual, other than a Member, whose compensation is disbursed by the Clerk;

(15) "officer or employee of the Senate" means an individual, other than a Senator or the Vice President, whose compensation is disbursed by the Secretary; and

(16) "designated committee of the House of Representatives" and "designated committee of the Senate" means the committee of the House or Senate, as the case may be, assigned

responsibility for administering the reporting requirements of this chapter.

§ 708. State laws affected

The provisions added by this chapter, and the regulations issued thereunder, shall supersede and preempt any State or local law with respect to financial disclosure by reason of holding the office of Member or candidacy for Federal office or employment by the United States Government.

§ 709. Study by Comptroller General

(a) Before November 30, 1980, and regularly thereafter, the Comptroller General of the United States shall conduct a study to determine whether this chapter is being carried out effectively and whether timely and accurate reports are being filed by individuals subject to this chapter.

(b) Within thirty days after completion of the study, the Comptroller General shall transmit a report to each House of Congress containing a detailed statement of his findings and conclusions, together with his recommendations for such legislative and administrative actions as he deems appropriate. The first such study shall include the Comptroller General's findings and recommendations on the feasibility and potential need for a requirement that systematic random audits be conducted of financial disclosure reports filed under this chapter, including a thorough discussion of the type and nature of audits that might be conducted; the personnel and other costs of audits; the value of an audit to Members, the appropriate House and Senate committees, and the public; and, if conducted, whether a governmental or nongovernmental unit should perform the audits, and under whose supervision.

Maximum Honoraria Acceptable by Members of Congress, 2 U.S.C. §31-1

§ 31-1. Maximum amount of honoraria which may be accepted by Members of Congress

(a) Definitions

For the purposes of this section—

(1) "charitable organization" means an organization described in section 170(c) of title 26;

(2) "honorarium" means a payment of money or anything of value to a Member for an appearance, speech, or article, by the Member; but there shall not be taken into account for the purposes of this section any actual and necessary travel expenses, incurred by the Member, and spouse or an aide to the extent that such expenses are paid or reimbursed by any other person, and the amount otherwise determined shall be reduced by the amount of any such expenses to the extent that such expenses are not paid or reimbursed;

(3) "Member" means a United States Senator, a Member of the House of Representatives, a Delegate to the House of Representa-

tives, or the Resident Commissioner from Puerto Rico; and

(4) "travel expenses" means with respect to a Member, and spouse or an aide, the cost of transportation, and the cost of lodging and meals while away from his or her residence or the metropolitan area of Washington, District of Columbia.

(b) Maximum as percentage of aggregate salary

(1) Notwithstanding any other provision of law, except as provided in paragraph (2), on and after January 1, 1984, a Member shall not accept honoraria which are attributable to any calendar year and total more than the amount that is equal to 40 percent of the aggregate salary paid to such Member for service as a Member during such calendar year.

(2) An individual who becomes a Member on a date after the first day of a calendar year shall not accept honoraria which are attributable to the remaining portion of that calendar year on and after the date such individual becomes a Member and total more than the amount that is equal to 40 percent of the aggregate salary

paid to the Member for service as a Member during such calendar year.

(3) For the purposes of this subsection, an honorarium shall be attributable to the period or calendar year in which payment is received.

(c) Honoraria paid to charitable organizations

Any honorarium, or any part thereof, paid by or on behalf of a Member to a charitable organization shall be deemed not to be accepted for the purposes of subsection (b) of this section.

Acceptance of Excessive Honoraria, 2 U.S.C. §441i

§ 441i.　Acceptance of excessive honorariums

(a)　No person while an elected or appointed officer or employee of any branch of the Federal Government shall accept any honorarium of more than $2,000 (excluding amounts accepted for actual travel and subsistence expenses for such person and his spouse or an aide to such person, and excluding amounts paid or incurred for any agents' fees or commissions) for any appearance, speech, or article.

(b)　Any honorarium, or any part thereof, paid by or on behalf of an elected or appointed officer or employee of any branch of the Federal Government to a charitable organization shall be deemed not to be accepted for the purposes of this section.

(c)　For purposes of determining the aggregate amount of honorariums received by a person during any calendar year, amounts returned to the person paying an honorarium before the close of the calendar year in which it was received shall be disregarded.

(d)　For purposes of paragraph (2) of subsection (a) of this section, an honorarium shall be treated as accepted only in the year in which that honorarium is received.

Receipt of Foreign Gifts, 5 U.S.C. §7342

§ 7342.　Receipt and disposition of foreign gifts and decorations

(a) For the purpose of this section—

(1) "employee" means—

(A) an employee as defined by section 2105 of this title and an officer or employee of the United States Postal Service or of the Postal Rate Commission;

(B) an expert or consultant who is under contract under section 3109 of this title with the United States or any agency, department, or establishment thereof, including, in the case of an organization performing services under such section, any individual involved in the performance of such services;

(C) an individual employed by, or occupying an office or position in, the government of a territory or possession of the United States or the government of the District of Columbia;

(D) a member of a uniformed service;

(E) the President and the Vice President;

(F) a Member of Congress as defined by section 2106 of this title (except the Vice President) and any Delegate to the Congress; and

(G) the spouse of an individual described in subparagraphs (A) through (F) (unless such individual and his or her spouse are separated) or a dependent (within the meaning of section 152 of the Internal Revenue Code of 1986) of such an individual, other than a spouse or dependent who is an employee under subparagraphs (A) through (F);

(2) "foreign government" means—

(A) any unit of foreign governmental authority, including any foreign national, State, local, and municipal government;

(B) any international or multinational organization whose membership is composed of any unit of foreign government described in subparagraph (A); and

(C) any agent or representative of any such unit or such organization, while acting as such;

(3) "gift" means a tangible or intangible present (other than a decoration) tendered by, or received from, a foreign government;

(4) "decoration" means an order, device, medal, badge, insignia, emblem, or award tendered by, or received from, a foreign government;

(5) "minimal value" means a retail value in the United States at the time of acceptance of $100 or less, except that—

(A) on January 1, 1981, and at 3 year intervals thereafter, "minimal value" shall be redefined in regulations prescribed by the Administrator of General Services, in consultation with the Secretary of State, to reflect changes in the consumer price index for the immediately preceding 3-year period; and

(B) regulations of an employing agency may define "minimal value" for its employees to be less than the value established under this paragraph; and

(6) "employing agency" means—

(A) the Committee on Standards of Official Conduct of the House of Representatives, for Members and employees of the House of Representatives, except that those responsibilities specified in subsections (c)(2)(A), (e)(1), and (g)(2)(B) shall be carried out by the Clerk of the House;

(B) the Select Committee on Ethics of the Senate, for Senators and employees of the Senate, except that those responsibilities (other than responsibilities involving approval of the employing agency) specified in subsections (c)(2), (d), and (g)(2)(B) shall be carried out by the Secretary of the Senate;

(C) the Administrative Office of the United States Courts, for judges and judicial branch employees; and

(D) the department, agency, office, or other entity in which an employee is employed, for other legislative branch employees and for all executive branch employees.

(b) An employee may not—

(1) request or otherwise encourage the tender of a gift or decoration; or

(2) accept a gift or decoration, other than in accordance with the provisions of subsections (c) and (d).

(c)(1) The Congress consents to—

(A) the accepting and retaining by an employee of a gift of minimal value tendered and received as a souvenir or mark of courtesy; and

(B) the accepting by an employee of a gift of more than minimal value when such gift is in the nature of an educational scholarship or medical treatment or when it appears that to refuse the gift would likely cause offense or embarrassment or otherwise adversely affect the foreign relations of the United States, except that—

(i) a tangible gift of more than minimal value is deemed to have been accepted on behalf of the United States and, upon acceptance, shall become the property of the United States; and

(ii) an employee may accept gifts of travel or expenses for travel taking place entirely outside the United States (such as transportation, food, and lodging) of more than minimal value if such acceptance is appropriate, consistent with the interests of the United States, and permitted by the employing agency and any regulations which may be prescribed by the employing agency.

(2) Within 60 days after accepting a tangible gift of more than minimal value (other than a gift described in paragraph (1)(B)(ii)), an employee shall—

(A) deposit the gift for disposal with his or her employing agency; or

(B) subject to the approval of the employing agency, deposit the gift with that agency for official use.

Within 30 days after terminating the official use of a gift under subparagraph (B), the employing agency shall forward the gift to the Administrator of General Services in accordance with subsection (e)(1) or provide for its disposal in accordance with subsection (e)(2).

(3) When an employee deposits a gift of more than minimal value for disposal or for official use pursuant to paragraph (2), or within 30 days after accepting travel or travel expenses as provided in paragraph (1)(B)(ii) unless such travel or travel expenses are accepted in accordance with specific instructions of his or her employing agency, the employee shall file a statement with his or her employing agency or its delegate containing the information prescribed in subsection (f) for that gift.

(d) The Congress consents to the accepting, retaining, and wearing by an employee of a decoration tendered in recognition of active field service in time of combat operations or awarded for other outstanding or unusually meritorious performance, subject to the approval of the employing agency of such employee. Without this approval, the decoration is deemed to have been accepted on behalf of the United States, shall become the property of the

United States, and shall be deposited by the employee, within sixty days of acceptance, with the employing agency for official use, for forwarding to the Administrator of General Services for disposal in accordance with subsection (e)(1), or for disposal in accordance with subsection (e)(2).

(e)(1) Except as provided in paragraph (2), gifts and decorations that have been deposited with an employing agency for disposal shall be (A) returned to the donor, or (B) forwarded to the Administrator of General Services for transfer, donation, or other disposal in accordance with the provisions of the Federal Property and Administrative Services Act of 1949. However, no gift or decoration that has been deposited for disposal may be sold without the approval of the Secretary of State, upon a determination that the sale will not adversely affect the foreign relations of the United States. Gifts and decorations may be sold by negotiated sale.

(2) Gifts and decorations received by a Senator or an employee of the Senate that are deposited with the Secretary of the Senate for disposal, or are deposited for an official use which has terminated, shall be disposed of by the Commission on Arts and Antiquities of the United States Senate. Any such gift or decoration, may be returned by the Commission to the donor or may be transferred or donated by the Commission, subject to such terms and conditions as it may prescribe, (A) to an agency or instrumentality of (i) the United States, (ii) a State, territory, or possession of the United States, or a political subdivision of the foregoing, or (iii) the District of Columbia, or (B) to an organization described in section 501(c)(3) of the Internal Revenue Code of 1954 which is exempt from taxation under section 501(a) of such Code. Any such gift or decoration not disposed of as provided in the preceding sentence shall be forwarded to the Administrator of General Services for disposal in accordance with paragraph (1). If the Administrator does not dispose of such gift or decoration within one year, he shall, at the request of the Commission, return it to the Commission and the Commission may dispose of such gift or decoration in such manner as it considers proper, except that such gift or decoration may be sold only with the approval of the Secretary of State upon a determination that the sale will not adversely affect the foreign relations of the United States.

(f)(1) Not later than January 31 of each year, each employing agency or its delegate shall compile a listing of all statements filed during the preceding year by the employees of that agency pursuant to subsection (c)(3) and shall transmit such listing to the Secretary of State who shall publish a comprehensive listing of all such statements in the Federal Register.

(2) Such listings shall include for each tangible gift reported—

(A) the name and position of the employee;

(B) a brief description of the gift and the circumstances justifying acceptance;

(C) the identity, if known, of the foreign government and the name and position of the individual who presented the gift;

(D) the date of acceptance of the gift;

(E) the estimated value in the United States of the gift at the time of acceptance; and

(F) disposition or current location of the gift.

(3) Such listings shall include for each gift of travel or travel expenses—

(A) the name and position of the employee;

(B) a brief description of the gift and the circumstances justifying acceptance; and

(C) the identity, if known, of the foreign government and the name and position of the individual who presented the gift.

(4) In transmitting such listings for the Central Intelligence Agency, the Director of Central Intelligence may delete the information described in subparagraphs (A) and (C) of paragraphs (2) and (3) if the Director certifies in writing to the Secretary of State that the publication of such information could adversely affect United States intelligence sources.

(g)(1) Each employing agency shall prescribe such regulations as may be necessary to carry out the purpose of this section. For all employing agencies in the executive branch, such regulations shall be prescribed pursuant to guidance provided by the Secretary of State. These regulations shall be implemented by each employing agency for its employees.

(2) Each employing agency shall—

(A) report to the Attorney General cases in which there is reason to believe that an employee has violated this section;

(B) establish a procedure for obtaining an appraisal, when necessary, of the value of gifts; and

(C) take any other actions necessary to carry out the purpose of this section.

(h) The Attorney General may bring a civil action in any district court of the United States against any employee who knowingly solicits or accepts a gift from a foreign government not consented to by this section or who fails to deposit or report such gift as required by this section. The court in which such action is brought may assess a penalty against such employee in any amount not to exceed the retail value of the gift improperly solicited or received plus $5,000.

(i) The President shall direct all Chiefs of a United States Diplomatic Mission to inform their host governments that it is a general policy of the United States Government to prohibit United States Government employees from receiving gifts or decorations of more than minimal value.

(j) Nothing in this section shall be construed to derogate any regulation prescribed by any employing agency which provides for more stringent limitations on the receipt of gifts and decorations by its employees.

(k) The provisions of this section do not apply to grants and other forms of assistance to which section 108A of the Mutual Educational and Cultural Exchange Act of 1961 applies.

Political Contributions by Government Employees (Hatch Act), 5 U.S.C. §§7321–7328

§ 7321. Political contributions and services

The President may prescribe rules which shall provide, as nearly as conditions of good administration warrant, that an employee in an Executive agency or in the competitive service is not obliged, by reason of that employment, to contribute to a political fund or to render political service, and that he may not be removed or otherwise prejudiced for refusal to do so.

§ 7322. Political use of authority or influence; prohibition

The President may prescribe rules which shall provide, as nearly as conditions of good administration warrant, that an employee in an Executive agency or in the competitive service may not use his official authority or influence to coerce the political action of a person or body.

§ 7323. Political contributions; prohibition

An employee in an Executive agency (except one appointed by the President, by and with the advice and consent of the Senate) may not request or receive from, or give to, an employee, a Member of Congress, or an officer of a uniformed service a thing of value for political purposes. An employee who violates this section shall be removed from the service.

§ 7324. Influencing elections; taking part in political campaigns; prohibitions; exceptions

(a) An employee in an Executive agency or an individual employed by the government of the District of Columbia may not—

(1) use his official authority or influence for the purpose of interfering with or affecting the result of an election; or

(2) take an active part in political management or in political campaigns.

For the purpose of this subsection, the phrase "an active part in political management or in political campaigns" means those acts of political management or political campaigning which were prohibited on the part of employees in the competitive service before July 19, 1940, by determinations of the Civil Service Commission under the rules prescribed by the President.

(b) An employee or individual to whom subsection (a) of this section applies retains the right to vote as he chooses and to express his opinion on political subjects and candidates.

(c) Subsection (a) of this section does not apply to an individual employed by an educational or research institution, establishment, agency, or system which is supported in whole or in part by the District of Columbia or by a recognized religious, philanthropic, or cultural organization.

(d) Subsection (a)(2) of this section does not apply to—

(1) an employee paid from the appropriation for the office of the President;

(2) the head or the assistant head of an Executive department or military department;

(3) an employee appointed by the President, by and with the advice and consent of the Senate, who determines policies to be pursued by the United States in its relations with foreign powers or in the nationwide administration of Federal laws;

(4) the Mayor of the District of Columbia, the members of the Council of the District of Columbia, or the Chairman of the Council of the District of Columbia, as established by the District of Columbia Self-Government and Governmental Reorganization Act; or

(5) the Recorder of Deeds of the District of Columbia.

§ 7325. Penalties

An employee or individual who violates section 7324 of this title shall be removed from his position, and funds appropriated for the position from which removed thereafter may not be used to pay the employee or individual. However, if the Merit Systems Protection Board finds by unanimous vote that the violation does not warrant removal, a penalty of not less than 30 days' suspension without pay shall be imposed by direction of the Board.

§ 7326. Nonpartisan political activity permitted

Section 7324(a)(2) of this title does not prohibit political activity in connection with—

(1) an election and the preceding campaign if none of the candidates is to be nominated or elected at that election as representing a party any of whose candidates for presidential elector received votes in the last preceding election at which presidential electors were selected; or

(2) a question which is not specifically identified with a National or State political party or political party of a territory or possession of the United States.

For the purpose of this section, questions relating to constitutional amendments, referendums, approval of municipal ordinances, and others of a similar character, are deemed not specifically identified with a National or State political party or political party of a territory or possession of the United States.

§ 7327. Political activity permitted; employees residing in certain municipalities

(a) Section 7324(a)(2) of this title does not apply to an employee of The Alaska Railroad who resides in a municipality on the line of the railroad in respect to political activities involving that municipality.

(b) The Office of Personnel Management may prescribe regulations permitting employees and individuals to whom section 7324 of this title applies to take an active part in political management and political campaigns involving the municipality or other political subdivision in which they reside, to the extent the Office considers it to be in their domestic interest, when—

(1) the municipality or political subdivision is in Maryland or Virginia and in the immediate vicinity of the District of Columbia, or is a municipality in which the majority of voters are employed by the Government of the United States; and

(2) the Office determines that because of special or unusual circumstances which exist in the municipality or political subdivision it is in the domestic interest of the employees and individuals to permit that political participation.

Limitation on Voluntary Services by Government Employees, 31 U.S.C. §1342

§ 1342. Limitation on voluntary services

An officer or employee of the United States Government or of the District of Columbia government may not accept voluntary services for either government or employ personal services exceeding that authorized by law except for emergencies involving the safety of human life or the protection of property. This section does not apply to a corporation getting amounts to make loans (except paid in capital amounts) without legal liability of the United States Government.

Elections and Political Activities, 18 U.S.C. §§591–607

§ 591.   Definitions

Except as otherwise specifically provided, when used in this section and in sections 597, 599, 600, and 602 of this title—

(a) "election" means (1) a general, special, primary, or runoff election, (2) a convention or caucus of a political party held to nominate a candidate, (3) a primary election held for the selection of delegates to a national nominating convention of a political party, or (4) a primary election held for the expression of a preference for the nomination of persons for election to the office of President;

(b) "candidate" means an individual who seeks nomination for election, or election, to Federal office, whether or not such individual is elected, and, for purposes of this paragraph, an individual shall be deemed to seek nomination for election, or election, to Federal office, if he has (1) taken the action necessary under the law of a State to qualify himself for nomination for election, or election, or (2) received contributions or made expenditures, or has given his consent for any other person to receive contributions or make expenditures, with a view to bringing about his nomination for election, or election, to such office;

(c) "Federal office" means the office of President or Vice President of the United States, or Senator or Representative in, or Delegate or Resident Commissioner to, the Congress of the United States;

(d) "political committee" means any committee, club, association, or other group of persons which receives contributions or makes expenditures during a calendar year in an aggregate amount exceeding $1,000;

(e) "contribution"—

(1) means a gift, subscription, loan, advance, or deposit of money or anything of value (except a loan of money by a national or State bank made in accordance with the applicable banking laws and regulations and in the ordinary course of business, which shall be considered a loan by each endorser or guarantor, in that proportion of the unpaid balance thereof that each endorser or guarantor bears to the total number of endorsers or guarantors), made for the purpose of influencing the nomination for election, or election, of any person to Federal office or for the purpose of influencing the results of a primary held for the selection of delegates to a national nominating convention of a political party or for the expression of a preference for the nomination of persons for election to the office of President of the United States;

(2) means a contract, promise, or agreement, express or implied, whether or not legally enforceable, to make a contribution for such purposes;

(3) means funds received by a political committee which are transferred to such committee from another political committee or other source;

(4) means the payment, by any person other than a candidate or a political committee, of compensation for the personal services of another person which are rendered to such candidate or political committee without charge for any such purpose, except that this paragraph shall not apply in the case of legal or accounting services rendered to or on behalf of the national committee of a political party (unless the person paying for such services is a person other than the regular employer of the individual rendering such services), other than services attributable to activities which directly further the election of a designated candidate or candidates to Federal office, nor shall this paragraph apply in the case of legal or accounting services rendered to or on behalf of a candidate or political committee solely for the purpose of ensuring compliance with the provisions of the Federal Election Campaign Act of 1971 or chapter 95 or chapter 96 of the Internal Revenue Code of 1954 (unless the person paying for such services is a person other than the regular employer of the individual rendering such services), but amounts paid or incurred for such legal or accounting services shall be reported in accordance with the requirements of section 304(b) of the Federal Election Campaign Act of 1971; but

(5) does not include—

(A) the value of services provided without compensation by individuals who volunteer a portion or all of their time on behalf of a candidate or political committee;

(B) the use of real or personal property and the cost of invitations, food, and beverages, voluntarily provided by an individual to a candidate in rendering voluntary personal services on the individual's residential premises for candidate-related activities;

(C) the sale of any food or beverage by a vendor for use in a candidate's campaign at a charge less than the normal comparable charge, if such charge for use in a candidate's campaign is at least equal to the cost of such food or beverage to the vendor;

(D) any unreimbursed payment for travel expenses made by an individual who on his own behalf volunteers his personal services to a candidate, or

(E) the payment by a State or local committee of a political party of the costs of preparation, display, or mailing or other distribution incurred by such committee with respect to a printed slate card or sample ballot, or other printed listing, of 3 or more candidates for any public office for which an election is held in the State in which such committee is organized, except that this clause shall not apply in the case of costs incurred by such committee with respect to a display of any such listing made on broadcasting stations, or in newspapers, magazines or other similar types of general public political advertising;

to the extent that the cumulative value of activities by any person on behalf of any candidate under each of clauses (B), (C), and (D) does not exceed $500 with respect to any election;

(f) "expenditure"—

(1) means a purchase, payment, distribution, loan, advance, deposit, or gift of money or anything of value (except

a loan of money by a national or State bank made in accordance with the applicable banking laws and regulations and in the ordinary course of business), made for the purpose of influencing the nomination for election, or election, of any person to Federal office or for the purpose of influencing the results of a primary held for the selection of delegates to a national nominating convention of a political party or for the expression of a preference for the nomination of persons for election to the office of President of the United States;

(2) means a contract, promise, or agreement, express or implied, whether or not legally enforceable, to make any expenditure; and

(3) means the transfer of funds by a political committee to another political committee; but

(4) does not include—

(A) any news story, commentary, or editorial distributed through the facilities of any broadcasting station, newspaper, magazine, or other periodical publication, unless such facilities are owned or controlled by any political party, political committee, or candidate;

(B) nonpartisan activity designed to encourage individuals to register to vote or to vote;

(C) any communication by any membership organization or corporation to its members or stockholders, if such membership organization or corporation is not organized primarily for the purpose of influencing the nomination for election, or election, of any person to Federal office;

(D) the use of real or personal property and the cost of invitations, food, and beverages, voluntarily provided by an individual to a candidate in rendering voluntary personal services on the individual's residential premises for candidate-related activities;

(E) any unreimbursed payment for travel expenses made by an individual who on his own behalf volunteers his personal services to a candidate;

(F) the payment, by any person other than a candidate or political committee, of compensation for legal or accounting services rendered to or on behalf of the national committee of a political party (unless the person paying for such services is a person other than the regular employer of the individual rendering such services), other than services attributable to activities which directly further the election of a designated candidate or candidates to Federal office, or the payment for legal or accounting services rendered to or on behalf of a candidate or political committee solely for the purpose of ensuring compliance with the provisions of the Federal Election Campaign Act of 1971 or of chapter 95 or chapter 96 of the Internal Revenue Code of 1954 (unless the person paying for such services is a person other than the regular employer of the individual rendering such services), but amounts paid or incurred for such legal or accounting services shall be reported under section 304(b) of the Federal Election Campaign Act of 1971;

(G) any communication by any person which is not made for the purpose of influencing the nomination for election, or election, of any person to Federal office;

(H) the payment by a State or local committee of a political party of the costs of preparation, display, or mailing or other distribution incurred by such committee with respect to a printed slate card or sample ballot, or other printed listing, of 3 or more candidates for any public office for which an election is held in the State in which such committee is organized, except that this clause shall not apply in the case of costs incurred by such committee with respect to a display of any such listing made on broadcasting stations, or in newspapers, magazines or other similar types of general public political advertising;

(I) any costs incurred by a candidate in connection with the solicitation of contributions by such candidate, except that this clause shall not apply with respect to costs incurred by a candidate in excess of an amount equal to 20 percent of the expenditure limitation applicable to such candidate under section 320(b) of the Federal Election Campaign Act of 1971; or

(J) any costs incurred by a political committee (as such term is defined under section 320(a)(2) of the Federal Election Campaign Act of 1971) with respect to the solicitation of contributions to such political committee or to any general political fund controlled by such political committee, except that this clause shall not apply to exempt costs incurred with respect to the solicitation of contributions o any such political committee made through broadcasting stations, newspapers, magazines, outdoor advertising facilities, and other similar types of general public political advertising;

to the extent that the cumulative value of activities by any individual on behalf of any candidate under each of clauses (D) or (E) does not exceed $500 with respect to any election;

(g) "person" and "whoever" mean an individual, partnership, committee, association, corporation, or any other organization or group of persons;

(h) "State" means each State of the United States, the District of Columbia, the Commonwealth of Puerto Rico, and any territory or possession of the United States; and

(i) "political party" means any association, committee, or organization which nominates a candidate for election to any Federal office whose name appears on the election ballot as the candidate of such association, committee, or organization;

(j) "State committee" means the organization which, by virtue of the bylaws of a political party, is responsible for the day-to-day operation of such political party at the State level, as determined by the Federal Election Commission;

(k) "national committee" means the organization which, by virtue of the bylaws of the political party, is responsible for the day-to-day operation of such political party at the national level, as determined by the Federal Election Commission established under section 309(a) of the Federal Election Campaign Act of 1971; and

(l) "principal campaign committee" means the principal campaign committee designated by a candidate under section 302(f)(1) of the Federal Election Campaign Act of 1971.

§ 592. Troops at polls

Whoever, being an officer of the Army or Navy, or other person in the civil, military, or naval service of the United States, orders, brings, keeps, or has under his authority or control any troops or armed men at any place where a general or special election is held, unless such force be necessary to repel armed enemies of the United States, shall be fined not more than $5,000 or imprisoned not more than five years, or both; and be disqualified from holding any office of honor, profit, or trust under the United States.

This section shall not prevent any officer or member of the armed forces of the United States from exercising the right of suffrage in any election district to which he may belong, if otherwise qualified according to the laws of the State in which he offers to vote.

§ 593. Interference by armed forces

Whoever, being an officer or member of the Armed Forces of the United States, prescribes or fixes or attempts to prescribe or fix, whether by proclamation, order or otherwise, the qualifications of voters at any election in any State; or

Whoever, being such officer or member, prevents or attempts to prevent by force, threat, intimidation, advice or otherwise any qualified voter of any State from fully exercising the right of suffrage at any general or special election; or

Whoever, being such officer or member, orders or compels or attempts to compel any election officer in any State to receive a vote from a person not legally qualified to vote; or

Whoever, being such officer or member, imposes or attempts to impose any regulations for conducting any general or special election in a State, different from those prescribed by law; or

Whoever, being such officer or member, interferes in any manner with an election officer's discharge of his duties—

Shall be fined not more than $5,000 or imprisoned not more than five years, or both; and disqualified from holding any office of honor, profit or trust under the United States.

This section shall not prevent any officer or member of the Armed Forces from exercising the right of suffrage in any district to which he may belong, if otherwise qualified according to the laws of the State of such district.

§ 594. Intimidation of voters

Whoever intimidates, threatens, coerces, or attempts to intimidate, threaten, or coerce, any other person for the purpose of interfering with the right of such other person to vote or to vote as he may choose, or of causing such other person to vote for, or not to vote for, any candidate for the office of President, Vice President, Presidential elector, Member of the Senate, Member of the House of Representatives, Delegate from the District of Columbia, or Resident Commissioner, at any election held solely or in part for the purpose of electing such candidate, shall be fined not more than $1,000 or imprisoned not more than one year, or both.

§ 595. Interference by administrative employees of Federal, State, or Territorial Governments

Whoever, being a person employed in any administrative position by the United States, or by any department or agency thereof, or by the District of Columbia or any agency or instrumentality thereof, or by any State, Territory, or Possession of the United States, or any political subdivision, municipality, or agency thereof, or agency of such political subdivision or municipality (including any corporation owned or controlled by any State, Territory, or Possession of the United States or by any such political subdivision, municipality, or agency), in connection with any activity which is financed in whole or in part by loans or grants made by the United States, or any department or agency thereof, uses his official authority for the purpose of interfering with, or affecting, the nomination or the election of any candidate for the office of President, Vice President, Presidential elector, Member of the Senate, Member of the House of Representatives, Delegate from the District of Columbia, or Resident Commissioner, shall be fined not more than $1,000 or imprisoned not more than one year, or both.

This section shall not prohibit or make unlawful any act by any officer or employee of any educational or research institution, establishment, agency, or system which is supported in whole or in part by any state or political subdivision thereof, or by the District of Columbia or by any Territory or Possession of the United States; or by any recognized religious, philanthropic or cultural organization.

§ 596. Polling armed forces

Whoever, within or without the Armed Forces of the United States, polls any member of such forces, either within or without the United States, either before or after he executes any ballot under any Federal or State law, with reference to his choice of or his vote for any candidate, or states, publishes, or releases any result of any purported poll taken from or among the members of the Armed Forces of the United States or including within it the statement of choice for such candidate or of such votes cast by any member of the Armed Forces of the United States, shall be fined not more than $1,000 or imprisoned for not more than one year, or both.

The word "poll" means any request for information, verbal or written, which by its language or form of expression requires or implies the necessity of an answer, where the request is made with the intent of compiling the result of the answers obtained, either for the personal use of the person making the request, or for the purpose of reporting the same to any other person, persons, political party, unincorporated association or corporation, or for the purpose of publishing the same orally, by radio, or in written or printed form.

§ 597. Expenditures to influence voting

Whoever makes or offers to make an expenditure to any person, either to vote or withhold his vote, or to vote for or against any candidate; and

Whoever solicits, accepts, or receives any such expenditure in consideration of his vote or the withholding of his vote—

Shall be fined not more than $1,000 or imprisoned not more than one year, or both; and if the violation was willful, shall be fined not more than $10,000 or imprisoned not more than two years, or both.

§ 598. Coercion by means of relief appropriations

Whoever uses any part of any appropriation made by Congress for work relief, relief, or for increasing employment by providing loans and grants for public-works projects, or exercises or administers any authority conferred by any Appropriation Act for the purpose of interfering with, restraining, or coercing any individual in the exercise of his right to vote at any election, shall be fined not more than $1,000 or imprisoned not more than one year, or both.

§ 599. Promise of appointment by candidate

Whoever, being a candidate, directly or indirectly promises or pledges the appointment, or the use of his influence or support for the appointment of any person to any public or private position or employment, for the purpose of procuring support in his candidacy shall be fined not more than $1,000 or imprisoned not more than one year, or both; and if the violation was willful, shall be fined not more than $10,000 or imprisoned not more than two years, or both.

§ 600. Promise of employment or other benefit for political activity

Whoever, directly or indirectly, promises any employment, position, compensation, contract, appointment, or other benefit, provided for or made possible in whole or in part by any Act of Congress, or any special consideration in obtaining any such benefit, to any person as consideration, favor, or reward for any political activity or for the support of or opposition to any candidate or any political party in connection with any general or special election to any political office, or in connection with any primary election or political convention or caucus held to select candidates for any political office, shall be fined not more than $1,000 or imprisoned not more than one year, or both.

§ 601. Deprivation of employment or other benefit for political activity

Whoever, except as required by law, directly or indirectly, deprives, attempts to deprive, or threatens to deprive any person of any employment, position, work, compensation, or other benefit provided for or made possible by any Act of Congress appropriating funds for work relief or relief purposes, on account of race, creed, color, or any political activity, support of, or opposition to any candidate or any political party in any election, shall be fined not more than $1,000 or imprisoned not more than one year, or both.

§ 602.   Solicitation of political contributions

Whoever, being a Senator or Representative in, or Delegate or Resident Commissioner to, or a candidate for Congress, or individual elected as, Senator, Representative, Delegate, or Resident Commissioner, or an officer or employee of the United States or any department or agency thereof, or a person receiving any salary or compensation for services from money derived from the Treasury of the United States, directly or indirectly solicits, receives, or is in any manner concerned in soliciting or receiving, any assessment, subscription, or contribution for any political purpose whatever, from any other such officer, employee, or person, shall be fined not more than $5,000 or imprisoned not more than three years or both.

§ 603.   Place of solicitation

Whoever, in any room or building occupied in the discharge of official duties by any person mentioned in section 602 of this title, or in any navy yard, fort, or arsenal, solicits or receives any contribution of money or other thing of value for any political purpose, shall be fined not more than $5,000 or imprisoned not more than three years, or both.

§ 604.   Solicitation from persons on relief

Whoever solicits or receives or is in any manner concerned in soliciting or receiving any assessment, subscription, or contribution for any political purpose from any person known by him to be entitled to, or receiving compensation, employment, or other benefit provided for or made possible by any Act of Congress appropriating funds for work relief or relief purposes, shall be fined not more than $1,000 or imprisoned not more than one year, or both.

§ 605.   Disclosure of names of persons on relief

Whoever, for political purposes, furnishes or discloses any list or names of persons receiving compensation, employment or benefits provided for or made possible by any Act of Congress appropriating, or authorizing the appropriation of funds for work relief or relief purposes, to a political candidate, committee, campaign manager, or to any person for delivery to a political candidate, committee, or campaign manager; and

Whoever receives any such list or names for political purposes—

Shall be fined not more than $1,000 or imprisoned not more than one year, or both.

§ 606.   Intimidation to secure political contributions

Whoever, being one of the officers or employees of the United States mentioned in section 602 of this title, discharges, or promotes, or degrades, or in any manner changes the official rank or compensation of any other officer or employee, or promises or threatens so to do, for giving or withholding or neglecting to make any contribution of money or other valuable thing for any political purpose, shall be fined not more than $5,000 or imprisoned not more than three years, or both.

§ 607.   Making political contributions

Whoever, being an officer, clerk, or other person in the service of the United States or any department or agency thereof, directly or indirectly gives or hands over to any other officer, clerk, or person in the service of the United States, or to any Senator or Member of or Delegate to Congress, or Resident Commissioner, any money or other valuable thing on account of or to be applied to the promotion of any political object, shall be fined not more than $5,000 or imprisoned not more than three years, or both.

Appendix F

Excerpts From the U.S. Constitution

Article I, Section 5, Clause 2

Each House may determine the Rules of its Proceedings, punish its Members for disorderly Behavior, and, with the Concurrence of two thirds, expel a Member.

Article I, Section 9, Clause 8

No Title of Nobility shall be granted by the United States: And no Person holding any Office of Profit or Trust under them, shall, without the Consent of the Congress, accept of any present, Emolument, Office, or Title, of any kind whatever, from any King, Prince, or foreign State.

Appendix G

Excerpts From Federal Election Campaign Act, 2 U.S.C. §§432, 433, 437d, 437f, 437g, 441a, 441b

§ 432. Organization of political committees

(a) *Treasurer; vacancy; official authorizations.* Every political committee shall have a treasurer. No contribution or expenditure shall be accepted or made by or on behalf of a political committee during any period in which the office of treasurer is vacant. No expenditure shall be made for or on behalf of a political committee without the authorization of the treasurer or his or her designated agent.

(b) *Account of contributions; segregated funds.*

(1) Every person who receives a contribution for an authorized political committee shall, no later than 10 days after receiving such contribution, forward to the treasurer such contribution, and if the amount of the contribution is in excess of $50 the name and address of the person making the contribution and the date of receipt.

(2) Every person who receives a contribution for a political committee which is not an authorized committee shall—

(A) if the amount of the contribution is $50 or less, forward to the treasurer such contribution no later than 30 days after receiving the contribution; and

(B) if the amount of the contribution is in excess of $50, forward to the treasurer such contribution, the name and address of the person making the contribution, and the date of receipt of the contribution, no later than 10 days after receiving the contribution.

(3) All funds of a political committee shall be segregated from, and may not be commingled with, the personal funds of any individual.

(c) *Recordkeeping.* The treasurer of a political committee shall keep an account of—

(1) all contributions received by or on behalf of such political committee;

(2) the name and address of any person who makes any contribution in excess of $50, together with the date and amount of such contribution by any person;

(3) the identification of any person who makes a contribution or contributions aggregating more than $200 during a calendar year, together with the date and amount of any such contribution;

(4) the identification of any political committee which makes a contribution, together with the date and amount of any such contribution; and

(5) the name and address of every person to whom any disbursement is made, the date, amount, and purpose of the disbursement, and the name of the candidate and the office sought by the candidate, if any, for whom the disbursement was made, including a receipt, invoice, or cancelled check for each disbursement in excess of $200.

(d) *Preservation of records and copies of reports.* The treasurer shall preserve all records required to be kept by this section and copies of all reports required to be filed by this subchapter for 3 years after the report is filed.

(e) *Principal and additional campaign committees; designations, status of candidate, authorized committees, etc.*

(1) Each candidate for Federal office (other than the nominee for the office of Vice President) shall designate in writing a political committee in accordance with paragraph (3) to serve as the principal campaign committee of such candidate. Such designation shall be made no later than 15 days after becoming a candidate. A candidate may designate additional political committees in accordance with paragraph (3) to serve as authorized committees of such candidate. Such designation shall be in writing and filed with the principal campaign committee of such candidate in accordance with subsection (f)(1) of this section.

(2) Any candidate described in paragraph (1) who receives a contribution, or any loan for use in connection with the campaign of such candidate for election, or makes a disbursement in connection with such campaign, shall be considered, for purposes of this Act, as having received the contribution or loan, or as having made the disbursement, as the case may be, as an agent of the authorized committee or committees of such candidate.

(3) (A) No political committee which supports or has supported more than one candidate may be designated as an authorized committee, except that—

(i)   the candidate for the office of President nominated by a political party may designate the national committee of such political party as a principal campaign committee, but only if that national committee maintains separate books of account with respect to its function as a principal campaign committee; and

(ii)   candidates may designate a political committee established solely for the purpose of joint fundraising by such candidates as an authorized committee.

(B)   As used in this section, the term "support" does not include a contribution by any authorized committee in amounts of $1,000 or less to an authorized committee of any other candidate.

(4)   The name of each authorized committee shall include the name of the candidate who authorized such committee under paragraph (1). In the case of any political committee which is not an authorized committee, such political committee shall not include the name of any candidate in its name.

(5)   The name of any separate segregated fund established pursuant to section 441b(b) shall include the name of its connected organization.

(f)   *Filing with and receipt of designations, statements, and reports by principal campaign committees.*

(1)   Notwithstanding any other provision of this Act, each designation, statement, or report of receipts or disbursements made by an authorized committee of a candidate shall be filed with the candidate's principal campaign committee.

(2)   Each principal campaign committee shall receive all designations, statements, and reports required to be filed with it under paragraph (1) and shall compile and file such designations, statements, and reports in accordance with this Act.

(g)   *Filing with and receipt of designations, statements, and reports by Clerk of House of Representatives or Secretary of Senate; forwarding to Commission; filing requirements with Commission; public inspection and preservation of designations, etc.*

(1)   Designations, statements, and reports required to be filed under this Act by a candidate or by an authorized committee of a candidate for the office of Representative in, or Delegate or Resident Commissioner to, the Congress, and by the principal campaign committee of such a candidate, shall be filed with the Clerk of the House of Representatives, who shall receive such designations, statements, and reports as custodian for the Commission.

(2) Designations, statements, and reports required to be filed under this Act by a candidate for the office of Senator, and by the principal campaign committee of such candidate, shall be filed with the Secretary of the Senate, who shall receive such designations, statements, and reports, as custodian for the Commission.

(3) The Clerk of the House of Representatives and the Secretary of the Senate shall forward a copy of any designation, statement, or report filed with them under this subsection to the Commission as soon as possible (but no later than 2 working days) after receiving such designation, statement, or report.

(4) All designations, statements, and reports required to be filed under this Act, except designations, statements, and reports filed in accordance with paragraphs (1) and (2), shall be filed with the Commission.

(5) The Clerk of the House of Representatives and the Secretary of the Senate shall make the designations, statements, and reports received under this subsection available for public inspection and copying in the same manner as the Commission under section 438(a)(4), and shall preserve such designations, statements, and reports in the same manner as the Commission under section 438(a)(5).

(h) *Campaign depositories; designations, maintenance of accounts, etc.; petty cash fund for disbursements; record of disbursements.*

(1) Each political committee shall designate one or more State banks, federally chartered depository institutions, or depository institutions the deposits or accounts of which are insured by the Federal Deposit Insurance Corporation, the Federal Savings and Loan Insurance Corporation, or the National Credit Union Administration, as its campaign depository or depositories. Each political committee shall maintain at least one checking account and such other accounts as the committee determines at a depository designated by such committee. All receipts received by such committee shall be deposited in such accounts. No disbursements may be made (other than petty cash disbursements under paragraph (2)) by such committee except by check drawn on such accounts in accordance with this section.

(2) A political committee may maintain a petty cash fund for disbursements not in excess of $100 to any person in connection with a single purchase or transaction. A record of all petty cash disbursements shall be maintained in accordance with subsection (c)(5) of this section.

(i) When the treasurer of a political committee shows that best efforts have been used to obtain, maintain, and submit the information required by this Act for the political committee, any report or any records of such committee shall be considered in compliance with this Act or chapter 95 or chapter 96 of title 26.

§ 433. Registration of political committees

(a) *Statements of organization.* Each authorized campaign committee shall file a statement of organization no later than 10 days after designation pursuant to section 432(e)(1). Each separate segregated fund established under the provisions of section 441b(b) shall file a statement of organization no later than 10 days after establishment. All other committees shall file a statement of organization within 10 days after becoming a political committee within the meaning of section 431(4).

(b) *Contents of statements.* The statement of organization of a political committee shall include—

(1) the name, address, and type of committee;

(2) the name, address, relationship, and type of any connected organization or affiliated committee;

(3) the name, address, and position of the custodian of books and accounts of the committee;

(4) the name and address of the treasurer of the committee;

(5) if the committee is authorized by a candidate, the name, address, office sought, and party affiliation of the candidate; and

(6) a listing of all banks, safety deposit boxes, or other depositories used by the committee.

(c) *Change of information in statements.* Any change in information previously submitted in a statement of organization shall be reported in accordance with section 432(g) no later than 10 days after the date of the change.

(d) *Termination, etc., requirements and authorities.*

(1) A political committee may terminate only when such a committee files a written statement, in accordance with section 432(g), that it will no longer receive any contributions or make any disbursement and that such committee has no outstanding debts or obligations.

(2) Nothing contained in this subsection may be construed to eliminate or limit the authority of the Commission to establish procedures for—

(A) the determination of insolvency with respect to any political committee;

(B) the orderly liquidation of an insolvent political committee, and the orderly application of its assets for the reduction of outstanding debts; and

(C) the termination of an insolvent political committee after such liquidation and application of assets.

§ 437d. Powers of the Commission

(a) *Specific authorities.* The Commission has the power—

(1) to require by special or general orders, any person to submit, under oath, such written reports and answers to questions as the Commission may prescribe;

(2) to administer oaths or affirmations;

(3) to require by subpoena, signed by the chairman or the vice chairman, the attendance and testimony of witnesses and the production of all documentary evidence relating to the execution of its duties;

(4) in any proceeding or investigation, to order testimony to be taken by deposition before any person who is designated by the Commission and has the power to administer oaths and, in such instances, to compel testimony and the production of evidence in the same manner as authorized under paragraph (3);

(5) to pay witnesses the same fees and mileage as are paid in like circumstances in the courts of the United States;

(6) to initiate (through civil actions for injunctive, declaratory, or other appropriate relief), defend (in the case of any civil action brought under section 437g(a)(8) of this title) or appeal any civil action in the name of the Commission to enforce the provisions of this Act and chapter 95 and chapter 96 of title 26, through its general counsel;

(7) to render advisory opinions under section 437f of this title;

(8) to develop such prescribed forms and to make, amend, and repeal such rules, pursuant to the provisions of chapter 5 of title 5, United States Code, as are necessary to carry out the provisions of this Act and chapter 95 and chapter 96 of title 26; and

(9) to conduct investigations and hearings expeditiously, to encourage voluntary compliance, and to report apparent violations to the appropriate law enforcement authorities.

(b) *Judicial orders for compliance with subpoenas and orders of Commission; contempt of court.* Upon petition by the Commission, any United States district court within the jurisdiction of which any inquiry is being carried on may, in case of refusal to obey a subpoena or order of the Commission issued under subsection (a) of this section, issue an order requiring compliance. Any failure to obey the order of the court may be punished by the court as a contempt thereof.

(c) *Civil liability for disclosure of information.* No person shall be subject to civil liability to any person (other than the Commission or the United States) for disclosing information at the request of the Commission.

(d) *Concurrent transmissions to Congress or member of budget estimates, etc.; prior submission of legislative recommendations, testimony, or comments on legislation.*

(1) Whenever the Commission submits any budget estimate or request to the President or the Office of Management and Budget, it shall concurrently transmit a copy of such estimate or request to the Congress.

(2) Whenever the Commission submits any legislative recommendation, or testimony, or comments on legislation, requested by the Congress or by any Member of the Congress, to the President or the Office of Management and Budget, it shall concurrently transmit a copy thereof to the Congress or to the Member requesting the same. No officer or agency of the United States shall have any authority to require the Commission to submit its legislative recommendations, testimony, or comments on legislation, to any office or agency of the United States for approval, comments, or review, prior to the submission of such recommendations, testimony, or comments to the Congress.

(e) *Exclusive civil remedy for enforcement.* Except as provided in section 437g(a)(8) of this title, the power of the Commission to initiate civil actions under subsection (a)(6) of this section shall be the exclusive civil remedy for the enforcement of the provisions of this Act.

§ 437f. Advisory opinions

(a) *Requests by persons, candidates, or authorized committees; subject matter; time for response.*

(1) Not later than 60 days after the Commission receives from a person a complete written request concerning the application of this Act, chapter 95 or chapter 96 of title 26, or a rule or regulation prescribed by the Commission, with respect to a specific transaction or activity by the person, the Commission shall render a written advisory opinion relating to such transaction or activity to the person.

(2) If an advisory opinion is requested by a candidate, or any authorized committee of such candidate, during the 60-day period before any election for Federal office involving the requesting party, the Commission shall render a written advisory opinion relating to such request no later than 20 days after the Commission receives a complete written request.

(b) *Procedures applicable to initial proposal of rules or regulations, and advisory opinions.* Any rule of law which is not stated in this Act or in chapter 95 or chapter 96 of title 26 may be initially proposed by the Commission only as a rule or regulation pursuant to procedures established in section 438(d) of this title. No opinion of an advisory nature may be issued by the Commission or any of its employees except in accordance with the provisions of this section.

(c) *Persons entitled to rely upon opinions; scope of protection for good faith reliance.*

(1) Any advisory opinion rendered by the Commission under subsection (a) of this section may be relied upon by—

(A) any person involved in the specific transaction or activity with respect to which such advisory opinion is rendered; and

(B) any person involved in any specific transaction or activity which is indistinguishable in all its material aspects from the transaction or activity with respect to which such advisory opinion is rendered.

(2) Notwithstanding any other provisions of law, any person who relies upon any provision or finding of an advisory opinion in accordance with the provisions of paragraph (1) and who acts in good faith in accordance with the provisions and findings of such advisory opinion shall not, as a result of any such act, be subject to any sanction provided by this Act or by chapter 95 or chapter 96 of title 26.

(d) *Requests made public; submission of written comments by interested public.* The Commission shall make public any requests made under subsection (a) of this section for an advisory opinion. Before rendering an advisory opinion, the Commission shall accept written comments submitted by any interested party within the 10-day period following the date the request is made public.

§ 437g. Enforcement

(a) *Administrative and judicial practice and procedure.*

(1) Any person who believes a violation of this Act or of chapter 95 or chapter 96 of title 26 has occurred, may file a complaint with the Commission. Such complaint shall be in writing, signed and sworn to by the person filing such complaint, shall be notarized, and shall be made under penalty of perjury and subject to the provisions of section 1001 of title 18, United States Code. Within 5 days after receipt of a complaint, the Commission shall notify, in writing, any person alleged in the complaint to have committed such a violation. Before the Commission conducts any vote on the complaint, other than a vote to dismiss, any person so notified shall have the opportunity to demonstrate, in writing, to the Commission within 15 days after notification that no action should be taken against such person on the basis of

the complaint. The Commission may not conduct any investigation or take any other action under this section solely on the basis of a complaint of a person whose identity is not disclosed to the Commission.

(2) If the Commission, upon receiving a complaint under paragraph (1) or on the basis of information ascertained in the normal course of carrying out its supervisory responsibilities, determines, by an affirmative vote of 4 of its members, that it has reason to believe that a person has committed, or is about to commit, a violation of this Act or chapter 95 or chapter 96 of title 26, the Commission shall, through its chairman or vice chairman, notify the person of the alleged violation. Such notification shall set forth the factual basis for such alleged violation. The Commission shall make an investigation of such alleged violation, which may include a field investigation or audit, in accordance with the provisions of this section.

(3) The general counsel of the Commission shall notify the respondent of any recommendation to the Commission by the general counsel to proceed to a vote on probable cause pursuant to paragraph (4)(A)(i). With such notification, the general counsel shall include a brief stating the position of the general counsel on the legal and factual issues of the case. Within 15 days of receipt of such brief, respondent may submit a brief stating the position of such respondent on the legal and factual issues of the case, and replying to the brief of general counsel. Such briefs shall be filed with the Secretary of the Commission and shall be considered by the Commission before proceeding under paragraph (4).

(4) (A) (i) Except as provided in clause (ii), if the Commission determines, by an affirmative vote of 4 of its members, that there is probable cause to believe that any person has committed, or is about to commit, a violation of this Act or of chapter 95 or chapter 96 of title 26, the Commission shall attempt, for a period of at least 30 days, to correct or prevent such violation by informal methods of conference, conciliation, and persuasion, and to enter into a conciliation agreement with any person involved. Such attempt by the Commission to correct or prevent such violation may continue for a period of not more than 90 days. The Commission may not enter into a conciliation agreement under this clause except pursuant to an affirmative vote of 4 of its members. A conciliation agreement, unless violated, is a complete bar to any further action by the Commission, including

the bringing of a civil proceeding under paragraph (6)(A).

(ii) If any determination of the Commission under clause (i) occurs during the 45-day period immediately preceding any election, then the Commission shall attempt, for a period of at least 15 days, to correct or prevent the violation involved by the methods specified in clause (i).

(B) (i) No action by the Commission or any person, and no information derived, in connection with any conciliation attempt by the Commission under subparagraph (A) may be made public by the Commission without the written consent of the respondent and the Commission.

(ii) If a conciliation agreement is agreed upon by the Commission and the respondent, the Commission shall make public any conciliation agreement signed by both the Commission and the respondent. If the Commission makes a determination that a person has not violated this Act or chapter 95 or chapter 96 of title 26, the Commission shall make public such determination.

(5) (A) If the Commission believes that a violation of this Act or of chapter 95 or chapter 96 of title 26 has been committed, a conciliation agreement entered into by the Commission under paragraph (4)(A) may include a requirement that the person involved in such conciliation agreement shall pay a civil penalty which does not exceed the greater of $5,000 or an amount equal to any contribution or expenditure involved in such violation.

(B) If the Commission believes that a knowing and willful violation of this Act or of chapter 95 or chapter 96 of title 26 has been committed, a conciliation agreement entered into by the Commission under paragraph (4)(A) may require that the person involved in such conciliation agreement shall pay a civil penalty which does not exceed the greater of $10,000 or an amount equal to 200 percent of any contribution or expenditure involved in such violation.

(C) If the Commission by an affirmative vote of 4 of its members, determines that there is probable cause to believe that a knowing and willful violation of this Act which is subject to subsection (d) of this section, or a knowing and willful violation of chapter 95 or chapter 96 of title 26, has occurred or is about to occur, it may refer such apparent violation to the Attorney General of the United States without regard to any limitations set forth in paragraph (4)(A).

(D) In any case in which a person has entered into a conciliation agreement with the Commission under paragraph (4)(A), the Commission may institute a civil action for relief under paragraph (6)(A) if it believes that the person has violated any provision of such conciliation agreement. For the Commission to obtain relief in any civil action, the Commission need only establish that the person has violated, in whole or in part, any requirement of such conciliation agreement.

(6) (A) If the Commission is unable to correct or prevent any violation of this Act or of chapter 95 or chapter 96 of title 26, by the methods specified in paragraph (4)(A), the Commission may, upon an affirmative vote of 4 of its members, institute a civil action for relief, including a permanent or temporary injunction, restraining order, or any other appropriate order (including an order for a civil penalty which does not exceed the greater of $5,000 or an amount equal to any contribution or expenditure involved in such violation) in the district court of the United States for the district in which the person against whom such action is brought is found, resides, or transacts business.

(B) In any civil action instituted by the Commission under subparagraph (A), the court may grant a permanent or temporary injunction, restraining order, or other order, including a civil penalty which does not exceed the greater of $5,000 or an amount equal to any contribution or expenditure involved in such violation, upon a proper showing that the person involved has committed, or is about to commit (if the relief sought is a permanent or temporary injunction or a restraining order), a violation of this Act or chapter 95 or chapter 96 of title 26.

(C) In any civil action for relief instituted by the Commission under subparagraph (A), if the court determines that the Commission has established that the person involved in such civil action has committed a knowing and willful violation of this Act or of chapter 95 or chapter 96 of title 26, the court may impose a civil penalty which does not exceed the greater of $10,000 or an amount equal to 200 percent of any contribution or expenditure involved in such violation.

(7) In any action brought under paragraph (5) or (6), subpoenas for witnesses who are required to attend a United States district court may run into any other district.

(8) (A) Any party aggrieved by an order of the Commission dismissing a complaint filed by such party under paragraph (1), or by a failure of the Commission to act on such complaint during the 120-day period beginning on the date the complaint is filed, may file a petition with the United States District Court for the District of Columbia.

(B) Any petition under subparagraph (A) shall be filed, in the case of a dismissal of a complaint by the Commission, within 60 days after the date of the dismissal.

(C) In any proceeding under this paragraph the court may declare that the dismissal of the complaint or the failure to act is contrary to law, and may direct the Commission to conform with such declaration within 30 days, failing which the complainant may bring, in the name of such complainant, a civil action to remedy the violation involved in the original complaint.

(9) Any judgment of a district court under this subsection may be appealed to the court of appeals, and the judgment of the court of appeals affirming or setting aside, in whole or in part, any such order of the district court shall be final, subject to review by the Supreme Court of the United States upon certiorari or certification as provided in section 1254 of title 28, United States Code.

(10) *Repealed.*[1]

(11) If the Commission determines after an investigation that any person has violated an order of the court entered in a proceeding brought under paragraph (6), it may petition the court for an order to hold such person in civil contempt, but if it believes the violation to be knowing and willful it may petition the court for an order to hold such person in criminal contempt.

(12) (A) Any notification or investigation made under this section shall not be made public by the Commission or by any person without the written consent of the person receiving such notification or the person with respect to whom such investigation is made.

(B) Any member or employee of the Commission, or any other person, who violates the provisions of subparagraph (A) shall be fined not more than $2,000. Any such member, employee, or other person

---

[1] *Expedited Judicial Review.* Section 402(1)(A) of Pub. L. No. 98–620, effective November 11, 1984, repealed subparagraph (a)(10). The repealed provision had required that actions brought under this subsection be advanced on the docket of the court in which filed and put ahead of all other actions.

who knowingly and willfully violates the provisions of subparagraph (A) shall be fined not more than $5,000.

(b) *Notice to persons not filing reports prior to institution of enforcement action; publication of identity of persons and unfiled reports.* Before taking any action under subsection (a) of this section against any person who has failed to file a report required under section 434(a)(2)(A)(iii) of this title for the calendar quarter immediately preceding the election involved, or in accordance with section 434(a)(2)(A)(i), the Commission shall notify the person of such failure to file the required reports. If a satisfactory response is not received within 4 business days after the date of notification, the Commission shall, pursuant to section 438(a)(7) of this title, publish before the election the name of the person and the report or reports such person has failed to file.

(c) *Reports by Attorney General of apparent violations.* Whenever the Commission refers an apparent violation to the Attorney General, the Attorney General shall report to the Commission any action taken by the Attorney General regarding the apparent violation. Each report shall be transmitted within 60 days after the date the Commission refers an apparent violation, and every 30 days thereafter until the final disposition of the apparent violation.

(d) *Penalties; defenses; mitigation of offenses.*

(1) (A) Any person who knowingly and willfully commits a violation of any provision of this Act which involves the making, receiving, or reporting of any contribution or expenditure aggregating $2,000 or more during a calendar year shall be fined, or imprisoned for not more than one year, or both. The amount of this fine shall not exceed the greater of $25,000 or 300 percent of any contribution or expenditure involved in such violation.

(B) In the case of a knowing and willful violation of section 441b(b)(3), the penalties set forth in this subsection shall apply to a violation involving an amount aggregating $250 or more during a calendar year. Such violation of section 441b(b)(3) may incorporate a violation of section 441c(b), 441f or 441g of this title.

(C) In the case of a knowing and willful violation of section 441h of this title, the penalties set forth in this subsection shall apply without regard to whether the making, receiving, or reporting of a contribution or expenditure of $1,000 or more is involved.

(2) In any criminal action brought for a violation of any provision of this Act or of chapter 95 or chapter 96 of this title 26, any defendant may evidence their lack of knowledge or intent to commit the alleged violation by in-

troducing as evidence a conciliation agreement entered into between the defendant and the Commission under subsection (a)(4)(A) which specifically deals with the act or failure to act constituting such violation and which is still in effect.

(3) In any criminal action brought for a violation of any provision of this Act or of chapter 95 or chapter 96 of title 26, the court before which such action is brought shall take into account, in weighing the seriousness of the violation and in considering the appropriateness of the penalty to be imposed if the defendant is found guilty, whether—

(A) the specific act or failure to act which constitutes the violation for which the action was brought is the subject of a conciliation agreement entered into between the defendant and the Commission under subparagraph (a)(4)(A);

(B) the conciliation agreement is in effect; and

(C) the defendant is, with respect to the violation involved, in compliance with the conciliation agreement.

§ 441a.   Limitations on contributions and expenditures

(a) *Dollar limits on contributions.*

(1) No person shall make contributions—

(A) to any candidate and his authorized political committees with respect to any election for Federal office which, in the aggregate, exceed $1,000.

(B) to the political committees established and maintained by a national political party, which are not the authorized political committees of any candidate, in any calendar year which, in the aggregate, exceed $20,000; or

(C) to any other political committee in any calendar year, which in the aggregate, exceed $5,000.

(2) No multicandidate political committee shall make contributions—

(A) to any candidate and his authorized political committees with respect to any election for Federal office which, in the aggregate, exceed $5,000;

(B) to the political committees established and maintained by a national political party, which are not the authorized political committees of any candidate, in any calendar year, which, in the aggregate, exceed $15,000; or

(C) to any other political committee in any calendar year which, in the aggregate, exceed $5,000.

(3) No individual shall make contributions aggregat-

ing more than $25,000 in any calendar year. For purposes of this paragraph, any contribution made to a candidate in a year other than the calendar year in which the election is held with respect to which such contribution is made, is considered to be made during the calendar year in which such election is held.

(4) The limitations on contributions contained in paragraphs (1) and (2) do not apply to transfers between and among political committees which are national, State, district, or local committees (including any subordinate committee thereof) of the same political party. For purposes of paragraph (2), the term "multicandidate political committee" means a political committee which has been registered under section 433 of this title for a period of not less than 6 months, which has received contributions from more than 50 persons, and except for any State political party organization, has made contributions to 5 or more candidates for Federal office.

(5) For purposes of the limitations provided by paragraph (1) and paragraph (2), all contributions made by political committees established or financed or maintained or controlled by any corporation, labor organization, or any other person, including any parent, subsidiary, branch, division, department, or local unit of such corporation, labor organization, or any other person, or by any group of such persons, shall be considered to have been made by a single political committee, except that—

(A) nothing in this sentence shall limit transfers between political committees of funds raised through joint fundraising efforts;

(B) for purposes of the limitations provided by paragraph (1) and paragraph (2) all contributions made by a single political committee established or financed or maintained or controlled by a national committee of a political party and by a single political committee established or financed or maintained or controlled by the State committee of a political party shall not be considered to have been made by a single political committee; and

(C) nothing in this section shall limit the transfer of funds between the principal campaign committee of a candidate seeking nomination or election to a Federal office and the principal campaign committee of that candidate for nomination or election to another Federal office if—

(i) such transfer is not made when the candidate is actively seeking nomination or election to both such offices;

(ii)   the limitations contained in this Act on contributions by persons are not exceeded by such transfer; and

(iii)   the candidate has not elected to receive any funds under chapter 95 or chapter 96 of title 26.

In any case in which a corporation and any of its subsidiaries, branches, divisions, departments or local units, or a labor organization and any of its subsidiaries, branches, divisions, departments, or local units establish or finance or maintain or control more than one separate segregated fund, all such separate segregated funds shall be treated as a single separate segregated fund for purposes of the limitations provided by paragraph (1) and paragraph (2).

(6)   The limitations on contributions to a candidate imposed by paragraphs (1) and (2) of this subsection shall apply separately with respect to each election, except that all elections held in any calendar year for the office of President of the United States (except a general election for such office) shall be considered to be one election.

(7)   For purposes of this subsection—

(A)   contributions to a named candidate made to any political committee authorized by such candidate to accept contributions on his behalf shall be considered to be contributions made to such candidate;

(B)   (i)   expenditures made by any person in cooperation, consultation, or concert, with, or at the request or suggestion of, a candidate, his authorized political committees, or their agents, shall be considered to be a contribution to such candidate;

(ii)   the financing by any person of the dissemination, distribution, or republication, in whole or in part, of any broadcast or any written, graphic, or other form of campaign materials prepared by the candidate, his campaign committees, or their authorized agents shall be considered to be an expenditure for purposes of this paragraph; and

(C)   contributions made to or for the benefit of any candidate nominated by a political party for election to the office of Vice President of the United States shall be considered to be contributions made to or for the benefit of the candidate of such party for election to the office of President of the United States.

(8)   For purposes of the limitations imposed by this section, all contributions made by a person, either directly or indirectly, on behalf of a particular candidate, including contributions which are in any way earmarked or otherwise directed through an intermediary or conduit to such candi-

date, shall be treated as contributions from such person to such candidate. The intermediary or conduit shall report the original source and the intended recipient of such contribution to the Commission and to the intended recipient.

(b) *Dollar limits on expenditures by candidates for office of President of the United States.*

(1) No candidate for the office of President of the United States who is eligible under section 9003 of title 26 (relating to condition for eligibility for payments) or under section 9033 of title 26 (relating to eligibility for payments) to receive payments from the Secretary of the Treasury may make expenditures in excess of—

(A) $10,000,000 in the case of a campaign for nomination for election to such office, except the aggregate of expenditures under this subparagraph in any one State shall not exceed the greater of 16 cents multiplied by the voting age population of the State (as certified under subsection (e) of this section), or $200,000; or

(B) $20,000,000 in the case of a campaign for election to such office.

(2) For purposes of this subsection—

(A) expenditures made by or on behalf of any candidate nominated by a political party for election to the office of Vice President of the United States shall be considered to be expenditures made by or on behalf of the candidate of such party for election to the office of President of the United States; and

(B) an expenditure is made on behalf of a candidate, including a vice presidential candidate, if it is made by—

(i) an authorized committee or any other agent of the candidate for purposes of making any expenditure; or

(ii) any person authorized or requested by the candidate, an authorized committee of the candidate, or an agent of the candidate, to make the expenditure.

(c) *Increases on limits based on increases in price index.*

(1) At the beginning of each calendar year (commencing in 1976), as there become available necessary data from the Bureau of Labor Statistics of the Department of Labor, the Secretary of Labor shall certify to the Commission and publish in the Federal Register the percent difference between the price index for the 12 months preceding the beginning of such calendar year and the price index for the base period. Each limitation established by subsection

(b) of this section and subsection (d) of this section shall be increased by such percent difference. Each amount so increased shall be the amount in effect for such calendar year.

(2)   For purposes of paragraph (1)—

(A) the term "price index" means the average over a calendar year of the Consumer Price Index (all items—United States city average) published monthly by the Bureau of Labor Statistics; and

(B) the term "base period" means the calendar year of 1974.

(d)   *Expenditures by national committee, State committee, or subordinate committee of State committee in connection with general election campaign of candidates for Federal office.*

(1)   Notwithstanding any other provision of law with respect to limitations on expenditures or limitations on contributions, the national committee of a political party and a State committee of a political party, including any subordinate committee of a State committee, may make expenditures in connection with the general election campaign of candidates for Federal office, subject to the limitations contained in paragraphs (2) and (3) of this subsection.

(2)   The national committee of a political party may not make any expenditure in connection with the general election campaign of any candidate for President of the United States who is affiliated with such party which exceeds an amount equal to 2 cents multiplied by the voting age population of the United States (as certified under subsection (e) of this section). Any expenditure under this paragraph shall be in addition to any expenditure by a national committee of a political party serving as the principal campaign committee of a candidate for the office of President of the United States.

(3)   The national committee of a political party, or a State committee of a political party, including any subordinate committee of a State committee, may not make any expenditure in connection with the general election campaign of a candidate for Federal office in a State who is affiliated with such party which exceeds—

(A)   in the case of a candidate for election to the office of Senator, or of Representative from a State which is entitled to only one Representative, the greater of—

(i)   2 cents multiplied by the voting age population of the State (as certified under subsection (e) of this section); or

(ii) $20,000; and

(B) in the case of a candidate for election to the office of Representative, Delegate, or Resident Commissioner of any other State, $10,000. .

(e) *Certification and publication of estimated voting age population.* During the first week of January 1975, and every subsequent year, the Secretary of Commerce shall certify to the Commission and publish in the Federal Register an estimate of the voting age population of the United States, of each State, and of each congressional district as of the first day of July next preceding the date of certification. The term "voting age population" means resident population, 18 years of age or older.

(f) *Prohibited contributions and expenditures.* No candidate or political committee shall knowingly accept any contribution or make any expenditure in violation of the provisions of this section. No officer or employee of a political committee shall knowingly accept a contribution made for the benefit or use of a candidate, or knowingly make any expenditure on behalf of a candidate, in violation of any limitation imposed on contributions and expenditures under this section.

(g) *Attribution of multi-state expenditures to candidate's expenditure limitation in each State.* The Commission shall prescribe rules under which any expenditure by a candidate for presidential nominations for use in 2 or more States shall be attributed to such candidate's expenditure limitation in each such State, based on the voting age population in such State which can reasonably be expected to be influenced by such expenditure.

(h) *Senatorial candidates.* Notwithstanding any other provision of this Act, amounts totaling not more than $17,500 may be contributed to a candidate for nomination for election, or for election, to the United States Senate during the year in which an election is held in which he is such a candidate, by the Republican or Democratic Senatorial Campaign Committee, or the national committee of a political party, or any combination of such committees.

§ 441b. Contributions or expenditures by national banks, corporations, or labor organizations

(a) It is unlawful for any national bank, or any corporation organized by authority of any law of Congress, to make a contribution or expenditure in connection with any election to any political office, or in connection with any primary election or political convention or caucus held to select candidates for any political office, or for any corporation whatever, or any labor organization, to make a contribution or expenditure in connection with any election at which presidential and vice presidential electors or a Senator or Representative in, or a Delegate or Resident Commissioner to, Congress are to be voted for, or in connection with any primary election or political convention or caucus held to select candidates for any of the foregoing offices, or for any candidate, political committee, or other person knowingly to accept or receive any contribution prohibited by this section, or any officer or any director of any corporation or any national bank or any officer of any labor organization to consent to any contribution or expenditure by the corporation, national bank, or labor organization, as the case may be, prohibited by this section.

(b) (1) For the purposes of this section the term "labor organization" means any organization of any kind, or any agency or employee representation committee or plan, in which employees participate and which exists for the purpose, in whole or in part, of dealing with employers concerning grievances, labor disputes, wages, rates of pay, hours of employment, or conditions of work.

(2) For purposes of this section and section 79*l*(h) of title 15, the term "contribution or expenditure" shall include any direct or indirect payment, distribution, loan, advance, deposit, or gift of money, or any services, or anything of value (except a loan of money by a national or State bank made in accordance with the applicable banking laws and regulations and in the ordinary course of business) to any candidate, campaign committee, or political party or organization, in connection with any election to any of the offices referred to in this section, but shall not include—

(A) communications by a corporation to its stockholders and executive or administrative personnel and their families or by a labor organization to its members and their families on any subject;

(B) nonpartisan registration and get-out-the-vote campaigns by a corporation aimed at its stockholders and executive or administrative personnel and their families, or by a labor organization aimed at its members and their families; and

(C) the establishment, administration, and solicitation of contributions to a separate segregated fund to be utilized for political purposes by a corporation, labor organization, membership organization, cooperative, or corporation without capital stock.

(3) It shall be unlawful—

(A) for such a fund to make a contribution or expenditure by utilizing money or anything of value secured by physical force, job discrimination, financial reprisals, or the threat of force, job discrimination, or financial reprisal; or by dues, fees, or other moneys required as a condition of membership in a labor organization or as a condition of employment, or by moneys obtained in any commercial transaction;

(B) for any person soliciting an employee for a contribution to such a fund to fail to inform such employee of the political purposes of such fund at the time of such solicitation; and

(C) for any person soliciting an employee for a contribution to such a fund to fail to inform such employee, at the time of such solicitation, of his right to refuse to so contribute without any reprisal.

(4) (A) Except as provided in subparagraphs (B), (C), and (D), it shall be unlawful—

 (i) for a corporation, or a separate segregated fund established by a corporation, to solicit contributions to such a fund from any person other than its stockholders and their families and its executive or administrative personnel and their families, and

 (ii) for a labor organization, or a separate segregated fund established by a labor organization, to solicit contributions to such a fund from any person other than its members and their families.

(B) It shall not be unlawful under this section for a corporation, a labor organization, or a separate segregated fund established by such corporation or such labor organization, to make 2 written solicitations for contributions during the calendar year from any stockholder, executive or administrative personnel, or employee of a corporation or the families of such persons. A solicitation under this subparagraph may be made only by mail addressed to stockholders, executive or administrative personnel, or employees at their residence and shall be so designed that the corporation, labor organization, or separate segregated fund conducting such solicitation cannot determine who makes a contribution of $50 or less as a result of such solicitation and who does not make such a contribution.

(C) This paragraph shall not prevent a membership organization, cooperative, or corporation without capital stock, or a separate segregated fund established by a membership organization, cooperative, or corporation without capital stock, from soliciting contributions to such a fund from members of such organization, cooperative, or corporation without capital stock.

(D) This paragraph shall not prevent a trade association or a separate segregated fund established by a trade association from soliciting contributions from the stockholders and executive or administrative personnel of the member corporations of such trade association and the families of such stockholders or personnel to the extent that such solicitation of such stockholders and personnel, and their families, has been separately and specifically approved by the member corporation involved, and such member corporation does not approve any such solicitation by more than one such trade association in any calendar year.

(5) Notwithstanding any other law, any method of soliciting voluntary contributions or of facilitating the making of voluntary contributions to a separate segregated fund established by a corporation, permitted by law to corporations with regard to stockholders and executive or administrative personnel, shall also be permitted to labor organizations with regard to their members.

(6) Any corporation, including its subsidiaries, branches, divisions, and affiliates, that utilizes a method of soliciting voluntary contributions or facilitating the making of voluntary contributions, shall make available such method, on written request and at a cost sufficient only to reimburse the corporation for the expenses incurred thereby, to a labor organization representing any members working for such corporation, its subsidiaries, branches, divisions, and affiliates.

(7) For purposes of this section, the term "executive or administrative personnel" means individuals employed by a corporation who are paid on a salary, rather than hourly, basis and who have policymaking, managerial, professional, or supervisory responsibilities.

Appendix H

Federal Election Commission Regulations Regarding Submission of Requests for Advisory Opinions, 11 C.F.R. Part 112

§ 112.1 Requests for advisory opinions (2 U.S.C. 437f(a)(1)).

(a) Any person may request in writing an advisory opinion concerning the application of the Act, chapters 95 or 96 of the Internal Revenue Code of 1954, or any regulation prescribed by the Commission. An authorized agent of the requesting person may submit the advisory opinion request, but the agent shall disclose the identity of his or her principal.

(b) The written advisory opinion request shall set forth a specific transaction or activity that the requesting person plans to undertake or is presently undertaking and intends to undertake in the future. Requests presenting a general question of interpretation, or posing a hypothetical situation, or regarding the activities of third parties, do not qualify as advisory opinion requests.

(c) Advisory opinion requests shall include a complete description of all facts relevant to the specific transaction or activity with respect to which the request is made.

(d) The Office of General Counsel shall review all requests for advisory opinions submitted under 11 CFR 112.1. If the Office of General Counsel determines that a request for an advisory opinion is incomplete or other-

wise not qualified under 11 CFR 112.1, it shall, within 10 calendar days of receipt of such request, notify the requesting person and specify the deficiencies in the request.

(e) Advisory opinion requests should be sent to the Federal Election Commission, Office of General Counsel, 999 E Street, NW., Washington, DC 20463.

(f) Upon receipt by the Commission, each request which qualifies as an advisory opinion request (AOR) under 11 CFR 112.1 shall be assigned an AOR number for reference purposes.

§ 112.2 Public availability of requests (2 U.S.C. 437f(d)).

(a) Advisory opinion requests which qualify under 11 CFR 112.1 shall be made public at the Commission promptly upon their receipt.

(b) A copy of the original request and any supplements thereto, shall be available for public inspection and purchase at the Public Disclosure Division of the Commission.

§ 112.3 Written comments on requests (2 U.S.C. 437f(d)).

(a) Any interested person may submit written comments concerning advisory opinion requests made public at the Commission.

(b) The written comments shall be

submitted within 10 calendar days following the date the request is made public at the Commission. However, if the 10th calendar day falls on a Saturday, Sunday, or Federal holiday, the 10 day period ends at the close of the business day next following the weekend or holiday. Additional time for submission of written comments may be granted upon written request for an extension by the person who wishes to submit comments or may be granted by the Commission without an extension request.

(c) Comments on advisory opinion requests should refer to the AOR number of the request, and statutory references should be to the United States Code citations, rather than to Public Law citations.

(d) Written comments and requests for additional time to comment shall be sent to the Federal Election Commission, Office of General Counsel, 999 E Street, NW., Washington, DC 20463.

(e) Before it issues an advisory opinion the Commission shall accept and consider all written comments submitted within the 10 day comment period or any extension thereof.

§ 112.4 Issuance of advisory opinions (2 U.S.C. 437f(a) and (b)).

(a) Within 60 calendar days after receiving an advisory opinion request that qualifies under 11 CFR 112.1, the Commission shall issue to the requesting person a written advisory opinion or shall issue a written response stating that the Commission was unable to approve an advisory opinion by the required affirmative vote of 4 members.

(b) The 60 calendar day period of 11 CFR 112.4(a) is reduced to 20 calendar days for an advisory opinion request qualified under 11 CFR 112.1 provided the request:

(1) is submitted by any candidate, including any authorized committee of the candidate (or agent of either), within the 60 calendar days preceding the date of any election for Federal office in which the candidate is seeking nomination or election; and

(2) presents a specific transaction or activity related to the election that may invoke the 20 day period if the connection is explained in the request.

(c) The 60 day and 20 day periods referred to in 11 CFR 112.4(a) and (b) only apply when the Commission has received a qualified and complete advisory opinion request under 11 CFR 112.1, and when the 60th or 20th day occurs on a Saturday, Sunday or Federal holiday, the respective period ends at the close of the business day next following the weekend or holiday.

(d) The Commission may issue advisory opinions pertaining only to the Federal Election Campaign Act of 1971, as amended, chapters 95 or 96 of the Internal Revenue Code of 1954, or rules or regulations duly prescribed under those statutes.

(e) Any rule of law which is not stated in the Act or in chapters 95 or 96 of the Internal Revenue Code of 1954, or in a regulation duly prescribed by the Commission, may be initially proposed only as a rule or regulation pursuant to procedures established in 2 USC 438(d) or 26 USC 9009(c) and 9039(c) as applicable.

(f) No opinion of an advisory nature may be issued by the Commission or any of its employees except in accordance with 11 CFR Part 112; however, this limitation does not preclude distribution by the Commission of information consistent with the Act and chapters 95 or 96 of the Internal Revenue Code of 1954.

(g) When issued by the Commission, each advisory opinion or other response under 11 CFR 112.4(a) shall be made public and sent by mail, or personally delivered to the person who requested the opinion.

§ 112.5 Reliance on advisory opinions (2 U.S.C. 437f(c)).

(a) An advisory opinion rendered by the Commission under 11 CFR Part 112 may be relied upon by:

(1) any person involved in the specific transaction or activity with respect to which such advisory opinion is rendered, and

(2) any person involved in any specific transaction or activity which is indistinguishable in all its material aspects from the transaction or activity with respect to which such advisory opinion is rendered.

(b) Notwithstanding any other provision of law, any person who relies upon an advisory opinion in accordance with 11 CFR 112.5(a) and who acts in good faith in accordance with that advisory opinion shall not, as a result of any such act, be subject to any sanction provided by the Federal

Election Campaign Act of 1971, as amended, or by chapters 95 or 96 of the Internal Revenue Code of 1954.

§ 112.6 Reconsideration of advisory opinions.

(a) The Commission may reconsider an advisory opinion previously issued if the person to whom the opinion was issued submits a written request for reconsideration within 30 calendar days of receipt of the opinion and if, upon the motion of a Commissioner who voted with the majority that originally approved the opinion, the Commission adopts the motion to reconsider by the affirmative vote of 4 members.

(b) The Commission may reconsider an advisory opinion previously issued if, upon the motion of a Commissioner who voted with the majority that originally approved the opinion and within 30 calendar days after the date the Commission approved the opinion, the Commission adopts the motion to reconsider by the affirmative vote of 4 members.

(c) In the event an advisory opinion is reconsidered pursuant to 11 CFR 112.6(b), the action taken in good faith reliance on that advisory opinion by the person to whom the opinion was issued shall not result in any sanction provided by the Act or chapters 95 or 96 of the Internal Revenue Code of 1954. 11 CFR 112.6(c) shall not be effective after the date when the person to whom the advisory opinion was issued has received actual notice of the Commission's decision to reconsider that advisory opinion.

(d) Adoption of a motion to reconsider vacates the advisory opinion to which it relates.

Appendix I

OMB Circular A-122, Cost Principles for Nonprofit Organizations

45 Fed. Reg. 46,022–46,034 (July 8, 1980)

OFFICE OF MANAGEMENT AND BUDGET

Circular A-122, "Cost Principles for Nonprofit Organizations"

[Note: This reprint incorporates corrections published at 46 FR 17185, Tuesday, March 17, 1981.]

AGENCY: Office of Management and Budget.

ACTION: Final Policy.

SUMMARY: This notice advises of a new OMB Circular dealing with principles for determining costs of grants, contracts, and other agreements with nonprofit organizations.

The Circular is the product of an interagency review conducted over a two-year period. Its purpose is to provide a set of cost principles to replace existing principles issued by individual agencies. These have often contained varying and conflicting requirements, and created confusion among agency administrators, auditors, and nonprofit officials. The new Circular will provide a uniform approach to the problem of determining costs, and promote efficiency and better understanding between recipients and the Federal Government.

EFFECTIVE DATE: The Circular becomes effective on issuance.

FOR FURTHER INFORMATION CONTACT: Palmer A. Marcantonio, Financial Management Branch, Office of Management and Budget, Washington, D.C. 20503, (202) 395–4773.

SUPPLEMENTARY INFORMATION: Before the Circular became final there was extensive coordination with the affected nonprofit organizations, professional associations, Federal agencies and others. All interested persons were given an opportunity to comment on the proposed Circular through informal consultations and a notice in the Federal Register. In response to our requests for comment, we received about 100 letters from Federal agencies, nonprofit organizations, associations, and other interested members of the public. These comments were considered in the final version of the Circular. There follows a summary of the major comments and the action taken on each.

In addition to the changes described, other changes have been made to improve the clarity and readability of the Circular. To the extent possible, we have tried to make the language of this Circular consistent with that of cost principles for educational institutions (Circular A–21), and State and local governments (Circular 74–4).

Summary of Significant Changes:

Set forth are changes that have been made in the final Circular as a result of

231

public comments. The more significant changes to the basic Circular and Attachment A include:

1. Paragraph 2. "Supersession" was added to the basic Circular to make it clear that this Circular supersedes cost principles issued by individual agencies.

2. Paragraph 4 of the basic Circular has been amended to make it clear that the absence of an advance agreement on any element of cost will not in itself affect the reasonableness of allocability of that element. Also, this paragraph was amended to make it clear that where an item of cost requiring prior approval is specified in the budget, approval of the budget constitutes approval of the cost.

3. Paragraph 5 of the basic Circular has been changed to remove any doubt as to which nonprofit organizations would not be covered by the Circular. Now, Appendix C to the Circular lists all exclusions.

4. Paragraph 8 was added to the basic Circular to permit Federal agencies to request exceptions from the requirements of the Circular.

5. Paragraph E.2. was added to Attachment A to cover the negotiation and approval of indirect cost rates, and to provide for cognizance arrangements.

The more significant changes to Attachment B to the Circular include:

1. Paragraph 6, *Compensation for Personal Services*, was modified to:

a. Permit Federal agencies to accept a substitute system for documenting personnel costs through means other than personnel activity reports.

b. Clarify provisions covering the allowability of costs for unemployment compensation or workers' compensation, and costs of insurance policies on the lives of trustees, officers, or other employees.

c. Make unallowable any increased costs of pension plans caused by delayed funding.

d. Delete a paragraph dealing with review and approval of compensation of individual employees.

2. Paragraph 7, *Contingencies*, was changed to make it clear that the term "contingency reserves" excludes self-insurance reserves or pension funds.

3. Paragraph 10 was modified to provide that the value of donated services used in the performance of a direct cost activity shall be allocated a share of indirect cost only when (a) the aggregate value of the service is material, (b) the services are supported by a significant amount of the indirect cost incurred by the organization, and (c) the direct cost activity is not pursued primarily for the benefit of the Federal Government. Provisions were also added to this paragraph for the cognizant agency and the recipient to negotiate when there is no basis for determining the fair market value of the services rendered, and to permit indirect costs allocated to donated services to be charged to an agreement or used to meet cost sharing or matching requirements.

4. Paragraph 13, *Equipment and Other Capital Expenditures*, was changed. Capital equipment is now defined as having an acquisition cost of $500 and a useful life of more than two years.

5. Paragraph 24, *Meetings, Conferences*. The prior approval requirement for charging meetings and conferences as a direct cost was deleted. A sentence was added to make it clear such costs were allowable provided they meet the criterion for the allowability of cost shown in Attachment A.

6. Paragraph 26, *Organization Costs*, was amended to provide that organization costs may be allowable when approved in writing by the awarding agency.

7. Paragraph 28, *Page Charges in Professional Journals*, was revised to provide that page charges may be allowable.

8. Paragraph 36, *Public Information Service Costs*, was modified to make public information costs allowable as direct costs with awarding agency approval.

9. Paragraph 42, *Rental Costs*, was rewritten to:

a. Make it clear that rental costs under leases which create a material equity on the leased property are allowable only up to the amount that the organization would have been allowed had it purchased the property; e.g., depreciation or use allowances, maintenance, taxes, insurance, etc.

b. Clarify the criteria for material equity leases.

10. Paragraph 50, *Travel Costs*, was amended to delete the prior approval requirement for domestic travel. In

addition to the above, a number of editorial changes were made to the original document.

Suggested Changes Not Considered Necessary.

Comment. Several respondents questioned the provision that, for "less than arm's length" leases, rental costs are allowable only up to the amount that would be allowed had title to the property been vested in the grantee organization. In their opinion this rule will result in unnecessary cost to the Federal Government, since it would encourage an organization to lease space on the commercial market at a higher rate.

Response. The cost principles are designed to cover most situations; however, there are always exceptions that must be considered on a case-by-case basis. The Circular contains a provision for Federal agencies to request exceptions.

Comment. Several respondents questioned why interest is not an allowable cost, since it is an ordinary and necessary cost of doing business.

Response. It has been a longstanding policy not to recognize interest as a cost. However, this policy has recently been revised for State and local governments in Circular 74–4, with respect to the cost of office space. The revision provides that "rental" rates for publicly owned buildings may be based on actual costs, including depreciation, interest, operation and maintenace costs, and other allowable costs. This revision was under consideration for some time. It was studied extensively by OMB, the General Accounting Office and others, and considerable analysis went into its formulation. Suggestions for extending it to nonprofit organizations would have to be examined with equal care. This has not yet been done; and we were reluctant to further delay issuance of this Circular.

Comment. Several respondents questioned why public information costs were not allowable as an indirect cost.

Response. Public information costs are often direct services to an organization's other programs. They are allowable, however, as a direct charge when they are within the scope of work of a particular agreement.

Comment. One respondent suggested that smaller grantees be excluded from complying with the Circular.

Response. Similar rules for the 50 selected items of cost would be needed regardless of the size of the grantee. To the extent possible, the Circular provides simplified methods for smaller grantees.

Comment. One respondent said the requirements of the Cost Accounting Standards Board should be applied to cover contracts with nonprofit organizations.

Response. It is unlikely that the type of grantees covered by this Circular would have contracts large enough to be covered by the CASB. In the event that they do, however, the regulations of the CASB would apply.

Comment. One respondent said the allocation of indirect cost to donated services would pose a tremendous difficulty to the organization. The organization relies on a corps of approximately 8,000 committee members to carry out obligations in response to Government requests. There is no employer relationship in the arrangements for this assistance, nor are there committee members normally reimbursed for such services. Further, it was pointed out the committee members spend many thousands of hours outside the organization's premises conducting research.

Response. It would appear that this type of committee arrangement would not be considered in the determination of the organization's indirect cost rate provided that Federal agreements do not bear an unreasonable share of indirect cost. However, the cognizant agency will be responsible for evaluating the allocation of indirect cost where there are committee-type arrangements on a case-by-case basis.

Comment. One respondent suggested that wherever possible the language in the *Federal Procurement Regulations* be used for nonprofit organizations.

Response. The language in the *Federal Procurement Regulations* was designated primarily for commercial firms, and is not necessarily well suited to nonprofit organizations. At the suggestion of the General Accounting Office, the nonprofit cost principles were written to conform as closely as possible to those of educational institutions (Circular A–21), and State and local governments (Circular 74–4).

John J. Lordan,
Chief, Financial Management Branch.

[Circular No. A–122]

June 27, 1980

To The Heads of Executive Departments and Establishments

Subject: Cost principles for nonprofit organizations.

1. *Purpose.* This Circular establishes principles for determining costs of grants, contracts and other agreements with nonprofit organizations. It does not apply to colleges and universities which are covered by Circular A–21; State, local, and federally recognized Indian tribal governments which are covered by Circular 74–4; or hospitals. The principles are designed to provide that the Federal Government bear its fair share of costs except where restricted or prohibited by law. The principles do not attempt to prescribe the extent of cost sharing or matching on grants, contracts, or other agreements. However, such cost sharing or matching shall not be accomplished through arbitrary limitations on individual cost elements by Federal agencies. Provision for profit or other increment above cost is outside the scope of this Circular.

2. *Supersession.* This Circular supersedes cost principles issued by individual agencies for nonprofit organization.

3. *Applicability.* a. These principles shall be used by all Federal agencies in determining the costs of work performed by nonprofit organizations under grants, cooperative agreements, cost reimbursement contracts, and other contracts in which costs are used in pricing, administration, or settlement. All of these instruments are hereafter referred to as awards. The principles do not apply to awards under which an organization is not required to account to the Government for actual costs incurred.

b. All cost reimbursement subawards (subgrants, subcontracts, etc.) are subject to those Federal cost principles applicable to the particular organization concerned. Thus, if a subaward is to a nonprofit organization, this Circular shall apply; if a subaward is to a commercial organization, the cost principles applicable to commercial concerns shall apply; if a subaward is to a college or university, Circular A–21 shall apply; if a subaward is to a State, local, or federally recognized Indian tribal government, Circular 74–4 shall apply.

4. *Definitions.* a. *"Nonprofit organization"* means any corporation, trust, association, cooperative, or other organization which (1) is operated primarily for scientific, educational, service, charitable, or similar purposes in the public interest; (2) is not organized primarily for profit; and (3) uses its net proceeds to maintain, improve, and/or expand its operations. For this purpose, the term "nonprofit organization" excludes (i) colleges and universities; (ii) hospitals; (iii) State, local, and federally recognized Indian tribal governments; and (iv) those nonprofit organizations which are excluded from coverage of this Circular in accordance with paragraph 5 below.

b. *"Prior approval"* means securing the awarding agency's permission in advance to incur cost for those items that are designated as requiring prior approval by the Circular. Generally this permission will be in writing. Where an item of cost requiring prior approval is specified in the budget of an award, approval of the budget constitutes approval of that cost.

5. *Exclusion of some nonprofit organizations.* Some nonprofit organizations, because of their size and nature of operations, can be considered to be similar to commercial concerns for purpose of applicability of cost principles. Such nonprofit organizations shall operate under Federal cost principles applicable to commercial concerns. A listing of these organizations is contained in Attachment C. Other organizations may be added from time to time

6. *Responsibilities.* Agencies responsible for administering programs that involve awards to nonprofit organizations shall implement the provisions of this Circular. Upon request, implementing instruction shall be furnished to the Office of Management and Budget. Agencies shall designate a liaison official to serve as

the agency representative on matters relating to the implementation of this Circular. The name and title of such representative shall be furnished to the Office of Management and Budget within 30 days of the date of this Circular.

7. *Attachments.* The principles and related policy guides are set forth in the following Attachments:

Attachment A—General Principles
Attachment B—Selected Items of Cost
Attachment C—Nonprofit Organizations Not Subject to This Circular

8. *Requests for exceptions.* The Office of Management and Budget may grant exceptions to the requirements of this Circular when permissible under existing law. However, in the interest of achieving maximum uniformity, exceptions will be permitted only in highly unusual circumstances.

9. *Effective Date.* The provisions of this Circular are effective immediately. Implementation shall be phased in by incorporating the provisions into new awards made after the start of the organization's next fiscal year. For existing awards the new principles may be applied if an organization and the cognizant Federal agency agree. Earlier implementation, or a delay in implementation of individual provisions is also permitted by mutual agreement between an organization and the cognizant Federal agency.

10. *Inquiries.* Further information concerning this Circular may be obtained by contacting the Financial Management Branch, Budget Review Division, Office of Management and Budget, Washington, D.C. 20503, telephone (202) 395–4773.

James T. McIntyre, Jr.,
Director.
[Circular No. A–122]

Attachment A

General Principles

Table of Contents

A. Basic Considerations

1. Composition of total costs
2. Factors affecting allowability of costs
3. Reasonable costs
4. Allocable costs
5. Applicable credits
6. Advance understandings

B. Direct Costs

C. Indirect Costs

D. Allocation of Indirect Costs and Determination of Indirect Cost Rates

1. General
2. Simplified allocation method
3. Multiple allocation base method
4. Direct allocation method
5. Special indirect cost rates

E. Negotiation and Approval of Indirect Cost Rates

1. Definitions
2. Negotiations and approval of rates

[Circular No. A–122]

Attachment A

General Principles

A. Basic Considerations.

1. *Composition of total costs.* The total cost of an award is the sum of the allowable direct and allocable indirect costs less any applicable credits.

2. *Factors affecting allowability of costs.* To be allowable under an award, costs must meet the following general criteria:

a. Be reasonable for the performance of the award and be allocable thereto under these principles.

b. Conform to any limitations or exclusions set forth in these principles or in the award as to types or amount of cost items.

c. Be consistent with policies and procedures that apply uniformly to both federally financed and other activities of the organization.

d. Be accorded consistent treatment.

e. Be determined in accordance with generally accepted accounting principles.

f. Not be included as a cost or used to meet cost sharing or matching requirements of any other federally financed program in either the current or a prior period.

g. Be adequately documented.

3. *Reasonable costs.* A cost is reasonable if, in its nature or amount, it does not exceed that which would be incurred by a prudent person under the circumstances prevailing at the time the decision was made to incur the costs. The question of the reasonableness of specific costs must be scrutinized with particular care in connection with organizations or separate divisions thereof which receive the preponderance of their support from awards made by Federal agencies. In determining the reasonableness of a given cost, consideration shall be given to:

a. Whether the cost is of a type generally recognized as ordinary and necessary for the operation of the organization or the performance of the award.

b. The restraints or requirements imposed

by such factors as generally accepted sound business practices, arms length bargaining, Federal and State laws and regulations, and terms and conditions of the award.

c. Whether the individuals concerned acted with prudence in the circumstances, considering their responsibilities to the organization, its members, employees, and clients, the public at large, and the Government.

d. Significant deviations from the established practices of the organization which may unjustifiably increase the award costs.

4. *Allocable costs.*

a. A cost is allocable to a particular cost objective, such as a grant, project, service, or other activity, in accordance with the relative benefits received. A cost is allocable to a Government award if it is treated consistently with other costs incurred for the same purpose in like circumstances and if it:

(1) Is incurred specifically for the award.

(2) Benefits both the award and other work and can be distributed in reasonable proportion to the benefits received, or

(3) Is necessary to the overall operation of the organization, although a direct relationship to any particular cost objective cannot be shown.

b. Any cost allocable to a particular award or other cost objective under these principles may not be shifted to other Federal awards to overcome funding deficiencies, or to avoid restrictions imposed by law or by the terms of the award.

5. *Applicable credits.*

a. The term applicable credits refers to those receipts, or reduction of expenditures which operate to offset or reduce expense items that are allocable to awards as direct or indirect costs. Typical examples of such transactions are: purchase discounts, rebates or allowances, recoveries or indemnities on losses, insurance refunds, and adjustments of overpayments or erroneous charges. To the extent that such credits accruing or received by the organization relate to allowable cost they shall be credited to the Government either as a cost reduction or cash refund as appropriate.

b. In some instances, the amounts received from the Federal Government to finance organizational activities or service operations should be treated as applicable credits. Specifically, the concept of netting such credit items against related expenditures should be applied by the organization in determining the rates or amounts to be charged to Federal awards for services rendered whenever the facilities or other resources used in providing such services have been financed directly, in whole or in part, by Federal funds.

(c) For rules covering program income (i.e., gross income earned from federally supported activities) see Attachment D of OMB Circular A–110.

6. *Advance understandings.* Under any given award the reasonableness and allocability of certain items of costs may be difficult to determine. This is particularly true in connection with organizations that receive a preponderance of their support from Federal agencies. In order to avoid subsequent disallowance or dispute based on unreasonableness or nonallocability, it is often desirable to seek a written agreement with the cognizant or awarding agency in advance of the incurrence of special or unusual costs. The absence of an advance agreement on any element of cost will not, in itself, affect the reasonableness or allocability of that element.

B. Direct Costs

1. Direct costs are those that can be identified specifically with a particular final cost objective: i.e., a particular award, project, service, or other direct activity of an organization. However, a cost may not be assigned to an award as a direct cost if any other cost incurred for the same purpose, in like circumstances, has been allocated to an award as an indirect cost. Costs identified specifically with awards are direct costs of the awards and are to be assigned directly thereto. Costs identified specifically with other final cost objectives of the organization are direct costs of those cost objectives and are not to be assigned to other awards directly or indirectly.

2. Any direct cost of a minor amount may be treated as an indirect cost for reasons of practicality where the accounting treatment for such cost is consistently applied to all final cost objectives.

3. The cost of certain activities are not allowable as charges to Federal awards (see, for example, fund raising costs in paragraph 19 of Attachment B). However, even though these costs are unallowable for purposes of computing charges to Federal awards, they nonetheless must be treated as direct cost for purposes of determining indirect cost rates and be allocated their share of the organization's indirect costs if they represent activities which (1) include the salaries of personnel, (2) occupy space, and (3) benefit from the organization's indirect costs.

4. The costs of activities performed primarily as a service to members, clients, or the general public when significant and necessary to the organization's mission must be treated as direct costs whether or not allowable and be allocated an equitable share of indirect costs. Some examples of these types of activities include:

a. Maintenance of membership rolls, subscriptions, publications, and related functions.

b. Providing services and information to

members, legislative or administrative bodies, or the public.

c. Promotion, lobbying, and other forms of public relations.

d. Meetings and conferences except those held to conduct the general administration of the organization.

3. Maintenance, protection, and investment of special funds not used in operation of the organization.

f. Administration of group benefits on behalf of members or clients including life and hospital insurance, annuity or retirement plans, financial aid, etc.

C. Indirect Cost.

1. Indirect costs are those that have been incurred for common or joint objectives and cannot be readily identified with a particular final cost objective. Direct cost of minor amounts may be treated as indirect costs under the conditions described in paragraph B.2. above. After direct costs have been determined and assigned directly to awards or other work as appropriate, indirect costs are those remaining to be allocated to benefiting cost objectives. A cost may not be allocated to an award as an indirect cost if any other cost incurred for the same purpose, in like circumstances, has been assigned to an award as a direct cost.

2. Because of the diverse characteristics and accounting practices of nonprofit organizations, it is not possible to specify the types of costs which may be classified as indirect cost in all situations. However, typical examples of indirect cost for many nonprofit organizations may include depreciation or use allowances on buildings and equipment, the costs of operating and maintaining facilities, and general administration and general expenses, such as the salaries and expenses of executive officers, personnel administration, and accounting.

D. Allocation of Indirect Costs and Determination of Indirect Cost Rates.

1. *General.*

a. Where a nonprofit organization has only one major function, or where all its major functions benefit from its indirect costs to approximately the same degree, the allocation of indirect costs and the computation of an indirect cost rate may be accomplished through simplified allocation procedures as described in paragraph 2 below.

b. Where an organization has several major functions which benefit from its indirect costs in varying degrees, allocation of indirect costs may require the accumulation of such costs into separate cost groupings which then are allocated individually to benefiting functions by means of a base which best measures the relative degree of benefit. The

indirect costs allocated to each function are then distributed to individual awards and other activities included in that function by means of an indirect cost rate(s).

c. The determination of what constitutes an organization's major functions will depend on its purpose in being; the types of services it renders to the public, its clients, and its members; and the amount of effort it devotes to such activities as fund raising, public information and membership activities.

d. Specific methods for allocating indirect costs and computing indirect cost rates along with the conditions under which each method should be used are described in paragraphs 2 through 5 below.

e. The base period for the allocation of indirect costs is the period in which such costs are incurred and accumulated for allocation to work performed in that period. The base period normally should coincide with the organization's fiscal year, but in any event, shall be so selected as to avoid inequities in the allocation of the costs.

2. *Simplified allocation method.*

a. Where an organization's major functions benefit from its indirect costs to approximately the same degree, the allocation of indirect costs may be accomplished by (i) separating the organization's total costs for the base period as either direct or indirect, and (ii) dividing the total allowable indirect costs (net of applicable credits) by an equitable distribution base. The result of this process is an indirect cost rate which is used to distribute indirect costs to individual awards. The rate should be expressed as the percentage which the total amount of allowable indirect costs bears to the base selected. This method should also be used where an organization has only one major function encompassing a number of individual projects or activities, and may be used where the level of Federal awards to an organization is relatively small.

b. Both the direct costs and the indirect costs shall exclude capital expenditures and unallowable costs. However, unallowable costs which represent activities must be included in the direct costs under the conditions described in paragraph B.3. above.

c. The distribution base may be total direct costs (excluding capital expenditures and other distorting items, such as major subcontracts or subgrants), direct salaries and wages, or other base which results in an equitable distribution. The distribution base shall generally exclude participant support costs as defined in paragraph 29 of Attachment B.

d. Except where a special rate(s) is required in accordance with paragraph D.5 below, the indirect cost rate developed under the above principles is applicable to all awards at the organization. If a special rate(s) is required, appropriate modifications shall be made in order to develop the special rate(s).

3. *Multiple allocation base method.*

a. Where an organization's indirect costs benefit its major functions in varying degrees, such costs shall be accumulated into separate cost groupings. Each grouping shall then be allocated individually to benefiting functions by means of a base which best measures the relative benefits.

b. The groupings shall be established so as to permit the allocation of each grouping on the basis of benefits provided to the major functions. Each grouping should constitute a pool of expenses that are of like character in terms of the functions they benefit and in terms of the allocation base which best measures the relative benefits provided to each function. The number of separate groupings should be held within practical limits, taking into consideration the materiality of the amounts involved and the degree of precision desired.

c. Actual conditions must be taken into account in selecting the base to be used in allocating the expenses in each grouping to benefiting functions. When an allocation can be made by assignment of a cost grouping directly to the function benefited, the allocation shall be made in that manner. When the expenses in a grouping are more general in nature, the allocation should be made through the use of a selected base which produces results that are equitable to both the Government and the organization. In general, any cost element or cost related factor associated with the organization's work is potentially adaptable for use as an allocation base provided (i) it can readily be expressed in terms of dollars or other quantitative measures (total direct costs, direct salaries and wages, staff hours applied, square feet used, hours of usage, number of documents processed, population served, and the like) and (ii) it is common to the benefiting functions during the base period.

d. Except where a special indirect cost rate(s) is required in accordance with paragraph D.5. below, the separate groupings of indirect costs allocated to each major function shall be aggregated and treated as a common pool for that function. The costs in the common pool shall then be distributed to individual awards included in that function by use of a single indirect cost rate.

e. The distribution base used in computing the indirect cost rate for each function may be total direct costs (excluding capital expenditures and other distorting items such as major subcontracts and subgrants), direct salaries and wages, or other base which results in an equitable distribution. The distribution base shall generally exclude participant support costs as defined in paragraph 29, Attachment B. An indirect cost rate should be developed for each separate indirect cost pool developed. The rate in each case should be stated as the percentage which the amount of the particular indirect cost pool is of the distribution base identified with that pool.

4. *Direct allocation method.*

a. Some nonprofit organizations, treat all costs as direct costs except general administration and general expenses. These organizations generally separate their costs into three basic categories: (i) General administration and general expenses, (ii) fund raising, and (iii) other direct functions (including projects performed under Federal awards). Joint costs, such as depreciation, rental costs, operation and maintenance of facilities, telephone expenses, and the like are prorated individually as direct costs to each category and to each award or other activity using a base most appropriate to the particular cost being prorated.

b. This method is acceptable provided each joint cost is prorated using a base which accurately measures the benefits provided to each award or other activity. The bases must be established in accordance with reasonable criteria, and be supported by current data. This method is compatible with the Standards of Accounting and Financial Reporting for Voluntary Health and Welfare Organizations issued jointly by the National Health Council, Inc., the National Assembly of Voluntary Health and Social Welfare Organizations, and the United Way of America.

c. Under this method, indirect costs consist exclusively of general administration and general expenses. In all other respects, the organization's indirect cost rates shall be computed in the same manner as that described in paragraph D.2 above.

5. *Special indirect cost rates.* In some instances, a single indirect cost rate for all activities of an organization or for each major function of the organization may not be appropriate, since it would not take into account those different factors which may substantially affect the indirect costs applicable to a particular segment of work. For this purpose, a particular segment of work may be that performed under a single award or it may consist of work under a group of awards performed in a common environment. The factors may include the physical location of the work, the level of administrative support required, the nature of the facilities or other resources employed, the scientific disciplines or technical skills involved, the organizational arrangements used, or any combination thereof. When a particular segment of work is performed in an environment which appears to generate a significantly different level of indirect costs, provisions should be made for a separate indirect cost pool applicable to such work.

The separate indirect cost pool should be developed during the course of the regular allocation process, and the separate indirect cost rate resulting therefrom should be used provided it is determined that (i) the rate differs significantly from that which would have been obtained under paragraph D.2, 3, and 4 above, and (ii) the volume of work to which the rate would apply is material.

E. Negotiation and Approval of Indirect Cost Rates.

1. *Definitions.* As used in this section, the following terms have the meanings set forth below:

a. "Cognizant agency" means the Federal agency responsible for negotiating and approving indirect cost rates for a nonprofit organization on behalf of all Federal agencies.

b. "Predetermined rate" means an indirect cost rate, applicable to a specified current or future period, usually the organization's fiscal year. The rate is based on an estimate of the costs to be incurred during the period. A predetermined rate is not subject to adjustment.

c. "Fixed rate" means an indirect cost rate which has the same characteristics as a predetermined rate, except that the difference between the estimated costs and the actual costs of the period covered by the rate is carried forward as an adjustment to the rate computation of a subsequent period.

d. "Final rate" means an indirect cost rate applicable to a specified past period which is based on the actual costs of the period. A final rate is not subject to adjustment.

e. "Provisional rate" or billing rate means a temporary indirect cost rate applicable to a specified period which is used for funding, interim reimbursement, and reporting indirect costs on awards pending the establishment of a final rate for the period.

f. "Indirect cost proposal" means the documentation prepared by an organization to substantiate its claim for the reimbursement of indirect costs. This proposal provides the basis for the review and negotiation leading to the establishment of an organization's indirect cost rate.

g. "Cost objective" means a function, organizational subdivision, contract, grant, or other work unit for which cost data are desired and for which provision is made to accumulate and measure the cost of processes, projects, jobs and capitalized projects.

2. *Negotiation and approval of rates.*

a. Unless different arrangements are agreed to by the agencies concerned, the Federal agency with the largest dollar value of awards with an organization will be designated as the cognizant agency for the negotiation and approval of indirect cost rates and, where necessary, other rates such

as fringe benefit and computer charge-out rates. Once an agency is assigned cognizance for a particular nonprofit organization, the assignment will not be changed unless there is a major long-term shift in the dollar volume of the Federal awards to the organization. All concerned Federal agencies shall be given the opportunity to participate in the negotiation process, but after a rate has been agreed upon it will be accepted by all Federal agencies. When a Federal agency has reason to believe that special operating factors affecting its awards necessitate special indirect cost rates in accordance with paragraph D.5 above, it will, prior to the time the rates are negotiated, notify the cognizant agency.

b. A nonprofit organization which has not previously established an indirect cost rate with a Federal agency shall submit its initial indirect cost proposal to the cognizant agency. The proposal shall be submitted as soon as possible after the organization is advised that an award will be made and, in no event, later than three months after the effective date of the award.

c. Organizations that have previously established indirect cost rates must submit a new indirect cost proposal to the cognizant agency within six months after the close of each fiscal year.

d. A predetermined rate may be negotiated for use on awards where there is reasonable assurance, based on past experience and reliable projection of the organization's costs, that the rate is not likely to exceed a rate based on the organization's actual costs.

e. Fixed rates may be negotiated where predetermined rates are not considered appropriate. A fixed rate, however, shall not be negotiated if (i) all or a substantial portion of the organization's awards are expected to expire before the carry-forward adjustment can be made; (ii) the mix of Government and non-government work at the organization is too erratic to permit an equitable carry-forward adjustment; or (iii) the organization's operations fluctuate significantly from year to year.

f. Provisional and final rates shall be negotiated where neither predetermined nor fixed rates are appropriate.

g. The results of each negotiation shall be formalized in a written agreement between the cognizant agency and the nonprofit organization. The cognizant agency shall distribute copies of the agreement to all concerned Federal agencies.

h. If a dispute arises in a negotiation of an indirect cost rate between the cognizant agency and the nonprofit organization, the dispute shall be resolved in accordance with the appeals procedures of the cognizant agency.

i. To the extent that problems are encountered among the Federal agencies in connection with the negotiation and approval process, the Office of Management and Budget will lend assistance as required to resolve such problems in a timely manner.

[Circular No. A–122]

Attachment B

Selected Items of Cost

Table of Contents

[Circular No. A–122]

Attachment B

Selected Items of Cost

Paragraphs 1 through 50 provide principles to be applied in establishing the allowability of certain items of cost. These principles apply whether a cost is treated as direct or indirect. Failure to mention a particular item of cost is not intended to imply that it is unallowable; rather determination as to allowability in each case should be based on the treatment or principles provided for similar or related items of cost.

1. *Advertising costs.*

a. Advertising costs mean the costs of media services and associated costs. Media advertising includes magazines, newspapers, radio and television programs, direct mail, exhibits, and the like.

b. The only advertising costs allowable are those which are solely for (i) the recruitment of personnel when considered in conjunction with all other recruitment costs, as set forth in paragraph 40; (ii) the procurement of goods and services; (iii) the disposal of surplus materials acquired in the performance of the award except when organizations are reimbursed for disposals at a predetermined amount in accordance with Attachment N of OMB Circular A–110; or (iv) specific requirements of the award.

2. *Bad debts.* Bad debts, including losses (whether actual or estimated) arising from uncollectible accounts and other claims, related collection costs, and related legal costs, are unallowable.

3. *Bid and proposal costs.* (reserved)

4. *Bonding costs.*

a. Bonding costs arise when the Government requires assurance against financial loss to itself or others by reason of the act or default of the organization. They arise also in instances where the organization requires similar assurance. Included are such bonds as bid, performance, payment, advance payment, infringement, and fidelity bonds.

b. Costs of bonding required pursuant to the terms of the award are allowable.

c. Costs of bonding required by the organization in the general conduct of its operations are allowable to the extent that such bonding is in accordance with sound business practice and the rates and premiums are reasonable under the circumstances.

5. *Communication costs.* Costs incurred for telephone services, local and long distance telephone calls, telegrams, radiograms, postage and the like, are allowable.

6. *Compensation for personal services.*

a. *Definition.* Compensation for personal

services includes all compensation paid currently or accrued by the organization for services of employees rendered during the period of the award (except as otherwise provided in paragraph g. below). It includes, but is not limited to, salaries, wages, director's and executive committee member's fees, incentive awards, fringe benefits, pension plan costs, allowances for off-site pay, incentive pay, location allowances, hardship pay, and cost of living differentials.

b. *Allowability.* Except as otherwise specifically provided in this paragraph, the costs of such compensation are allowable to the extent that:

(1) Total compensation to individual employees is reasonable for the services rendered and conforms to the established policy of the organization consistently applied to both Government and non-Government activities; and

(2) Charges to awards whether treated as direct or indirect costs are determined and supported as required in this paragraph.

c. *Reasonableness.*

(1) When the organization is predominantly engaged in activities other than those sponsored by the Government, compensation for employees on Government-sponsored work will be considered reasonable to the extent that it is consistent with that paid for similar work in the organization's other activities.

(2) When the organization is predominantly engaged in Government-sponsored activities and in cases where the kind of employees required for the Government activities are not found in the organization's other activities, compensation for employees on Government-sponsored work will be considered reasonable to the extent that it is comparable to that paid for similar work in the labor markets in which the organization competes for the kind of employees involved.

d. *Special considerations in determining allowability.* Certain conditions require special consideration and possible limitations in determining costs under Federal awards where amounts or types of compensation appear unreasonable. Among such conditions are the following:

(1) Compensation to members of nonprofit organizations, trustees, directors, associates, officers, or the immediate families thereof. Determination should be made that such compensation is reasonable for the actual personal services rendered rather than a distribution of earnings in excess of costs.

(2) Any change in an organization's compensation policy resulting in a substantial increase in the organization's level of compensation, particularly when it was concurrent with an increase in the ratio of Government awards to other activities of the organization or any change in the treatment of allowability of specific types of

compensation due to changes in Government policy.

e. *Unallowable costs.* Costs which are unallowable under other paragraphs of this Attachment shall not be allowable under this paragraph solely on the basis that they constitute personal compensation.

f. *Fringe benefits.*

(1) Fringe benefits in the form of regular compensation paid to employees during periods of authorized absences from the job, such as vacation leave, sick leave, military leave, and the like, are allowable provided such costs are absorbed by all organization activities in proportion to the relative amount of time or effort actually devoted to each.

(2) Fringe benefits in the form of employer contributions or expenses for social security, employee insurance, workmen's compensation insurance, pension plan costs (see paragraph g. below), and the like, are allowable provided such benefits are granted in accordance with established written organization policies. Such benefits whether treated as indirect costs or as direct costs, shall be distributed to particular awards and other activities in a manner consistent with the pattern of benefits accruing to the individuals or group of employees whose salaries and wages are chargeable to such awards and other activities.

(3)(a) Provisions for a reserve under a self-insurance program for unemployment compensation or workers' compensation are allowable to the extent that the provisions represent reasonable estimates of the liabilities for such compensation, and the types of coverage, extent of coverage, and rates and premiums would have been allowable had insurance been purchased to cover the risks. However, provisions for self-insured liabilities which do not become payable for more than one year after the provision is made shall not exceed the present value of the liability.

(b) Where an organization follows a consistent policy of expensing actual payments to, or on behalf of, employees or former employees for unemployment compensation or workers' compensation, such payments are allowable in the year of payment with the prior approval of the awarding agency provided they are allocated to all activities of the organization.

(4) Costs of insurance on the lives of trustees, officers, or other employees holding positions of similar responsibility are allowable only to the extent that the insurance represents additional compensation. The costs of such insurance when the organization is named as beneficiary are unallowable.

g. *Pension plan costs.*

(1) Costs of the organization's pension plan which are incurred in accordance with the

established policies of the organization are allowable, provided:

(a) Such policies meet the test of reasonableness;

(b) The methods of cost allocation are not discriminatory;

(c) The cost assigned to each fiscal year is determined in accordance with generally accepted accounting principles as prescribed in Accounting Principles Board Opinion No. 8 issued by the American Institute of Certified Public Accountants; and

(d) The costs assigned to a given fiscal year are funded for all plan participants within six months after the end of that year. However, increases to normal and past service pension costs caused by a delay in funding the actuarial liability beyond 30 days after each quarter of the year to which such costs are assignable are unallowable.

(2) Pension plan termination insurance premiums paid pursuant to the Employee Retirement Income Security Act of 1974 (Pub. L. 93–406) are allowable. Late payment charges on such premiums are unallowable.

(3) Excise taxes on accumulated funding deficiencies and other penalties imposed under the Employee Retirement Income Security Act are unallowable.

h. *Incentive compensation.* Incentive compensation to employees based on cost reduction, or efficient performance, suggestion awards, safety awards, etc., are allowable to the extent that the overall compensation is determined to be reasonable and such costs are paid or accrued pursuant to an agreement entered into in good faith between the organization and the employees before the services were rendered, or pursuant to an established plan followed by the organization so consistently as to imply, in effect, an agreement to make such payment.

i. *Overtime, extra pay shift, and multishift premiums.* See paragraph 27.

j. *Severance pay.* See paragraph 44.

k. *Training and education costs.* See paragraph 48.

l. *Support of salaries and wages.*

(1) Charges to awards for salaries and wages, whether treated as direct costs or indirect costs, will be based on documented payrolls approved by a responsible official(s) of the organization. The distribution of salaries and wages to awards must be supported by personnel activity reports as prescribed in subparagraph (2) below, except when a substitute system has been approved in writing by the the cognizant agency. (See paragraph E.2 of Attachment A)

(2) Reports reflecting the distribution of activity of each employee must be maintained for all staff members (professionals and nonprofessionals) whose compensation is charged, in whole or in part, directly to awards. In addition, in order to support the allocation of indirect costs, such reports must also be maintained for other employees whose work involves two or more funcitons or activities if a distribution of their compensation between such functions or activities is needed in the determination of the organization's indirect cost rate(s) (e.g., an employee engaged part-time in indirect cost activities and part-time in a direct function). Reports maintained by nonprofit organizations to satisfy these requirements must meet the following standards:

(a) The reports must reflect an *after-the-fact* determination of the actual activity of each employee. Budget estimates (i.e., estimates determined before the services are performed) do not qualify as support for charges to awards.

(b) Each report must account for the total activity for which employees are compensated and which is required in fulfillment of their obligations to the organization.

(c) The reports must be signed by the individual employee, or by a responsible supervisory official having first hand knowledge of the activities performed by the employee, that the distribution of activity represents a reasonable estimate of the actual work performed by the employee during the periods covered by the reports.

(d) The reports must be prepared at least monthly and must coincide with one or more pay periods.

(3) Charges for the salaries and wages of nonprofessional employees, in addition to the supporting documentation described in subparagraphs (1) and (2) above, must also be supported by records indicating the total number of hours worked each day maintained in conformance with Department of Labor regulations implementing the Fair Labor Standards Act (29 CFR Part 516). For this purpose, the term "nonprofessional employee" shall have the same meaning as "nonexempt employee," under the Fair Labor Standards Act.

(4) Salaries and wages of employees used in meeting cost sharing or matching requirements on awards must be supported in the same manner as salaries and wages claimed for reimbursement from awarding agencies.

7. *Contingency provisions.* Contributions to a contingency reserve or any similar provision made for events the occurrence of which cannot be foretold with certainty as to time, intensity, or with an assurance of their happening, are unallowable. The term "contingency reserve" excludes self-insurance reserves (see paragraph 6.f.(3) and 18.a.(2)(d)); pension funds (see paragraph 6.(g)); and reserves for normal severance pay (see paragraph 44.(b)(1).

8. *Contributions.* Contributions and donations by the organization to others are unallowable.

9. *Depreciation and use allowances.*

a. Compensation for the use of buildings, other capital improvements, and equipment on hand may be made through use allowances or depreciation. However, except as provided in paragraph f. below a combination of the two methods may not be used in connection with a single class of fixed assets (e.g., buildings, office equipment, computer equipment, etc.).

b. The computation of use allowances or depreciation shall be based on the acquisition cost of the assets involved. The acquisition cost of an asset donated to the organization by a third party shall be its fair market value at the time of the donation.

c. The computation of use allowances or depreciation will exclude.

(1) The cost of land;

(2) Any portion of the cost of buildings and equipment borne by or donated by the Federal Government irrespective of where title was originally vested or where it presently resides; and

(3) Any portion of the cost of buildings and equipment contributed by or for the organization in satisfaction of a statutory matching retirement.

d. Where the use allowance method is followed, the use allowance for buildings and improvement (including land improvements such as paved parking areas, fences, and sidewalks) will be computed at an annual rate not exceeding two percent of acquisition cost. The use allowance for equipment will be computed at an annual rate not exceeding six and two-thirds percent of acquisition cost. When the use allowance method is used for buildings, the entire building must be treated as a single asset; the building's components (e.g. plumbing system, heating and air conditioning, etc.) cannot be segregated from the building's shell. The two percent limitation, however, need not be applied to equipment which is merely attached or fastened to the building but not permanently fixed to it and which is used as furnishings or decorations or for specialized purposes (e.g., dentist chairs and dental treatment units, counters, laboratory benches bolted to the floor, dishwashers, carpeting, etc.). Such equipment will be considered as not being permanently fixed to the building if it can be removed without the need for costly or extensive alterations or repairs to the building or the equipment. Equipment that meets these criteria will be subject to the six and two-thirds percent equipment use allowance limitation.

e. Where depreciation method is followed, the period of useful service (useful life) established in each case for usable capital assets must take into consideration such factors as type of construction, nature of the equipment used, technological developments in the particular program area, and the renewal and replacement policies followed for the the individual items or classes of assets involved. The method of depreciation used to assign the cost of an asset (or group of assets) to accounting periods shall reflect the pattern of consumption of the asset during its useful life. In the absence of clear evidence indicating that the expected consumption of the asset will be significantly greater or lesser in the early portions of its useful life than in the later portions, the straight-line method shall be presumed to be the appropriate method. Depreciation methods once used shall not be changed unless approved in advance by the cognizant Federal agency. When the depreciation method is introduced for application to assets previously subject to a use allowance, the combination of use allowances and depreciation applicable to such assets must not exceed the total acquisition cost of the assets. When the depreciation method is used for buildings, a building's shell may be segregated from each building component (e.g., plumbing system, heating, and air conditioning system, etc.) and each item depreciated over its estimated useful life; or the entire building (i.e., the shell and all components) may be treated as a single asset and depreciated over a single useful life.

f. When the depreciation method is used for a particular class of assets, no depreciation may be allowed on any such assets that, under paragraph e. above, would be viewed as fully depreciated. However, a reasonable use allowance may be negotiated for such assets if warranted after taking into consideration the amount of depreciation previously charged to the Government, the estimated useful life remaining at time of negotiation, the effect of any increased maintenance charges or decreased efficiency due to age, and any other factors pertinent to the utilization of the asset for the purpose contemplated.

g. Charges for use allowances or depreciation must be supported by adequate property records and physical inventories must be taken at least once every two years (a statistical sampling basis is acceptable) to ensure that assets exist and are usable and needed. When the depreciation method is followed, adequate depreciation records indicating the amount of depreciation taken each period must also be maintained.

10. *Donations*

a. *Services received.*

(1) Donated or volunteer services may be furnished to an organization by professional and technical personnel, consultants, and other skilled and unskilled labor. The value of these services is not reimbursable either as a direct or indirect cost.

(2) The value of donated services utilized in the performance of a direct cost activity shall be considered in the determination of

the organization's indirect cost rate(s) and, accordingly, shall be allocated a proportionate share of applicable indirect costs when the following circumstances exist:

(a) The aggregate value of the services is material;

(b) The services are supported by a significant amount of the indirect costs incurred by the organization;

(c) The direct cost activity is not pursued primarily for the benefit of the Federal Government.

(3) In those instances where there is no basis for determining the fair market value of the services rendered, the recipient and the cognizant agency shall negotiate an appropriate allocation of indirect cost to the services.

(4) Where donated services directly benefit a project supported by an award, the indirect costs allocated to the services will be considered as a part of the total costs of the project. Such indirect costs may be reimbursed under the award or used to meet cost sharing or matching requirements.

(5) The value of the donated services may be used to meet cost sharing or matching requirements under conditions described in Attachment E, OMB Circular No. A–110. Where donated services are treated as indirect costs, indirect cost rates will separate the value of the donations so that reimbursement will not be made.

(6) Fair market value of donated services shall be computed as follows:

(a) *Rates for volunteer services.* Rates for volunteers shall be consistent with those regular rates paid for similar work in other activities of the organization. In cases where the kinds of skills involved are not found in the other activities of the organization, the rates used shall be consistent with those paid for similar work in the labor market in which the organization competes for such skills.

(b) *Services donated by other organizations.* When an employer donates the services of an employee, these services shall be valued at the employee's regular rate of pay (exclusive of fringe benefits and indirect costs) provided the services are in the same skill for which the employee is normally paid. If the services are not in the same skill for which the employee is normally paid, fair market value shall be computed in accordance with subparagraph (a) above.

b. *Goods and space.*

(1) Donated goods; i.e., expendable personal property/supplies, and donated use of space may be furnished to an organization. The value of the goods and space is not reimbursable either as a direct or indirect cost.

(2) The value of the donations may be used to meet cost sharing or matching share requirements under the conditions described in Attachment E, OMB Circular No. A–110.

The value of the donations shall be determined in accordance with Attachment E. Where donations are treated as indirect costs, indirect cost rates will separate the value of the donations so that reimbursement will not be made.

11. *Employee morale, health, and welfare, costs and credits.* The costs of house publications, health or first-aid clinics, and/or infirmaries, recreational activities, employees' counseling services, and other expenses incurred in accordance with the organization's established practice or custom for the improvement of working conditions, employer-employee relations, employee morale, and employee performance are allowable. Such costs will be equitably apportioned to all activities of the organization. Income generated from any of these activities will be credited to the cost thereof unless such income has been irrevocably set over to employee welfare organizations.

12. *Entertainment costs.* Costs of amusement, diversion, social activities, ceremonials, and costs relating thereto, such as meals, lodging, rentals, transportation, and gratuities are unallowable (but see paragraphs 11 and 25).

13. *Equipment and other capital expenditures.*

a. As used in this paragraph, the following terms have the meanings set forth below:

(1) "Equipment" means an article of nonexpendable tangible personal property having a useful life of more than two years and an acquisition cost of $500 or more per unit. An organization may use its own definition provided that it at least includes all nonexpendable tangible personal property as defined herein.

(2) "Acquisition cost" means the net invoice unit price of an item of equipment, including the cost of any modifications, attachments, accessories, or auxiliary apparatus necessary to make it usable for the purpose for which it is acquired. Ancillary charges, such as taxes, duty, protective in-transit insurance, freight, and installation shall be included in or excluded from acquisition cost in accordance with the organization's regular written accounting practices.

(3) "Special purpose equipment" means equipment which is usable only for research, medical, scientific, or technical activities. Examples of special purpose equipment include microscopes, x-ray machines, surgical instruments, and spectrometers.

(4) "General purpose equipment" means equipment which is usable for other than research, medical, scientific, or technical activities, whether or not special modifications are needed to make them suitable for a particular purpose. Examples of general purpose equipment include office

equipment and furnishings, air conditioning equipment, reproduction and printing equipment, motor vehicles, and automatic data processing equipment.

b. (1) Capital expenditures for general purpose equipment are unallowable as a direct cost except with the prior approval of the awarding agency.

(2) Capital expenditures for special purpose equipment are allowable as direct costs provided that items with a unit cost of $1000 or more have the prior approval of the awarding agency.

c. Capital expenditures for land or buildings are unallowable as a direct cost except with the prior approval of the awarding agency.

d. Capital expenditures for improvements to land, buildings, or equipment which materially increase their value or useful life are unallowable as a direct cost except with the prior approval of the awarding agency.

e. Equipment and other capital expenditures are unallowable as indirect costs. However, see paragraph 9 for allowability of use allowances or depreciation on buildings, capital improvements, and equipment. Also, see paragraph 42 for allowability of rental costs for land, buildings, and equipment.

14. *Fines and penalties.* Costs of fines and penalties resulting from violations of, or failure of the organization to comply with Federal, State, and local laws and regulations are unallowable except when incurred as a result of compliance with specific provisions of an award or instructions in writing from the awarding agency.

15. *Fringe benefits.* See paragraph 6. f.

16. *Idle facilities and idle capacity.*

a. As used in this paragraph the following terms have the meanings set forth below:

(1) "Facilities" means land and buildings or any portion thereof, equipment individually or collectively, or any other tangible capital asset, wherever located, and whether owned or leased by the organization.

(2) "Idle facilities" means completely unused facilities that are excess to the organization's current needs.

(3) "Idle capacity" means the unused capacity of partially used facilities. It is the difference between that which a facility could achieve under 100 per cent operating time on a one-shift basis less operating interruptions resulting from time lost for repairs, setups, unsatisfactory materials, and other normal delays, and the extent to which the facility was actually used to meet demands during the accounting period. A multishift basis may be used if it can be shown that this amount of usage could normally be expected for the type of facility involved.

(4) "Costs of idle facilities or idle capacity" means costs such as maintenance, repair,

housing, rent, and other related costs; e.g., property taxes, insurance, and depreciation or use allowances.

b. The costs of idle facilities are unallowable except to the extent that:

(1) They are necessary to meet fluctuations in workload; or

(2) Although not necessary to meet fluctuations in workload, they were necessary when acquired and are now idle because of changes in program requirements, efforts to achieve more economical operations, reorganization, termination, or other causes which could not have been reasonably foreseen. Under the exception stated in this subparagraph, costs of idle facilities are allowable for a reasonable period of time, ordinarily not to exceed one year, depending upon the initiative taken to use, lease, or dispose of such facilities (but see paragraphs 47.D. and d.).

c. The costs of idle capacity are normal costs of doing business and are a factor in the normal fluctuations of usage or indirect cost rates from period to period. Such costs are allowable, provided the capacity is reasonably anticipated to be necessary or was originally reasonable and is not subject to reduction or elimination by subletting, renting, or sale, in accordance with sound business, economics, or security practices. Widespread idle capacity throughout an entire facility or among a group of assets having substantially the same function may be idle facilities.

17. *Independent research and development* [Reserved].

18. *Insurance and indemnification.*

a. Insurance includes insurance which the organization is required to carry, or which is approved, under the terms of the award and any other insurance which the organization maintains in connection with the general conduct of its operations. This paragraph does not apply to insurance which represents fringe benefits for employees (see paragraph 6.f. and 6.g.(2)).

(1) Costs of insurance required or approved, and maintained, pursuant to the award are allowable.

(2) Costs of other insurance maintained by the organization in connection with the general conduct of its operations are allowable subject to the following limitations.

(u) Types and extent of coverage shall be in accordance with sound business practice and the rates and premiums shall be reasonable under the circumstances.

(b) Costs allowed for business interruption or other similar insurance shall be limited to exclude coverage of management fees.

(c) Costs of insurance or of any provisions for a reserve covering the risk of loss or damage to Government property are allowable only to the extent that the organization is liable for such loss or damage.

(d) Provisions for a reserve under a self-insurance program are allowable to the extent that types of coverage, extent of coverage, rates, and premiums would have been allowed had insurance been purchased to cover the risks. However, provision for known or reasonably estimated self-insured liabilities, which do not become payable for more than one year after the provision is made shall not exceed the present value of the liability.

(e) Costs of insurance on the lives of trustees, officers, or other employees holding positions of similar responsibilities are allowable only to the extent that the insurance represents additional compensation (see paragraph 6). The cost of such insurance when the organization is identified as the beneficiary is unallowable.

(3) Actual losses which could have been covered by permissible insurance (through the purchase of insurance or a self-insurance program) are unallowable unless expressly provided for in the award, except:

(a) Costs incurred because of losses not covered under nominal deductible insurance coverage provided in keeping with sound business practice are allowable.

(b) Minor losses not covered by insurance, such as spoilage, breakage, and disappearance of supplies, which occur in the ordinary course of operations, are allowable.

b. Indemnification includes securing the organization against liabilities to third persons and any other loss or damage, not compensated by insurance or otherwise. The Government is obligated to indemnify the organization only to the extent expressly provided in the award.

19. *Interest, fund raising, and investment management costs.*

a. Costs incurred for interest on borrowed capital or temporary use of endowment funds, however represented, are unallowable.

b. Costs of organized fund raising, including financial campaigns, endowment drives, solicitation of gifts and bequests, and similar expenses incurred solely to raise capital or obtain contributions are unallowable.

c. Costs of investment counsel and staff and similar expenses incurred solely to enhance income from investments are unallowable.

d. Fund raising and investment activities shall be allocated an appropriate share of indirect costs under the conditions described in paragraph B of Attachment A.

20. *Labor relations costs.* Costs incurred in maintaining satisfactory relations between the organization and its employees, including costs of labor management committees,

employee publications, and other related activities are allowable.

21. *Losses on other awards.* Any excess of costs over income on any award is unallowable as a cost of any other award. This includes, but is not limited to, the organization's contributed portion by reason of cost sharing agreements or any underrecoveries through negotiation of lump sums for, or ceilings on, indirect costs.

22. *Maintenance and repair costs.* Costs incurred for necessary maintenance, repair, or upkeep of buildings and equipment (including Government property unless otherwise provided for) which neither add to the permanent value of the property nor appreciably prolong its intended life, but keep it in an efficient operating condition, are allowable. Costs incurred for improvements which add to the permanent value of the buildings and equipment or appreciably prolong their intended life shall be treated as capital expenditures (see paragraph 13).

23. *Materials and supplies.* The costs of materials and supplies necessary to carry out an award are allowable. Such costs should be charged at their actual prices after deducting all cash discounts, trade discounts, rebates, and allowances received by the organization. Withdrawals from general stores or stockrooms should be charged at cost under any recognized method of pricing consistently applied. Incoming transportation charges may be a proper part of material cost. Materials and supplies charged as a direct cost should include only the materials and supplies actually used for the performance of the contract or grant, and due credit should be given for any excess materials or supplies retained, or returned to vendors.

24. *Meetings, conferences.*

a. Costs associated with the conduct of meetings and conferences, include the cost of renting facilities, meals, speakers' fees, and the like. But see paragraph 12, *Entertainment costs*, and paragraph 29, *Participant support costs.*

b. To the extent that these costs are identifiable with a particular cost objective, they should be charged to that objective. (See paragraph B. of Attachment A.) These costs are allowable provided that they meet the general tests of allowability, shown in Attachment A to this Circular.

c. Costs of meetings and conferences held to conduct the general administration of the organization are allowable.

25. *Memberships, subscriptions, and professional activity costs.*

a. Costs of the organization's membership in civic, business, technical and professional organizations are allowable.

b. Costs of the organization's subscriptions

to civic, business, professional, and technical periodicals are allowable.

c. Costs of attendance at meetings and conferences sponsored by others when the primary purpose is the dissemination of technical information, are allowable. This includes costs of meals, transportation, and other items incidental to such attendance.

26. *Organization costs.* Expenditures, such as incorporation fees, brokers' fees, fees to promoters, organizers or management consultants, attorneys, accountants, or investment counselors, whether or not employees of the organization, in connection with establishment or reorganization of an organization, are unallowable except with prior approval of the awarding agency.

27. *Overtime, extra-pay shift, and multishift premiums.* Premiums for overtime, extra-pay shifts, and multishift work are allowable only with the prior approval of the awarding agency except:

a. When necessary to cope with emergencies, such as those resulting from accidents, natural disasters, breakdowns of equipment, or occasional operational bottlenecks of a sporadic nature.

b. When employees are performing indirect functions such as administration, maintenance, or accounting.

c. In the performance of tests, laboratory procedures, or other similar operations which are continuous in nature and cannot reasonably be interrupted or otherwise completed.

d. When lower overall cost to the Government will result.

28. *Page charges in professional journals.* Page charges for professional journal publications are allowable as a necessary part of research costs, where:

a. The research papers report work supported by the Government; and

b. The charges are levied impartially on all research papers published by the journal, whether or not by Government-sponsored authors.

29. *Participant support costs.* Participant support costs are direct costs for items such as stipends or subsistence allowances, travel allowances, and registration fees paid to or on behalf of participants or trainees (but not employees) in connection with meetings, conferences, symposia, or training projects. These costs are allowable with the prior approval of the awarding agency.

30. *Patent costs.*

a. Costs of (i) preparing disclosures, reports, and other documents required by the award and of searching the art to the extend necessary to make such disclosures, (ii) preparing documents and any other patent costs in connection with the filing and prosecution of a United states patent

application where title or royalty-free license is required by the Government to be conveyed to the Government, and (iii) general counseling services relating to patent and copyright matters, such as advice on patent and copyright laws, regulations, clauses, and employee agreements are allowable (but see paragraph 34).

b. Cost of preparing disclosures, reports, and other documents and of searching the art to the extent necessary to make disclosures, if not required by the award, are unallowable. Costs in connection with (i) filing and prosecuting any foreign patent application, or (ii) any United States patent application, where the award does not require conveying title or a royalty-free license to the Government, are unallowable (also see paragraph 43).

31. *Pension plans.* See paragraph 6. g.

32. *Plant security costs.* Necessary expenses incurred to comply with Government security requirements or for facilities protection, including wages, uniforms, and equipment of personnel are allowable.

33. *Preaward costs.* Preaward costs are those incurred prior to the effective date of the award directly pursuant to the negotiation and in anticipation of the award where such costs is necessary to comply with the proposed delivery schedule or period of performance. Such costs are allowable only to the extent that they would have been allowable if incurred after the date of the award and only with the written approval of the awarding agency.

34. *Professional service costs.*

a. Costs of professional and consultant services rendered by persons who are members of a particular profession or possess a special skill, and who are not officers or employees of the organization, are allowable, subject to b, c, and d, of this paragraph when reasonable in relation to the services rendered and when not contingent upon recovery of the costs from the Government.

b. In determing the allowability of costs in a particular case, no single factor or any special combination of factors is necessarily determinative. However, the following factors are relevant:

(1) The nature and scope of the service rendered in relation to the service required.

(2) The necessity of contracting for the service, considering the organization's capability in the particular area.

(3) The past pattern of such costs, particularly in the years prior to Government awards.

(4) The impact of Government awards on the organization's business (i.e., what new problems have arisen).

(5) Whether the proportion of Government

work to the organization's total business is such as to influence the organization in favor of incurring the cost, particularly where the services rendered are not of a continuing nature and have little relationship to work under Government grants and contracts.

(6) Whether the service can be performed more economically by direct employment rather than contracting.

(7) The qualifications of the individual or concern rendering the service and the customary fees charged, especially on non-Government awards.

(8) Adequacy of the contractual agreement for the service (e.g., description of the service, estimate of time required, rate of compensation, and termination provisions).

c. In addition to the factors in paragraph b above, retainer fees to be allowable must be supported by evidence of bona fide services available or rendered.

d. Cost of legal, accounting, and consulting services, and related costs incurred in connection with defense of antitrust suits, and the prosecution of claims against the Government, are unallowable. Costs of legal, accounting and consulting services, and related costs, incurred in connection with patent infringement litigation, organization and reorganization, are unallowable unless otherwise provided for in the award (but see paragraph 47e).

35. *Profits and losses on disposition of depreciable property or other capital assets.*

a. (1) Gains and losses on sale, retirement, or other disposition of depreciable property shall be included in the year in which they occur as credits or charges to cost grouping(s) in which the depreciation applicable to such property was included. The amount of the gain or loss to be included as a credit or charge to the appropriate cost grouping(s) shall be the difference between the amount realized on the property and the undepreciated basis of the property.

(2) Gains and losses on the disposition of depreciable property shall not be recognized as a separate credit or charge under the following conditions.

(a) The gain or loss is processed through a depreciation reserve account and is reflected in the depreciation allowable under paragraph 9.

(b) The property is given in exchange as part of the purchase price of a similar item and the gain or loss is taken into account in determining the depreciation cost basis of the new item.

(c) A loss results from the failure to maintain permissible insurance, except as otherwise provided in paragraph 18.a.(3).

(d) Compensation for the use of the property was provided through use allowances in lieu of depreciation in accordance with paragraph 9.

(e) Gains and losses arising from mass or extraordinary sales, retirements, or other dispositions shall be considered on a case-by-case basis.

b. Gains or losses of any nature arising from the sale or exchange of property other than the property covered in paragraph a. above shall be excluded in computing award costs.

36. *Public information service costs.*

a. Public information service costs include the cost associated with pamphlets, news releases, and other forms of information services. Such costs are normally incurred to:

(1) Inform or instruct individuals, groups, or the general public.

(2) Interest individuals or groups in participating in a service program of the organization.

(3) Disseminate the results of sponsored and nonsponsored activities.

b. Public information service costs are allowable as direct costs with the prior approval of the awarding agency. Such costs are unallowable as indirect costs.

37. *Publication and printing costs.*

a. Publication costs include the costs of printing (including the processes of composition, plate-making, press work, binding, and the end products produced by such processes), distribution, promotion, mailing, and general handling.

b. If these costs are not identifiable with a particular cost objective, they should be allocated as indirect costs to all benefiting activities of the organization.

c. Publication and printing costs are unallowable as direct costs except with the prior approval of the awarding agency.

d. The cost of page charges in journals is addressed paragraph 28.

38 *Rearrangement and alteration costs.* Costs incurred for ordinary or normal rearrangement and alteration of facilities are allowable. Special arrangement and alteration costs incurred specifically for the project are allowable with the prior approval of the awarding agency.

39 *Reconversion costs.* Costs incurred in the restoration or rehabilitation of the organization's facilities to approximately the same condition existing immediately prior to commencement of Government awards, fair wear and tear excepted, are allowable.

40. *Recruiting costs.* The following recruiting costs are allowable: cost of "help wanted" advertising, operating costs of an employment office, costs of operating an educational testing program, travel expenses including food and lodging of employees while engaged in recruiting personnel, travel costs of applicants for interviews for prospective employment, and relocation costs incurred incident to recruitment of new employees (see paragraph 41c). Where the organization uses employment agencies,

costs not in excess of standard commercial rates for such services are allowable.

41. *Relocation costs.*

a. Relocation costs are costs incident to the permanent change of duty assignment (for an indefinite period or for a stated period of not less than 12 months) of an existing employee or upon recruitment of a new employee. Relocation costs are allowable, subject to the limitation described in paragraphs b, c, and d, below, provided that:

(1) The move is for the benefit of the employer.

(2) Reimbursement to the employee is in accordance with an established written policy consistently followed by the employer.

(3) The reimbursement does not exceed the employee's actual (or reasonably estimated) expenses.

b. Allowable relocation costs for current employees are limited to the following:

(1) The costs of transportation of the employee, members of his immediate family and his household, and personal effects to the new location.

(2) The costs of finding a new home, such as advance trips by employees and spouses to locate living quarters and temporary lodging during the transition period, up to a maximum period of 30 days, including advance trip time.

(3) Closing costs, such as brokerage, legal, and appraisal fees, incident to the disposition of the employee's former home. These costs, together with those described in (4) below, are limited to 8 per cent of the sales price of the employee's former home.

(4) The continuing costs of ownership of the vacant former home after the settlement or lease date of the employee's new permanent home, such as maintenance of buildings and grounds (exclusive of fixing up expenses), utilities, taxes, and property insurance.

(5) Other necessary and reasonable expenses normally incident to relocation, such as the costs of cancelling an unexpired lease, disconnecting and reinstalling household appliances, and purchasing insurance against loss of or damages to personal property. The cost of cancelling an unexpired lease is limited to three times the monthly rental.

c. Allowable relocation costs for new employees are limited to those described in (1) and (2) of paragraph b. above. When relocation costs incurred incident to the recruitment of new employees have been allowed either as a direct or indirect cost and the employee resigns for reasons within his control within 12 months after hire, the organization shall refund or credit the Government for its share of the cost. However, the costs of travel to an overseas location shall be considered travel costs in accordance with paragraph 50 and not relocation costs for the purpose of this paragraph if dependents are not permitted at the location for any reason and the costs do not include costs of transporting household goods.

d. The following costs related to relocation are unallowable:

(1) Fees and other costs associated with acquiring a new home.

(2) A loss on the sale of a former home.

(3) Continuing mortgage principal and interest payments on a home being sold.

(4) Income taxes paid by an employee related to reimbursed relocation costs.

42. *Rental costs.*

a. Subject to the limitations described in paragraphs b. through d. of this paragraph, rental costs are allowable to the extent that the rates are reasonable in light of such factors as: rental costs of comparable property, if any; market conditions in the area; alternatives available; and the type, life expectancy, condition, and value of the property leased.

b. Rental costs under sale and leaseback arrangements are allowable only up to the amount that would be allowed had the organization continued to own the property.

c. Rental costs under less-than-length leases are allowable only up to the amount that would be allowed had title to the property vested in the organization. For this purpose, a less-than-arms-length lease is one under which one party to the lease agreement is able to control or substantially influence the actions of the other. Such leases include, but are not limited to those between (i) divisions of an organization; (ii) organizations under common control through common officers, directors, or members; and (iii) an organization and a director, trustee, officer, or key employee of the organization or his immediate family either directly or through corporations, trusts, or similar arrangements in which they hold a controlling interest.

d. Rental costs under leases which create a material equity in the leased property are allowable only up to the amount that would be allowed had the organization purchased the property on the date the lease agreement was executed; e.g., depreciation or use allowances, maintenance, taxes, insurance but excluding interest expense and other unallowable costs. For this purpose, a material equity in the property exists if the lease in noncancelable or is cancelable only upon the occurrence of some remote contingency and has one or more of the following characteristics:

(1) The organization has the right to purchase the property for a price which at the beginning of the lease appears to be substantially less than the probable fair market value at the time it is permitted to

purchase the property (commonly called a lease with a bargain purchase option);

(2) Title to the property passes to the organization at some time during or after the lease period;

(3) The term of the lease (initial term plus periods covered by bargain renewal options, if any) is equal to 75 per cent or more of the economic life of the leased property; i.e., the period the property is expected to be economically usable by one or more users.

43. *Royalties and other costs for use of patents and copyrights.*

a. Royalties on a patent or copyright or amortization of the cost of acquiring by purchase a copyright, patent, or rights thereto, necessary for the proper performance of the award are allowable unless:

(1) The Government has a license or the right to free use of the patent or copyright.

(2) The patent or copyright has been adjudicated to be invalid, or has been administratively determined to be invalid.

(3) The patent or copyright is considered to be unenforceable.

(4) The patent or copyright is expired.

b. Special care should be exercised in determining reasonableness where the royalties may have been arrived at as a result of less then arm's length bargaining; e.g.:

(1) Royalties paid to persons, including corporations, affiliated with the organization.

(2) Royalties paid to unaffiliated parties, including corporations, under an agreement entered into in contemplation that a Government award would be made.

(3) Royalties paid under an agreement entered into after an award is made to an organization.

c. In any case involving a patent or copyright formerly owned by the organization, the amount of royalty allowed should not exceed the cost which would have been allowed had the organization retained title thereto.

44. *Severance pay.*

a. Severance pay, also commonly referred to as dismissal wages, is a payment in addition to regular salaries and wages, by organizations to workers whose employment is being terminated. Costs of severance pay are allowable only to the extent that in each case, it is required by (i) law, (ii) employer-employee agreement, (iii) established policy that constitutes, in effect, an implied agreement on the organization's part, or (iv) circumstances of the particular employment.

b. Costs of severance payments are divided into two categories as follows:

(1) Actual normal turnover severance payments shall be allocated to all activities; or, where the organization provides for a reserve for normal severances such method will be acceptable if the charge to current operations is reasonable in light of payments actually made for normal severances over a representative past period, and if amounts charged are allocated to all activities of the organization.

(2) Abnormal or mass severance pay is of such a conjectural nature that measurement of costs by means of an accrual will not achieve equity to both parties. Thus, accruals for this purpose are not allowable. However, the Government recognizes its obligation to participate to the extent of its fair share, in any specific payment. Thus, allowability will be considered on a case-by-case basis in the event of occurrence.

45. *Specialized service facilities.*

a. The costs of services provided by highly complex or specialized facilities operated by the organization, such as electronic computers and wind tunnels, are allowable provided the charges for the services meet the conditions of either b. or c. of this paragraph and, in addition, take into account any items of income or Federal financing that qualify as applicable credits under paragraph A.5. of Attachment A.

b. The costs of such services, when material, must be charged directly to applicable awards based on actual usage of the services on the basis of a schedule of rates or established methodology that (i) does not discriminate against federally supported activities of the organization, including usage by the organization for internal purposes, and (ii) is designed to recover only the aggregate costs of the services. The costs of each service shall consist normally of both its direct costs and its allocable share of all indirect costs. Advance agreements pursuant to paragraph A.6. of Attachment A are particularly important in this situation.

c. Where the costs incurred for a service are not material, they may be allocated as indirect costs.

46. *Taxes.*

a. In general, taxes which the organization is required to pay and which are paid or accrued in accordance with generally accepted accounting principles, and payments made to local governments in lieu of taxes which are commensurate with the local government services received are allowable, except for (i) taxes from which exemptions are available to the organization directly or which are available to the organization based on an exemption afforded the Government and in the latter case when the awarding agency makes available the necessary exemption certificates, (ii) special assessments on land which represent capital improvements, and (iii) Federal income taxes.

b. Any refund of taxes, and any payment to the organization of interest thereon, which were allowed as award costs, will be credited either as a cost reduction or cash refund, as appropriate, to the Government.

47. *Termination costs.* Termination of awards generally give rise to the incurrence

of costs, or the need for special treatment of costs, which would not have arisen had the award not been terminated. Cost principles covering these items are set forth below. They are to be used in conjunction with the other provisions of this Circular in termination situations.

a. *Common items.* The cost of items reasonably usable on the organization's other work shall not be allowable unless the organization submits evidence that it would not retain such items at cost without sustaining a loss. In deciding whether such items are reasonably usable on other work of the organization, the awarding agency should consider the organization's plans and orders for current and scheduled activity. Contemporaneous purchases of common items by the organization shall be regarded as evidence that such items are reasonably usable on the organization's other work. Any acceptance of common items as allocable to the terminated portion of the award shall be limited to the extent that the quantities of such items on hand, in transit, and on order are in excess of the reasonable quantitative requirements of other work.

b. *Costs continuing after termination.* If in a particular case, despite all reasonable efforts by the organization, certain costs cannot be discontinued immediately after the effective date of termination, such costs are generally allowable within the limitations set forth in this Circular, except that any such costs continuing after termination due to the negligent or willful failure of the organization to discontinue such costs shall be unallowable.

c. *Loss of useful value.* Loss of useful value of special tooling, machinery and equipment which was not charged to the award as a capital expenditure is generally allowable if:

(1) Such special tooling, machinery, or equipment is not reasonably capable of use in the other work of the organization.

(2) The interest of the Government is protected by transfer of title or by other means deemed appropriate by the awarding agency;

d. *Rental costs.* Rental costs under unexpired leases are generally allowable where clearly shown to have been reasonably necessary for the performance of the terminated award less the residual value of such leases, if (i) the amount of such rental claimed does not exceed the reasonable use value of the property leased for the period of the award and such further period as may be reasonable, and (ii) the organization makes all reasonable efforts to terminate, assign, settle, or otherwise reduce the cost of such lease. There also may be included the cost of alterations of such leased property, provided such alterations were necessary for the performance of the award, and of reasonable

restoration required by the provisions of the lease.

e. *Settlement expenses.* Settlement expenses including the following are generally allowable:

(1) Accounting, legal, clerical, and similar costs reasonably necessary for:

(a) The preparation and presentation to awarding agency of settlement claims and supporting data with respect to the terminated portion of the award, unless the termination is for default. (See paragraph 4.a. of Attachment L, OMB Circular No. A–110; and

(b) The termination and settlement of subawards.

(2) Reasonable costs for the storage, transportation, protection, and disposition of property provided by the Government or acquired or produced for the award; except when grantees are reimbursed for disposals at a predetermined amount in accordance with Attachment N of OMB Circular A–110.

(3) Indirect costs related to salaries and wages incurred as settlement expenses in subparagraphs (1) and (2) of this paragraph. Normally, such indirect costs shall be limited to fringe benefits, occupancy cost, and immediate supervision.

f. *Claims under subawards.* Claims under subawards, including the allocable portion of claims which are common to the award, and to other work of the organization are generally allowable. An appropriate share of the organization's indirect expense may be allocated to the amount of settlements with subcontractor/subgrantees; provided that the amount allocated is otherwise consistent with the basic guidelines contained in Attachment A. The indirect expense so allocated shall exclude the same and similar costs claimed directly or indirectly as settlement expenses.

48. *Training and education costs.*

a. Costs of preparation and maintenance of a program of instruction including but not limited to on-the-job, classroom, and apprenticeship training, designed to increase the vocational effectiveness of employees, including training materials, textbooks, salaries or wages of trainees (excluding overtime compensation which might arise therefrom), and (i) salaries of the director of -training and staff when the training program is conducted by the organization; or (ii) tuition and fees when the training is in an institution not operated by the organization, are allowable.

b. Costs of part-time education, at an undergraduate or postgraduate college level, including that provided at the organization's own facilities, are allowable only when the course or degree pursued is relative to the field in which the employee is now working or may reasonably be expected to work, and are limited to:

(1) Training materials.

(2) Textbooks.

(3) Fees charges by the educational institution.

(4) Tuition charged by the educational institution, or in lieu of tuition, instructors' salaries and the related share of indirect costs of the educational institution to the extent that the sum thereof is not in excess of · the tuition which would have ben paid to the participating educational institution.

(5) Salaries and related costs of instructors who are employees of the organization.

(6) Straight-time compensation of each employee for time spent attending classes during working hours not in excess of 156 hours per year and only to the extent that circumstances do not permit the operation of classes or attendance at classes after regular working hours; otherwise such compensation is unallowable.

c. Costs of tuition, fees, training materials, and textbooks (but not subsistence, salary, or any other emoluments) in connection with full-time education, including that provided at the organization's own facilities, at a postgraduate (but not undergraduate) college level, are allowable only when the course or degree pursued is related to the field in which the employee is now working or may reasonably be expected to work, and only where the costs receive the prior approval of the awarding agency. Such costs are limited to the costs attributable to a total period not to exceed one school year for each employee so trained. In unusual cases the period may be extended.

d. Costs of attendance of up to 16 weeks per employee per year at specialized programs specifically designed to enhance the effectiveness of executives or managers or to prepare employees for such positions are allowable. Such costs include enrollment fees, training materials, textbooks and related charges, employees' salaries, subsistence, and travel. Costs allowable under this paragraph do not include those for courses that are part of a degree-oriented curriculum, which are allowable only to the extent set forth in b. and c. above.

e. Maintenance expense, and normal depreciation or fair rental, on facilities owned or leased by the organization for training purposes are allowable to the extent set forth in paragraphs 9, 22, and 42.

f. Contributions or donations to educational or training institutions, including the donation of facilities or other properties, and scholarships or fellowships, are unallowable.

g. Training and education costs in excess of those otherwise allowable under paragraphs b. and c. of this paragraph may be allowed with prior approval of the awarding agency. To be considered for approval, the organization must demonstrate that such costs are consistently incurred pursuant to an established training and education program, and that the course or degree pursued is relative to the field in which the employee is now working or may reasonably be expected to work.

49. *Transportation costs.* Transportation costs include freight, express, cartage, and postage charges relating either to goods purchased, in process, or delivered. These costs are allowable. When such costs can readily be identified with the items involved, they may be directly charged as transportation costs or added to the cost of such items (see paragraph 23). Where identification with the materials received cannot readily be made, transportation costs may be charged to the appropriate indirect cost accounts if the organization follows a consistent, equitable procedure in this respect.

50. *Travel costs.*

a. Travel costs are the expenses for transportation, lodging, subsistence, and related items incurred by employees who are in travel status on official business of the organization. Travel costs are allowable subject to paragraphs b. through e. below, when they are directly attributable to specific work under an award or are incurred in the normal course of administration of the organization.

b. Such costs may be charged on an actual basis, on a per diem or mileage basis in lieu of actual costs incurred, or on a combination of the two, provided the method used results in charges consistent with those normally allowed by the organization in its regular operations.

c. The difference in cost between first-class air accommodations and less than first-class air accommodations is unallowable except when less than first-class air accommodations are not reasonably available to meet necessary mission requirements, such as where less than first-class accommodations would (i) require circuitous routing, (ii) require travel during unreasonable hours, (iii) greatly increase the duration of the flight, (iv) result in additional costs which would offset the transportation savings, or (v) offer accommodations which are not reasonably adequate for the medical needs of the traveler.

d. Necessary and reasonable costs of family movements and personnel movements of a special or mass nature are allowable, pursuant to paragraphs 40 and 41, subject to allocation on the basis of work or time period benefited when appropriate. Advance agreements are particularly important.

e. Direct charges for foreign travel costs are allowable only when the travel has received prior approval of the awarding agency. Each separate foreign trip must be approved. For purposes of this provision, foreign travel is defined as any travel outside of Canada and the United States and its territories and possessions. However, for an organization located in foreign countries, the term "foreign travel" means travel outside that country.

[Circular No. A-122]

Attachment C

Nonprofit Organizations not Subject to this Circular

Aerospace Corporation, El Segundo, California

Argonne Universities Association, Chicago, Illinois

Associated Universities, Incorporated, Washington, D.C.

Associated Universities for Research and Astronomy, Tucson, Arizona

Atomic Casualty Commission, Washington, D.C.

Battelle Memorial Institute, Headquartered in Columbus, Ohio

Brookhaven National Laboratory, Upton, New York

Center for Energy and Environmental Research (CEER), (University of Puerto Rico) Commonwealth of Puerto Rico

Charles Stark Draper Laboratory, Incorporated, Cambridge, Massachusetts

Comparative Animal Research Laboratory (CARL) (University of Tennessee), Oak Ridge, Tennessee

Environmental Institute of Michigan, Ann Arbor, Michigan

Hanford Environmental Health Foundation, Richland, Washington

IIT Research Institute, Chicago, Illinois

Institute for Defense Analysis, Arlington, Virginia

Institute of Gas Technology, Chicago, Illinois

Midwest Research Institute, Headquartered in Kansas City, Missouri

Mitre Corporation, Bedford, Massachusetts

Montana Energy Research and Development Institute, Inc., (MERDI), Butte, Montana

National Radiological Astronomy Observatory, Green Bank, West Virginia

Oak Ridge Associated Universities, Oak Ridge, Tennessee

Project Management Corporation, Oak Ridge, Tennessee

Rand Corporation, Santa Monica, California

Research Triangle Institute, Research Triangle Park, North Carolina

Riverside Research Institute, New York, New York

Sandia Corporation, Albuquerque, New Mexico

Southern Research Institute, Birmingham, Alabama

Southwest Research Institute, San Antonio, Texas

SRI International, Menlo Park, California

Syracuse Research Corporation, Syracuse, New York

Universities Research Association, Incorporated (National Acceleration Lab), Argonne, Illinois

Universities Corporation for Atmospheric Research, Boulder, Colorado

Nonprofit Insurance Companies such as Blue Cross and Blue Shield Organizations

Other nonprofit organizations as negotiated with awarding agencies.

---

49 Fed. Reg. 18,268–18,277 (April 27, 1984)

OFFICE OF MANAGEMENT AND BUDGET

Circular A-122; Cost Principles for Nonprofit Organizations—"Lobbying" Revision

[NOTE: This reprint incorporates corrections that are published in the Federal Register of Tuesday, May 8, 1984.]

AGENCY: Office of Management and Budget, Executive Office of the President.

ACTION: Publication of Revision to the Circular.

SUMMARY: This notice sets forth the final version of the Office of Management and Budget's (OMB) "Lobbying" revision to Circular A-122, "Cost Principles for Nonprofit Organizations." The revison makes unallowable for Federal reimbursement the costs associated with most kinds of lobbying and political activities, but does not restrict lobbying or political activities paid for with non-Federal funds.

A parallel revision is being made to the Federal Acquisition Regulation (FAR) to cover all defense and civilian contractors. The FAR revision appears

on the pages immediately following the
Circular A–122 revision.

EFFECTIVE DATE: This revision will
become effective May 29, 1984. The
revision will affect only grants,
contracts, and other agreements entered
into after the effective date. Existing
grants, contracts, and other agreements
will not be affected. Agency contracts
and regulations will incorporate these
provisions to the same extent and in the
same manner as they do other
provisions of Circular A–122.

FOR FURTHER INFORMATION CONTACT:
John J. Lordan, Financial Management
Branch, Office of Management and
Budget, Washington, D.C. 20503. (202)
395–6823.

SUPPLEMENTARY INFORMATION: The
attached text sets forth the final
language for the revision to Circular A–
122 that was proposed on November 3,
1983. 48 FR 50860–50874. Significant
modifications have been made to the
proposed language after a thorough
review of the approximately 93,600
public comments received and extensive
discussions with the General
Accounting Office and cognizant
Congressional committees.

I. Background of Circular A–122

Circular A–122, "Cost Principles for
Nonprofit Organizations," establishes
uniform rules for determining the costs
of grants, contracts, and other
agreements. Like other OMB cost
principle circulars for state and local
governments and educational
institutions, Circular A–122 is a
management directive addressed to the
heads of Federal departments and
agencies and constitutes the legal basis
by which they define allowable and
unallowable costs and how such costs
are calculated.

Circular A–122 was first issued in June
1980. It was developed by an
interagency team chosen from the major
grant-making agencies and led by OMB.
Before issuance, public comments were
sought and received, and consultations
were held with the General Accounting
Office. The cost principles built upon
accounting rules previously in use by
Federal agencies in their dealings with
nonprofit organizations. The Circular
standardized and simplified those rules.
In general, the Circular provides that, to
be recovered from the Federal
government, costs incurred by grantees
and contractors must be necessary,
reasonable, and related to the federally-
sponsored activity. In addition, costs
must be legal, proper, and consistent
with the policies that govern the
organization's other expenditures.

The disallowance of lobbying costs in
this revision is comparable to the
disallowance by Circular A–122 of other
costs which are not reimbursed on
grounds of public policy, such as
advertising, fundraising expenses and
entertainment. In each of these
instances, a determination has been

made that it would not be appropriate or cost-efficient to permit Federal tax dollars to be used for these purposes. In any event, it should be noted that lobbying costs are currently unallowable; as indicated throughout, this revision is intended to clarify and make more uniform the meaning and application of that bar.

II. History of the Revision

On January 24, 1983, OMB published a proposal to revise Circular A-122's treatment of the costs of lobbying activities by defining as unallowable the costs of advocacy activities performed by Federal nonprofit grantees and contractors with appropriated funds. 48 FR 3348-3351. Following publication, OMB received approximately 48,300 comments from the public, from nonprofit and commercial organizations and from government agencies. Approximately 16,500 comments opposed the proposed revision, and approximately 31,800 supported it. Many of the comments opposing the revision expressed support for the general principle that Federal tax dollars should not be used for lobbying and related purposes, but objected that the proposals contained in the January 1983 notice would disrupt the legitimate activities of Federal nonprofit grantees and contractors. On the other hand, many of the supporting comments suggested a need for controls significantly more restrictive than those proposed.

In order to permit further study of the issues raised by these comments, OMB withdrew the January 1983 proposal at the end of the 45-day public comment period. In the intervening months, OMB conducted numerous discussions with nonprofit organizations, business groups, trade associations, the General Accounting Office, and interested Committees of the Congress and their staffs. After further consideration of the comments and discussions, OMB published a second proposal on November 3, 1983, to revise the Circular's cost standards. The November proposal represented a fundamental revision of the original January proposal as a result of the

lengthy dialogue between OMB and affected groups.

The most important changes from the January proposal were:

- Adoption of an allocation method of accounting for the costs of lobbying and related activities;
- A more limited definition of unallowable costs; and
- Clarifications and limits on reporting and recordkeeping requirements in the spirit of the Paperwork Reduction Act.

The November 1983 proposal initially provided for a 45-day public comment period. 48 FR 50860-50874. As a result of the interest shown by the public and Congress and the large volume of comments received by OMB, the comment period was extended for thirty days until January 18, 1984. 48 FR 56463-56464.

By the end of the public comment period, OMB had received some 93,600 separate comments. Of these, some 87,500 (93.5%) favored the proposed revision without further changes; some 4,175 (4.5%) opposed the revision or sought further modifications; and some 1,925 (2.0%) did not clearly express either support or criticism. These totals include only individually mailed comments; bulk packages of letters, including form letters and petitions, were counted as single comments.

In finalizing the revision, OMB has carefully reviewed each of the comments received. The November proposal has been further amended in several significant respects, and the final version addresses many of the concerns raised by the critical comments. OMB also has conducted extensive discussions with interested members of Congress and their staffs, particularly members of the House Government Operations Committee and the Senate Subcommittee on Intergovernmental Relations. Prior to publication of the November proposal, OMB had met extensively with Committee staff to review their concerns, and several major modifications were made to the proposal to accommodate their suggestions. OMB has continued to meet with the Committee staffs during the public comment period and, following development of the final language of the revision, OMB has reviewed this language with the Committees on several occasions. In addition, OMB has met with the General Accounting Office at various stages of the process and is authorized to state that the Comptroller General believes that OMB has the clear legal authority to issue the Circular amendment published today, and that he supports it.

III. Summary of the Revision

The revision amends Circular A-122 to define certain lobbying activities by nonprofit Federal grantees and contractors as unallowable costs which cannot be paid for with Federal funds. The most significant provisions make costs of the following activities unallowable:

- Federal, state or local electioneering and support of such entities as campaign organizations and political action committees;
- Most direct lobbying of Congress and, with the exceptions noted below, state legislatures, to influence legislation;
- Lobbying of the Executive Branch in connection with decisions to sign or veto enrolled legislation;
- Efforts to utilize state or local officials to lobby Congress or state legislatures;
- Grassroots lobbying concerning either Federal or state legislation; and
- Legislative liaison activities in support of unallowable lobbying activities.

The revision is considerably less encompassing than the earlier proposals and the current regulations of other agencies governing for-profit contractors, in that it does not cover:

- Lobbying at the local level (unallowable under both the Federal Acquisition Regulation (FAR) and the Defense Acquisition Regulation (DAR) supplement to the FAR);
- Lobbying to influence state legislation, in order to directly reduce the cost of performing the grant or contract, or to avoid impairing the organization's authority to do so (covered under the current FAR, DAR supplement, and the January 1983 proposal);
- Lobbying in the form of a technical and factual presentation to Congress or state legislatures, at their request (unallowable under the current DAR supplement to the FAR);

- Contacts with Executive Branch officials other than lobbying for the veto or signing of enrolled bills (covered under the January 1983 proposal); and
- Lobbying on regulatory actions (covered under the January 1983 proposal).

In particular, the revision will make unallowable only the portion of costs attributable to lobbying (the "allocation" approach)—not, as in the January 1983 proposal, entire cost items used in part for political advocacy (the so-called "tainting" approach).

The revision will provide relief from paperwork and audit burdens for nonprofit organizations (and, under a simultaneous change being made in the FAR, for government contractors). For example, indirect cost employees (such as executive directors) will not be required to maintain time logs or calendars (for the portion of their time treated as an indirect cost) if they certify in good faith that they spend less than 25% of their work time in defined lobbying activities. Moreover, the clear standards provided by the revision will prove of substantial benefit to nonprofit grantees in audit situations by reducing the resources necessary to resolve whether Federal funds were spent on unallowable activities.

The penalties for violating the revision will be the same as for any other cost principle in OMB Circular A-122. The standard remedy is recovery of the misspent money. In cases of serious abuse, however, the grant or contract may be suspended or terminated, or the recipient may be debarred from receiving further Federal grants or contracts for a certain period.

IV. Significant Changes From the November Proposal

After review of the comments submitted during the comment period, OMB has made further significant changes to the revision. Among the most noteworthy amendments are the following:

1. *The definitional term "lobbying and related activities" has been changed to "lobbying."*

Numerous commenters expressed concern that the term "related activities" could be used in the future to expand the scope of unallowable acivities beyond what is explicitly defined as unallowable. This was not OMB's intent, which was merely to use the most appropriate term for describing the unallowable activities, which include electioneering and activities supporting unallowable lobbying, as well as what is normally thought of as "lobbying."

The original term for the activities defined as unallowable (in the January 1983 proposal) was "political advocacy." That term was changed to "lobbying and related activities" in the November proposal and has now been revised to "lobbying." Deletion of the term "related activities" does not affect the continuing disallowance of "costs associated with" unallowable lobbying—including those activities undertaken to facilitate that lobbying.

2. *The restrictions on direct legislative lobbying and grassroots lobbying have been clarified to cover attempts to influence "the introduction of legislation" and "the enactment or modification of * * * pending legislation."* Sections a(3) and a(4).

This change makes more precise the scope of the activities disallowed, and conforms to the IRS definition of lobbying.

3. *The "legislative liaison" provision has been made less restrictive, and clarified.* Section a(5).

In the November proposal, all legislative liaison was deemed to be unallowable unless it did not relate to otherwise unallowable activities. Commenters complained that this section was both too confusing, because it employed a double negative, and too restrictive. Section a(5) has been revised to clarify that legislative liaison is unallowable only "when such activities are carried on in support of or in knowing preparation for an effort to engage in unallowable lobbying," as defined in the revision.

4. *The exception for providing assistance in response to a "specific written request" has been broadened to facilitate easier usage and has been narrowed in other respects.* Section b(1).

The final version has been broadened by deleting the "specific written request" requirement and permitting oral requests, if properly documented; allowing "cognizant staff members" (in addition to Congressmen) to make such requests; and making *Congressional Record* notices sufficient to invoke the exception.

The exception also has been narrowed in certain respects by limiting it to information derived from grant or contract performance that is conveyed in "hearing testimony, statements or letters" and requested by legislative sources; requiring presentations to be "technical and factual," and further requiring that the information is "readily obtainable and can be readily put in deliverable form." Further, the use of the term "technical and factual presentation" avoids use of the exception whenever technical and factual information is provided in any manner of lobbying presentation and likewise avoids the requirement that brief advocacy conclusions following technical and factual presentations require separate accountings and disallowances.

The costs of travel, lodging or meals involved in lobbying activities which would otherwise be unallowable under the terms of section a(3) are nonetheless made allowable if expended for the purpose of offering Congressional hearing testimony pursuant to written request of the Committee's Chairman or Ranking Minority Member for a technical and factual presentation.

5. *The state waiver clause in the state lobbying exception has been deleted and the scope of the exception clarified.* Section b(2).

The state waiver clause was added to the November 1983 notice in response to concerns raised by some nonprofit organizations. It would have permitted states to make allowable all state lobbying by their subgrantees. Upon further review, however, the clause was determined to be confusing and superfluous. Further, under none of Circular A–122's other 50 cost categories do states have the right to override Federal cost standards.

Two significant clarifying changes have been made in new section b(2). First, the "lobbying" covered by the exception has been explicitly limited to lobbying made unallowable by section a(3); thus, for example, grassroots lobbying (covered under section a(4)) does not come within the exception. Second, the exception has been reworded to apply to efforts to influence state legislation affecting an organization's authority to perform a grant, contract, or other agreement, and efforts to reduce the costs to the organization of such performance. The original language, applying to an organization's "ability" to perform the grant, contract, or other agreement, was deemed too broad.

6. *The exception for "activity in connection with an employee's service as an elected or appointed official or member of a governmental advisory board" was deleted.* Section c(3) in November proposal.

This provision was put in the January 1983 proposal to prevent part-time government officials from being subject to complete non-reimbursement as a result of the "tainting" principle. Since the allocation method is now used, the exception is irrelevant and would open major loopholes.

7. *The "disclosure" requirement relating to the indirect cost rate proposal has been clarified and explicitly tied to existing accounting guidelines.* Section c(1).

The November proposal had required a statement "identifying by category, costs attributable in whole or in part to lobbying" and "stating how they are accounted for."

Section c(1) now simply requires that total lobbying costs "be separately identified" in the indirect cost rate proposal and treated consistently with other unallowable activity costs, as required by the operative Circular A–122 accounting provision.

8. *The Circular A–122 certification requirement has been changed to conform to the Defense and GSA November 1983 proposal.* Section c(2).

The November proposal's certification requirement pertains to the "Financial Status Report," which is prepared on an individual grant basis. However, most lobbying activities are accounted for in an entity's indirect costs, which are calculated on an organization-wide basis. Thus, the appropriate place to certify such costs is in the Indirect Cost Rate Proposal, as required under the Defense and GSA·(FAR) approach. The final version has been changed to reflect this fact.

9. *The language explaining the "25%*

Rule" exception for recordkeeping has been clarified. Section c(4).

Some commenters said that the annual period the 25% rule covered created retroactivity problems, in that intensive late-year lobbying could remove the rule's paperwork protections for persons who had previously estimated that the 25% trigger would not be exceeded. Other commenters said it was unclear whether the rule was to be based on 40-hour weeks or the actual hours worked. In response, the phrase "25% of the time" has been revised to "25% of his compensated hours of employment during that calendar month."

V. Purpose of the Revision

As set forth at greater length in the preambles to the January and November notices, the purpose of this revision is to establish comprehensive, government-wide cost principles to ensure that nonprofit Federal grantees and contractors do not use appropriated funds for lobbying activities. This principle is achieved by disallowing the recovery of lobbying costs in a manner consistent with the treatment under Circular A–122 of other costs which are disallowed on grounds of public policy. In adopting this revision, OMB does not intend to discourage or penalize nonprofit organizations from conducting lobbying efforts with their own non-Federal funds. The sole purpose of this revision is to require that those efforts be paid for with funds raised from other sources and to ensure that the Federal government does not subsidize such lobbying activities with appropriated funds. In addition, this revision seeks, for the sake of auditors and auditees both, to clarify definitions and thereby to make the current provisions against use of funds for lobbying purposes both easier to comply with and to enforce.

In recent years, Congress and the Comptroller General have recognized that the use of Federal monies by grantees and contractors to engage in lobbying is inappropriate. The voluminous comments OMB received on the revision demonstrate that there is little disagreement on this score. Use of appropriated funds for lobbying diverts scarce resources from the purpose for which the grant or contract was awarded. By permitting such a use of its funds, the government subsidizes the lobbying efforts of its contractors and grantees. This improperly distorts the political process, by favoring the political expression of some—organizations with contracts or grants—relative to others, who must conduct their political expression at their own expense.

Government subsidization of certain participants the debate over legislative outcomes may contradict important principles of government neutrality in political debate, and use of Federal funds for private lobbying can give the appearance of Federal support of one political position over another. As the comments indicate, subsidizing such lobbying can create misunderstanding and interfere with the neutral, nonpartisan administration of Federally-funded programs. The revision seeks to avoid the appearance that, by awarding Federal grants, contracts, or other agreements to organizations engaged in political advocacy on particular sides of public issues, the government has endorsed, fostered, or "prescribe[d] [as] orthodox" a particular view on such issues. *West Virginia State Board of Education* v. *Barnette*, 319 U.S. 624, 645 (1943).

Requiring grantees and contractors to bear the costs of their own lobbying efforts does not infringe upon their constitutional rights. No person or group has a First Amendment right to receive government funding for political expression. As the Supreme Court has recently emphasized in a unanimous opinion, free speech does not mean subsidized speech. The Federal government "is not required by the First Amendment to subsidize lobbying. * * * We again reject the 'notion that the First Amendment rights are somehow not fully realized unless they are subsidized by the State.'" *Regan* v. *Taxation with Representation of Washington*, 103 S.Ct. 1997, 2001 (1983).

In recent years, the problem of the use of taxpayer funds for lobbying purposes has become of increasing concern, and steps have been taken in a variety of different contexts to address the problem. There has been increasing public concern that limited grant and contract resources should not be used in projects that involve political organizing.

Congress has responded to this problem by adopting numerous appropriations restrictions to address some of the more flagrant abuses and problems raised by lobbying activities with Federal funds. Indeed, over the past ten years, some 40–50 riders have been attached to appropriations bills to address different aspects of the problem. These appropriations riders use many different formulations, but have as a common element prohibiting the use of appropriated funds for publicity or propaganda purposes designed to support or defeat legislation. The agencies affected by specific appropriations riders include Defense, the District of Columbia, the Legal Services Corporation, and agencies covered by the State-Justice-Commerce Appropriations Acts. For example, the current Labor-HHS-Education-Related Agencies Appropriations Act, dealing with agencies that dispense the large proportion of grant funds, reads as follows:

No part of any appropriation contained in this Act shall be used to pay the salary or expenses of any grant or contract recipient or agency acting for such recipient to engage in any activity designed to influence legislation or appropriations pending before the Congress. (Section 502, Pub. L. 98–139.)

This provision has been construed by the Justice Department to extend the ban on grantee activities significantly beyond the conduct of "grassroots" campaigns. Moreover, as to many of the appropriations riders which prohibit agencies from using public funds for their own lobbying activities, clear policies regarding grantee and contractor expenditures for lobbying may be needed in order for the agencies not to be in violation, albeit indirect, of their statutory restrictions. Enforcement of these appropriations provisions, and of the consensus principle that Federal funds should not be used to support lobbying activities, has proved to be very difficult, because of the absence of any clear definitions or standards for determining which activities by grantees and contractors violate the lobbying restrictions.

Furthermore, when audits are undertaken, the lack of clear standards imposes substantial burdens on the grantees. Auditors can have great discretion and significant leverage over the grantees in negotiations to determine which factors should be included in allowable costs. If auditors decide to inquire into lobbying activities, nonprofit entities can be compelled to provide elaborate factual backup from their records to refute any claims that may be raised. In light of the enormous expansion of Inspector General staffs and the sensitivity of this issue, significantly more auditing activity can reasonably be expected in this area in the future. Accordingly, the current practices do not serve the current need to assure that Federal funds are not used for lobbying purposes and, as well, impose potentially heavy burdens on agencies, their auditors and the nonprofit entities themselves.

As the Investigations Subcommittee of the House Armed Services Committee recently concluded:

[T]here is a deficiency in the appropriations acts' prohibition of lobbying with appropriated funds. A review of the legislative history of the publicity-propaganda appropriations acts restrictions provides no definition of the critical terms 'publicity' and 'propaganda.' Thus, there appears to be no firm distinction between the conduct which is permissible and that which is prohibited. Thus the clear signal from Congress through the appropriations laws and other actions has not been translated into effective management controls.

In the commercial field, several steps recently have been taken to facilitate the need to be sure that Federal funds are not used for lobbying. For example:

• On December 18, 1981, the Department of Defense issued revisions to its Defense Acquisition Regulation (DAR), addressing for the first time the issue of lobbying activities, and making certain such costs unallowable under Defense contracts.

• On April 27, 1982 and October 22, 1982, Defense further toughened its rules disallowing lobbying costs by eliminating certain exceptions from coverage.

• On May 28, 1982, NASA issued a new cost principle in the NASA Procurement Regulation (NASAPR) making certain lobbying costs unallowable for NASA contractors.

• On November 2, 1982, the General Services Administration issued a new cost principle in the Federal Procurement Regulation (FPR) making certain lobbying costs unallowable for civilian agency contracts with commercial organizations.

• On April 1, 1984, the three sets of cost principles that had governed Federal contracts—the DAR, FPR and NASAPR—were replaced by the new Federal Acquisition Regulation (FAR). The FAR is the product of several years of inter-agency negotiations to create a uniform set of guidelines for all Federal contractors. The procurement agencies are required to use the new FAR regulation except in those cases where they issue a formal deviation to a specified FAR section. The FAR adopted the former FPR lobbying cost principle. The Defense Acquisition Regulation Council, however, issued a deviation so that the former DAR lobbying cost principle continues to be operative for Defense contractors.

These initiatives, however, affect only defense and civilian contracts with commercial entities. No generally applicable cost principle has been issued to cover the Federal funding of lobbying under contracts and grants to nonprofit organizations. These entities, however, are in the same position with respect to most Federal government cost guidelines as profit-making grantees and contractors, and the comments received by OMB clearly and overwhelmingly support the view that the same lobbying cost principles should likewise apply to them. Therefore, in keeping with sound management practices, it is important that the lobbying cost principles be extended to these nonprofit entities and harmonized, to the maximum extent practicable, with the principles already applicable to commercial concerns.

Given the vagueness of the existing A-122 standards, the need for a clear cost principle on lobbying for nonprofit grantees was addressed explicitly by the Comptroller General in September 1982, after a GAO investigation of whether funds under Title X of the Public Health Services Act were used to finance lobbying activities or abortion-related activities:

Clear Federal guidance is needed both to ensure that Title X program funds are not used for lobbying and to preclude unnecessary controversy over whether grantees are violating Federal restrictions. *The move to revise and make more specific the cost principles applicable to all Federal grantees is the appropriate mechanism to achieve these ends.* GAO/HRD–82–106 (Sept. 24. 1982) at 27 (emphasis added).

This revision thus addresses the major area in which Federal cost principles have not yet been adopted to ensure that appropriated funds are not used to subsidize lobbying by Federal grantees and contractors. This revision is intended to provide lines of demarcation so that nonprofit entities can know in advance what is allowable. The revision protects their First Amendment rights and in significant respects strongly advances their interests. By giving nonprofit entities clear guidance and limiting the bookkeeping work that can be required to refute an auditor's claim of unallowable costs, the revision removes a potentially severe burden from these entities, especially the smaller and less well financed groups. In addition, although the revision cannot resolve in advance every problem which may arise in this complex field, a mechanism has been provided by which nonprofits may obtain advance rulings whether certain costs are unallowable.

The revision is similar in critical respects to the current Defense and FAR procurement regulations, although—as noted elsewhere in this premble— provisions added in the past two years to the cost principles governing all Federal contractors are far more restrictive than the revision adoped here. Since parallel revisions are being issued for Circular A–122 and FAR sets of cost principles, the present initiative guarantees uniformity of lobbying cost rules for both nonprofit and profit-making recipients of Federal funds. This principle of uniformity has been urged by Congressional commenters and by the GAO.

VI. Principal Objections to the Proposal

A. *Legal Authority*

Numerous commenters suggested that OMB lacks authority to issue this revision to Circular A–122. Most of these comments appear to have been based upon a report of the Congressional Research Service, which suggested that this might be a potential legal issue but ultimately reached no conclusion on the matter. OMB, supported by the

Comptroller General, believes that its legal authority to issue the amendment is clear.

The responsibility for implementing grant programs, including the power of administration, has been delegated by Congress to the various grant- and contract-making agencies. It has long been settled that the Federal government may impose terms and conditions upon grants and contracts it awards, including those given to State or local government instrumentalities. *See, e.g., King* v. *Smith,* 392 U.S. 309 (1968). Accordingly, those agencies have the direct legal authority to establish cost principles and, prior to the late 1970s, did so in a piecemeal fashion without coordinated government-wide standards.

OMB's legal authority for establishing cost principles derives from the President's constitutional authority to "take care that the laws be faithfully executed." U.S. Constitution, Article II, Section 3; his authority under section 205(a) of the Federal Property and Administrative Services Act, 40 U.S.C. 486(a); and from the general supervisory responsibilities over the Executive Branch vested by Congress in the President and in OMB. In particular, in its capacity as the President's managing agent for the Executive Branch, OMB is authorized by 31 U.S.C. 1111(2) to assist the President in improving economy and efficiency throughout the government by developing plans for the improved organization, coordination, and management of the Executive Branch. This revision constitutes an effort to develop government-wide cost principles that are uniform, to the maximum extent practicable, and treat similarly situated organizations alike.

The President assigned responsibility for grants management to OMB by Executive Order No. 11541 (July 1, 1970), pursuant to Reorganization Plan No. 2 of 1970, 5 U.S.C. App. Subsequently, grants management authority was transferred to GSA by Executive Order No. 11717 (May 9, 1973) and transferred back to OMB by Executive Order No. 11893 (December 31, 1975). Relevant statutory authorities include section 209 of the Budget and Accounting Act of 1921, 31 U.S.C. 1111(1); and section 104 of the Budget and Accounting Procedures Act of 1950, 31 U.S.C. 1111(2). Under these and other general management authorities. OMB may develop plans for implementing better management with "a view to efficient and economical service" and may issue supplementary interpretative guidelines "to promote consistent and efficient use of procurement contracts, grant agreements, and cooperative agreements."

In its capacity of exercising the President's general management functions over the Executive Branch, OMB has the power to supervise and direct the management activities of Federal agencies. OMB has issued a series of Circulars over the years in discharging these delegated responsibilities, and these Circulars serve as one of the primary means of informing the agencies how to exercise their authority in administrative and managerial matters. The cost principles set forth in Circular A-122 exemplify OMB's traditional budget and management policy authority.

OMB Circulars are binding upon the Executive agencies as a matter of Presidential policy. Agencies, in turn, incorporate the provisions and requirements of applicable OMB Circulars into grant and contract agreements through regulations, grant or contract terms, or other means. In this manner, the Circular provisions become legally binding upon contractors and grantees. Indeed, provisions of OMB Circulars have been held legally applicable to grantees even when the grant-making agency has not explicitly implemented the Circular. *Qonaar Corporation* v. *Metropolitan Atlanta Rapid Transit Authority*, 441 F. Supp. 1168, 1172 (N.D. Ga. 1977).

This revision, like the cost principles disallowing advertising, fundraising, entertainment, and investment management costs, is directly related to the efficient and economical administration of grants, contracts, and other agreements. By prohibiting the use of grant and contract monies for lobbying (unless specifically authorized by statute), funds can be directed toward their proper uses, thereby achieving greater public benefit. As the Comptroller General has noted, "The cost principles applicable to all Federal grantees is the appropriate mechanism to achieve these ends [of ensuring that

program funds are not used for lobbying]." GAO/HRD-82-106 (September 24, 1982), at 27.

As noted, the Comptroller General believes that OMB has the clear legal authority to issue the Circular amendment published today, and supports it.

B. First Amendment Considerations

Some commenters suggested that the revision might, under certain circumstances, be construed as imposing unconstitutional burdens on First Amendment freedoms of speech, association, and the right to petition Congress. Most of these objections appear to follow, in large measure, an analysis of the proposed revision prepared by the Congressional Research Service (CRS) which, as indicated, noted that constitutional questions might be raised but ultimately did not conclude that the proposal was unconstitutional in any respect. Constitutional objections to the revised November proposal were sharply reduced, apparently in response to the May 1983 decision of the Supreme Court in *Regan* v. *Taxation With Representation of Washington*, 103 S. Ct. 1997. That case reemphasized that nonprofit entities do not have a First Amendment right to have their political advocacy activities subsidized by the Federal government and essentially satisfies the principal constitutional concerns raised during the comment period. OMB, however, has carefully reviewed the comments and, where improvements in phrasing could be made to eliminate ambiguity or provide clarity, appropriate changes have been made.

Intent Underlying the Circular. Some commenters suggested that the revision was the product of an unconstitutional discriminatory purpose, an alleged intent to "defund the left." Assuming, *arguendo*, that the allegation is relevant as a matter of law in overriding the actual effect of the revision, this concern is without foundation. As more fully explained in the November 1983 notice, the intent behind the revision is nondiscriminatory, and its effects are politically neutral. It is designed, as a matter of sound management practice, to extend to nonprofit grantees and contractors a cost reimbursement policy already applicable to similarly situated profit-making entities. The revision is intended only to ensure that Federal funds are not used to subsidize lobbying efforts. The revision is content neutral and is not intended "to discourage or in any way penalize organizations for lobbying efforts conducted with their own funds." 48 FR at 50860. Furthermore, nothing in these neutral accounting principles provides any basis for concern that they will be applied in anything but an impartial, objective fashion. Accordingly, the revision passes constitutional muster. *Regan* v. *Taxation With Representation of Washington*, 103 S. Ct. 1997, 2002–2003.

Overbreadth. Some commenters claimed that the revision violates the First Amendment because its provisions are overbroad and not drafted "precisely" and "narrowly" enough. For example, the League of Women Voters expressed concern that the language of the revision somehow might require "disclosures concerning the source of funds for private lobbying and certain other political activities," in violation of its freedom of association and right of privacy.

Upon review of the comments, OMB believes that the "overbreadth" claims are defective. This is particularly so in light of the elimination of the so-called "tainting" theory, under which Federal reimbursement would have been disallowed for the entire cost of any supplies, equipment, or services of a nonprofit organization used even partially for lobbying or advocacy activities. The November proposal and this final version have dropped the "tainting" approach in favor of a much more narrowly crafted "allocation" approach, in which only the actual amounts expended are deemed unallowable—an amendment that more than satisfies all overbreadth concerns. Moreover, this allegation applies with greater force to the current, vague bar in the Circular and to the statutory bars earlier noted.

Vagueness. Other commenters suggested that the proposed revision was impermissibly vague. For example, the National Education Association contended that "the revised proposal is so ambiguous and vague that organizations would not know how to comply with them and OMB could interpret them arbitrarily and apply them unequally," and the American

Friends Service Committee alleged that "[t]his [proposal] will tend to chill advocacy efforts of organizations for fear of jeopardizing Federal grants and contracts." Some commenters, including the League of Women Voters, also claimed that the proposal leaves nonprofits with no better guidance on unallowable costs than before.

Upon review of the comments, OMB finds these claims wholly unpersuasive. As noted above, the management consideration driving this revision is the desire to provide a clear, uniform definition of unallowable activities, so that grantees and contractors will know what is expected of them and can conform their conduct to the guidelines, and so that agencies and auditors will have more explicit standards to which to refer than are now available. The suggestions about vagueness are wholly speculative and without any real basis. However, in order to avoid any possible ambiguity and provide explicit guidance to nonprofit entities, the final revision has been revised in several respects, and a section-by-section explanation of the operation of the revision provided. In particular, as described in detail below, the proposed definitional phrase "lobbying and related activities" has been changed to "lobbying," and the standard "costs associated with" term has been used to clarify application of subparagraphs a and b. Finally, section (c)(5) of the proposal provides for advance clarification procedures between agencies and grantees, which should further assist in the development of a fair evolutionary process of implementing the final revision and its objective of limiting Federal subsidization of lobbying.

Recordkeeping. Finally, some commenters suggested that the revision's reporting and recordkeeping requirements somehow would burden or chill the First Amendment rights of nonprofit entities. These recordkeeping requirements comply fully, however, with the Supreme Court's decision in *Regan, see* 103 S. Ct. at 2000 n.6, and are consistent with accepted accounting principles. In fact, they constitute one of the major factors which eliminates any alleged potential for "unfettered administrative discretion" about which other commenters, notably CRS, objected. These requirements have been intentionally made *less* onerous and far more explicit than those provided by OMB management circulars in other circumstances for other types of costs. *See* the current Circular A–122, and Circular A–110: "Uniform Administrative Requirements" for nonprofit organizations, and compare with section c(4) of the revision. As noted above, one of OMB's primary goals has been to reduce the burden on nonprofit entities during the audit process and to reduce the amount of bookkeeping material auditors may demand in challenging the allowability of their lobbying costs.

The revision simply requires nonprofit entities to "maintain adequate records to demonstrate that the determination of costs as being allowable or unallowable pursuant to paragraph B21 complies with the requirements of this Circular." The paragraph does not call for separate establishment of the lobbying and non-lobbying activities of an entity. Indeed, in the case of indirect-cost employees who spend 25% or less of their time engaging in lobbying, there is no requirement that they maintain time logs, calendars, or similar records. The grantee or contractor, in such instances, exercises full discretion over its recordkeeping activities.

In sum, the recordkeeping requirements are lawful, reasonable, and by no means burdensome relative to other unallowable cost activities.

C. Relationship With Internal Revenue Code Provisions

Some commenters suggested that the Circular A–122 revision was not necessary because the Internal Revenue Code's restrictions regarding "influencing legislation" by 501(c)(3) organizations already provide sufficient protection against lobbying abuse. Others claimed that the revision could create confusion or needlessly increase the paperwork burden on grantees and contractors already regulated by the Code provisions. Neither of these arguments is valid.

The lobbying restrictions of the Internal Revenue Code and Circular A–122 serve entirely different functions. The Code has no direct bearing on preventing the use of grantee funds for lobbying purposes, because it governs only the use of private funds and does not concern the use of Federal monies. The sole purpose of the Code provisions is to define the character and status of organizations that will be entitled to favorable tax treatment. As long as lobbying expenditures do not exceed a certain portion of its revenues, an organization is eligible for tax-exempt status under the Code (assuming it also meets the qualifying tests in other areas). The Code's lobbying provisions determine only whether an organization is sufficiently devoted to a public purpose to justify preferential tax treatment.

The Code does not address the distinct question of whether Federal grant monies should be used to reimburse lobbying costs—the sole problem addressed by the Circular A–122 cost standards. The Code's lobbying provisions thus do not preempt or otherwise make unnecessary the promulgation of cost standards in this area. Indeed, the fact that the Code's lobbying provisions do not address the use of grant monies for lobbying has been implicitly recognized by Congress on numerous occasions through appropriation bill riders prohibiting such expenditures. *See, e.g.,* Pub. L. 97–377, section 509; Pub. L. 96–74, section 607.

The fact that certain expenditures by nonprofit organizations are lawful under the Code does not mean that Federal grant monies should be spent for those purposes. For example, the Code does not prohibit tax-exempt organizations from spending their revenues on advertising or entertainment. Circular A–122, however, allows only certain advertising costs, and disallows all entertainment costs, from reimbursement from Federal awards. Moreover, the Code does not preclude additional conditions from being imposed on tax-exempt organizations. For example, Section 503 of the Code denies tax-exempt status in certain instances to organizations using their revenues for the private gain of controlling individuals. That provision does not prevent disallowance of the use of Federal grant monies for the advancement of private partisan or financial interests. This point is perhaps best highlighted by the fact that nothing in the Code would prevent some grantees from spending all of their grant funds for lobbying purposes.

Similarly, the fact that the Code and other provisions of law regulate lobbying activities of business firms (*e.g.*, 26 U.S.C. 162(e); Federal Election Campaign Act, 2 U.S.C. 431–456) does not mean that there should be no provisions in the FAR regarding such activities. Some members of the business community suggested that any provisions in Circular A-122 regarding the unallowability of lobbying expenditures should be superseded by definitions of lobbying set forth in the Federal Regulation of Lobbying Act, 2 U.S.C. 261–270. The commenters have cited no authority, however, to support the view that the Code, lobbyist registration laws, or any other statutes obviate the propriety of the government's assuring that Federal grant and contract funds are spent only for authorized purposes and, to the degree feasible, that they be used to provide direct goods and services to intended beneficiaries.

Although the Code and Circular A-122 lobbying provisions serve different purposes, in practice the information and accounting practices necessary to satisfy these two authorities largely overlap so that it will generally be possible for both provisions to operate harmoniously. The Code provides a set of operational principles with which nonprofit organizations are already familiar. Thus, wherever possible, the final revision brings Circular A-122 into greater conformity with those sections of the Code dealing with nonprofit entities. Where differences remain, Circular A-122 is generally narrower in its application than the Code—and often far narrower. Thus, nonprofit entities should be able to adhere to the lobbying cost standard using existing accounting and bookkeeping systems.

While some commenters argued that Circular A-122 as revised would require all nonprofits to maintain multiple sets of books, no commenter was able to specify why simultaneous compliance with the Code and A-122 required such double recordkeeping. As discussed in the section concerning Paperwork Reduction Act considerations, a nonprofit organization maintaining adequate financial records should be able to comply fully with information requests from the Internal Revenue Service or its granting Federal agency.

Further, section c(4) of the revision effectively exempts almost all employees (those that spend less than 25% of their time on unallowable lobbying activities) from any requirements to keep time logs, calendars, or similar records relating to indirect cost time.

D. Restricting the Flow of Information

Many of the critical nonprofit commenters asserted that it is crucial for them to be allowed to "educate" policymakers on pending legislation, and that the revision will impede their testimony and other assistance to legislators, by restricting the use of Federal grant and contract funds for lobbying activities. The National Education Association, for example, alleged that "the proposed revisions would have an adverse effect on the government and on nonprofit organizations through discouraging communication with Congress and disallowing activities that are vitally important to nonprofit organizations." Most such commenters seemed to premise their comments on the ground that the proposal would prevent them from even attending legislative hearings or analyzing legislation. Others claimed that, should Federal funds not be available, there would be no other manner in which legislators could receive their valuable information.

OMB has repeatedly stated that the only effect of the revision is intended to prevent *Federal funds* being expended for lobbying purposes, and that nothing in the revision limits the ability of nonprofit entities to lobby with their own funds. OMB has made every effort to clarify the terms of the revision so as to eliminate such misconceptions about the scope of what is unallowable. Hence, various language changes have been made in the revision, especially in sections a(5) and b(1). It was never intended, for example, that funding for all attendance at legislative hearings would be proscribed, but only that that funding for attendance connected with or in knowing preparation for a lobbying effort would be precluded. The final version removes any doubt on this score.

The revision will not restrict the legitimate flow of factual information requested by the legislators, who are in the best position to know what they need to discharge their functions in our system of government. Even in the context of contractor and grantee lobbying, section b(1) has been designed to avoid such interference with formal congressional hearing and normal informational interchange processes.

E. Evidence of Confusion Regarding Current Lobbying Restrictions

Several commenters argued that too few instances of the use of Federal funds for lobbying activities had been cited to justify the revision. However, as noted in the November proposal, the number of adjudicated violations was limited by enforcement difficulties, not necessarily an absence of abuses. Before the revision, it has been very difficult for auditors to obtain evidence of outright violations or fraud that could be prosecuted, or of mistakes in application, so they could be corrected. Such items were typically carried on the books as part of an organization's indirect costs, and not broken out by category.

While various statutes mandate that taxpayer funds not be used for lobbying on legislation and electioneering, and while there is clear policy consensus that no Federal funds should be spent for these purposes, the Inspectors General have reported that effective auditing of the use of Federal funds for lobbying is not possible under the existing Circular. For example, Charles Dempsey, HUD's Inspector General and Chairman of the Prevention Committee of the President's Council on Integrity and Efficiency, has stated that:

> We do not believe that effective auditing of the use of Federal funds for lobbying purposes is possible under the current OMB Circular A-122. Moreover, we do not believe that, given the current Circular, it is possible to know or otherwise assess the extent to which Federal funds are used for lobbying purposes.

However, even with the current auditing difficulties, a number of instances have been uncovered in which there is, at a minimum, confusion on the part of agencies and grantees as to allowable and unallowable costs in the area of lobbying. Examples include:

• A Department of Education grantee under the Women's Educational Equity Act Program recently conducted a two-day conference in Washington, D.C. According to the conference program, one afternoon was largely devoted to a discussion of "political action and participation." The other afternoon was devoted in its entirety to "a visit to Capitol Hill and meeting with legislators." The program itself noted that the conference had been funded by the Department of Education.

• A September 1982 GAO study of grantees under Title X of the Public Health Service Act audited representative grantees, and found that some incurred "expenses that, in our opinion, raised questions as to adherence with Federal lobbying restrictions." GAO/HRD-82-106.

• GAO found that a mass transportation grantee prepared and distributed a newsletter, a portion of which urged its readers to write to the Congress to support continued funding of a "People Mover Project." *The agency was deemed responsible* for not informing its grantees that expenditures of grant funds for this purpose were not permissible. (B-202 975, November 3, 1981.)

As noted, the GAO in September 1982, recommended a cost circular revision on lobbying. And, as further noted, the current revison has been prepared in active consultation with the GAO, which supports it. The revision will now make it possible for the Federal government to better ensure that appropriated monies reach their proper objective, while limiting the amount of documentation auditors may demand from nonprofit entities in auditing and negotiating situations. Similarly, for the first time, organizations will have clarified responsibilities and incentives for proper documentation, which will benefit both the private sector and the government.

F. The Proposed Revision Was Not Sufficiently Restrictive

Many commenters argued that the proposed revision was not sufficiently restrictive to curb abuses in this area. For example, the American Legislative Exchange Council, the largest individual membership organization of state legislators, argued that the revised proposal would not achieve the necessary fundamental reforms. "There is a tremendous concern across the country that some groups are using Federal dollars to advance their own narrow political interests before Congress and State legislatures • • • we believe these regulations should be stronger in requiring a strict accounting of Federal grant money."

Similarly, Taxpayers for Less Government recommended broadening the definition of unallowable lobbying to include the lobbying of several types of government entities not covered under the November proposal, such as school boards and independent regulatory commissions. It also recommended that all forms of legislation be explicitly covered, including bills, appropriations, declarations, ratifications and calls for conventions. It also contended that, "[c]ourt cases on any of these areas should also be prohibited with the use of tax funds; if a group has a legal dispute, the taxpayer should not have to underwrite the extensive litigation process."

The Stockholder Sovereignty Society advocated several changes to tighten the revision: (1) Assess double or treble damages against violators; (2) debar violators from participating for five years in the particular program from which funds were diverted for lobbying or related activities; and (3) debar any parent, subsidiary, or other controlled organization of violators.

Many other commenters opposed the omission of local level lobbying from the revision, contending that there is no rational basis for funding one level of lobbying (local) when another (Federal) is made unallowable. Many also argued that the revised Circular should reflect the principle of "preemption." For example, the United States Business and Industrial Council stated "[n]onprofit organizations should be required to choose between political activism and Federal subsidies. Preemption would allow nonprofits to lobby, but only on condition that they disavow Federal funds." Such an approach would be far more restrictive than OMB's January 1983 proposal.

Braddock Publications argued that, with adoption of the allocation method,

the 25% recordkeeping rule created an unfortunate loophole. "A '10% rule' would be more reasonable and would still address the concerns of those groups which lobby very little."

OMB has carefully considered but not accepted these suggestions. In OMB's judgment, the November 1983 revision, as modified in this final publication, constitutes a major, workable management initiative which represents the best achievable compromise among the interested parties, while fully protecting their interests. OMB also considered and rejected more extensive "sunshine" provisions which would have called for full disclosure by recipient organizations of detailed information concerning their personnel, public policy positions, affiliations of officers and directors, publications, and other such information. OMB believes such reporting requirements would exceed those necessary to achieve the purpose of this revision to ensure that Federally appropriated funds are not used for lobbying activities by grantees and contractors.

VII. Analysis of Comments and Resulting Changes to Proposal

The revision creates a new paragraph in Attachment B to Circular A-122, to be called "B21 Lobbying." Paragraph B21 consists of three subparagraphs, which in turn contain a total of thirteen sections.

A. Unallowable Lobbying— Subparagraph a

Enforcement of the current restrictions on tax-funded lobbying has been hampered by the lack of a clear definition of what activities are unallowable. In constructing the definitions and standards in this revision, OMB has drawn where appropriate upon experience with the Internal Revenue Code, statutory provisions, Defense, GSA, and NASA procurement regulations, and similar authorities. Great care has been taken to avoid prohibiting reimbursement for activities that are legitimately necessary to fulfill the purposes of a grant or contract.

Subparagraph a defines five categories of lobbying activities that are unallowable for reimbursement. It should be read in conjunction with subparagraph b. which establishes exceptions to these provisions.

B. Electioneering—Sections a (1) and a(2).

Section a(1) makes unallowable certain electioneering activities at the Federal, state, or local levels. It applies both to referenda, initiatives and similar campaigns, as well as to elections of candidates to office. The restrictions should be familiar to nonprofit organizations, since they are prohibited by 26 U.S.C 501(c)(3). This section is narrower than the Code in one respect, however, because it is confined to "contributions, endorsements, publicity, or similar activity," while the Code broadly prohibits "participat[ing] or interven[ing], directly or indirectly" * *."

Section a(2) makes unallowable the financial or administrative support of political entities—including political parties, campaigns, political action committees, or other organizations—for the purpose of influencing elections. Thus, it bars indirect support of electioneering activities through intermediaries. This section also follows the definition of disqualifying activities under the Internal Revenue Code.

Very few commenters disagreed with the principle that use of Federal funds for electioneering and political activities should be disallowed. Some, however, argued against the "disallowance of costs associated with participation in referenda, initiatives, and similar procedures." For instance, the Catholic Social Service of Santa Clara asserted that lobbying expenditures should be allowable if incurred for an educational purpose. OMB agrees that the cost of educational activities should be allowable if they are educational and nothing more. But if the activities go further than helping persons accumulate data or comprehend its meaning, and involve partisan political activity or steps designed to influence the outcome of an election, they constitute activity that should not receive Federal funding.

The American Jewish Congress also argued that section a(1) would severely restrict political campaign involvement by organizations classified under the Internal Revenue Code as 501(c)(4) groups, which face minimal restrictions as to their political involvement. As

noted above, the Code's restrictions serve merely to classify organizations for purposes of taxability. By contrast, the cost principles established through Circular A-122—including this revision—define permissable uses of Federal grant or contract money, without regard to the organization's tax status. The revision does not in any respect limit an organization's right to engage in campaign activities with its own funds.

C. Attempts To Influence Legislation—Sections a(3) and a(4)

Section a(3) makes unallowable the costs of attempts to influence Federal or state legislation through contacts with government officials. This section confines the reach of unallowable lobbying to legislative decisionmaking, and does not apply to Executive Branch lobbying, with the exception of attempts to influence a decision to sign or veto legislation, and attempts to use state and local officials as conduits for grantee and contractor lobbying of Congress or state legislatures. The coverage of section a(3) is more limited than the current prohibitions in the Internal Revenue Code, and the FAR, in that it does not apply to legislative lobbying at the local level (e.g., matters such as obtaining zoning changes, police protection, or permits). Since there is no rigorous separation between legislative and executive authority at the local level, it would be difficult to construct or enforce a rule regarding legislative lobbying at that level.

Efforts to influence state and local officials to accomplish the lobbying activities defined in section a(3) are likewise unallowable. Thus, the Federal government will not reimburse an organization for the cost of meeting with mayors or city council representatives if the purpose is to convince them to lobby the Congress for legislation that the grantee or contractor favors.

The comments raised few objections to the basic soundness of the proscriptions in section a(3), although some argued that the broad coverage of the January 1983 proposal was more appropriate than the more-limited scope of the November proposal. The Conservative Caucus suggested that the costs of attempts to influence rulemakings (as well as legislation) and of local level lobbying should be added to the list of unallowable activities. Similarly, the Fairness Committee argued that reimbursement should not be allowed for *any* Executive Branch lobbying, and not simply decisions to sign or veto legislation. After careful consideration, OMB has decided not to expand the scope of this section. Rulemakings frequently have direct implications for a grantee's technical performance of its award. Furthermore, recipient organizations are likely to require regular contacts with Executive oficials in the ordinary course of managing and performing the terms of the grant or contract. As stated above, this is even more certain to be the case at the local level. The granting or witholding of Executive consent to a bill is an integral part of the legislative process, however, so that this limitation on Executive lobbying is appropriate.

One commenter, the Concho Valley Center for Human Development, objected that "prohibiting lobbying at the state level would interfere with business that is more appropriately the purview of the state legislature." Ample allowance is made in section b(2) of this revision for activities at the state level affecting the authority of an entity or the costs of performing Federal grants or contracts. Likewise, as recognized in section b(3), specific grant or contract provisions may, pursuant to Federal statutory law, make allowable certain lobbying with grant or contract funds. Apart from these exceptions, it is not the business of the Federal Government to subsidize lobbying of state legislatures.

Section a(4) deals with grass roots lobbying, and is applicable only to grass roots campaigns concerning legislation. Similar provisions are found in many appropriations riders and have been interpreted and applied by GAO on many occasions. The definition of grass roots lobbying in section a(4), however, is less inclusive than that of the Internal Revenue Code. It is limited to efforts to obtain concerted actions on the part of the public and, unlike the Code, it does ot include attempts "to affect the *opinions* of the general public," if such attempts are not intended or designed in such fashion as to have the reasonably foreseeable consequence of leading to concerted action. 26 U.S.C. 4911(d)(1)(A). The narrower reach of this

section is consistent with GAO's interpretation of the prohibitions in appropriations riders on the use of funds for "publicity or propaganda." *See, e.g.,* Comp. Gen. Op. B–202975 (Nov. 3, 1981).

It was suggested that use of the term "legislation pending," in sections a(3) and a(4) of the proposal, was ambiguous and questioned whether that phrase applied only to bills formally introduced before a deliberative assembly, or included legislation in the process of development. In response to that concern, these sections have been amended to specify that they apply when the activity in question constitutes an attempt to influence either "the introduction of Federal or state legislation" or "the enactment or modification of any pending Federal or state legislation." This language, especially when considered in conjunction with the phrase "costs associated with" which commences subparagraph a, should clarify that the costs of preparing, instigating or urging legislation not yet formally introduced are just as unallowable as lobbying with regard to bills that have already been introduced.

Several commenters, including CARE and the National Association of Manufacturers, expressed concern that costs of an activity not originally intended to promote legislative advocacy might be disallowed, after the fact, if it were later discovered that the activity or its proximate effects did in fact lead to the development and promulgation of legislation. The revision addresses this problem. The limitation on "costs associated with * * * any attempt to influence * * * legislation," as used in sections a(3) and a(4), includes costs which support or facilitate pursuing or developing legislation before its formal introduction. However, the key phrase in the final version of sections a(3) and a(4) is "attempt to." This phrase requires intent or conduct with the reasonably foreseeable consequence of initiating legislative action, or to support or facilitate such ongoing action, in order for its actions to be categorized as "unallowable."

The language of sections a(3) and a(4) has been amended in minor respects so that it tracks more closely those provisions of the Internal Revenue Code which establish the activities that constitute "influencing legislation." Section a(3) tracks 26 U.S.C. 4911(d)(1)(B), which prohibits "an attempt to influence any [Federal, state or local] legislation through communication with any member or employee of a legislative body, or with any government official or employee who may participate in the formulation of the legislation." Similarly, section a(4) follows 26 U.S.C 4911(d)(1)(A), which defines "influencing legislation" to include "any attempt to influence any [Federal, state, or local] legislation through any attempt to affect the opinions of the general public or any segment thereof." As previously noted, sections a(3) and a(4) are narrower than the comparable Code provisions in several respects.

D. Legislative Liaison—section a(5)

Section a(5) makes unallowable the cost of legislative liaison activities when they are in furtherance of unallowable activities as defined in sections a(1)–(4). While a key purpose of an organization's "legislative liaison" activity may be to direct and prepare for what has been defined in this revision as unallowable lobbying, it may also serve other functions that this revision does not make unallowable. By contrast, under the current Defense Department Supplement to the FAR, *all* legislative liaison activities are deemed unallowable.

OMB received more technical comments on this section than any other part of the proposal. Some commenters argued that, since the Internal Revenue Code does not disallow "legislative liaison" for purposes of determining organizations' tax-exempt status, neither should Circular A–122. However, the IRS does not exempt legislative liaison activities from treatment as lobbying—it merely does not recognize legislative liaison as a separate category of lobbying. Legislative liaison activities which, in the language of section a(5), were "in support of or in knowing preparation for an effort to engage in unallowable lobbying" would be covered by the IRS bar. In any event, however, and as discussed above, the revision is concerned not with determining the tax status of entities, but with the proper use of Federal funds

by recipient organizations. Use of the term "legislative liaison" in section a(5)—in its present narrow sense—can now not excuse or mask lobbying activities by grantees or contractors.

Many other commenters argued that the proposed section a(5) was ambiguous. In particular, they objected that the compound effect of prohibiting "legislative liaison" contributing to support "lobbying and related activity" was vague, and that the proposal was difficult to construe because it employed a double negative—that is, all "legislative liaison" costs were unallowable unless the activity was unrelated to lobbying. The final version of section a(5) has been revised to accommodate these concerns. The new language provides that "legislative liaison" is unallowable only "when such activities are carried on in support of or in knowing preparation for an effort to engage in unallowable lobbying."

The "knowing preparation" requirement in the final revison should avoid unintended retroactivity problems by not permitting auditors to automatically disallow legislative liaison costs in every instance where they are associated with later efforts at lobbying. While responsibility for establishing the allowability of costs rests, here as in all aspects of cost reimbursement, with the parties seeking it, the "knowing preparation" standard of section a(5) is a particularly favorable one for grantees and contractors. Thus, only those legislative liaison activities which, from their timing and subject matter, can reasonably be inferred to have had a clearly forseeable link with later lobbying fall within the "knowing preparation" standard of section a(5).

Finally, it should be noted in connection with section a(5) that the term "costs associated with," which commences subparagraph a, is fully applicable. This means that the proscription in section a(5) extends not only to costs directly attributable to performing a "legislative liaison" activity, but also to costs that support or facilitate its performance. Likewise, the technical status of a piece of legislation (*i.e.*, whether it is formally introduced, referred or enrolled) is not dispositive of the issue whether the costs of "legislative liaison activities" are unallowable within the meaning of section a(5).

E. Exceptions to Unallowable Lobbying—Subparagraph b

Subparagraph b contains three exceptions to activities disallowed under subparagraph a. The subparagraph does not necessarily make the costs of these activities *allowable;* allowability or unallowability of such costs will be determined by the terms of the grant, contract, or other agreement involved. Circular A-122 does not authorize costs or expenditures; it merely limits the allowability of costs or expenditures.

Some commenters noted that the use of the term "not unallowable" in the introductory clause to this subparagraph in the November proposal might indicate a fine legal distinction which grassroots volunteers would be unlikely to comprehend or which would lead to needless confusion. For clarity, the introduction of subparagraph b has accordingly been modified to provide that "the following activities are excepted from the coverage of subparagraph a." For this reason, activities which are not defined as lobbying by subparagraph a, *e.g.,* informational communications by organizations with its members or the distribution by organizations of nonpartisan analyses, are not set forth as separate sections of subparagraph b. To the extent that those, or any other activities, otherwise fall within the definitional terms of any section of subparagraph a, they are deemed unallowable unless they fall within the exceptions defined by subparagraph b.

F. Legislative Requests for Technical and Factual Information—Section b(1)

Section b(1) exempts from subparagraph a technical and factual presentations to a legislative audience on a topic directly related to grant or contract performance and offered upon a documented request, even though the presentation would otherwise constitute unallowable lobbying. Since contacts with legislative sources are not made unallowable in the first place unless they are for purposes of influencing legislation, this exception is relevant only to those legislative contacts made unallowable under section a(3). The

exception is meant to fulfill the specific informational needs of legislatures, and members and staffs thereof, and has been revised extensively to reflect concerns expressed in the comments and by members of the interested Congressional committees.

The term "technical advice or assistance," used in the November 1983 proposal to define the scope of the exception, has been changed to provide that costs of rendering "technical and factual presentation of information" may be excepted. The term "factual" was added after "technical" to clarify that, to be reimbursable, the services rendered in a section b(1) situation must be overridingly informational in purpose and content, and not advocatory. However, the fact that an advocatory conclusion is reached does not in itself make the presentation unallowable. As previously indicated, this exception will avoid separate accountings and disallowances for each kernel of information provided in a lobbying effort, and will restrict the exception to "presentation[s]" which are in fact and which would be clearly seen as "technical and factual" in character. This change will allow and advocatory conclusion to be communicated with no disallowance for the time and effort involved in preparing or communicating the conclusion, provided of course that it clearly and naturally flows from the technical and factual data presented and is a distinctly minor aspect of the overall presentation. In addition, the lobbying effort excepted by section b(1) is confined to information on a topic directly related to the performance of a grant, contract or other agreement.

A requirement that the presentation of such information is to be provided through "hearing testimony, statements or letters" also has been added to the scope provision, in response to a Congressional suggestion. This change helps clarify that, with the exception of travel, meals and lodging costs in connection with a(3) lobbying, such information need not necessarily be tendered in formal testimony to fall within this exception.

Discussions with Congressional staffs revealed concerns that legislators' routine business of information gathering in connection with hearings, drafting bills and other legislative functions might be hampered if the types of requests sufficient to invoke the section b(1) exception did not include oral requests; especially by telephone. Accordingly, the condition that the request be "written" has been changed to a requirement that it be "documented." The final version of section b(1) de-emphasizes the necessity for stringent request documentation requirements. The section also now states explicitly that the technical information exception is invoked by notices in the *Congressional Record* requesting testimony or statements for the record at regularly scheduled hearings. Some persons suggested that some of the routine information-gathering functions of the legislative bodies might be disrupted if such notices and responses to them were not specifically included in section b(1). As indicated below, for its costs to be excepted, the presentation must not only be of a "technical and factual" nature, but must also be "readily obtainable and can be readily put in deliverable form."

Several commenters expressed uncertainty about the requirement that, to fall within the exception, technical advice or assistance to legislative bodies must be "in response to a *specific* * * * request." The term "specific" has therefore been deleted from this final version of section b(1). This change does not affect the underlying intent that requests sufficient to invoke this exception must be *bona fide*, may not be open-ended or indeterminate, and must not be made for the purpose of circumventing the subparagraph a restrictions.

Section b(1) now requires that the request for information be "made by the *recipient* member, legislative body or subdivision, or a cognizant staff member thereof." This language, articulating a condition implicit in the November 1983 version, makes explicit that the person or committee requesting the information should be the recipient, so that, for example, a request by one employee of the legislative branch could not be advanced as justification for allowing the costs of a lobbying mailing to each Member of Congress.

The term "cognizant staff member" has been inserted in response to

Congressional comments that the November 1983 language might require personal attention by legislators to each request for factual or technical information. Linking the request from a staff member to that person's "cognizance" of the matters for which the information is sought is intended to ensure that the request is a *bona fide* request for information of a truly factual and technical nature, not otherwise readily available to the legislators.

When the above changes were made to greatly ease the implementation of the exception, it became necessary to put some limit on the costs that grantees and contractors could charge the Federal government when undertaking such lobbying. With the elimination of the requirement for a written request, and the addition of the provision allowing *Congressional Record* notices to suffice for providing such information at government expense, a corresponding potential was created for unduly substantial Federal financing of lobbying.

In order to ensure that the information and its preparation are the true bases of the cost, section b(1) has been revised to require that the response must be information that "is readily obtainable and can be put in readily deliverable form." (This provision is intended to restrict and relate to the costs of acquisition and delivery of information, not the time involved in responding to requests.) Provision of such assistance justifies invoking the exception only when the information is known or obtainable—and in such form—as to be readily produced and delivered. The section b(1) exception was included in order that legislators could draw on the expertise and data possessed by nonprofit organizations—even while offered as part of a lobbying effort. This section, however, does *not* justify paying for research projects or otherwise incurring significant charges to grants or contracts to develop information not readily at hand.

Likewise, in order to limit Federal payment for lobbying to technical and factual presentations most likely to produce expert information not readily obtainable elsewhere, the further requirement has been added that the presentation be linked to information "derived from the performance of a grant, contract or other agreement." This provision permits the exception to be invoked for information not only derived from grants or contracts presently in effect but also information on topics directly related to grant or contract performance. Nonetheless, a direct nexus between the topic of a grant, contract or other agreement and the technical and factual presentation will be required to be shown.

While the revision seeks to maximize the free flow of information from Federal fund recipients to Congress, this does not mean to allow grant funds to pay for lobbying trips to Washington simply because part of that trip was devoted to delivering information to a staff member, or delivering essentially unsolicited statements or testimony to a Committee hearing.

To deal with this problem, the revision provides that Federally-reimbursable costs under this exception could not include travel, lodging or meal costs, except when incurred for the purpose of providing Committee hearing-testimony upon written request for a technical and factual presentation. To help ensure that the Federal financing of lobbying trips to Washington is limited to those which Congress deems necessary to its decision-making, the revision provides that these otherwise restricted costs (travel, lodging and meals) can only be "incurred to offer testimony at a regularly scheduled Congressional hearing pursuant to a written request for such presentation made by the Chairman or Ranking Minority Member of the Committee or Subcommittee conducting such hearing." To the degree possible, the cost of providing information requested by legislators should be paid for out of the legislative budget. Both houses of the Congress have rules providing for payment of expenses relating to Congressional testimony. (*See,* Senate Resolution 538, 96–2; House Rule 35.)

The American Civil Liberties Union challenged the entire section b(1) exception on the grounds that linking the exception to a special legislative invitation constitutes an impermissible regulation of free speech on the basis of content. The reimbursement provisions set forth in section b(1) do not discriminate against any person's speech but turn instead on the type of assistance rendered. Under *Regan,* the

Supreme Court has ruled that no entity has a right to have its speech subsidized with Federal funds. Thus, it is constitutional to establish general cost guidelines to clarify the types of lobbying for which the government will provide reimbursement. Indeed, this section is based upon a similar provision in the Internal Revenue Code. It bears repeating that nothing in this revision prohibits grantees or contractors from conducting any form of lobbying or making any kind of communication to Congress they wish, as long as they do so with their own funds.

G. State Level Lobbying Related to Performance of Grant or Contract— Section b(2)

Section b(2) exempts lobbying otherwise unallowable under section a(3) to influence state legislation in order to directly reduce the cost or to avoid impairment of the organization's authority to perform a grant, contract, or other agreement. Such lobbying is permitted because it can directly benefit the Federal government by helping minimize the costs of award performance. The exception does *not,* however, permit the use of Federal funds to lobby state legislatures to promote an organization's ideological objectives merely because those objectives are consonant with the purposes of the grant or contract.

A primary concern for several national organizations that commented on this proposal was the problem of determining how closely legislation must directly affect the performance of a grant or contract in order to fall within the proposed exception. A related concern was the possibility that an activity could serve multiple purposes, some of which would and some of which would not "directly relate" to the organization's grant mission.

In the final version, the term "directly affecting" has been deleted, and other changes made to the language to clarify the precise scope of the exception. Thus, the lobbying affected by the exception is specified to be only that made unallowable by section a(3). Additionally, the phrase "at the state level" was deleted in favor of the greater clarity provided by the phrase "to influence state legislation." Finally, the phrase "or related activity" after "lobbying" has been dropped, consistent with changes throughout the revision.

The most significant substantive change made to this section was deletion of the phrase "ability of the organization," which several commenters argued was far too broad. For example, the "ability of the organization" to perform a grant, contract, or other agreement could be construed to include those secondary, tangential, or speculative aspects of the activity that the November 1983 preamble indicated did not fit properly within the exception. 48 FR at 50865. OMB has deleted this language and replaced it with a reference to an organization's basic "authority" to perform the activity, thus eliminating the potentially overbroad applications that could be associated with the term "ability." The potential for such abuse is made evident by the incident described below:

ANNAPOLIS, March 7—Administrators of two community-based programs for the mentally retarded led several hundred clients in a demonstration here today in support of bills that would raise employes' salaries and exempt their organizations from state procurement laws * * *

[The demonstration organizer] said that all participants in today's demonstration had been "educated intensively" about the reason for the demonstration and had elected to come, although some might have forgotten by the time they arrived, he said * * *

Demonstration organizers defended the tactic saying the bills, if approved, will directly affect the clients by improving the quality of care they receive * * * [See, *Washington Post,* March 8, 1984, pp. Cl, C5.]

Under the November 1983 proposal, a strained argument could be made under the concept of "ability to perform" that the lobbying on the bills described above should fit within the exemption—a wholly unintended and inappropriate result. By focusing on an organization's "authority" instead of its "ability" to perform, the revised language should eliminate any confusion as to what was intended by the exception. Moreover, by modifying the reference to "cost" to include only cost reductions, the revised language precludes lobbying for higher salaries and reflects the point made in the November 1983 preamble, that the

exception is intended to allow lobbying for lower costs or better performance of grants or contracts. These changes guarantee that the only lobbying costs reimbursable under the exception will be those that relate to the organization's direct performance of the grant or contract in the most cost-efficient manner possible, or its very authority to perform the grant or contract.

A state waiver clause was added to the November 1983 notice in response to concerns raised by some nonprofit organizations. That clause would have permitted states to make Federally reimbursable the costs of all state lobbying by their Federally-funded subgrantees. Upon further review, however, the clause was determined to be superfluous, and potentially troublesome for several reasons. Some nonprofit commenters found the exception confusing, subject to partisan political pressures, and a needless cause of complexity for grant rules. Under none of Circular A-122's other 50 cost categories do states have the right to determine which costs will be eligible for Federal reimbursement. Furthermore, any lobbying "to influence State legislation in order to directly reduce the cost, or to avoid material impairment of the organization's authority to perform the grant, contract or other agreement," is already excepted by the remainder of section b(2).

H. Lobbying Authorized by Statute— Section b(3)

Section b(3) exempts any activity specifically authorized by statute to be undertaken with funds from Federal grants, contracts, or other agreements. This technical section reflects that the provisions of this Circular do not override statutory law. Only minor wording changes—with no change of substance—were made from the wording of this provision in the November proposal.

I. Exceptions Deleted from November Proposal

Section c(2) in the November 1983 proposal specified that communications with Executive Branch officials would not be unallowable, with two exceptions now set out in section a(3): (1) To influence a decision to sign or veto legislation, or (2) to influence state or local officials to serve as conduits for unallowable lobbying activities. This section had been inserted solely for the purpose of clarifying that the only Executive Branch communications regulated by the revision are those relating to signing or vetoing legislation, or serving as a lobbying conduit.

On the other hand, it is not intended that proscriptions should be created by implication from the fact that a type of activity is not specifically excepted in subparagraph b. Hence, section c(2) has been omitted entirely, since the only Executive Branch contacts unallowable in the first place are those dealing with a decision to sign or veto enrolled bills, as specified in section a(3). As indicated by the new language introducing subparagraph b, the final version of the subparagraph contains only exceptions to activities which are otherwise unallowable.

Section c(3) of the November proposal also has been deleted, since other provisions of the revision make it superfluous. This section concerned the application of the "tainting" principle of the Janury proposal which was eliminated in the November proposal and replaced by the current proportional "allocation" principle. The inclusion of section c(3) in the November revision was inadvertent and has been corrected.

J. Accounting Treatment of Unallowable Costs—Subparagraph c.

As with the Federal Acquisition Regulation and as is already the case under Circular A-122's general rules for unallowable costs, the costs identified as unallowable by this revision include not only costs of the direct activity itself but also the costs of other activities supporting that activity. For example, if a lobbyist spends four hours lobbying the Congress and an additional eight hours in study, consultation, and preparation for the lobying, the full twelve hours, with the cost of any support services and any other costs attributable to the lobbying activity, are disallowed.

As emphasized in the comment published with the text of the November proposal, only the portion of those cost items allocable to the lobbying activity is unallowable. Thus, if an employee spends 60% of his time on lobbying

activities and 40% on Federal grant activities, 40% of the salary may be allocated to the grant. This approach is consistent with the FAR lobbying cost treatment provision, as well as with the traditional accounting method of prorating costs between allowable and unallowable activities.

OMB considered and rejected an alternative method of allocating costs of items used for both lobbying activities and grant or contract purposes, namely, the concept that no Federal money can be used to pay for any portion of a cost item used for lobbying activities: (1) In any way, or (2) over 5% of the time. The OMB proposal published in January 1983 followed this stricter approach. Commenters argued that it would increase the cost of performing Federal grants and contracts by effectively requiring them to separate their lobbying activities from their grant or contract activities and could also lead to inefficient duplication of equipment and facilities. They also argued that it would burden the First Amendment rights of contractors and grantees because engaging in lobbying activities could result in otherwise legitimate costs being disallowed. As set forth in the November notice, OMB has adopted a different approach which alleviates these concerns and serves the goal of assuring government neutrality by disallowing reimbursement of Federally appropriated funds used for certain types of lobbying.

K. Indirect Cost Rate Proposal—section c(1)

Subparagraph c establishes an administrative framework for the overall revision. Section c(1) follows current cost allocation principles familiar to grantees and contractors and establishes a general format similar to that now applicable to comparable unallowable activities.

Indirect cost rate negotiations are conducted between an organization and a single cognizant agency on an organization-by-organization, rather than on a grant-by-grant basis. This approach saves agencies and recipient organizations considerable time and effort in cases where the organization receives more than one grant or contract. The revision has been modified to reflect this approach. Further, section c(1) follows existing accounting practice and emphasizes that lobbying costs must be identified and dealt with appropriately, in accordance with the Circular's indirect cost rate provisions.

Although very few commenters criticized section c(1), some—including Congressional sources—expressed concern that the November proposal's language could be broadly interpreted by agency auditors. Further, they suggested that lobbying costs, because of their political nature, should be subject to only very limited, if any, disclosure.

The purpose of section c(1) was simply to require accounting information necessary for the government to calculate the reimbursement of indirect (overhead) costs. Such information is already made available to auditors through existing recordkeeping requirements in Circulars A–122 and A–110.

However, to clarify OMB's intent to request only the minimum amount of accounting data to comply with existing accounting guidelines, OMB has rewritten section c(1) following consultation with GAO and Congressional staffs. In essence, only the minimal information that is needed for the calculation of Federally-reimbursed overhead costs is now required, and organizations are completely exempt from this section if they do not seek such Federal reimbursement.

The new section c(1) says that only the *total* lobbying costs must be identified in the indirect cost rate proposal. This will allay concerns of nonprofit groups that separate accountings and disclosures were mandated for each of the five component definitions of lobbying set forth in sections a(1)–a(5). Moreover, since this information is made necessary only for indirect cost calculations in order to avoid Federal subsidization of the lobbying process, this sentence also explicitly makes clear that no such disclosure is required by the revision unless the grantee seeks reimbursement for indirect costs. (See also, Internal Revenue Service Form 990, requiring lobbying cost disclosure, which many nonprofit organizations now submit.)

In comparison with the November proposal, the new section c(1) sharply reduces the accounting data requested, eliminates language that some thought gave agencies too much discretion in requesting information, and explicitly ties the treatment of lobbying costs to existing Circular A–122 requirements. The November proposal's requirement of "a statement, identifying by category, costs attributable in whole or in part" to lobbying, as well as the requirement of a statement of "how (lobbying costs) are accounted for," have been deleted.

When the existing Circular A–122 accounting requirements are reviewed in conjunction with the uniquely lenient recordkeeping treatment provided for lobbying in section c(4) of the revision, it becomes clear that such information is the minimum necessary to achieve an acceptable level of accounting integrity, and that the overall recordkeeping required for lobbying costs is much less than that required for any other type of allowable or unallowable cost.

It should of course be noted that the stated requirement that organizations must "separately identify" their total lobbying costs cannot be construed to limit auditors or indirect cost analysts from requiring more detailed breakdowns when such information would normally be required under existing indirect cost rate proposal guidelines. *See, e.g.,* the Department of Health and Human Services' "Guide for Nonprofit Organizations" (May 1983) at 73 (Sample Indirect Cost Proposal Format—Direct Allocation Method). Additionally, if auditors suspect that an organization may have misstated its unallowable lobbying costs, they are not constrained from requesting any data normally accessible under Circulars A–122 and A–110, as long as such data does not fall under the recordkeeping exemption provided in section c(4).

Section c(1) follows existing Circular A–122 requirements that provide for the general disclosure of the costs spent on unallowable activities. This requirement is necessary so that when the government calculates the amount of an organization's indirect costs (*i.e.,* overhead) that it will pay, it does not include the costs of unallowable activities that the organization happens to account for as indirect costs. Paragraph B.3 of the existing Attachment A to Circular A–122 now requires this:

The costs of certain activities are not allowable as charges to Federal awards (see, for example, fund raising costs in paragraph 19 of Attachment B). However, even though these costs are unallowable for purposes of computing charges to Federal awards, they nonetheless must be treated as direct costs for purposes of determining indirect cost rates and be allocated their share of the organization's indirect costs if they represent activities which: (1) Include the salaries of personnel, (2) occupy space, and (3) benefit from the organization's indirect costs.

Some persons argued that unallowable costs need not be reported, since they are not Federally reimbursed. However, it is impossible for the government to properly determine the extent to which it should pay for an organization's indirect costs unless it can determine what portion of the organization's total indirect costs are from allowable activities, and what portion are unallowable. Such treatment is currently required under Circular A-122's Attachment A, Section D: "Allocation of Indirect Costs and Determination of Indirect Cost Rates."

Further, some persons argued that the disclosure requirement should expressly authorize that initial submissions in indirect cost rate proposals set forth an aggregated figure representing both lobbying and other unallowable costs. Such an approach would codify the current practices of most (but, it should be pointed out, not all) grantees, a not unsurprising fact in light of the vagueness of the current standard and the relative lack of audit resources applied to determining whether lobbying activities are supported by Federal grants and contracts. There is agreement that auditors would be able to obtain and would indeed require disaggregated information on lobbying costs if they engage in specific auditing of lobbying disallowances.

In weighing this proposal against agency auditors' concerns that detailed breakdowns of lobbying costs are critical to proper cost analyses, OMB has resolved to require that only the total amount of lobbying costs be initially disclosed in the indirect cost rate proposal. OMB has determined that it would make no sense to rely on varying and what would almost certainly be inconsistent initiatives of individual auditors, regional offices and agencies to inquire, as a matter of standard practice, into whether lobbying activities are being improperly subsidized through indirect cost allocations—or to rely on random audits to accomplish this purpose. Thus, the final revision requires, consistent with paragraph B.3 of Attachment A and at a level of specificity less than that generally provided for fundraising activities, *i.e.*, disclosure only of a total, lump sum lobbying cost figure. Disclosure of such a figure will give auditors a basis for further inquiry into lobbying cost estimates set forth in particular indirect cost rate proposals, and will provide a level of detail that actually would be minimally required in every instance in which an auditor seeks to determine whether Federal subsidization of lobbying is taking place through the overhead mechanism. Given the 25% rule which makes more difficult auditor disallowances of lobbying estimates, this balanced compromise—and reduction in the level of detail called for in the November 1983 proposal—is in OMB's judgment a minimal requirement consistent with the Circular's accounting guidelines.

L. Certification Requirement—Section c(2)

The requirement in section a(2) of the November 1983 proposal, that certification accompany the Financial Status Report, has been changed in the final version to a requirement that certification accompany an organization's annual indirect cost rate proposal. Since a Financial Status Report is required for each grant that an organization has, while an organization must file only one indirect cost rate proposal per year to cover all of its grants, this change reduces paperwork and administrative effort.

Further, lobbying expenses are usually included in indirect costs, which are calculated on an organization-wide basis. Consequently, the appropriate place to certify such costs is in the annual indirect cost rate proposal, as required under the Defense and GSA proposed revisions. In addition, most future audits will be "single audits" of all Federal funds received by the grantee, so there will be less emphasis on the Financial Status Report and more on the indirect cost rate proposal.

M. Recordkeeping—Sections c(3) and c(4)

Documentation of the amounts of allowable and unallowable costs became a necessity when the method of cost treatment was changed from total disallowance of cost items partially involved in lobbying (the January 1983 proposal) to the typical "allocation" cost treatment. The principal alternative considered by OMB was to adopt the documentation philosophy of the restrictions on lobbying in the prior Defense, GSA, and NASA procurement regulations, *i.e.*, to place the burden on the grantee or the contractor to prove in all instances the appropriateness of a cost. This approach, while consistent with the cost principles in general, would entail an implied burden on some indirect cost employees to maintain records (time logs, calendars, or the like) to establish the proportion of their time spent on lobbying. This would be of particular concern for high level officials of grantees and contractors who, in the ordinary course of business, may engage in only a small amount of lobbying. OMB (along with Defense, GSA, and NASA) will therefore allow grantees and contractors to certify in good faith the amount of their employee's time attributable to lobbying activities.

No detailed recordkeeping requirements have been included in this revision, as these requirements are generally set forth for all nonprofit organizations in OMB Circular A-110: "Grants and Agreements with Institutions of Higher Education, Hospitals, and Other Nonprofit Organizations: Uniform Administrative Requirements" (*See, e.g.,* Circular A-110, Attachments C and F.) That Circular generally requires grantees, *inter alia,* to keep for a period of three years, "[f]inancial records, supporting documents, statistical records, and all other records pertinent to [grants]," and to access for audit purposes "pertinent books, documents, papers and records of * * * recipient organizations."

Section c(3) restates the general rule for cost documentation, but is modified by section c(4), which provides that for the purposes of complying with this revision, employees are not required to prepare or maintain time logs, calendars, or similar records to document the portion of their time treated as an indirect cost. This means that the agency and auditor must rely on the employee's good-faith estimates of time spent in lobbying, or upon other evidence not otherwise precluded. As noted earlier, the absence of time logs or comparable records for indirect cost time not kept pursuant to the discretion of the grantee or contractor will not serve as a basis for government auditors disallowing claims of allowable costs by contesting unallowable lobbying time' estimates except in two distinct situations: first, where the employee spends more than 25% of his compensated hours of employment during a month lobbying; and, second, where a material misstatement of costs has been found within the preceding five years. This avoids the necessity of employees who engage in only incidental lobbying having to account for all of their time to Federal agencies. Morever, by making each calendar month an independent, operative period under section c(4), problems of retroactivity are avoided by persons unexpectedly required to engage in intensive lobbying during the latter portions of a larger operative period such as a calendar year. Alternatively, persons engaged in intensive lobbying activities during the earlier portions of such a longer operative period will not lose the protection of section c(4) during latter months of the longer period when lobbying activities fall below the 25% trigger. However, it should be stressed that in the exemption from "records which are not kept," the primary sense of the word "kept" was "created." Thus, records that would otherwise be kept in the ordinary course of business cannot be destroyed simply to avoid audit inspection merely because they are not required under this exemption.

For two significant reasons, the last sentence of this section, as proposed in the November 1983 version, has been deleted. It stated:

Agency guidance regarding the extent and nature of documentation required pursuant to subparagraph (c)(3) shall be reviewed under the criteria of the Paperwork Reduction Act to ensure that requirements are the least burdensome necessary to satisfy the objectives of this subparagraph.

Commenters questioned why, if such a provision was necessary in the first place, other laws, such as the Regulatory Flexibility Act, were not included. Such a reference to compliance with existing laws is not necessary, and the reference to the Paperwork Reduction Act was included to emphasize OMB's commitment that the sprit of this law be followed in the revision's implementation.

Moreover, the Department of Health and Human Services noted that the sentence could have been read to give agencies the mandate to develop their own regulations. As there is no reason for agencies to deviate from or add to the Circular A-122 guidelines and as agency deviations could result in multiple rules for nonprofit entities—an outcome not intended by OMB and one which would create the potential for inconsistent enforcement and excessive paperwork—this sentence was eliminated from the final version.

N. Administrative Restrictions on Agencies—Section c(5)

Section c(5) requires agencies to establish procedures for advance resolution of definitional issues arising under this revision. This will alleviate the inevitable problems of interpretation at the margin and will avoid discouraging organizations from engaging in borderline activities merely because the application of the provisions may be uncertain.

Section c(5) is not intended to impose or authorize OMB micromanagement of agencies which award grants or contracts. Agencies typically have methods of resolving disagreements or differences with their grantees and contractors, and such methods shall be deemed adequate to meet the requirements of section c(5), unless OMB review of such procedures determines that changes are necessary to comply with the intent of this section.

O. Paragraph Renumbering Provision

Paragraph 2 renumbers paragraphs B21 through B50 of Circular A-122's Attachment B. Since the cost items covered under Attachment B are numbered in alphabetical order,

"Lobbying" is appropriately designated as paragraph B21, necessitating the renumbering of former paragraphs B21 through B50 as B22 through B51.

VIII. Paperwork Reduction Act Considerations

The November notice invited "comments about the appropriateness of collection of information requirements in this proposal" to be submitted to OMB's Office of Information and Regulatory Affairs. Forty-three such comments were received. Of these, twenty expressed general concerns similar to those of other commenters but raised no specific paperwork burden issues.

The twenty-three other commenters followed, almost verbatim, points raised by the Center for Non-Profit Corporations. These alleged that a "substantial increase" in paperwork would result from the recordkeeping mandated by Circular A-122. The commenters asserted that the additional paperwork burden would occur to: (1) Meet requirements for the annual indirect cost proposal, and (2) maintain the records required to demonstrate that costs are allowable or unallowable.

However, by establishing uniform and well-defined guidelines for lobbying costs, and by explicitly restricting the paperwork that auditors can require for documentation of such costs, this revision may significantly reduce the net paperwork burden to which grantees are now legally subject. Clearly, some grantees may avoid the existing paperwork requirements by ignoring the multiple—and oftern vague—sets of lobbying reimbursement restrictions that have been issued by the various agencies, and likewise ignore the existing accounting rules in Circular A-122 regarding treatment of such costs. Such non-compliance may currently exist in part because government auditors have found it difficult to efficiently enforce the myriad of vague restrictions on lobbying costs. With the clear guidelines provided by this revision, agency and audit enforcement will increase. Those grantees already in compliance with the differing sets of restrictions will enjoy a much-reduced paperwork burden: those who have previously ignored these restrictions will find that non-compliance is more likely to be questioned by government auditors.

Moreover, regardless of whether grantees currently choose to adhere to existing rules on lobbying, most routinely maintain detailed books regarding their expenditures. Annual financial planning by the nonprofit itself and filing requirements of the Internal Revenue Service already require maintenance of detailed records.

In general, Circular A–122 will not require employees to keep a second set of books, e.g., time logs, to record lobbying. In fact, most employees who engage in lobbying are explicitly exempted from any requirements to keep time logs or other similar documents. This is because most lobbying is done by indirect cost (e.g., headquarters staff) employees, and section c(4) states that employees who certify that they spend less than 25% of their compensated time lobbying do not have to keep such records documenting that portion of their time that is treated as an indirect cost. Since employees whose time is charged directly to contracts already must keep such records, no special rule for direct cost time is necessary.

The 23 critics of the revision also submitted identical comments to the effect that "[t]ax dollars will be diverted to unnecessary paperwork and needlessly drawn away from the purpose of the organizations by these requirements." As discussed above, the fact that the revision decreases, in general, existing paperwork requirements will reduce the current recordkeeping costs incurred to comply with existing restrictions.

Some commenters argued that differing Internal Revenue Code and Circular A–122 standards would require maintenance of two sets of financial books. No commenters were able to specify any situation in which a detailed set of expenditure records for lobbying would not provide sufficient information to serve the filing or audit requirements of the Internal Revenue Service as well as those of the various grant or contracting agencies implementing the revision.

OMB will review all agency information burden requests to implement Circular A–122 according to the standards of the Paperwork Reduction Act. None of the comments OMB received from agencies mentioned any specific concern over a possible increase in paperwork.

IX. Enforcement

Circular A–122 is a management directive to Federal agencies establishing cost principles for use in connection with grants and contracts with nonprofit organizations. It does not contain its own enforcement mechanism, though its terms are incorporated in grants and contracts through agency regulations or grant instruments. The degree and nature of enforcement of these anti-lobbying provisions will depend, therefore, on operational experience and competing demands on enforcement resources.

1. *Voluntary compliance.* The bedrock for enforcing these provisions is voluntary compliance by grantees and contractors. In the past, restrictions on the use of Federal funds for lobbying have been inadequately communicated and defined. Neither agencies nor recipient organizations devoted much attention to them. This revision is expected to improve compliance significantly by:

• Defining unallowable activities so that organizations can comply in good faith; and

• Providing occasions (indirect cost rate negotiations) in which responsible officials of the grantee or contractor will focus specifically on the issue of the organization's compliance.

To assist organizations in complying, agencies are to be prepared to resolve definitional questions concerning potential expenditures in advance. This procedure should reduce the inevitable difficulty of interpretations at the margin.

2. *Sanctions.* OMB considered and rejected as too stringent a penalty provision which would require the return to the Federal government of all grant or contract funds received by a nonprofit organization found to be using Federal funds to engage in lobbying. Instead, penalties for violating this revision are the same as for violations of existing Circular A–122 provisions. The principal sanction in the event of minor or unintentional violations is cost recovery, i.e., the Federal agency will

obtain reimbursement from the contractor or grantee of misspent funds. In more serious cases, contracts and grants can be suspended or terminated, or contractors and grantees can be debarred from further awards. The availability of these sanctions for violating the anti-lobbying restrictions of appropriations legislation has been confirmed by the Office of Legal Counsel of the Department of Justice.

3. *Audits.* Contractors and grantees are currently subject to audit requirements, and to the possibility of audit by agency Inspectors General or the Comptroller General; however, only rarely have audits focused on compliance with anti-lobbying provisions due to the difficulty of determining proper adherence to a myriad of frequently vague restrictions. After uniform cost principles are promulgated, it will become possible for uniform and effective audit enforcement to take place. Stratified audits and other strategies can be used to create an incentive for greater compliance among all grantees and contractors. Alternatively, promulgating a defined set of rules can and will serve as a protection against audit harassment, and will and should make for fairer and simpler audits for grantees and contractors. This should be of particular benefit to smaller grantees and contractors who lack the means and support staff to contend with audits under the vague, ambiguous, and diverse rules now in effect. With expanded Inspector General and agency audit staffs now in place, the protections afforded by the proposal are manifest.

X. Designation as "Non-Major" Rule

OMB Circulars are not "rules" within the meaning of the Administrative Procedures Act or Executive Order No. 12291. Instead, they are management directives by which OMB, on behalf of the President, instructs Executive Branch entities how to exercise their authority in matters subject to agency discretion. Even if the Circular were considered a "rule," however, OMB has determined that the revision to Circular A-122 would not qualify as a "major rule" under the criteria as listed in Executive Order No. 12291, which defines a "major rule" as "any regulation that is likely to result in:

(1) An annual effect on the economy of $100 million or more;

(2) A major increase in costs or prices for consumers, individual industries, Federal, state, or local government agencies, or geographic regions; or

(3) Significant adverse effects on competition, employment, investment, productivity, innovation, or on the ability of United States-based enterprises to compete with foreign-based enterprises in domestic or export markets.

The principal effect of the revision will be to ensure that Federal grant funds are used for the purposes for which they were intended, and not to facilitate lobbying activities. As noted above, current financial control procedures do not permit an accurate estimate of the amount of tax dollars now diverted to lobbying efforts by grantees and contractors. Whether large or small, correction of this problem will produce a net gain to the intended beneficiaries of Federal programs. The costs to be considered are primarily accounting and recordkeeping costs for grantees and contractors, as well as Federal agencies. These additional costs, however, are minimal in both absolute and relative terms. Indeed, in many instances, the revisions should reduce audit and compliance costs. Furthermore, much of the accounting work that the revision requires is already mandated by other sections of Circular A-122, Circular A-110, or other provisions of law.

Issued in Washington, D.C., April 25, 1984.
Candice C. Bryant,

Deputy Associate Director for Administration.

1. Insert a new paragraph in Attachment B, as follows: "B21 Lobbying"

a. Notwithstanding other provisions of this Circular, costs associated with the following activities are unallowable:

a.(1) Attempts to influence the outcomes of any Federal, State, or local election, referendum, initiative, or similar procedure, through in kind or cash contributions, endorsements, publicity, or similar activity;

a.(2) Establishing, administering, contributing to, or paying the expenses of a political party, campaign, political action committee, or other organization established for the purpose of influencing the outcomes of elections;

a.(3) Any attempt to influence: (i) The introduction of Federal or state legislation; or (ii) the enactment or modification of any pending Federal or state legislation through communication with any member or employee of the Congress or state legislature (including efforts to influence State or local officials to engage in similar lobbying activity), or with any government official or employee in connection with a decision to sign or veto enrolled legislation;

a.(4) Any attempt to influence: (i) The introduction of Federal or state legislation; or (ii) the enactment or modification of any pending Federal or state legislation by preparing, distributing or using publicity or propaganda, or by urging members of the general public or any segment thereof to contribute to or participate in any mass demonstration, march, rally, fundraising drive, lobbying campaign or letter writing or telephone campaign; or

a.(5) Legislative liaison activities, including attendance at legislative sessions or committee hearings, gathering information regarding legislation, and analyzing the effect of legislation, when such activities are carried on in support of or in knowing preparation for an effort to engage in unallowable lobbying.

b. The following activities are excepted from the coverage of subparagraph a:

b.(1) Providing a technical and factual presentation of information on a topic directly related to the performance of a grant, contract or other agreement through hearing testimony; statements or letters to the Congress or a state legislature, or subdivision, member, or cognizant staff member thereof, in response to a documented request (including a Congressional Record notice requesting testimony or statements for the record at a regularly scheduled hearing) made by the recipient member, legislative body or subdivision, or a cognizant staff member thereof: provided such information is readily obtainable and can be readily put in deliverable form; and further provided that costs under this section for travel, lodging or meals are unallowable unless incurred to offer

testimony at a regularly scheduled Congressional hearing pursuant to a written request for such presentation made by the Chairman or Ranking Minority Member of the Committee or Subcommittee conducting such hearing.

b.(2) Any lobbying made unallowable by section a.(3) to influence State legislation in order to directly reduce the cost, or to avoid material impairment of the organization's authority to perform the grant, contract, or other agreement.

b.(3) Any activity specifically authorized by statute to be undertaken with funds from the grant, contract, or other agreement.

c.(1) When an organization seeks reimbursement for indirect costs, total lobbying costs shall be separately identified in the indirect cost rate proposal, and thereafter treated as other unallowable activity costs in accordance with the procedures of paragraph B3 of Attachment A.

c.(2) Organizations shall submit as part of their annual indirect cost rate proposal a certification that the requirements and standards of this paragraph have been complied with.

c.(3) Organizations shall maintain adequate records to demonstrate that the determination of costs as being allowable or unallowable pursuant to paragraph B21 complies with the requirements of this Circular.

c.(4) Time logs, calendars, or similar records documenting the portion of an employee's time that is treated as an indirect cost shall not be required for the purposes of complying with subparagraph c, and the absence of such records which are not kept pursuant to the discretion of the grantee or contractor, will not serve as a basis for disallowing claims of allowable costs by contesting estimates of unallowable lobbying time spent by employees during any calendar month unless: (i) The employee engages in lobbying, as defined in subparagraphs a and b, more than 25% of his compensated hours of employment during that calendar month; or (ii) the organization has materially misstated allowable or unallowable costs within the preceding five year period.

c.(5) Agencies shall establish procedures for resolving in advance, in consultation with OMB, any significant questions or disagreements concerning the interpretation or application of paragraph B21. Any such advance resolution shall be binding in any subsequent settlements, audits or investigations with respect to that grant or contract for purposes of

interpretation of this Circular; provided, however, that this shall not be construed to prevent a contractor or grantee from contesting the lawfulness of such a determination.

2. Renumber subsequent paragraphs of Attachment B.

---

49 Fed. Reg. 19,588 (May 8, 1984)

OFFICE OF MANAGEMENT AND BUDGET

Circular A-122; Cost Principles for Nonprofit Organizations—"Lobbying" Revision

Correction

In FR Doc. 84-11594 beginning on page 18260 in the issue of Friday, April 27, 1984, make the following corrections:

1. On page 18263, third column, third line from the bottom, "regulations" should read "regulation"; and in the second line from the bottom, "deviaiton" should read "deviation".

2. On page 18265, first column, third paragraph, eighth line, "and" should read "an"; and in the fourth paragraph, fourth line, "and" should read "an".

3. On page 18266, second column, second line, "cost" should read "costs"; in the eighth line from the bottom, "statues" should read "statutes".

4. Also on page 18266, third column, third line from the bottom, "hearing" should read "hearings"; and in the second line from the bottom, "Other" should read "Others".

5. On page 18267, first column, first complete paragraph, 13th line, "section" should read "sections"; in the second column, fifth paragraph, second line, "transportatin" should read "transportation".

6. On page 18268, first column, first complete paragraph, first line, "condidered" should read "considered", and in the second column, first complete paragraph, fourth line, "compaigns" should read "campaigns".

7. On page 18269, second column, 12th line, "prusuing" should read "pursuing".

8. On page 18270, first column, third line from the bottom, "contracts" should read "contacts".

9. On page 18271, first column, second complete paragraph, 14th and 15th lines, "or other agreements" should read "performance".

10. On page 18272, third column, first complete paragraph, 11th line, "tht" should read "that".

11. On page 18273, second column, first complete paragraph, 16th line, "be" should read "have".

12. On page 18274, second column, fifth line, "Requirement" should read "Requirements"; and in the first complete paragraph, 18th line, "as basis" should read "as a basis".

13. On page 18275, second column, third complete paragraph, 10th and 11th lines, remove "sufficient information to serve the filing or audit requirements"; and in the third line from the bottom of the column, "agencies" should read "agency".

52 Fed. Reg. 19,788 (May 27, 1987)

OFFICE OF MANAGEMENT AND BUDGET

Revision of OMB Circular A–122, "Cost Principles for Nonprofit Organizations"

AGENCY: Office of Management and Budget.

ACTION: Revision of OMB Circular A–122, "Cost Principles for Nonprofit Organizations".

SUMMARY: This notice revises Office of Management and Budget (OMB) Circular A–122, "Cost Principles for Nonprofit Organizations." Based on recommendations by the Defense Acquisition Council and the Civilian Agency Acquisition Council, this revision clarifies requirements for maintenance and access to records for costs associated with legislative lobbying and political activities. It does not alter the originally intended meaning of the affected section and will not result in the imposition of any additional recordkeeping requirements.

This revision maintains consistency with an identical technical revision to the Federal Acquisition Regulation (FAR) to cover all defense and civilian contractors. The FAR revision appears elsewhere in this issue of the Federal Register.

SUPPLEMENTARY INFORMATION: OMB Circular A–122, "Cost Principles for Nonprofit Organizations," establishes uniform rules for determining the costs of grants, contracts and other agreements between the Federal Government and nonprofit organizations. Attachment B, section B21, "Lobbying" makes unallowable the costs associated with most kinds of legislative lobbying and political activities.

According to the Department of Defense, contractors are misinterpreting paragraph c.(4), the so-called "25 percent rule," to either stop keeping records maintained to comply with the prior cost principle, or to deny access to their regularly-maintained accounting data. The paragraph was only intended to restrict requirements for additional special records, such as time logs and calenders, and not intended to restrict

access to records regularly maintained in the ordinary course of business.

The Department of Defense, General Services Administration, and National Aeronautics and Space Administration published a proposed rule in the Federal Register on May 29, 1986 (51 FR 19506). Twenty-four comments were received, of which 20 were from Federal agencies. Twenty of the 24 either concurred or had no comment. The Defense Acquisition Regulatory Council and the Civilian Agency Acquisition Council considered the comments and incorporated technical changes to meet some of the recommendations in the four other comments.

The revision restructures paragraph c.(4) to make clear its original intent that records usually maintained to demonstrate the allowability of costs must continue to be maintained and made available for audit.

May 19, 1987.

[Circular No. A–122, Revised Transmittal Memorandum No. 2]

To the Heads of Executive Departments and Agencies

Subject: Cost Principles for Nonprofit Organizations.

This memorandum revises OMB Circular A–122, "Cost Principles for Nonprofit Organizations, to clarify requirements for maintenance and access to records for costs associated with legislative lobbying and political activities.

In attachment B, section B21, "Lobbying," paragraph c.(4) is revised as follows:

c.(4) Time logs, calendars, or similar records shall not be required to be created for purposes of complying with this section during any particular calendar month when: (1) the employee engages in lobbying (as defined in paragraphs (a) and (b) above) 25 percent or less of the employee's compensated hours of employment during that calendar month, and (2) within the preceding five-year period, the organization has not materially misstated allowable or unallowable costs of any nature, including legislative lobbying costs. When conditions (1) and (2) above are met, organizations are not required to establish records to support the allowability of claimed costs in addition to records already required or maintained. Also, when conditions (1) and (2) above are met, the absence of time logs, calendars, or similar records will not serve as a basis for disallowing costs by contesting estimates of lobbying time spent by employees during a calendar month.

Appendix J

Internal Revenue Code §162(e)

(e) Appearances, etc., with respect to legislation

(1) In general

The deduction allowed by subsection (a) shall include all the ordinary and necessary expenses (including, but not limited to, traveling expenses described in subsection (a)(2) and the cost of preparing testimony) paid or incurred during the taxable year in carrying on any trade or business—

(A) in direct connection with appearances before, submission of statements to, or sending communications to, the committees, or individual members, of Congress or of any legislative body of a State, a possession of the United States, or a political subdivision of any of the foregoing with respect to legislation or proposed legislation of direct interest to the taxpayer, or

(B) in direct connection with communication of information between the taxpayer and an organization of which he is a member with respect to legislation or proposed legislation of direct interest to the taxpayer and to such organization,

and that portion of the dues so paid or incurred with respect to any organization of which the taxpayer is a member which is attributable to the expenses of the activities described in subparagraphs (A) and (B) carried on by such organization.

(2) Limitation

The provisions of paragraph (1) shall not be construed as allowing the deduction of any amount paid or incurred (whether by way of contribution, gift, or otherwise)—

(A) for participation in, or intervention in, any political campaign on behalf of any candidate for public office, or

(B) in connection with any attempt to influence the general public, or segments thereof, with respect to legislative matters, elections, or referendums.

Appendix K

Proposed Treasury Regulations for Internal Revenue Code §§4911 and 4945, 53 Fed. Reg. 51,826–51,845 (December 23, 1988)

DEPARTMENT OF THE TREASURY

Internal Revenue Service

26 CFR Parts 1, 53 and 56

[EE-154-78]

Lobbying by Public Charities; Lobbying by Private Foundations

AGENCY: Internal Revenue Service, Treasury.

ACTION: Notice of proposed rulemaking and notice of public hearing.

SUMMARY: This document revises proposed regulations published in 1986 and also supersedes portions of proposed regulations published in 1980. The proposed regulations relate to lobbying expenditures by certain tax-exempt public charities and by private foundations. Changes to the tax laws governing lobbying by public charities were made by the Tax Reform Act of 1976 (the "Act"). The proposed regulations will provide organizations the guidance needed to comply with the Act, and will affect public charities electing the expenditure test under section 501(h) of the Internal Revenue Code of 1986 ("electing public charities"). The proposed regulations will also provide organizations with clearer guidance needed to comply with

the requirements of section 4945 (relating to lobbying expenditures by private foundations). Finally, in light of the unique charitable and educational purposes shared by all organizations described in section 501(c)(3) as well as the similarity of the statutory schemes governing lobbying by private foundations and by electing public charities, the regulations ensure that the rules regarding lobbying by private foundations are consistent with the rules regarding lobbying by electing public charities. However, these proposed regulations are not applicable to lobbying by ineligible or nonelecting public charities, which continue to be covered by the "substantial part" test regarding lobbying activities.

DATES: Written comments and/or requests to appear (with an outline of the oral comments to be presented) at a public hearing scheduled for Monday, April 3, 1989, at 10:00 a.m., and continuing, if necessay, at the same time on Tuesday, April 4, 1989, must be delivered or mailed by March 23, 1989. The proposed regulations published in the **Federal Register** on November 5, 1986 (51 FR 40211), as amended by this document, are proposed to be effective for tax years beginning after the publication of final regulations.

ADDRESS: Send comments, requests to

appear at the public hearing, and outlines of oral comments to be presented at the public hearing to: Commissioner of Internal Revenue, Attention: CC:CORP:T:R (EE–154–78), Washington, DC 20224. The public hearing will be held in the I.R.S. Auditorium, Seventh Floor, 7400 Corridor, Internal Revenue Building, 1111 Constitution Avenue NW., Washington, DC.

FOR FURTHER INFORMATION CONTACT: Jerome P. Walsh Skelly of the Office of Assistant Chief Counsel (Employee Benefits and Exempt Organizations), Internal Revenue Service, 1111 Constitution Avenue NW., Washington, DC 20224, Attention: CC:CORP:T:R (EE–154–78), telephone 202–535–3818 (not a toll-free call).

SUPPLEMENTARY INFORMATION:

Prior Law

A publicly supported charity is not an organization described in section 501(c)(3) ("a section 501(c)(3) organization") if its lobbying activities are more than an insubstantial part of its activities. If it is determined that a substantial part of a publicly supported section 501(c)(3) organization's activities consists of attempts to influence legislation, the organization will lose its tax-exempt status as a charity. Before the passage of the Tax Reform Act of 1976, there was uncertainty about what constituted a "substantial part" of an organization's activities. Congress was aware both of the severity of loss of tax exemption as a sanction and of the belief that the vague standards of the substantial part test tended to create uncertainty and allow subjective and selective enforcement.

Expenditure Test

Under sections 501(h) and 4911, which were added by section 1307 of the Tax Reform Act of 1976, certain publicly supported section 501(c)(3) organizations may elect to spend up to a certain percentage of their "exempt purpose expenditures" to influence legislation without incurring tax or losing qualification for tax-exempt status. Thus, if an eligible organization elects the "expenditure test" of sections 501(h) and 4911, specific statutory dollar limits on the organization's lobbying expenditures apply. Under the expenditure test, there are limits both upon the amount of the organization's grass roots lobbying expenditures and upon the total amount of the organization's direct and grass roots lobbying expenditures. In contrast to the substantial part test, however, the expenditure test imposes no limit on lobbying activities that do not require expenditures, such as certain unreimbursed lobbying activities conducted by bona fide volunteers. In general, if either or both of the expenditure test limits are exceeded, a 25 percent excise tax is imposed upon the greater of: (1) The amount by which the organization's grass roots lobbying expenditures exceed its grass roots lobbying limit, or (2) the amount by which an organization's total direct and grass roots lobbying expenditures exceed its total lobbying limit. Additionally, if an organization's grass roots expenditures or total lobbying expenditures normally exceed 150 percent of the applicable limitation on its lobbying expenditures, the organization will cease to be described in section 501(c)(3), and, therefore, will cease to be exempt from income tax and will no longer be eligible to receive tax deductible charitable contributions.

Background

On November 25, 1980, the **Federal Register** published proposed amendments to the Income Tax Regulations (26 CFR Part 1) under sections 162, 6001, and 6033 of the Internal Revenue Code of 1954 (relating to grass roots lobbying expenditures by business corporations) and to the Foundation and Similar Excise Taxes (26 CFR Part 53) under section 4945 of the Internal Revenue Code of 1954 (relating to lobbying expenditures by private foundations) (45 FR 78167) ("the 1980 NPRM").

On November 5, 1986, the **Federal Register** published proposed amendments to the Income Tax Regulations (26 CFR Part 1), Temporary Income Tax Regulations under the Tax Reform Act of 1976 (26 CFR Part 7), Estate Tax Regulations (26 CFR Part 20), Gift Tax Regulations (26 CFR Part 25), and Foundation and Similar Excise Taxes (26 CFR Part 53), and also proposed regulations on Public Charity Excise Taxes (26 CFR Part 56), under sections 170, 501(c)(3), 501(c)(4), 501(h),

504, 2055, 2522, 4911, 4945, 6001, 6011, and 6033 of the Internal Revenue Code of 1954 (51 FR 40211) ("the 1986 NPRM").

This document supersedes a portion of the 1980 NPRM and revises portions of the 1986 NPRM. Specifically, it supersedes that portion of the 1980 NPRM that proposed amendments to the regulations under section 4945 of the Internal Revenue Code (relating to lobbying expenditures by private foundations). It revises portions of the 1986 NPRM relating to proposed regulations on Public Charity Excise Taxes (26 CFR Part 56) under section 4911 of the Internal Revenue Code. In addition, it revises portions of the 1986 NPRM that proposed amendments to the regulations under sections 501(h) and 4945. Thus, where this document proposes to amend any portion of the regulations under section 501(h) or section 4945, the proposed amendment in this document supersedes any proposed amendment of that portion of the regulations that was published in the 1986 NPRM.

The amendments to the Foundation and Similar Excise Taxes are necessary to provide guidance to organizations that must comply with the requirements of section 4945 and will also ensure that the regulations regarding lobbying by private foundations are consistent with the regulations regarding lobbying by electing public charities. The amendments proposed on November 5, 1986, as amended in this document, are proposed to conform the regulations to section 1307 of the Tax Reform Act of 1976 (90 Stat. 1720) as well as to ensure consistency between the similar schemes governing lobbying expenditures by electing public charities and by private foundations. The proposed regulations are to be issued under the authority in sections 501(h)(6), 504(b), 4911(f)(3) and 7805 of the Internal Revenue Code of 1986 (26 U.S.C. 501(h)(6), 504(b), 4911(f)(3), 7805).

Public Comment Process of Previous Notices of Proposed Rulemaking

Several thousand written comments were received concerning the 1986 NPRM. Numerous written comments were also received concerning the 1980 NPRM. In addition, on May 11 and 12, 1987, the Internal Revenue Service ("Service") held public hearings concerning the 1986 NPRM.

The numerous public comments and the two days of public hearings have been helpful in formulating this revised notice of proposed rulemaking. In addition, possible revisions of the controversial sections of the proposed regulations have been discussed at length with the Commissioner's Exempt Organizations Advisory Group (comprised of legal and other representatives of exempt organizations as well as academics) at public meetings held on September 17, 1987, and February 26, 1988.

Every effort has been made in the drafting of this revised notice of proposed rulemaking to be as responsive as possible to the many comments received from the public. This effort required a careful balancing of the statutory mandate limiting the amount of lobbying expenditures by section 501(c)(3) organizations with the desire of the affected organizations and individuals to involve themselves in the public policymaking process to the greatest extent consistent with that statutory mandate. Extensive revisions have been made to the prior notices of proposed rulemaking in an effort to achieve this difficult balance. For example, the proposed regulations contain a definition of grass roots lobbying that is less inclusive than is permitted by the broad statutory language defining grass roots lobbying.

Numerous portions of the 1986 NPRM were not controversial, however, and gave rise to little or no public comment. Those portions of the proposed regulations have been retained and are, in general, not affected by the revisions proposed in this document. For example, proposed §§ 1.501(h)–1 and 1.501(h)–3, proposed in the 1986 NPRM, describe the application of the expenditure test to electing public charities, including that an electing public charity may undertake a certain amount of lobbying expenditures without being subject to tax or having its tax-exempt status revoked. With minor exceptions, these portions of the proposed regulations are not affected by the revisions proposed in this document.

Summary of Comments Received on the Previous Notices of Proposed Rulemaking and Explanation of Provisions

1. Proposed Effective Date

Many of the comments on the 1986 NPRM's proposed regulations regarding lobbying expenditures by electing public charities opposed the proposed effective date of the proposed regulations (generally for tax years beginning after December 31, 1976). On April 9, 1987, the Service issued an information release, IR–87–49, stating that final regulations will be effective only prospectively from the date of publication of final regulations. Accordingly, the amendments proposed in this document and in the 1986 NPRM, as revised by this document, are hereby proposed to be effective on a prospective-only basis for tax years beginning after the date of publication of final regulations.

2. Definition of Grass Roots Lobbying

The 1986 NPRM proposed to define grass roots lobbying as a communication that:

(i) Pertains to legislation being considered by a legislative body, or seeks or opposes legislation,

(ii) Reflects a view with respect to the desirability of the legislation (for this purpose, a communication that pertains to legislation but expresses no explicit view on the legislation shall be deemed to reflect a view on legislation if the communication is selectively disseminated to persons reasonably expected to share a common view of the legislation), and

(iii) Is communicated in a form and distributed in a manner so as to reach individuals as members of the general public, that is, as voters or constituents, as opposed to a communication designed for academic, scientific, or similar purposes. A communication may meet this test even if it reaches the public only indirectly, as in a news release submitted to the media.

Most commentators expressed opposition to the breadth of the definition of grass roots lobbying contained in the 1986 NPRM. The primary objections were that the definition did not require a communication to have a "call to action" or some other encouragement to action on the part of the communication's recipients; that the definition considered an otherwise balanced discussion of a piece of legislation to reflect a view on that legislation based on the persons to whom the discussion was disseminated; and that the definition did not require the legislation to be pending or imminently to be introduced. Several commentators also expressed concern that the third part of the proposed definition of grass roots lobbying, regarding communications that reach the public only indirectly, could include testimony on a bill before a legislative committee if the press was in attendance.

In response to the numerous comments on the 1986 NPRM, this document substantially revises the proposed definition of grass roots lobbying. The modifications include the removal of the phrases "pertains to," "seeks or opposes legislation," and "selectively disseminated to persons reasonably expected to share a common view of the legislation."

In place of the definition contained in the 1986 NPRM, this document proposes to define the term "grass roots lobbying communication" (except with regard to a limited number of mass media communications discussed below) to include only those communications that: (1) Refer to specific legislation; (2) reflect a view on such legislation; and (3) encourage the recipient of the communication to take action with respect to such legislation.

Thus, under the rules proposed in this document, a communication is not a grass roots lobbying communication unless the communication's reference to legislation is to "specific legislation." As indicated in this document, this term includes both legislation that has already been introduced in a legislative body and a specific legislative proposal that the organization either supports or opposes.

The rules proposed in this document also indicate that a communication is not a grass roots lobbying communication unless it encourages its recipients to take action with respect to the specific legislation. As indicated in this document, a communication encourages its recipients to take action only if the communication:

(1) States that the recipient should contact a legislator or an employee of a legislative body, or should contact any other government official or employee who may participate in the formulation of legislation (but only if the principal purpose of urging contact with the government official or employee is to influence legislation);

(2) States the address, telephone number, or similar information of a legislator or an employee of a legislative body;

(3) Provides a petition, tear-off postcard or similar material for the recipient to communicate his or her views to a legislator or an employee of a legislative body, or to any other government official or employee who may participate in the formulation of legislation (but only if the principal purpose of so facilitating contact with the government official or employee is to influence legislation); or

(4) Specifically identifies one or more legislators who will vote on the legislation as: (a) Opposing the communication's view with respect to the legislation; (b) being undecided with respect to the legislation; (c) being the recipient's representative in the legislature; or (d) being a member of the legislative committee that will consider the legislation. Encouraging the recipient to take action under this fourth category does not include naming the main sponsor(s) of the legislation for purposes of identifying the legislation.

Communications that are described in categories (1) through (3) above are deemed not only to encourage action with respect to legislation, but also to "directly encourage" action with respect to legislation. This distinction is important because only communications in category (4), which encourage the recipient to take action with respect to legislation without "directly encouraging" such action, may be within the exception for nonpartisan analysis, study or research and, as a result, not be grass roots lobbying communications.

This revised definition is a major modification to the definition proposed in the 1986 NPRM. The lobbying definition contained in this document (with an exception for a limited number of mass media communications

discussed below) not only requires that the communication contain a reference to specific legislation, but also requires that the communication both reflect a view with respect to such legislation and encourage the recipient to take action. Under such a definition, communications could advocate or oppose specific legislation and not be considered lobbying, so long as the communications do not encourage the recipients to take action with respect to the legislation. The 1986 NPRM, in contrast, included within the definition of lobbying certain communications that did not encourage the recipient to take action with respect to legislation. Also in contrast to this document's definition, the definition proposed in 1986 provided that a communication not directly taking a position on legislation could be lobbying based upon the selective dissemination of the communication.

The one exception to the above three-part definition of lobbying is a special rule for certain mass media communications. If within two weeks before a vote by a legislative body, or committee thereof, on a highly publicized piece of legislation, an organization makes a communication in the mass media that reflects a view on the general subject of such legislation and either (1) refers to the highly publicized legislation or (2) encourages the public to communicate with their legislators on the general subject of such legislation, then the communication will be presumed to be a grass roots lobbying communication. An organization can rebut this presumption by demonstrating that the communication is a type of communication regularly made by the organization in the mass media without regard to the timing of legislation (that is, a customary course of business exception) or that the timing of the communication was for reasons unrelated to the upcoming legislative action. For purposes of this special rule, the term "mass media" means television, radio, and certain general circulation newspapers and magazines. Any mass media communication that is not made within two weeks before a legislative vote on a highly publicized piece of legislation will be tested by the general three-part test for grass roots lobbying.

Under the proposed regulations, testimony on a bill before a legislative committee, which is often a direct lobbying communication, is not grass roots lobbying merely because the testimony indirectly reached the public through press coverage of the organization's testimony.

In addition to the rules discussed above, numerous examples are provided to assist organizations in evaluating the facts and circumstances of each individual case. In general, those examples amplify the rule that a communication that advocates or opposes specific legislation is generally not a grass roots lobbying communication unless it encourages the recipient to take action with respect to the legislation, such as by requesting recipients to contact legislators or by providing the names of undecided legislators.

As noted above, under the proposed regulations, a communication will be considered to encourage recipients to take action with respect to legislation only if the communication is described in one of the four listed categories. The Service will, however, continue to study communications and, if other methods of encouraging recipients to take action are identified, will propose amendments to the regulations.

In order to achieve the balance between the statutory mandate limiting expenditures for grass roots lobbying and the desire of many charitable organizations to participate in the public policy process, the definition of grass roots lobbying proposed in this document is a less inclusive definition than is permitted by the broad statutory language defining grass roots lobbying. The Service believes that any definition of grass roots lobbying less inclusive than that proposed in this document could, in effect, eliminate the statutory limitation Congress has placed on grass roots lobbying expenditures by electing public charities.

3. Definition of Direct Lobbying

Some commentators criticized the definition of direct lobbying contained in the 1986 NPRM in that the definition was based on the grass roots lobbying definition. The primary objections were that the definition considered an otherwise balanced discussion of a piece of legislation to reflect a view on legislation based on the dissemination of the communication, and that the definition did not require the legislation to be pending or imminently to be introduced.

This document proposes to modify the definition of direct lobbying by removing the phrases "pertains to," "seeks or opposes legislation," and "selectively disseminated to persons reasonably expected to share a common view of the legislation." In place of the definition contained in the 1986 NPRM, this document proposes to define the term "direct lobbying communication" to include only those communications to legislators or certain other government officials that (1) refer to specific legislation, and (2) reflect a view on such legislation.

4. Allocation Rules

Many commentators expressed concern about the allocation rules proposed in the 1986 NPRM, particularly the special rules relating to advertising, fundraising, and mixed lobbying purposes.

This document revises the proposed allocation rules. Under the allocation rule proposed in this document, a mixed grass roots and direct lobbying expenditure is to be treated as a grass roots expenditure, except to the extent that the organization demonstrates that the expenditure was incurred *primarily* (rather than the *solely* standard contained in the 1986 NPRM) for direct lobbying purposes, in which case a reasonable allocation shall be made between the direct and grass roots lobbying purposes served by the communication.

This document removes the two special rules with respect to fundraising and advertising contained in the 1986 NPRM. For lobbying communications that also serve a bona fide nonlobbying purpose, this document proposes two different allocation rules. Which rule is used depends upon whether the communication is sent primarily to members or nonmembers.

For communications that are sent primarily to bona fide members (that is, for communications sent to more members than nonmembers), an organization must make a reasonable allocation between the amount expended for the lobbying purpose and the amount spent for the nonlobbying purpose. Including as a lobbying expenditure only the amount expended for the specific sentence or sentences that encourage the recipient to action is not considered a reasonable allocation.

For lobbying communications that are not sent primarily to bona fide members, all costs attributable to those parts of the communication that are on the same specific subject as the lobbying message must be included as lobbying expenditures for allocation purposes. Under the rules proposed in this document, however, the costs attributable to parts of a lobbying communication that are not on the same specific subject as the lobbying message are not considered lobbying expenditures. Whether or not a portion of a communication is on the same specific subject as the lobbying message will depend on the surrounding facts and circumstances. In general, a portion of a communication will be on the same specific subject as the lobbying message if that portion discusses an activity that would be directly affected by the proposed legislation that is the subject of the lobbying message. Moreover, discussion of the background or consequences of either the proposed legislation or of an activity directly affected by the proposed legislation will also be considered to be on the same specific subject as the lobbying communication.

5. Research and Preparation Costs

Some commentators expressed concern that, under the 1986 NPRM, the research and preparation costs incurred in producing a nonlobbying communication could be treated as a lobbying expenditure because of subsequent use of the communication in a lobbying campaign by that organization, a related organization, or an unrelated organization.

This document attempts to make clear that the costs of researching and preparing nonlobbying communications would be treated as lobbying expenditures only in cases of abuse. Except in such cases, the regulations proposed in this document would not treat as lobbying expenditures the research and preparation costs of a communication that is not itself a lobbying communication merely because the communication was also used in a lobbying campaign.

A communication that reflects a view on specific legislation but that is not a lobbying communication will be treated as a lobbying communication because of subsequent use of the communication in a lobbying effort only if the primary purpose of the organization in preparing the communication was for use in lobbying. The primary purpose of an organization in preparing a document is not lobbying if, prior to or contemporaneously with the use of the communication in lobbying, the organization makes a substantial nonlobbying distribution of the communication.

Where a communication's nonlobbying distribution is not substantial, all of the facts and circumstances must be weighed to determine the organization's primary purpose in preparing the communication. Two factors of particular importance are (1) the relative scope of the nonlobbying and subsequent lobbying distributions, and (2) whether the subsequent lobbying distribution is made by the organization itself, a related organization or an unrelated organization. Where the subsequent distribution is made by an unrelated organization, clear and convincing evidence will be required to establish that the primary purpose for preparing the communication was for use in lobbying.

6. Communications with Members

With respect to the exception for an organization's communications with its members, many commentators stated that their organizations have only a mailing list of supporters, without a formal membership, or have a single mailing list that includes both formal members and nonmember supporters.

This document does not revise the proposed definition of membership because the statutory use of the term "bona fide member", combined with the legislative history, indicates Congress intended that the exception for communications with members not include persons simply included on a mailing list or those whose financial support of the organization is in the distant past. However, the proposed regulations relating to communications with members have been slightly modified to reflect the revisions to the definition of direct and grass roots lobbying.

7. Exception for Nonpartisan Analysis, Study or Research

Some commentators expressed concern that the statutory exception for nonpartisan analysis should apply to some of the examples under the 1986 NPRM's general definition section for grass roots lobbying

The section 4945 regulations currently provide that engaging in and making available nonpartisan analysis, study or research does not constitute lobbying. This same exception was included in the 1986 NPRM's proposed section 4911 regulations by cross-reference to the section 4945 regulations. This document proposes to include in the section 4911 regulations the full text of the section 4945 regulations' exception for nonpartisan analysis, study or research, rather than merely a cross-reference to the section 4945 regulations. As requested by the comments, the examples proposed in this document note where the nonpartisan analysis exception clearly applies. As a result of the narrow definition of grass roots lobbying proposed in this document, many communications addressing legislation will not be grass roots lobbying communications. Because fewer communications will be lobbying communications, organizations will not have to depend on the nonpartisan analysis exception to the extent necessary under the 1986 NPRM. That is to say, under the rules proposed in this document, many communications that address legislation will fail to be lobbying communications as a result of the narrow definition of lobbying rather than because of the nonpartisan analysis exception.

The comments received by the Service indicated some confusion regarding the scope of the nonpartisan analysis exception. To remove this confusion, this document proposes to clarify in both the section 4945 and section 4911 regulations that a communication is not within the nonpartisan analysis exception if the communication *directly* encourages recipients of the

communication to contact legislators or certain other governmental officials in favor of or in opposition to specific legislation. As stated above, a communication would encourage the recipient to take action with respect to legislation, but not *directly* encourage such action, if the communication does no more than specifically identify legislators as: Opposing the communication's view with respect to the legislation; being undecided with respect to the legislation; being the recipient's representative in the legislature; or being a member of the legislative committee that will consider the legislation.

This document proposes an additional amendment to the regulations regarding the nonpartisan analysis, study or research exception. Under the rules proposed in this document, analysis, study or research that reflects a view on specific legislation is not nonpartisan if an organization's primary purpose for undertaking the analysis, study or research is for use in lobbying *and* the analysis, study or research is subsequently used as, or with, a lobbying communication that directly encourages recipients to take action with respect to specific legislation. However, the primary purpose of the organization in undertaking analysis, study or research will not be considered to be lobbying if, prior to or contemporaneously with the use of the analysis, study or research in lobbying, the organization makes a substantial distribution of the analysis, study or research (without an accompanying lobbying message). Whether a distribution is substantial will be determined by reference to all of the facts and circumstances, including the normal distribution pattern of similar nonpartisan analyses, studies, or research.

8. Exception for Discussion of Broad Social, Economic and Similar Problems

Some commentators requested that the "discussion of broad social, economic and similar problems" exception to the definition of lobbying be included in the text of the section 4911 regulations (relating to lobbying expenditures by electing public charities). The section 4945 regulations currently provided that discussions of broad social, economic and similar problems are not lobbying activities. This document proposes that the full text of the exception be included in the section 4911 regulations. In response to confusion about the scope of the exception, this document proposes that the exception, for purposes of both section 4945 and section 4911, does not apply where a communication directly encourages recipients of the communication to contact legislators or certain other government officials in favor of or in opposition to specific legislation. Because of the revised definition of grass roots lobbying proposed in this document, many communications will not be grass roots lobbying, and thus very few, if any, communications that actually constitute grass roots lobbying communications will be within the exception for discussion of broad social, economic and similar problems. That is, the revised definition of grass roots lobbying will reduce or eliminate the need for organizations to depend upon the exception for discussion of broad social, economic and similar problems.

9. Grants by Private Foundations to Electing Public Charities

Some commentators noted that the 1986 NPRM would expand certain rules relating to restrictions on grants by private foundations to electing public charities beyond the scope of a private letter ruling issued by the Service in 1977. These commentators suggested that the additions to the Service's 1977 private ruling are inappropriate and unnecessary.

With respect to grants by private foundations to electing public charities, this document revises the 1986 NPRM to conform to the Service's 1977 private letter ruling by removing the additional restrictions. Additionally, this document states that a private foundation can rely on the assertions of the grantee regarding the nonlobbying nature of the funded activities, unless the private foundation doubts or, in light of all the facts and circumstances, reasonably should doubt the accuracy or reliability of the documents provided by the grantee.

10. Effect on 1980 Notice of Proposed Rulemaking

In the 1980 NPRM, the Service proposed amendments to the regulations on Foundations and Similar Excise Taxes in order to provide clearer guidance to organizations that must comply with the requirements of section 4945, relating to the making of lobbying expenditures by private foundations. Regulations under section 162(e)(2) were also proposed to be amended in that same notice of proposed rulemaking. This document proposes to revise the regulations regarding lobbying by private foundations by conforming them to the regulations governing lobbying by electing public charities. It does not propose any revisions to the regulations under section 162(e)(2).

11. Rules Regarding Affiliated Organizations

Several commentators objected to the 1986 NPRM's standard that organizations are affiliated where the governing instruments of the "controlled" organization require that the "controlled" organization "take into account" the position of the "controlling" organization on a legislative issue.

In response to those comments, this document slightly modifies the affiliation rules by removing the "take into account" language and directly tracking the statutory language.

12. Definition of Term "Separate Fundraising Units"

Several commentators objected to the use of the term "substantial" in the 1986 NPRM's definition of the term "separate fundraising units." Their objections were with regard to both the term's lack of precision and its expansive scope.

In response to such objections, this document slightly modifies the proposed rule to include only those persons who spend a majority, rather than a substantial part, of their time on fundraising for the organization.

13. Miscellaneous Technical Revisions

Finally, some commentators suggested that, for a variety of reasons, certain portions of the proposed regulations needed minor technical changes. In response to those comments, this document proposes several minor technical revisions to the 1986 NPRM. The Service specifically welcomes further comments suggesting any additional technical revisions necessary for proper implementation of the underlying statutes.

Several sections in the regulations have been reserved. This is simply for the convenience of the **Federal Register** reader.

Rulings Regarding Application of the Regulations

Under its ruling program (see Rev. Proc. 83–36, 1983–1 C.B. 763 and Rev. Proc. 88–8, 1988–4 I.R.B. 22), the Service will consider requests for private letter rulings to clarify the application of these regulations to particular fact patterns.

Comments, Requests To Appear at the Public Hearing, and Outline of Oral Comments To Be Presented at the Public Hearing

Before adopting these prposed regulations, consideration will be given to any written comments that are submitted (preferably nine copies) to the Commissioner of Internal Revenue. All comments, requests to appear at, and outlines of oral comments to be presented at the public hearing will be available for public inspection and copying. In light of the extensive comments upon and full discussion of the issues in this document since the enactment of the Tax Reform Act of 1976 and the publication of the 1986 NPRM, the Service has scheduled a publich hearing to be held on Monday, April 3, 1989, at 10:00 a.m., and continuing, if necessary, at the same time on Tuesday, April, 4, 1989, in the I.R.S. Auditorium, Seventh Floor, 7400 Corridor, Internal Revenue Building, 1111 Constitution Avenue, NW., Washington, DC.

Special Analyses

The Commissioner of Internal Revenue has determined that this proposed rule is not a major rule as defined in Executive Order 12291 and that a regulatory impact analysis is therefore not required. Although this document is a notice of proposed rulemaking that solicits public comment, the Internal Revenue Service has concluded that the regulations proposed

herein are interpretative and that the notice and public procedure requirements of 5 U.S.C. 553 do not apply. Accordingly, these proposed regulations do not constitute regulations subject to the Regulatory Flexibility Act (5 U.S.C. chapter 6).

Supersession

These regulations, when published in final form in the **Federal Register**, will supersede section 7.0(c)(4) of the Temporary Income Tax Regulations under the Tax Reform Act of 1976. This document supersedes that portion of the notice of proposed rulemaking published in the **Federal Register** on November 25, 1980 (45 FR 78167) that proposed amendments to the regulations on Foundations and Similar Excise Taxes (26 CFR Part 53). Where this document proposes to amend any portion of the regulations under Title 26 of the Code of Federal Regulations, the proposed amendment in this document supersedes any proposed amendment of that portion of the regulations that was previously published in the **Federal Register** on November 5, 1986 (51 FR 40211).

Drafting Information

The principal author of this document was Jerome P. Walsh Skelly of the Office of Assistant Chief Counsel (Employee Benefits and Exempt Organizations Division). Other offices of the Internal Revenue Service and Treasury Department participated in developing the regulations, both on matters of substance and style.

List of Subjects

26 CFR 1.501(a)–1—1.528–10

Income taxes, Exempt organizations, Foundations, Nonprofit organizations, Cooperatives, Political organizations, Homeowners associations.

26 CFR Part 53

Excise taxes, Foundations, Investments, Trusts and trustees.

26 CFR Part 56

Excise tax, Lobbying expenditures, Exempt purpose expenditures, Affiliated organizations, Administration and procedure.

Proposed Amendments to the Regulations

Accordingly, (I) the proposed amendments to 26 CFR Part 53 that were published on November 25, 1980 (45 FR 78167) are withdrawn, and (II) the notice of proposed rulemaking (to amend 26 CFR Parts 1 and 53 and add a new Part 56) that was published on November 5, 1986 (51 FR 40211), is amended, and additional amendments of Part 53 are proposed, as follows:

PART 1—[AMENDED]

Paragraph 1. The authority citation for Part 1 is amended by adding the following citation:

Authority: 26 U.S.C. 7805. * * * Sections 1.504–1 and 1.504–2 also issued under 26 U.S.C. 504(b).

Par. 2. Proposed § 1.501(h)–2 is amended by revising paragraph (b)(2)(vi) to read:

§ 1.501(h)–2 Electing the expenditure test.

* * * * *

(b) *Organizations eligible to elect the expenditure test.* * * *

(2) *Certain organizations listed.* * * *

(vi) Section 509(a)(3) (relating to organizations supporting public charities), except that for purposes of this paragraph (b)(2), section 509(a)(3) shall be applied without regard to the last sentence of section 509(a).

* * * * *

Par. 3. Proposed § 1.501(h)–3 is amended by revising paragraph (c)(4) and adding new Examples (4) and (5) to paragraph (e), to read:

§ 1.501(h)–3 Lobbying or grass roots expenditures normally in excess of ceiling amount.

* * * * *

(c) *Definitions.* * * *

(4) The term "grass roots expenditures" means expenditures for grass roots lobbying communications as defined in section 4911(c)(3) or section 4911(f)(4)(A) and §§ 56.4911–2 and 3.

* * * * *

(e) *Examples.* * * *

Example (4) Organization M made the expenditure test election under section 501(h) effective for taxable years beginning with 1977 and has not revoked the election. M has $500,000 of exempt purpose expenditures during each of the years 1981 through 1984. In addition, during each of those years, M spends $75,000 for direct lobbying and $25,000 for grass roots lobbying. Since the amount expended for M's lobbying (both total lobbying and grass roots lobbying) is within the respective nontaxable expenditure limitations, M is not liable for the 25 percent excise tax imposed under section 4911(a) upon excess lobbying expenditures, nor is M denied tax-exempt status by reason of section 501(h).

Example (5) Assume the same facts as in Example (4), except that, on behalf of M, numerous unpaid volunteers conduct substantial lobbying activities with no reimbursement. Since the substantial lobbying activities of the unpaid volunteers are not counted towards the expenditure limitations and the amount expended for M's lobbying is within the respective nontaxable expenditure limitations, M is not liable for the 25 percent excise tax under section 4911, nor is M denied tax-exempt status by reason of section 501(h).

PART 53—[AMENDED]

Par. 4. The authority citation for Part 53 continues to read in part:

Authority: 26 U.S.C. 7805. * * *

Par. 5. Section 53.4945–2 is amended as follows:

1. Paragraph (a)(1) is revised, paragraph (a)(2) is removed and reserved, proposed paragraph (a)(6) is revised, and, in proposed paragraph (a)(7)(ii), Examples (1), (2), and (3) are revised and new Examples (10) through (13) are added and the introductory text is republished to read as set forth below.

2. Paragraphs (b) and (c) are removed and reserved.

3. Paragraph (d)(1)(i) is revised to read as set forth below.

4. In paragraph (d)(1)(iv), the last sentence is revised to read as set forth below.

5. Paragraph (d)(1)(v), *Examples,* is redesignated as paragraph (d)(1)(vii), Examples (4) and (5) are revised, and new Examples (8) through (11) are added, to read as set forth below.

6. New paragraphs (d)(1)(v) and (d)(1)(vi) are added, to read as set forth below.

7. Paragraph (d)(4) is revised to read as set forth below.

§ 53.4945–2 Propaganda influencing legislation.

(a) *Propaganda influencing legislation, etc.*—(1) *In general.* Under section 4945(d)(1) the term "taxable expenditure" includes any amount paid or incurred by a private foundation to carry on propaganda, or otherwise to attempt, to influence legislation. An expenditure is an attempt to influence legislation if it is for a direct or grass roots lobbying communication, as defined in § 56.4911-2 (without reference to §§ 56.4911-2(b)(3) and 56.4911-2(c)) and § 56.4911-3. See, however, paragraph (d) of this section for exceptions to the general rule of this paragraph (a)(1).

(2) [Reserved]

* * * * *

(6) *Grants to public organizations that attempt to influence legislation*—(i) *General Support Grant.* A general support grant by a private foundation to an organization described in section 509(a)(1), (2), or (3) (a "public charity" for purposes of paragraphs (a) (6) and (7) of this section) does not constitute a taxable expenditure under section 4945(d)(1) to the extent that the grant is not earmarked, within the meaning of § 53.4945-2(a)(5)(i), to be used in an attempt to influence legislation. The preceding sentence applies without regard to whether the public charity has made the election under section 501(h).

(ii) *Specific Project Grant.* A grant by a private foundation to fund a specific project of a public charity is not a taxable expenditure by the foundation under section 4945(d)(1) to the extent that—

(A) The grant is not earmarked, within the meaning of § 53.4945-2(a)(5)(i), to be used in an attempt to influence legislation, and

(B) The amount of the grant, together with other grants by the same private foundation for the same project for the same year, does not exceed the amount budgeted, for the year of the grant, by the grantee organization for activities of the project that are not attempts to influence legislation. If the grant is for more than one year, the preceding sentence applies to each year of the grant with the amount of the grant divided equally between years, or as otherwise actually disbursed by the private foundation. This paragraph (a)(6)(ii) applies without regard to whether the public charity has made the election under section 501(h)

(iii) *Reliance upon grantee's budget.* For purposes of determining the amount budgeted by a prospective grantee for specific project activities that are not attempts to influence legislation under paragraph (a)(6)(ii) of this section, a private foundation may rely on budget documents or other sufficient evidence supplied by the grantee organization (such as a signed statement by an authorized officer, director or trustee of such grantee organization) showing the proposed budget of the specific project, unless the private foundation doubts or, in light of all the facts and circumstances, reasonably should doubt the accuracy or reliability of the documents.

(7) *Grants to organizations that cease to be described in 501(c)(3)*— * * *

(ii) *Examples.* The provisions of paragraphs (a)(6) and (a)(7) of this section are illustrated by the following examples:

Example (1). W, a private foundation, makes a general support grant to Z, a public charity described in section 509(a)(1). Z informs W that, as an insubstantial portion of its activities, Z attempts to influence the State legislature with regard to changes in the mental health laws. The use of the grant is not earmarked by W to be used in a manner that would violate section 4945(d)(1). Even if the grant is subsequently devoted by Z to its legislative activities, the grant by W is not a taxable expenditure under section 4945(d).

Example (2). X, a private foundation, makes a specific project grant to Y University for the purpose of conducting research on the potential environmental effects of certain pesticides. X does not earmark the grant for any purpose that would violate section 4945(d)(1) and there is no oral or written agreement or understanding whereby X may cause Y to engage in any activity described in section 4945(d) (1), (2), or (5), or to select any recipient to which the grant may be devoted. Further, X determines, based on budget information supplied by Y, that Y's budget for the project does not contain any amount for attempts to influence legislation. X has no reason to doubt the accuracy or reliability of the budget information. Y uses most of the funds for the research project; however, Y expends a portion of the grant funds to send a representative to testify at Congressional hearings on a specific bill proposing certain pesticide control measures. The portion of the grant funds expended with respect to the Congressional hearings is not treated as a taxable expenditure by X under section 4945(d)(1).

Example (3). M, a private foundation, makes a specific project grant of $150,000 to

P, a public charity described in section 509(a)(1). In requesting the grant from M, P stated that the total budgeted cost of the project is $200,000, and that of this amount $20,000 is allocated to attempts to influence legislation related to the project. M relies on the budget figures provided by P in determining the amount P will spend on influencing legislation and M has no reason to doubt the accuracy or reliability of P's budget figures. In making the grant, M did not earmark any of the funds from the grant to be used for attempts to influence legislation. M's grant of $150,000 to P will not constitute a taxable expenditure under section 4945(d)(1) because M did not earmark any of the funds for attempts to influence legislation and because the amount of its grant ($150,000) does not exceed the amount allocated to specific project activities that are not attempts to influence legislation ($200,000 − $20,000 = $180,000).

*   *   *   *   *

Example (10). X, a private foundation, makes a specific project grant to Y, a public charity described in section 509(a). In requesting the grant, X stated that it planned to use the funds to purchase a computer for purposes of computerizing its research files and that the grant will not be used to influence legislation. Two years after X makes the grant, X discovers that Y has also used the computer for purposes of maintaining and updating the mailing list for Y's lobbying newsletter. Because X did not earmark any of the grant funds to be used for attempts to influence legislation and because X had no reason to doubt the accuracy or reliability of Y's documents representing that the grant would not be used to influence legislation, X's grant is not treated as a taxable expenditure.

Example (11). G, a private foundation, makes a specific project grant of $300,000 to L, a public charity described in section 509(a)(1) for a three-year specific project studying child care problems. L provides budget material indicating that the specific project will expend $200,000 in each of three years. L's budget materials indicate that attempts to influence legislation will amount to $10,000 in the first year, $20,000 in the second year and $100,000 in the third year. G intends to pay its $300,000 grant over three years as follows: $200,000 in the first year, $50,000 in the second year and $50,000 in the third year. Since the amount of the grant in each of the three years, when divided equally between the three years ($100,000 for each year), is not more than the nonlobbying expenditures of L on the specific project for any of the three years, none of the grant is treated as a taxable expenditure under section 4945(d)(1).

Example (12). P, a private foundation, makes a $120,000 specific project grant to C, a public charity described in section 509(a) for a three-year project. P intends to pay its grant to C in three equal annual installments of $40,000. C provides budget material indicating that the specific project will expend $100,000 in each of three years. C's budget materials, which P reasonably does not doubt, indicate that the project's attempts to influence legislation will amount to $50,000 in each of the three years. After P pays the first annual installment to C, but before P pays the second installment to C, reliable information comes to P's attention that C has spent $90,000 of the project's $100,000 first-year budget on attempts to influence legislation. This information causes P to doubt the accuracy and reliability of C's budget materials. Because of the information, P does not pay the second-year installment to C, P's payment of the first installment of $40,000 is not a taxable expenditure under section 4945(d)(1) because the grant in the first year is not more than the nonlobbying expenditures C projected in its lobbying materials that P reasonably did not doubt.

Example (13). Assume the same facts as in Example (12), except that P pays the second-year installment of $40,000 to C. In the project's second year, C once again spends $90,000 of the project's $100,000 annual budget in attempts to influence legislation. Because P doubts or reasonably should doubt the accuracy or reliability of C's budget materials when P makes the second-year grant payment, P may not rely upon C's budget documents at that time. Accordingly, although none of the $40,000 paid in the first installment is a taxable expenditure, only $10,000 ($100,000 minus $90,000) of the second-year grant payment is not a taxable expenditure. The remaining $30,000 of the second installment is a taxable expenditure within the meaning of section 4945(d)(1).

*   *   *   *   *

(b) [Reserved]

(c) [Reserved]

(d) * * *

(1) * * *

(i) *In general*. A communication is not a direct lobbying communication described in § 56.4911–2(b)(1) or a grass roots lobbying communication described in § 56.4911–2(b)(2) if the communication constitutes engaging in nonpartisan analysis, study or research and making available to the general public or a segment or members thereof or to governmental bodies, officials, or employees and results of such work. Accordingly, an expenditure for such a communication does not constitute a taxable expenditure under section 4945(d)(1) and § 53.4945–2(a)(1).

(ii) * * *

(iii) * * *

(iv) *Making available results of nonpartisan analysis, study, or research.* * * * For purposes of this paragraph (d)(1)(iv), such communications may not be limited to, or be directed toward, persons who are interested solely in one side of a particular issue.

(v) *Subsequent lobbying use of nonpartisan analysis, study or research.* For purposes of this paragraph, a nonlobbying communication is any communication that reflects a view on specific legislation but that is not a lobbying communication as described in § 56.4911–2(b). This § 56.4945–2(d)(1)(v) governs any nonlobbying communication that is nonpartisan analysis, study or research (within the meaning of § 56.4945–2(d)(1)) *and* that is: subsequently used with an accompanying lobbying communication that directly encourages recipients to take action with respect to legislation; or subsequently altered so that it is itself a lobbying communication that directly encourages recipients to take action with respect to legislation. In such a case, the communication is not within the exception for nonpartisan analysis, study or research and will be treated as a lobbying communication if the organization's primary purpose in preparing the communication was for use in lobbying; consequently, the expenses of preparing and distributing the communication will be treated as lobbying expenditures. The primary purpose of the organization in undertaking analysis, study, or research will not be considered to be for use in lobbying if, prior to or contemporaneously with the use of the analysis, study, or research in lobbying, the organization makes a substantial distribution of the analysis, study, or research (without an accompanying lobbying message). Whether a distribution is substantial will be determined by reference to all of the facts and circumstances, including the normal distribution pattern of similar nonpartisan analyses, studies, or research. Where the nonlobbying distribution of a communication governed by this paragraph is not substantial, all of the facts and circumstances must be weighed to determine whether the organization's primary purpose in preparing the communication was for use in lobbying. While not the only factor, the extent of the organization's nonlobbying distribution of the communication is particularly relevant, especially when compared to the extent of the communication's distribution with the lobbying message. Another particularly relevant factor is whether the subsequent lobbying use of a communication is by the organization that prepared the document, a related organization, or an unrelated organization. Where the subsequent lobbying distribution is made by an unrelated organization, clear and convincing evidence will be required to establish that the primary purpose for preparing the communication was for use in lobbying.

(vi) *Directly encouraging action by recipients of a communication.* A communication that reflects a view on specific legislation is not within the nonpartisan analysis, study or research exception of this § 53.4945–2(d)(1) if the communication directly encourages the recipient to take action with respect to such legislation. For purposes of this section, a communication directly encourages the recipient to take action with respect to legislation if the communication is described in § 56.4911–2(b)(2)(iii)(A) through (C). As described in § 56.4911–2(b)(2)(iv), a communication would encourage the recipient to take action with respect to legislation, but not *directly* encourage such action, if the communication does no more than specifically identify one or more legislators who will vote on the legislation as: Opposing the communication's view with respect to the legislation; being undecided with respect to the legislation; being the recipient's representative in the legislature; or being a member of the legislative committee that will consider the legislation.

(vii) *Examples.* * * *

Example (4). Publishes a bi-monthly newsletter to collect and report all published materials, ongoing research, and new developments with regard to the use of pesticides in raising crops. The newsletter also includes notices of proposed pesticide legislation with impartial summaries of the provisions and debates on such legislation. The newsletter does not encourage recipients to take action with respect to such legislation, but is designed to present information on both sides of the legislative controversy and does present such information fully and fairly. It is within the exception for nonpartisan analysis, study, or research.

Example (5). X is satisfied that A, a member of the faculty of Y University, is exceptionally well qualified to undertake a project involving a comprehensive study of the effects of pesticides on crop yields. Consequently, X makes a grant to A to underwrite the cost of the study and of the preparation of a book on the effect of pesticides on crop yields. X does not take any position on the issues or control the content of A's output. A produces a book which concludes that the use of pesticides often has a favorable effect on crop yields, and on that basis argues against pending bills which would ban the use of pesticides. A's book contains a sufficiently full and fair exposition of the pertinent facts, including known or potential disadvantages of the use of pesticides, to enable the public or an individual to form an independent opinion or conclusion as to whether pesticides should be banned as provided in the pending bills. The book does not directly encourage readers to take action with respect to the pending bills. Consequently, the book is within the exception for nonpartisan analysis, study, or research.

Example (6). * * *

Example (7). * * *

Example (8). Organization Z researches, writes, prints and distributes a study on the use and effects of pesticide X. A bill is pending in the U.S. Senate to ban the use of pesticide X. Z's study leads to the conclusion that pesticide X is extremely harmful and that the bill pending in the U.S. Senate is an appropriate and much needed remedy to solve the problems caused by pesticide X. The study contains a sufficiently full and fair exposition of the pertinent facts, including known or potential advantages of the use of pesticide X, to enable the public or an individual to form an independent opinion or conclusion as to whether pesticides should be banned as provided in the pending bills. In its analysis of the pending bill, the study names certain undecided Senators on the Senate committee considering the bill. Although the study meets the three part test for determining whether a communication is a grass roots lobbying communication, the study is within the exception for nonpartisan analysis, study or research, because it does not directly encourage recipients of the communication to urge a legislator to oppose the bill.

Example (9). Assume the same facts as in Example (8), except that, after stating support for the pending bill, the study concludes:

"You should write to the undecided committee members to support this crucial bill." The study is not within the exception for nonpartisan analysis, study or research because it directly encourages the recipients to urge a legislator to support a specific piece of legislation.

Example (10). Organization X plans to conduct a lobbying campaign with respect to illegal drug use in the United States. It incurs $5,000 in expenses to conduct research and prepare an extensive report primarily for use in the lobbying campaign. Although the detailed report discusses specific pending legislation and reaches the conclusion that the legislation would reduce illegal drug use, the report contains a sufficiently full and fair exposition of the pertinent facts to enable the public or an individual to form an independent conclusion regarding the effect of the legislation. The report does not encourage readers to contact legislators regarding the legislation. Accordingly, the report does not, in and of itself, constitute a lobbying communication.

Copies of the report are available to the public at X's office, but X does not actively distribute the report or otherwise seek to make the contents of the report available to the general public. Whether or not X's distribution is sufficient to meet the requirement in § 53.4945–2(d)(1)(iv) that a nonpartisan communication be made available, X's distribution is not substantial (for purposes of § 53.4945–2(d)(v)) in light of all of the facts and circumstances, including the normal distribution pattern of similar nonpartisan reports. X then mails copies of the report, along with a letter, to 10,000 individuals on X's mailing list. In the letter, X requests that individuals contact legislators urging passage of the legislation discussed in the report. Because X's research and report were primarily undertaken by X for lobbying purposes and X did not make a substantial distribution of the report (without an accompanying lobbying message) prior to or contemporaneously with the use of the report in lobbying, the report is a grass roots lobbying communication that is not within the exception for nonpartisan analysis, study or research. Thus, the expenditures for preparing and mailing both the report and the letter are taxable expenditures under section 4945.

Example (11). Assume the same facts as in Example (10), except that before using the report in the lobbying campaign, X sends the research and report (without an accompanying lobbying message) to universities and newspapers. At the same time, X also advertises the availability of the report in its newsletter. This distribution is similar in scope to the normal distribution pattern of similar nonpartisan reports. In light of all of the facts and circumstances, X's distribution of the report is substantial. Because of X's substantial distribution of the report, X's primary purpose will be considered to be other than for use in lobbying and the report will not be considered a grass roots lobbying communication. Accordingly, only the expenditures for copying and mailing the report to the 10,000 individuals on X's mailing list, as well as for preparing and mailing the letter, are expenditures for grass roots lobbying communications.

* * * * *

(4) *Examinations and discussions of broad social, economic, and similar problems.* Examinations and discussions of broad social, economic, and similar problems are neither direct lobbying communications under § 56.4911–2(b)(1) nor grass roots lobbying communications under § 56.4911–2(b)(2) even if the problems are of the type with which government would be expected to deal ultimately. Thus, under §§ 56.4911–2(b) (1) and (2), lobbying communications with members of legislative bodies or governmental employees, the general subject of which is also the subject of legislation before a legislative body so long as such discussion does not address itself to the merits of a specific legislative proposal and so long as such discussion does not directly encourage recipients to take action with respect to legislation. For example, this paragraph excludes from grass roots lobbying under § 56.4911–2(b)(2) an organization's discussions of problems such as environmental pollution or population growth that are being considered by Congress and various State legislatures, but only where the discussions are not directly addressed to specific legislation being considered, and only where the discussions do not directly encourage recipients of the communication to contact a legislator, an employee of a legislative body, or a government official or employee who may participate in the formulation of legislation.

PART 56—[AMENDED]

Par. 6. Proposed §§ 56.4911–1 through 56.4911–3 are revised to read:

§ 56.4911–1 Tax on excess lobbying expenditures.

(a) *In general.* Section 4911(a) imposes an excise tax of 25 percent on the excess lobbying expenditures (as defined in paragraph (b) of this section) for a taxable year of an organization for which the expenditure test election under section 501(h) is in effect. The limit on expenditures for influencing legislation on which no tax is due from an organization for a taxable year is the lobbying nontaxable amount, or, on expenditures for influencing legislation through grass roots lobbying, the grass roots nontaxable amount (see paragraph (c) of this section). For rules concerning the application of the excise tax imposed by section 4911(a) to the members of an affiliated group of organizations (as defined in § 56.4911–7(e)), see § 56.4911–8.

(b) *Excess lobbying expenditures.* For any taxable year for which the expenditure test election under section 501(h) is in effect, the amount of an organization's excess lobbying expenditures is the greater of—

(1) The amount by which the organization's lobbying expenditures (within the meaning of § 56.4911–2(a)) exceed the organization's lobbying nontaxable amount, or

(2) The amount by which the organization's expenditures for grass roots lobbying communications (within the meaning of §§ 56.4911–2 and –3)) exceed the organization's grass roots nontaxable amount.

(c) *Nontaxable amounts*—(1) *Lobbying nontaxable amount.* Under section 4911(c)(2), the lobbying nontaxable amount for any taxable year for which the expenditure test election is in effect is the lesser of—

((i)) $ 1,000,000, or

(ii) To the extent of the organization's exempt purpose expenditures (within the meaning of § 56.4911–4) for that year, the sum of 20 percent of the first $500,000 of such expenditures, plus 15 percent of the second $500,000 of such expenditures, plus 10 percent of the third $500,000 of such expenditures, plus 5 percent of the remainder of such expenditures.

(2) *Grass roots nontaxable amount.* Under section 4911(c)(4), an organization's grass roots nontaxable amount for any taxable year is 25 percent of its lobbying nontaxable amount for that year.

(d) *Examples.* The provisions of this

section are illustrated by the examples in § 1.501(h)–3.

§ 56.4911–2 Lobbying expenditures, direct lobbying communications, and grass roots lobbying communications.

(a) *Lobbying expenditures.* If an organization has in effect for any year the expenditure test election under section 501(h), its lobbying expenditures for that year are the sum of its expenditures during that year for direct lobbying communications ("direct lobbying expenditures") plus its expenditures during that year for grass roots lobbying communications ("grass roots expenditures").

(b) *Influencing legislation: direct and grass roots lobbying communications defined*—(1) *Direct lobbying communication*—(i) *Definition.* A direct lobbying communication is any attempt to influence any legislation through communication with:

(A) Any member or employee of a legislative body; or

(B) Any government official or employee (other than a member or employee of a legislative body) who may participate in the formulation of the legislation, but only if the principal purpose of the communication is to influence legislation.

(ii) *Required elements.* A communication with a legislator or government official will be treated as a direct lobbying communication under this § 56.4911–2(b)(1) only if the communication:

(A) Refers to specific legislation; and

(B) Reflects a view on such legislation.

(iii) *Definition of specific legislation.* For purposes of paragraphs (b)(1) and (b)(2) of this section, specific legislation includes both legislation that has already been introduced in a legislative body and a specific legislative proposal that the organization either supports or opposes.

(2) *Grass roots lobbying communication*—(i) *Definition.* A grass roots lobbying communication is any attempt to influence any legislation through an attempt to affect the opinions of the general public or any segment thereof.

(ii) *Required elements.* A communication will be treated as a grass roots lobbying communication

under this § 56.4911–2(b)(2) only if the communication:

(A) Refers to specific legislation;

(B) Reflects a view on such legislation; and

(C) Encourages the recipient of the communication to take action with respect to such legislation. (For special rules regarding certain mass media communications, see § 57.4911–2(b)(5)).

(iii) *Definition of encouraging recipient to take action.* For purposes of this section, encouraging a recipient to take action with respect to legislation means that the communication:

(A) States that the recipient should contact a legislator or an employee of a legislative body, or should contact any other government official or employee who may participate in the formulation of legislation (but only if the principal purpose of urging contact with the government official or employee is to influence legislation);

(B) States the address, telephone number, or similar information of a legislator or an employee of a legislative body;

(C) Provides a petition, tear-off postcard or similar material for the recipient to communicate his or her views to a legislator or an employee of a legislative body, or to any other government official or employee who may participate in the formulation of legislation (but only if the principal purpose of so facilitating contact with the government official or employee is to influence legislation); or

(D) Specifically identifies one or more legislators who will vote on the legislation as: Opposing the communication's view with respect to the legislation; being undecided with respect to the legislation; being the recipient's representative in the legislature; or being a member of the legislative committee that will consider the legislation. Encouraging the recipient to take action under this paragraph (b)(2)(iii)(D) does not include naming the main sponsor(s) of the legislation for purposes of identifying the legislation.

(iv) *Definition of directly encouraging recipient to take action.* Communications described in § 56.4911–2(b)(2)(iii) (A) through (C) not only "encourage," but also "directly encourage" the recipient to take action with respect to legislation.

Communications described in § 56.4911–2(b)(2)(iii)(D), however, do not directly encourage the recipient to take action with respect to legislation. Thus, a communication would encourage the recipient to take action with respect to legislation, but not *directly* encourage such action, if the communication does no more than identify one or more legislators who will vote on the legislation as: Opposing the communication's view with respect to the legislation; being undecided with respect to the legislation; being the recipient's representative in the legislature; or being a member of the legislative committee that will consider the legislation. Communications that encourage the recipient to take action with respect to legislation but that do not *directly* encourage the recipient to take action with respect to legislation may be within the exception for nonpartisan analysis, study or research (see § 56.4911–2(c)(1)) and thus not be grass roots lobbying communications.

(v) *Subsequent lobbying use of nonlobbying communication that is not nonpartisan analysis, study or research.* For purposes of this paragraph, a nonlobbying communication is any communication that reflects a view on specific legislation but that is not a lobbying communication as described in § 56.4911–2(b). This § 56.4911–2(b)(2)(v) governs any nonlobbying communication that is not nonpartisan analysis, study or research (within the meaning of § 56.4911–2(c)(1)) *and* that is subsequently used with an accompanying lobbying communication or is altered so that it is itself a lobbying communication. In such a case, the communication will be treated as a lobbying communication if the organization's primary purpose in preparing the communication was for use in lobbying, and the expenses of preparing and distributing the communication will be treated as lobbying expenditures. The primary purpose of the organization in preparing a communication governed by this paragraph will not be considered to be for use in lobbying if, prior to or contemporaneously with the use of the communication in lobbying, the organization makes a substantial distribution of the communication (without an accompanying lobbying message). Whether a distribution is substantial will be determined by reference to all of the facts and circumstances. Solely for purposes of this paragraph (b)(2)(v), the nonlobbying distribution of a communication will not be considered "substantial" unless that distribution is at least as extensive as the lobbying distribution of the communication. Where the nonlobbying distribution of a communication governed by this paragraph is not substantial, all of the facts and circumstances must be weighed to determine whether the organization's primary purpose in preparing the communication was for use in lobbying. While not the only factor, the extent of the organization's nonlobbying distribution of the communication is particularly relevant, especially when compared to the extent of the communication's distribution with the lobbying message. Another particularly relevant factor is whether the lobbying use of a communication is by the organization that prepared the document, a related organization, or an unrelated organization. Where the subsequent lobbying distribution is made by an unrelated organization, clear and convincing evidence will be required to establish that the primary purpose for preparing the communication was for use in lobbying. To illustrate this paragraph, assume a nonlobbying "report" (that is not nonpartisan analysis, study or research) is prepared by an organization, but distributed to only 50 people. The organization then sends the report to 10,000 people along with a letter urging recipients to write their Senators about the legislation discussed in the report. Because the report's nonlobbying distribution is not as extensive as its lobbying distribution, the report's nonlobbying distribution is not substantial for purposes of this paragraph. Accordingly, the organization's primary purpose in preparing the report must be determined by weighing all of the facts and circumstances. In light of the relatively minimal nonlobbying distribution and the fact that the lobbying distribution is by the preparing organization rather than by an unrelated organization, and in the absence of evidence to the contrary, both the report and the letter are grass roots lobbying communications. Accordingly, the organization's expenditures for preparing and mailing the two documents are grass roots lobbying expenditures.

(3) *Exceptions to the definition of influencing legislation.* A communication is not a direct or grass roots lobbying communication under § 56.4911-2(b) (1) or (2) if it falls within one of the exceptions listed in paragraph (c) of this section. See paragraph (c)(1), Nonpartisan analysis, study or research; paragraph (c)(2), Examinations and discussions of broad social, economic and similar problems; paragraph (c)(3), Requests for technical advice; and paragraph (c)(4), Communications pertaining to self-defense by the organization. In addition, see § 56.4911-5, which provides special rules regarding the treatment of certain lobbying communications directed in whole or in part to members of an electing public charity.

(4) *Examples.* This paragraph (b)(4) provides examples to illustrate the rules set forth in this section regarding direct and grass roots lobbying. Except where otherwise explicitly stated, the expenditure test election under section 501(h) is assumed to be in effect for all organizations discussed in the examples in this paragraph (b)(4). In addition, it is assumed that the special rules of § 56.4911-5, regarding certain of a public charity's communications with its members, do not apply to any of the examples in this paragraph (b)(4).

(i) *Direct lobbying.* The provisions of this section regarding direct lobbying communications are illustrated by the following examples:

Example (1). Organization P's employee, X, is assigned to approach members of Congress to gain their support for a pending bill. X drafts and P prints a position letter on the bill. P distributes the letter to members of Congress. Additionally, X personally contacts several members of Congress or their staffs to seek support for P's position on the bill. The letter and the personal contacts are direct lobbying communications.

Example (2). Organization M's president writes a letter to the Congresswoman representing the district in which M is headquartered, requesting that the Congresswoman write an administrative agency regarding proposed regulations recently published by that agency. M's president also requests that the Congresswoman's letter to the agency state the Congresswoman's support of M's application for a particular type of permit granted by the agency. The letter written by M's president is not a direct lobbying communication.

Example (3). Organization Z prepares a paper on a particular state's environmental problems. The paper does not reflect a view on any specific pending legislation or on any specific legislative proposal that Z either supports or opposes. Z's representatives give the paper to a state legislator. Z's paper is not a direct lobbying communication.

Example (4). State X enacts a statute that requires the licensing of all day care providers. Agency B in State X is charged with preparing rules to implement the bill enacted by State X. One week after enactment of the bill, organization C sends a letter to Agency B providing detailed proposed rules that organization C suggests to Agency B as the appropriate standards to follow in implementing the statute on licensing of day care providers. Organization C's letter to Agency B is not a lobbying communication.

Example (5). Organization B researches, prepares and prints a code of standards of minimum safety requirements in an area of common electrical wiring. Organization B sells the code of standards booklet to the public and it is widely used by professionals in the subject area. A number of states have codified all, or part, of the code of standards as mandatory safety standards. On occasion, B lobbies state legislators for passage of the code of standards for safety reasons. The research, preparation, printing and public distribution of the code of standards is not an expenditure for a direct (or grass roots) lobbying communication. Costs incurred in lobbying state legislators for passage of the code of standards into law are expenditures for direct lobbying communications.

Example (6). On the organization's own initiative, representatives of organization F, present written testimony to a Congressional committee. The news media reports on the testimony of organization F detailing F's opposition to a pending bill. The testimony is a direct lobbying communication but is not a grass roots lobbying communication.

(ii) *Grass roots lobbying.* The provisions of this section regarding grass roots lobbying communications are illustrated in paragraph (b)(4)(ii)(A) of this section by examples of communications that are not grass roots lobbying communications and in paragraph (b)(4)(ii)(B) by examples of communications that are grass roots lobbying communications. The provisions of this section are further illustrated in paragraph (b)(4)(ii)(C), with particular regard to the exception for nonpartisan analysis, study, or research:

(A) Communications that are not grass roots lobbying communications

Example (1). Organization L places in its newsletter an article that asserts that lack of new capital is hurting State W's economy. The article recommends that State W residents either invest more in local businesses or increase their savings so that funds will be available to others interested in making investments. The article is an attempt to influence opinions with respect to a general problem that might receive legislative attention and is distributed in a manner so as to reach and influence many individuals. However, the article does not refer to specific legislation that is pending in a legislative body, nor does the article refer to a specific legislative proposal the organization either supports or opposes.

Example (2). Assume the same facts as Example (1), except that the article refers to a bill pending in State W's legislature that is intended to provide tax incentives for private savings. The article praises the pending bill and recommends that it be enacted. However, the article does not encourage readers to take action with respect to the legislation.

Example (3). Organization B sends a letter to all persons on its mailing list. The letter includes an update on numerous environmental issues with a discussion of general concerns regarding pollution, proposed federal regulations affecting the area, and several pending legislative proposals. The letter endorses two pending bills and opposes another pending bill, but does not name any legislator involved (other than the sponsor of one bill, for purposes of identifying the bill), nor does it otherwise encourage the reader to take action with respect to the legislation.

Example (4). A pamphlet distributed by organization Z discusses the dangers of drugs and encourages the public to send their legislators a coupon, printed with the statement "I support a drug-free America." The term "drug-free America" is not widely identified with any of the many specific pending legislative proposals regarding drug issues. The pamphlet does not refer to any of the numerous pending legislative proposals, nor does the organization support or oppose a specific legislative proposal.

Example (5). A pamphlet distributed by organization B encourages readers to join an organization and "get involved in the fight against drugs." The text states, in the course of a discussion of several current drug issues,

that organization B supports a specific bill before Congress that would establish an expanded drug control program. The pamphlet does not encourage readers to communicate with legislators about the bill (such as by including the names of undecided or opposed legislators).

Example (6). Organization E, an evnronmental organization, routinely summarizes in each edition of its newsletter the new environment-related bills that have been introduced in Congress since the last edition of the newsletter. The newsletter identifies each bill by a bill number and the name of the legislation's sponsor. The newsletter also reports on the status of previously introduced environment-related bills. The summaries and status reports do not encourage recipients of the newsletter to take action with respect to legislation, as described in paragraphs (b)(2)(iii) (A) through (D) of this section. Although the summaries and status reports refer to specific legislation and often reflect a view on such legislation, they do not encourage the newsletter recipients to take action with respect to such legislation

(B) Communications that are grass roots lobbying communications

Example (1). A pamphlet distributed by organization Y states that the "President's plan for a drug-free America," which will establish a drug control program, should be passed. The pamphlet encourages readers to "write or call your senators and representatives and tell them to vote for the President's plan." No legislative proposal formally bears the name "President's plan for a drug-free America," but that and similar terms have been widely used in connection with specific legislation pending in Congress that was initially proposed by the President. Thus, the pamphlet refers to specific legislation, reflects a view on the legislation, and encourages readers to take action with respect to the legislation.

Example (2). Assume the same facts as in Example (1), except that the pamphlet does not encourage the public to write or call representatives, but does list the members of the committee that will consider the bill.

Example (3). Assume the same facts as in Example (1), except that the pamphlet encourages readers to "write the President to urge him to make the bill a top legislative priority" rather than encouraging readers to communicate with members of Congress.

Example (4). Organization B, a nonmembership organization, includes in one of three sections of its newsletter an endorsement of two pending bills and opposition to another pending bill and also identifies several legislators as undecided on the three bills. The section of the newsletter devoted to the three pending bills is a grass roots lobbying communication.

Example (5). Organization D, a nonmembership organization, sends a letter to all persons on its mailing list. The letter includes an extensive discussion concluding that a significant increase in spending for the Air Force is essential in order to provide an adequate defense of the nation. Prior to a concluding fundraising request, the letter encourages readers to write their Congressional representatives urging increased appropriations to build the B–1 bomber.

Example (6). State Y plans to conduct a binding voter referendum on a proposition to permit gambling in the state. Organization Z places an advertisement in a general circulation newspaper encouraging voters to vote against the proposition.

Example (7). Organization F mails letters requesting that each recipient contribute money to or join F. In addition, the letters express F's opposition to a pending bill that is to be voted upon by the U.S. House of Representatives. Although the letters are form letters sent as a mass mailing, each letter is individualized to report to the recipient the name of the recipient's congressional representative.

(C) Additional examples

Example (1). The newsletter of an organization concerned with drug issues is circulated primarily to individuals who are not members of the organization. A story in the newsletter reports on the prospects for passage of a specifically identified bill, stating that the organization supports the bill. The newsletter story identifies certain legislators as undecided, but does not state that readers should contact the undecided legislators. The story does not provide a full and fair exposition sufficient to qualify as nonpartisan analysis, study or research. The newsletter story is a grass roots lobbying communication.

Example (2). Assume the same facts as in Example (1), except that the newsletter story provides a full and fair exposition sufficient to qualify as nonpartisan analysis, study or research. The newsletter story is *not* a grass roots lobbying communication because it is within the exception for nonpartisan analysis, study or research.

Example (3). Assume the same facts as in Example (2), except that the newsletter story explicitly asks readers to contact the undecided legislators. Because the newsletter story directly encourages readers to take action with respect to the legislation, the newsletter story is not within the exception for nonpartisan analysis, study or research. Accordingly, the newsletter story is a grass roots lobbying communication.

Example (4). Assume the same facts as in Example (1), except that the story does not identify any undecided legislators. The story is not a grass roots lobbying communication.

Example (5). X organization places an advertisement that specifically identifies and opposes a bill that X asserts would harm the farm economy. The advertisement is not a mass media communication described in § 56.4911–2(b)(5)(ii) and does not directly encourage readers to take action with respect to the bill. However, the advertisement does state that Senator Y favors the legislation. Because the advertisement refers to and reflects a view on specific legislation, and also encourages the readers to take action with respect to the legislation by specifically identifying a legislator who opposes X's views on the legislation, the advertisement in a grass roots lobbying communication.

Example (6). Assume the same facts as in Example (5), except that instead of identifying Senator Y as favoring the legislation, the advertisement identifies the "junior Senator from State Z" as favoring the legislation. The advertisement is a grass roots lobbying communication.

Example (7). Assume the same facts as in Example (5), except that instead of identifying Senator Y as favoring the legislation, the advertisement states: "Even though this bill will have a devastating effect upon the farm economy, most of the Senators from the Farm Belt states are inexplicably in favor of the bill." The advertisement does not specifically identify one or more legislators as opposing the advertisement's view on the bill in question. Accordingly, the advertisement is not a grass roots lobbying communication because it does not encourage readers to take action with respect to the legislation.

(5) *Mass media communications*—(i) *In general.* All mass media communications, other than those described in paragraph (b)(5)(ii) of this section, are evaluated by the three-part grass roots lobbying definition contained in paragraph (b)(2) of this section.

(ii) *Special rule for certain mass media communications.* If within two weeks before a vote by a legislative body, or committee thereof, on a highly publicized piece of legislation, an organization makes a communication in the mass media that reflects a view on the general subject of such legislation and either: Refers to the highly publicized legislation; or encourages the public to communicate with legislators on the general subject of such legislation, then the communication will be presumed to be a grass roots lobbying communication. An organization can rebut this presumption by demonstrating that the communication is a type of communication regularly made by the organization in the mass media without regard to the timing of legislation (that is, a customary course of business exception) or that the timing of the communication was unrelated to the upcoming legislative action. Notwithstanding the fact that an organization successfully rebuts the presumption, a mass media communication described in this paragraph (b)(5)(ii) is a grass roots lobbying communication if the communication would be a grass roots lobbying communication under the rules contained in paragraph (b)(2) of this section.

(iii) *Definitions*—(A) *Mass media*. For purposes of this paragraph (b)(5), "mass media" means television, radio, and general circulation newspapers and magazines. General circulation newspapers and magazines do not include newspapers or magazines published by an organization for which the expenditure test election under section 501(h) is in effect, except where both: The total circulation of the newspaper or magazine is greater than 100,000; and fewer than one-half of the recipients are members of the organization (as defined in § 56.4911–5(f)).

(B) *Highly publicized*. For purposes of this paragraph (b)(5), "highly publicized" means frequent coverage on television, radio, and general circulation newspapers and magazines during the two weeks preceding the vote by the legislative body.

(iv) *Examples*. The special rule of this paragraph (b)(5) is illustrated by the following examples. The expenditure test election under section 501(h) is assumed to be in effect for all organizations discussed in the examples in this paragraph (b)(5)(iv):

Example (1). Organization X places a television advertisement advocating one of the President's major foreign policy initiatives, as outlined by the President in a series of speeches. The initiative is popularly known as "the President's World Peace Plan," and is voted upon by the Senate four days after X's advertisement. The advertisement concludes: "SUPPORT THE PRESIDENT'S WORLD PEACE PLAN!" The President's plan and position are highly publicized during the two weeks before the Senate vote, as evidenced by: coverage of the plan on several nightly television network news programs; more than one article about the plan on the front page of a majority of the country's ten largest daily general circulation newspapers; and an editorial about the plan in four of the country's ten largest daily general circulation newspapers. Although the advertisement does not encourage readers to contact legislators or other government officials, the advertisement does refer to specific legislation and reflects a view on the general subject of the legislation. The communication is presumed to be a grass roots lobbying communication.

Example (2). Assume the same facts as in Example (1), except that the advertisement appears three weeks before the Senate's vote on the plan. Because the advertisement appears more than two weeks before the legislative vote, the advertisement is *not* within the scope of the special rule for mass media communications on highly publicized legislation. Accordingly, the advertisement is a grass roots lobbying communication only if it is described in the general definition contained in paragraph (b)(2) of this section. Because the advertisement does not encourage recipients to take action with respect to the legislation in question, the advertisement is not a grass roots lobbying communication.

Example (3). Organization Y places a newspaper advertisement advocating increased government funding for certain public works projects the President has proposed and that are being considered by a legislative committee. The advertisement explains the President's proposals and concludes: "SUPPORT FUNDING FOR THESE VITAL PROJECTS!" The advertisement does not encourage readers to contact legislators or other government officials nor does it name any undecided legislators, but it does name the legislation being considered by the committee. The issue of funding public works, however, is not highly publicized during the two weeks before the vote: there has been little coverage of the issue on nightly television network news programs, only one front-page article on the issue in the country's ten largest daily general circulation newspapers, and only one editorial about the issue in the country's ten largest daily general circulation newspapers. Two days after the advertisement appears, the committee votes to approve funding of the projects. Although the advertisement appears less than two weeks before the legislative vote, the advertisement is *not* within the scope of the special rule for mass media communications on highly publicized legislation because the issue of funding for public works projects is not highly publicized. Thus, the advertisement is a grass roots lobbying communication only if it is described in the general definition contained in paragraph (b)(2) of this section. Because the advertisement does not encourage recipients to take action with respect to the legislation in question, the advertisement is not a grass roots lobbying communication.

Example (4). A binding referendum is held in State X. At issue is Proposition 1, a citizen initiated proposition that, if enacted, would ban the manufacture and sale of handguns in State X. The proposition is controversial and highly publicized during the two weeks preceding the vote, as evidenced by numerous front-page articles, editorials, and letters to the editor published in the state's general circulation daily newspapers, as well as frequent coverage of the proposition by the television and radio stations serving the state. During the two weeks before the election, Organization Y places advertisements on radio stations serving the state. The advertisements do not encourage listeners to vote against the proposition, but do attack the legislation as being unconstitutional and ineffective. Because the advertisements are mass media communications made within two weeks of a vote on highly publicized legislation and because the advertisements refer to that highly publicized legislation and reflect a view on the general subject of such legislation, the advertisements are presumed to be grass roots lobbying communications.

(c) *Exceptions to the definitions of direct lobbying communication and grass roots lobbying communication*— (1) *Nonpartisan analysis, study, or research exception*—(i) *In general.* Engaging in nonpartisan analysis, study, or research and making available to the general public or a segment or members thereof or to governmental bodies, officials, or employees the results of such work constitute neither a direct lobbying communication under § 56.4911–2(b)(1) nor a grass roots lobbying communication under § 56.4911–2(b)(2).

(ii) *Nonpartisan analysis, study, or research.* For purposes of this section, "nonpartisan analysis, study, or research" means an independent and objective exposition of a particular subject matter, including any activity that is "educational" within the meaning of § 1.501(c)(3)–1(d)(3). Thus, "nonpartisan analysis, study, or research" may advocate a particular position or viewpoint so long as there is a sufficiently full and fair exposition of the pertinent facts to enable the public or an individual to form an independent opinion or conclusion. The mere presentation of unsupported opinion, however, does not qualify as "nonpartisan analysis, study, or research". Activities of a noncommercial educational broadcasting station or network (television or radio) constitute "nonpartisan analysis, study, or research" if the station or network adheres to the Federal Communications Commission regulations and its "fairness doctrine," interpreted as in effect on January 1, 1987 (requiring balanced, fair, and objective presentation of issues).

(iii) *Presentation as part of a series.* Normally, whether a publication or broadcast qualifies as "nonpartisan analysis, study, or research" will be determined on a presentation-by-presentation basis. However, if a publication or broadcast is one of a series prepared or supported by an electing organization and the series as a whole meets the standards of paragraph (c)(1)(ii) of this section, then any individual publication or broadcast within the series is not a direct or grass roots lobbying communication even though such individual broadcast or publication does not, by itself, meet the standards of paragraph (c)(1)(ii) of this section. Whether a broadcast or publication is considered part of a series will ordinarily depend upon all the facts and circumstances of each particular situation. However, with respect to broadcast activities, all broadcasts within any period of six consecutive months will ordinarily be eligible to be considered as part of a series. If an electing organization times or channels a part of a series which is described in this paragraph (c)(1)(iii) in a manner designed to influence the general public or the action of a legislative body with respect to a specific legislative proposal, the expenses of preparing and distributing such part of the analysis, study, or research will be expenditures for a direct or grass roots lobbying communication, as the case may be.

(iv) *Making available results of nonpartisan analysis, study, or research.* An organization may choose any suitable means, including oral or written presentations, to distribute the results of its nonpartisan analysis, study, or research, with or without charge. Such means include distribution of reprints of speeches, articles and reports; presentation of information through conferences, meetings and discussions; and dissemination to the news media, including radio, television and newspapers, and to other public forums. For purposes of this paragraph (c)(1)(iv), such communications may not be limited to, or be directed toward, persons who are interested solely in one side of a particular issue.

(v) *Subsequent lobbying use of nonpartisan analysis, study or research.* For purposes of this paragraph, a nonlobbying communication is any communication that reflects a view on specific legislation but that is not a lobbying communication as described in § 56.4911–2(b). This § 56.4911–2(c)(1)(v) governs any nonlobbying communication that is nonpartisan analysis, study or research (within the meaning of § 56.4911–2(c)(1)) *and* that is: subsequently used with an accompanying lobbying communication that directly encourages recipients to take action with respect to legislation; or subsequently altered so that it is itself a lobbying communication that directly encourages recipients to take action with respect to legislation. In such a case, the communication is not within the exception for nonpartisan analysis, study or research and will be treated as a lobbying communication if the organization's primary purpose in preparing the communication was for use in lobbying; consequently, the expenses of preparing and distributing the communication will be treated as lobbying expenditures. The primary purpose of the organization in undertaking analysis, study, or research will not be considered to be for use in lobbying if, prior to or contemporaneously with the use of the analysis, study, or research in lobbying, the organization makes a substantial distribution of the analysis, study, or research (without an accompanying lobbying message). Whether a distribution is substantial will be determined by reference to all of the facts and circumstances, including the normal distribution pattern of similar nonpartisan analyses, studies, or research. Where the nonlobbying distribution of a communication governed by this paragraph is not

substantial, all of the facts and circumstances must be weighed to determine whether the organization's primary purpose in preparing the communication was for use in lobbying. While not the only factor, the extent of the organization's nonlobbying distribution of the communication is particularly relevant, especially when compared to the extent of the communication's distribution with the lobbying message. Another particularly relevant factor is whether the lobbying use of a communication is by the organization that prepared the document, a related organization, or an unrelated organization. Where the subsequent lobbying distribution is made by an unrelated organization, clear and convincing evidence will be required to establish that the primary purpose for preparing the communication was for use in lobbying.

(vi) *Directly encouraging action by recipients of a communication.* A communication that reflects a view on specific legislation is not within the nonpartisan analysis, study, or research exception of this paragraph (c)(1) if the communication directly encourages the recipient to take action with respect to such legislation. For purposes of this section, a communication directly encourages the recipient to take action with respect to legislation if the communication is described in § 56.4911–2(b)(2)(iii) (A) through (C). As described in § 56.4911–2(b)(2)(iv), a communication would encourage the recipient to take action with respect to legislation, but not *directly* encourage such action, if the communication does no more than specifically identify one or more legislators who will vote on the legislation as: Opposing the communication's view with respect to the legislation; being undecided with respect to the legislation; being the recipient's representative in the legislature; or being a member of the legislative committee that will consider the legislation.

(vii) *Examples.* The provisions of this paragraph (c)(1) may be illustrated by the following examples:

Example (1). Organization M establishes a research project to collect information for the purpose of showing the dangers of the use of pesticides in raising crops. The information collected includes data with respect to proposed legislation, pending before several State legislatures, which would ban the use of pesticides. The project takes favorable positions on such legislation without producing a sufficiently full and fair exposition of the pertinent facts to enable the public or an individual to form an independent opinion or conclusion on the pros and cons of the use of pesticides. This project is not within the exception for nonpartisan analysis, study, or research because it is designed to present information merely on one side of the legislative controversy.

Example (2). Organization N establishes a research project to collect information concerning the dangers of the use of pesticides in raising crops for the ostensible purpose of examining and reporting information as to the pros and cons of the use of pesticides in raising crops. The information is collected and distributed in the form of a published report which analyzed the effects and costs of the use and nonuse of various pesticides under various conditions on humans, animals and crops. The report also presents the advantages, disadvantages, and economic cost of allowing the continued use of pesticides unabated, of controlling the use of pesticides, and of developing alternatives to pesticides. Even if the report sets forth conclusions that the disadvantages as a result of using pesticides are greater than the advantages of using pesticides and that prompt legislative regulation of the use of pesticides is needed, the project is within the exception for nonpartisan analysis, study, or research since it is designed to present information on both sides of the legislative controversy and presents a sufficiently full and fair exposition of the pertinent facts to enable the public or an individual to form an independent opinion or conclusion.

Example (3). Organization O establishes a research project to collect information on the presence or absence of disease in humans from eating food grown with pesticides and the presence or absence of disease in humans from eating food not grown with pesticides. As part of the research project, O hires a consultant who prepares a "fact sheet" which calls for the curtailment of the use of pesticides and which addresses itself to the merits of several specific legislative proposals to curtail the use of pesticides in raising crops which are currently pending before State Legislatures. The "fact sheet" presents reports of experimental evidence tending to support its conclusions but omits any reference to reports of experimental evidence tending to dispute its conclusions. O distributes ten thousand copies to citizens' groups. Expenditures by O in connection with this work of the consultant are not within the exception for nonpartisan analysis, study, or research.

Example (4). P publishes a bi-monthly newsletter to collect and report all published materials, ongoing research, and new developments with regard to the use of pesticides in raising crops. The newsletter also includes notices of proposed pesticide legislation with impartial summaries of the provisions and debates on such legislation. The newsletter does not encourage recipients to take action with respect to such legislation, but is designed to present information on both sides of the legislative controversy and does present such information fully and fairly. It is within the exception for nonpartisan analysis, study, or research.

Example (5). X is satisfied that A, a member of the faculty of Y University, is exceptionally well qualified to undertake a project involving a comprehensive study of the effects of pesticides on crop yields. Consequently, X makes a grant to A to underwrite the cost of the study and of the preparation of a book on the effect of pesticides on crop yields. X does not take any position on the issues or control the content of A's output. A produces a book which concludes that the use of pesticides often has a favorable effect on crop yields, and on that basis argues against pending bills which would ban the use of pesticides. A's book contains a sufficiently full and fair exposition of the pertinent facts, including known or potential disadvantages of the use of pesticides, to enable the public or an individual to form an independent opinion or conclusion as to whether pesticides should be banned as provided in the pending bills. The book does not directly encourage readers to take action with respect to the pending bills. Consequently, the book is written the exception for nonpartisan analysis, study, or research.

Example (6). Assume the same facts as Example (2), except that, instead of issuing a report, X presents within a period of 6 consecutive months a two-program television series relating to the pesticide issue. The first program contains information, arguments, and conclusions favoring legislation to restrict the use of pesticides. The second program contains information, arguments, and conclusions opposing legislation to restrict the use of pesticides. The programs are broadcast within 6 months of each other during commensurate periods of prime time. X's programs are within the exception for nonpartisan analysis, study, or research. Although neither program individually could be regarded as nonpartisan, the series of two programs constitutes a balanced presentation.

Example (7). Assume the same facts as in Example (6), except that X arranged for televising the program favoring legislation to restrict the use of pesticides at 8:00 on a

Thursday evening and for televising the program opposing such legislation at 7:00 on a Sunday morning. X's presentation is not within the exception for nonpartisan analysis, study, or research, since X disseminated its information in a manner prejudicial to one side of the legislative controversy.

Example (8). Organization Z researches, writes, prints and distributes a study on the use and effects of pesticide X. A bill is pending in the U.S. Senate to ban the use of pesticide X. Z's study leads to the conclusion that pesticide X is extremely harmful and that the bill pending in the U.S. Senate is an appropriate and much needed remedy to solve the problems caused by pesticide X. The study contains a sufficiently full and fair exposition of the pertinent facts, including known or potential advantages of the use of pesticide X, to enable the public or an individual to form an independent opinion or conclusion as to whether pesticides should be banned as provided in the pending bills. In its analysis of the pending bill, the study names certain undecided Senators on the Senate committee considering the bill. Although the study meets the three part test for determining whether a communication is a grass roots lobbying communication, the study is within the exception for nonpartisan analysis, study or research, because it does not directly encourage recipients of the communication to urge a legislator to oppose the bill.

Example (9). Assume the same facts as in Example (8), except that, after stating support for the pending bill, the study concludes: "You should write to the undecided committee members to support this crucial bill." The study is not within the exception for nonpartisan analysis, study or research because it directly encourages the recipients to urge a legislator to support a specific piece of legislation.

Example (10). Organization X plans to conduct to lobbying campaign with respect to illegal drug use in the United States. It incurs $5,000 in expenses to conduct research and prepare an extensive report primarily for use in the lobbying campaign. Although the detailed report discusses specific pending legislation and reaches the conclusion that the legislation would reduce illegal drug use, the report contains a sufficiently full and fair exposition of the pertinent facts to enable the public or an individual to form an independent conclusion regarding the effect of the legislation. The report does not encourage readers to contact legislators regarding the legislation. Accordingly, the report does not, in and of itself, constitute a lobbying communication.

Copies of the report are available to the public at X's office, but X does not actively distribute the report or otherwise seek to make the contents of the report available to the general public. Whether or not X's distribution is sufficient to meet the requirement in § 56.4911–2(c)(1)(iv) that a nonpartisan communication be made available, X's distribution is not substantial (for purposes of § 56.4911–2(c)(1)(v)) in light of all of the facts and circumstances, including the normal distribution pattern of similar nonpartisan reports. X then mails copies of the report, along with a letter, to 10,000 individuals on X's mailing list. In the letter, X requests that individuals contact legislators urging passage of the legislation discussed in the report. Because X's research and report were primarily undertaken by X for lobbying purposes and X did not make a substantial distribution of the report (without an accompanying lobbying message) prior to or contemporaneously with the use of the report in lobbying the report is a grass roots lobbying communication that is not within the exception for nonpartisan analysis, study or research.

Example (11). Assume the same facts as in Example (10), except that before using the report in the lobbying campaign, X sends the research and report (without an accompanying lobbying message) to universities and newspapers. At the same time, X also advertises the availability of the report in its newsletter. This distribution is similar in scope to the normal distribution pattern of similar nonpartisan reports. In light of all of the facts and circumstances, X's distribution of the report is substantial. Because of X's substantial distribution of the report, X's primary purpose will be considered to be other than for use in lobbying and the report will not be considered a grass roots lobbying communication. Accordingly, only the expenditures for copying and mailing the report to the 10,000 individuals on X's mailing list, as well as for preparing and mailing the letter, are expenditures for grass roots lobbying communications.

(2) *Examinations and discussions of broad social, economic, and similar problems.* Examinations and discussions of board social, economic, and similar problems are neither direct lobbying communications under § 56.4911–2(b)(1) nor grass roots lobbying communications under § 56.4911–2(b)(2) even if the problems are of the type with which government would be expected to deal ultimately. Thus, under §§ 56.4911–2(b) (1) and (2), lobbying communications do not include public discussion, or communications with members of legislative bodies or governmental employees, the general subject of which is also the subject of legislation before a legislative body, so

long as such discussion does not address itself to the merits of a specific legislative proposal and so long as such discussion does not directly encourage recipients to take action with respect to legislation. For example, this paragraph excludes from grass roots lobbying under § 56.4911–2(b)(2) an organization's discussions of problems such as environmental pollution or population growth that are being considered by Congress and various State legislatures, but only where the discussions are not directly addressed to specific legislation being considered, and only where the discussions do not directly encourage recipients of the communication to contact a legislator, and employee of a legislative body, or a government official or employee who may participate in the formulation of legislation.

(3) *Requests for technical advice.* A communication is neither a direct lobbying communication under § 56.4911–2(b)(1) nor a grass roots lobbying communication under § 56.4911–2(b)(2) if the communication is the providing of technical advice or assistance to a governmental body, a governmental committee, or a subdivision of either in response to a written request by the body, committee, or subdivision, as set forth in § 53.4945–2(d)(2).

(4) *Communications pertaining to "self-defense" by the organization.* A communication is neither a direct lobbying communication under § 56.4911–2(b)(1) nor a grass roots lobbying communication under § 56.4911–2(b)(2) if:

(i) The communication is an appearance before, or communication with, any legislative body with respect to a possible action by the body that might affect the existence of the organization, its powers and duties, its tax-exempt status, or the deductibilty of contributions to the organization, as set forth in § 53.4945–2(d)(3);

(ii) The communication is by a member of an affiliated group of organizations (within the meaning of § 56.4911–7(e)), and is an appearance before, or communication with, a legislative body with respect to a possible action by the body that might affect the existence of any other member of the group, its powers and

duties, its tax-exempt status, or the deductibility of contributions to it;

(iii) The communication is by an organization that has a membership consisting solely of other organizations that are described in section 501(c)(3), and is an appearance before, or communication with, any legislative body with respect to a possible action by the body which might affect the existence of one or more of the member organizations, their powers, duties, or tax-exempt status, or the deductibility of contributions to one or more of the member organizations; or

(iv) The communication is by an organization that is a member of a limited affiliated group of organizations under § 56.4911–10, and is an appearnace before, or communication with, the Congress of the United States with respect to a possible action by the Congress that might affect the existence of any member of the limited affiliated group, its powers and duties, tax-exempt status, or the deductibility of contributions to it.

(d) *Certain transfers treated as lobbying expenditures—*(1) *Transfer earmarked for grass roots purposes.* A transfer is a grass roots expenditure to the extent that it is earmarked (as defined in § 56.4911–4(f)(4)) for grass roots lobbying purposes and is not described in § 56.4911–4(e).

(2) *Transfer earmarked for direct and grass roots lobbying.* A transfer that is earmarked for direct lobbying purposes or for direct lobbying and grass roots lobbying purposes is treated as a grass roots expenditure in full except to the extent the transferor demonstrates that the amounts transferred were expended for direct lobbying purposes. This paragraph (d)(2) shall not apply to any expenditure described in § 56.4911–4(e).

(3) *Certain transfers to organizations that lobby.* A transfer that is neither a controlled grant (as defined in § 56.4911–4(f)(3)) nor an expenditure described in § 56.4911–4(e), and that is made to an organization not described in section 501(c)(3) that engages in attempts to influence legislation, is treated as a grass roots expenditure to the extent of the lesser of the amount of the transfer or the transferee's expenditures for grass roots lobbying. If the amount of the transfer exceeds the transferee's expenditures for grass roots lobbying,

the excess will be treated as an expenditure for direct lobbying to the extent of the transferee's expenditures for direct lobbying. In applying the two preceding sentences, the expenditures of the transferee will be determined as if the regulations under section 4911 applied to the transferee.

(e) *Definitions.* For purposes of section 4911 and the regulations thereunder—

(1) *Legislation.* "Legislation" includes action by the Congress, any state legislature, any local council, or similar legislative body, or by the public in a referendum, initiative, constitutional amendment, or similar procedure. "Legislation" includes a proposed treaty required to be submitted by the President to the Senate for its advice and consent from the time the President's representative begins to negotiate its position with the prospective parties to the proposed treaty.

(2) *Action.* The term "action" is limited to the introduction, amendment, enactment, defeat or repeal of Acts, bills, resolutions, or similar items.

(3) *Legislative body.* "Legislative body" does not include executive, judicial, or administrative bodies.

(4) *Administrative bodies.* "Administrative bodies" includes school boards, housing authorities, sewer and water districts, zoning boards, and other similar Federal, State, or local special purpose bodies, whether elective or appointive. Thus, for example, for purposes of section 4911, the term "any attempt to influence any legislation" does not include attempts to persuade an executive body or department to form, support the formation of, or to acquire property to be used for the formation or expansion of, a public park or equivalent preserves (such as public recreation areas, game, or forest preserves, and soil demonstration areas) established or to be established by act of Congress, by executive action in accordance with an act of Congress, or by a State, municipality, or other governmental unit described in section 170(c)(1), as compared with attempts to persuade a legislative body, a member thereof, or other governmental offical or employee, to promote the appropriation of funds for such an acquisition or other legislative authorization of such an acquisition. Therefore, for example, an organization would not be influencing legislation for purposes of section 4911, if it proposed to a Park Authority that it purchase a particular tract of land for a new park, even though such an attempt would necessarily require the Park Authority eventually to seek appropriations to support a new park. However, in such a case, the organization would be influencing legislation, for purposes of section 4911, if it provided the Park Authority with a proposed budget to be submitted to a legislative body, unless such submission is described by one of the exceptions set forth in paragraph (c) of this section.

§ 56.4911-3. Expenditures for direct and/or grass roots lobbying communications.

(a) *Definition of term "expenditures for"*—(1) *In general.* Expenditures for a direct or grass roots lobbying communication ("lobbying expenditures") include amounts paid or incurred as current or deferred compensation for an employee's services attributable to the direct or grass roots lobbying communication, and the allocable portion of administrative, overhead, and other general expenditures attributable to the direct or grass roots lobbying communication. Except as otherwise indicated in this paragraph (a), all costs of preparing a direct or grass roots lobbying communication are included as expenditures for direct or grass roots lobbying. For example, except as otherwise provided in this paragraph (a), all expenditures for researching, drafting, reviewing, copying, publishing and mailing a direct or grass roots lobbying communication, as well as an allocable share of overhead expenses, are included as expenditures for direct or grass roots lobbying.

(2) *Allocation of mixed purpose expenditures*—(i) *Nonmembership communications.* Except as provided in paragraph (a)(2)(ii) of this section, lobbying expenditures for a communication that also has a bona fide nonlobbying purpose must include all costs attributable to those parts of the communication that are on the same specific subject as the lobbying message. All costs attributable to those parts of the communication that are not on the same specific subject as the lobbying message are not included as

lobbying expenditures for allocation purposes. Whether or not a portion of a communication is on the same specific subject as the lobbying message will depend on the surrounding facts and circumstances. In general, a portion of a communication will be on the same specific subject as the lobbying message if that portion discusses an activity or specific issue that would be directly affected by the proposed legislation that is the subject of the lobbying message. Moveover, discussion of the background or consequences of the proposed legislation, or discussion of the background or consequences of an activity or specific issue affected by the proposed legislation, is also considered to be on the same specific subject as the lobbying communication.

(ii) *Membership communications.* In the case of lobbying expenditures for a communication that also has a bona fide nonlobbying purpose and that is sent only or primarily to members, an organization must make a reasonable allocation between the amount expended for the lobbying purpose and the amount expended for the nonlobbying purpose. An organization that includes as a lobbying expenditure only the amount expended for the specific sentence or sentences that encourage the recipient to take action with respect to legislation has not made a reasonable allocation. For purposes of this paragraph, a communication is sent only or primarily to members if more than half of the recipients of the communication are members of the organization making the communication within the meaning of § 56.4911–5. See § 56.4911–5 for separate rules on communications sent only or primarily to members. Nothing in this paragraph shall change any allocation required by § 56.4911–5.

(3) *Allocation of mixed lobbying.* If a communication (to which § 56.4911–5 does not apply) is both a direct lobbying communication and a grass roots lobbying communication, the communication will be treated as a grass roots lobbying communication except to the extent that the organization demonstrates that the communication was made primarily for direct lobbying purposes, in which case a reasonable allocation shall be made between the direct and the grass roots

lobbying purposes served by the communication.

(b) *Examples.* The provisions of paragraph (a) of this section are illustrated by the following examples. Except where otherwise explicitly stated, the expenditure test election under section 501(h) is assumed to be in effect for all organizations discussed in the examples of this paragraph (b). See § 56.4911–5 for special rules applying to the member communications described in some of the following examples.

Example (1). Organization R makes the services of E, one of its paid executives, available to S, an organization described in section 501(c)(4) of the Code. E works for several weeks to assist S in developing materials that urge voters to contact their congressional representatives to indicate their support for specific legislation. In performing this work, E uses office space and clerical assistance provided by R. R pays full salary and benefits to E during this period and receives no reimbursement from S for these payments or for the other facilities and assistance provided. All expenditures of R, including allocable office and overhead expenses, that are attributable to this assignment are grass roots expenditures because E was engaged in an attempt to influence legislation.

Example (2). An organization distributes primarily to nonmembers a pamphlet with two articles on unrelated subjects. The total cost of preparing, printing and mailing the pamphlet is $11,000, $1,000 for preparation and $10,000 for printing and mailing. The cost of preparing one article, a nonlobbying communication, is $600. The article is printed on three of the four pages in the pamphlet. The cost of preparing the second article, a grassroots lobbying communication that addresses only one specific subject, is $400. This article is printed on one page of the four page pamphlet. In this situation, $400 of preparation costs and $2,500 (25% of $10,000) of printing and mailing costs are expenditures for a grass roots lobbying communication.

Example (3). Assume the same facts as in Example (2), except that the pamphlet is distributed only to members. In addition, assume the second article states that the recipient members should contact their congressional representatives. The organization allocates $400 of preparation costs and $2,500 of printing and mailing costs as expenditures for direct lobbying (see § 56.4911–5(c)). The allocation is reasonable for purposes of § 56.4911–3(a)(2)(ii).

Example (4). Organization J places a full-page advertisement in a newspaper. The advertisement urges passage of pending legislation to build three additional nuclear powered submarines, and states that readers should write their Congressional representatives in favor of the legislation. The advertisement also provides a general description of J's purposes and activities, invites readers to become members of J and asks readers to contribute money to J. Except for the cost of the portion of the advertisement describing J's purposes and activities and the portion specifically seeking members and contributions, the entire cost of the advertisement is an expenditure for grass roots lobbying communication, because the entire advertisement, except for the lines specifically describing J and specifically seeking members and contributions, is on the same specific subject as the grass roots lobbying message.

Example (5). Assume the same facts as in Example (4), except that J places in the newspaper two separate half-page advertisements instead of one full-page advertisement. One of the two advertisements discusses the need for three additional nuclear powered submarines and urges readers to write their Congressional representatives in favor of the pending legislation to build the three submarines. The other advertisement contains only the membership and fundraising appeals, along with a general description of J's purposes and activities. The half-page advertisement urging readers to write to Congress is a grass roots lobbying communication and all of J's expenditures for producing and placing that advertisement are expenditures for a grass roots lobbying communication. J's expenditures for the other half-page advertisement are not expenditures for a grass roots or direct lobbying communication.

Example (6). Assume the same facts as in Example (4), except that the communication by J is in a letter mailed only to members of J, rather than in a newspaper advertisement, and the invitation to become a member of I is an invitation to join a new membership category. In addition, assume that the communication states that the member recipients should ask nonmembers to write their Congressional representatives. J allocates one-half of the cost of the mailing as an expenditure for a grass roots lobbying communication (see § 56.4911–5(d)). Because the communication had both bona fide nonlobbying (e.g., membership solicitation and fundraising) purposes as well as lobbying purposes, J's allocation of one-half of the cost of the communication to grass roots lobbying and one-half to nonlobbying is reasonable for purposes of § 56.491–3(a)(2)(ii).

Example (7). A particular monthly issue of organization X's newsletter, which is distributed mainly to nonmembers of X, has three articles of equal length. The firt article is a grass roots lobbying communication, the sole specific subject of which is pending legislation to help protect seals from being slaughtered in certain foreign countries. The

second article discusses the rapid decline in the world's whale population, particularly because of the illegal hunting of whales by foreign countries. The third article deals with air pollution and the acid rain problem in North America. Because the first article is a grass roots lobbying communication, all of the costs allocable to that article (e.g., one-third of the newsletter's printing and mailing costs) are lobbying expenditures. The second article is not a lobbying communication and the pending legislation relating to seals addressed in the first article does not affect the illegal whale hunting activities. Because the second and third articles are not lobbying communications and are also not on the same specific subject as the first article, no portion of the costs attributable to those articles is a grass roots lobbying expenditure.

Example (8). Organization T, a nonmembership organization prepares a three page document that is mailed to 3,000 persons on T's mailing list. The first two pages of the three page document, titled "The Need for Child Care," support the need for additional child care programs, and include statistics on the number of children living in homes where both parents work or in homes with a single parent. The two pages also make note of the inadequacy of the number of day care providers to meet the needs of these parents. The third page of the document, titled "H.R. 1," indicates T's support of H.R. 1, a bill pending in the U.S. House of Representatives. The document states that H.R. 1 will provide for $10,000,000 in additional subsidies to child care providers, primarily for those providers caring for lower income children. The third page of the document also notes that H.R. 1 includes new federal standards regulating the quality of child care providers. The document ends with T's request that recipients contact their congressional representative in support of H.R. 1. The entire three page document is on the same specific subject, and, therefore, all expenditures of preparing and distributing the three page document are grass roots lobbying expenditures.

Example (9). Assume the same facts as in Example (8), except that T is a membership organization, 75 percent of the recipients of the three page document are members of T, and 25 percent of the recipients are nonmembers and are not subscribers within the meaning of § 56.4911–5(f)(5). Assume also that the document states that readers should write to Congress, but does not state that the readers should urge nonmembers to write to Congress. T treats the document as having a bona fide nonlobbying purpose, the purpose of educating its members about the need for child care. Accordingly, T allocates one-half of the cost of preparing and distributing the document as a lobbying expenditure (see § 56.4911–5(e)(2)(i), of which 75 percent is a direct lobbying expenditure (see § 56.4911–5(e)(2)(iii)) and 25 percent is a grass roots lobbying expenditure (see § 56.4911–5(e)(2)(ii)). The remaining one-half is allocated as a nonlobbying expenditure. T's allocation is reasonable for purposes of § 56.4911–3(a)(2)(ii) and is correct for purposes of § 56.4911–5(e).

Example (10). Assume the same facts as in Example (9), except that T allocates one percent of the cost of preparing and distributing the document as a lobbying expenditure (for purposes of § 56.4911–5(e)(2)) and 99 percent as a nonlobbying expenditure. T's allocation is based upon the fact that out of 200 lines in the document, only two lines state that the recipient should contact legislators about the pending legislation. T's allocation is unreasonable for purposes of § 56.4911–3(a)(2)(ii).

Example (11). Organization F, a nonmembership organization, sends a one page letter to all persons on its mailing list. The only subject of the letter is the organization's opposition to a pending bill allowing private uses of certain national parks. The letter requests recipients to send letters opposing the bill to their congressional representatives. A second one page letter is sent in the same envelope. The second letter discusses the broad educational activities and publications of the organization in all areas of environmental protection and ends by requesting the recipient to make a financial contribution to organization F. Since the separate second letter is on a different subject from the lobbying letter, and the letters are of equal length, 50 percent of the mailing costs must be allocated as an expenditure for a grass roots lobbying communication.

Example (12). Assume the same facts as in Example (11), except that F is a membership organization and the letters in question are sent primarily (90 percent) to members. The other 10 percent of the recipients are nonmembers and are not subscribers within the meaning of § 56.4911–5(f)(5). Assume also that the first letter does not state that readers should urge nonmembers to write to legislators. F allocates one-half of the mailing costs as a lobbying expenditure, of which 90 percent is a direct lobbying expenditure and 10 percent is a grass roots lobbying expenditure (see § 56.4911–5(e)(2)). F's allocation is reasonable for purposes of § 56.4911–3(a)(2)(ii) and is correct for purposes of § 56.4911–5.

Par. 7. Proposed § 56.4911–4 is amended by revising paragraphs (b)(2), (b)(5), (b)(6), (c)(7), and (f)(2) to read as follows:

§ 56.4911–4 Exempt purpose expenditures.

*   *   *   *   *

(b) *Included expenditures.* * * *
(2) Amounts paid or incurred as current or deferred compensation for an employee's services for a purpose enumerated in section 170(c)(2)(B).

*   *   *   *   *

(b) *Included expenditures.* * * *
(5) Amounts paid or incurred for activities described in § 56.4911–3,
(6) Amounts paid or incurred for activities described in § 56.4911–5 that are not lobbying expenditures, and

*   *   *   *   *

(c) *Included expenditures.* * * *
(7) Amounts paid or incurred for the production of income, whether or not described in section 512(a)(1).

*   *   *   *   *

(f) *Definitions.*
(2) For purposes of paragraph (c) of this section, a separate fund raising unit of any organization must consist of either two or more individuals a majority of whose time is spent on fund raising for the organization, or any separate accounting unit of the organization that is devoted to fund raising.

*   *   *   *   *

Par. 8 Proposed § 56.4911–5 is amended as follows, to read as set forth below:
1. Paragraphs (a) through (d) and paragraph (e)(1) are revised to read as set forth below.
2. Paragraph (f)(6) is revised to read as set forth below.
3. A new paragraph (f)(8) is added, to read as set forth below.

§ 56.4911–5 Communications with members.

(a) *In general.* For purposes of section 4911 and § 56.4911–2, expenditures for certain communications between an organization and its members are treated as expenditures for direct lobbying, as expenditures for grass roots lobbying, or as other than lobbying expenditures in accordance with this section.

(b) *Communication directed only to members; excepted communication.* Expenditures for a communication that refers to, and reflects a view on, specific legislation are not lobbying expenditures if the communication satisfies the following requirements:
(1) The communication is directed only to members of the organization;

(2) The specific legislation the communication refers to, and reflects a view on, is of direct interest to the organization and its members;

(3) The communication does not directly encourage the member to engage in direct lobbying (whether individually or through the organization); and

(4) The communication does not directly encourage the member to engage in grass roots lobbying (whether individually or through the organization).

(c) *Communication directed only to members: expenditures for direct lobbying.* Expenditures for a communication that refers to, and reflects a view on, specific legislation and that satisfies the requirements of paragraphs (b)(1), (b)(2), and (b)(4) of this section, but does not satisfy the requirements of paragraph (b)(3) of this section, are treated as expenditures for direct lobbying.

(d) *Communication directed only to members: grass roots expenditures.* Expenditures for a communication that refers to, and reflects a view on, specific legislation and that satisfies the requirements of paragraphs (b)(1) and (b)(2) of this section, but does not satisfy the requirements of paragraph (b)(4) of this section, are treated as grass roots expenditures (whether or not the communication satisfies the requirements of paragraph (b)(3) of this section.

(e) *Written communications directed to members and nonmembers*—(1) *In general.* Expenditures for any written communication that is designed primarily for members of an organization (but not directed only to members) and that refers to, and reflects a view on, specific legislation of direct interest to the organization and its members, are treated as expenditures for direct or grass roots lobbying in accordance with paragraph (e)(2) or (e)(3) of this section. For purposes of this section, a communication is designed primarily for members of an organization if more than half of the recipients of the communication are members of the organization.

* * * * *

(f) *Definitions and special rules.* * * *

* * * * *

(6) *Directly encourages*—(i) *Direct lobbying*—(A) *In general.* For purposes of this section, a communication directly encourages a recipient to engage in direct lobbying, whether individually or through the organization, if the communication:

(1) States that the recipient should contact a legislator or an employee of a legislative body, or should contact any other government official or employee who may participate in the formulation of legislation (but only if the principal purpose of urging contact with the government official or employee is to influence legislation);

(2) States the address, telephone number, or similar information of a legislator or an employee of a legislative body; or

(3) Provides a petition, tear-off postcard or similar material for the recipient to communicate his or her views to a legislator or an employee of a legislative body, or to any other government official or employee who may participate in the formulation of legislation (but only if the principal purpose of so facilitating contact with the government official or employee is to influence legislation).

(B) *"Self-defense" exception for communications with members.* Notwithstanding the provisions of paragraph (f)(6)(i)(A) of this section, for purposes of paragraphs (b)(3), (e)(2)(i), and (e)(3)(ii) of this section, a communication that directly encourages a member to engage in direct lobbying activities that are described in section 4911(d)(2)(C) and that would not be attempts to influence legislation if engaged in directly by the organization is treated as a communication that does not directly encourage a member to engage in direct lobbying.

(ii) *Grass roots lobbying.* For purposes of paragraphs (b)(4) and (e)(3)(i) of this section, a communication directly encourages recipients to engage individually or collectively (whether through the organization or otherwise) in grass roots lobbying if the communication:

(A) States that the recipient should encourage any nonmember to contact a legislator or an employee of a legislative body, or to contact any other government official or employee who may participate in the formulation of legislation (but only if the principal purpose of urging contact with the government official or employee is to influence legislation);

(B) States that the recipient should provide to any nonmember the address, telephone number, or similar information of a legislator or an employee of a legislative body; or

(C) Provides (or requests that the recipient provide to nonmembers) a petition, tear-off postcard or similar material for the recipient (or nonmember) to use to ask any nonmember to communicate views to a legislator or an employee of a legislative body, or to any other government official or employee who may participate in the formulation of legislation, but only if the principal purpose of so facilitating contact with the government official or employee is to influence legislation. For purposes of this paragraph, a petition is provided for the recipient to use to ask any nonmember to communicate views if, for example, the petition has an entire page of preprinted signature blocks. Similarly, for purposes of this paragraph, where a communication is distributed to a single member and provides several tear-off postcards addressed to a legislator, the postcards are presumed to be provided for the member to use to ask a nonmember to communicate with the legislator.

*　　*　　*　　*　　*

(8) *Reasonable allocation rule.* In the case of lobbying expenditures for a communication that also has a bona fide nonlobbying purpose and that is sent only or primarily to members, an organization must make a reasonable allocation between the amount expended for the lobbying purpose and the amount expended for the nonlobbying purpose. See § 56.4911-3(a)(2)(ii).

Par. 9. Proposed § 56.4911-6, paragraphs (a)(3), (a)(4), (b)(2), and (b)(3), are revised to read as follows:

§ 56.4911-6 Records of lobbying and grass roots expenditures.

(a) *Records of lobbying expenditures.* * * *

(3) The portion of amounts paid or incurred as current or deferred compensation for an employee's services for direct lobbying;

(4) Amounts paid for out-of-pocket expenditures incurred on behalf of the organization and for direct lobbying, whether or not incurred by an employee;

*　　*　　*　　*　　*

(b) *Records of grassroots expenditures.* * * *

(2) The portion of amounts paid or incurred as current or deferred compensation for an employee's services for grass roots lobbying;

(3) Amounts paid for out-of-pocket expenditures incurred on behalf of the organization and for grass roots lobbying, whether or not incurred by an employee;

*　　*　　*　　*　　*

Par. 10. Proposed § 56.4911-7 is amended by revising paragraph (c) to read:

§ 56.4911-7 Affiliated group of organizations.

*　　*　　*　　*　　*

(c) *Governing instrument.* One organization (the "controlling" organization) is affiliated with a second organization (the "controlled" organization) by reason of the governing instruments of the controlled organization if the governing instruments of the controlled organization expressly or by implication limit the independent action of the controlled organization on legislative issues by requiring it to be bound by decisions of the other organization on legislative issues.

*　　*　　*　　*　　*

Lawrence B. Gibbs,
Commissioner of Internal Revenue.

Table of Statutes

Index